Blood Inscriptions

JEWISH CULTURE AND CONTEXTS

Published in association with the Herbert D. Katz Center for Advanced Judaic Studies of the University of Pennsylvania

Series Editors
Shaul Magid, Francesca Trivellato, Steven Weitzman

A complete list of books in the series is available from the publisher.

Blood Inscriptions

Science, Modernity, and Ritual Murder at Europe's Fin de Siècle

Hillel J. Kieval

PENN

UNIVERSITY OF PENNSYLVANIA PRESS

PHILADELPHIA

Published by
University of Pennsylvania Press
Philadelphia, Pennsylvania 19104-4112
www.upenn.edu/pennpress

Printed in the United States of America on acid-free paper
10 9 8 7 6 5 4 3 2 1

A Cataloging-in-Publication record is available from the Library of Congress
ISBN 978-0-8122-5376-4 (hardback)
ISBN 978-0-8122-9838-3 (eBook)

For Debbie,

Who never asked when it would be finished.

Contents

A Note on Translation, Transliteration, and Orthography

All translations from foreign languages into English are the author's unless indicated otherwise.

Transliteration from Hebrew to Latin characters generally follows the guidelines issued by the *Encyclopaedia Judaica*, 2nd ed., eds. Michael Berenbaum and Fred Skolnik (Thomson Gale and Keter Publishing House, 2007), with the following exception: the letter *tsadi* is represented by ts.

Both Czech and Hungarian have undergone significant orthographic reforms over the course of the nineteenth (and even the twentieth) century. I have attempted, for the most part, to use modern orthographic conventions in this book.

Introduction

The Novelty of the Ritual Murder Trial in Fin de Siècle Europe

> One would have thought that in the nineteenth century a charge so gross could hardly have been listened to for a moment.
>
> —J. J. Stewart Berowne, Dean of Peterborough College, University of Cambridge (1883)

> Every century has its oddities and absurdities. The Tiszaeszlár trial is a baroque monstrosity, a horrible freak of the nineteenth century. One could almost describe it as a bloody mockery, a sickening satire on the powerful progress made in the industrial, political, and scientific realms, of which our era has justly been proud.
>
> —*Der Blut-Prozeß von Tisza Eszlár in Ungarn* (1883)

Mise-en-Scène

An adolescent girl or boy disappears, disrupting the regular pace of life and everyday social relations in a Central European village or market town. In the early stages of the event, close family members mobilize to resolve the problem. Neighboring residents, including Jewish families, are consulted or encountered; information is exchanged, but a growing sense of panic takes shape. The concerned families pressure local police and judicial authorities to conduct an investigation; these pressures are at times rebuffed; at any event, they do not always lead to the discovery of the missing person. In the meantime, local theories of what might have transpired begin to take shape, understandings that derive in part from the anthology of social knowledge that has long been at the disposal of the community, in part from suspicions born of the local history of social relations, and in part from chance encounters thought to have produced important information.

Eventually, a body is discovered—sometimes before, sometimes after the case moves to the investigative stage. Magistrates are summoned, newspaper reporters from the large cities arrive to issue serialized investigative stories, local and national politicians make reference to the "mysterious crime" in their speeches in parliament, and state's attorneys make preparations to prosecute a case for murder. If there is to be a criminal investigation and trial, scientific experts of various kinds are called upon to aid in the forensic evaluation of evidence or offer scientific testimony. When trials do ensue, they invariably attract crowds of spectators and are reported on energetically in the national and international press. The verdict rendered might acquit or convict, but rarely will it be the last word in either the judicial proceedings themselves or the public's discussion of the guilt or innocence of the accused. The local tragedy has grown into a widely publicized and engrossing criminal investigation and trial and in short order ballooned into an international affair.

This scenario might well be applied to any number of criminal trials for murder that took place at the turn of the past century, trials whose repercussions transcended the confines of the local town or village and, indeed, the state. But a subset of these criminal prosecutions from the last decades of the nineteenth century and the first decades of the twentieth stands out from the rest and is quite distinctive. In a handful of such trials in Germany, Austria-Hungary, and eventually Russia, Jewish defendants—either formally or by implication—were forced to answer to the accusation that they had committed murder for purposes of Jewish religious ritual. Over the centuries, popular belief in such religiously inspired, criminal behavior has been remarkably strong, if inconsistent. There was no single theory of Jewish ritual murder and no single ritual practice that it targeted, although it tended to be associated with the preparation of Passover matzah.[1] The response of political authorities to popular accusations of Jewish ritual murder, however, underwent a significant—if also inconsistent—shift in the aftermath of the Protestant Reformation and, later, Enlightenment-inspired criminal justice reform. With very few exceptions, states in Western and Central Europe abstained from prosecuting cases based on this theory after the sixteenth century, while in Poland-Lithuania, where the state did conduct prosecutions deriving from the "blood libel" in the seventeenth and even the eighteenth centuries (in connection with the country's own Counter-Reformation), these died out with the abolition of the use of torture to extract confessions in 1776.[2] Now, however, after a hiatus of some two to three centuries, shifting combinations of magistrates, criminal investigators, and state prosecutors appeared once again to be open to the suggestion that Jews committed homicide in the enactment of religious ritual.

As simple speech acts, accusations of Jewish ritual murder were surprisingly widespread at the fin de siècle, the object of a great deal of attention in newspapers and the popular press, and the instigation for much political commentary and debate. This particular construction of Jewish criminality and danger elicited numerous speeches and interpellations on the floor of parliament in Berlin, Vienna, Budapest, and St. Petersburg. To the best of my knowledge, no one has made a systematic tally of accusations of Jewish ritual murder in Europe from, say, 1880 to 1914—accusations that left behind a public record in the form of a criminal complaint or newspaper announcement. But the number must be in the hundreds. Friedrich Frank, a German Catholic priest and politician who eventually came to oppose the popular belief in the blood libel, claimed to have discovered no fewer than 128 public accusations of ritual murder that had been made against Jews between 1881 and 1900. For the preceding six hundred years, in contrast, he claimed to have been able to locate only forty-four such accusations![3] Writing around the same time, but focusing specifically on the last decade of the nineteenth century, the Berlin-based Verein zur Abwehr des Antisemitismus exposed seventy-nine "bona fide ritual murder charges" that had been leveled at Jews in various European countries, including Austria-Hungary, Germany, Bulgaria, Russia, Romania, Serbia, and France.[4]

One needs to be cautious, however, before concluding that popular accusations against Jews for ritual murder increased significantly at the close of the nineteenth century, because this was also a period in which the circulation of mass-market newspapers also grew. It is possible, then, that the numerous reports of, often evanescent, local rumors of ritual murder may simply have reflected a form of sensational news coverage and dissemination typical of the age. Nevertheless, whatever the actual number of accusations, the combination of fiery parliamentary politics and widely circulated newspapers that characterized public life in Central Europe in this period did produce what one might call a climate of growing fascination with a particular form of Jewish deviance and criminality.[5] The purpose of this book is not to offer an explanation for the growth in number of ritual murder accusations at the fin de siècle—if such expansion did occur—but rather to examine an important feature of this phenomenon. In light of all of the discussion—the background noise, if you will—of Jewish ritual murder, picked up by the popular press and debated in the public sphere, it is perhaps not surprising that some of these allegations managed to break through the legal, political, and institutional constraints of the modern, bureaucratic state to become full-fledged criminal proceedings.

In fact, relatively few of the hundreds of accusations made it all the way to trial. Just what it took to convince the state that an accusation was credible and, hence, worthy of prosecution and what happened in the course of these prosecutions are some of the questions that I pursue at some length in this book. In the end, Jewish defendants were formally prosecuted on six occasions between 1879 and 1913 for murder and related offenses, charges that either suggested or explicitly claimed that the crimes in question were carried out for ritual purposes and religious compulsion.

The first and the last of these trials took place in the Russian empire: Kutaisi (Russian Georgia) in 1879 and the well-known Beilis affair, which transpired in Kiev (Ukraine) between 1911 and 1913. The intervening four sets of trials, the events around which this book turns, were mounted in Central Europe: two in Imperial Germany (Xanten in 1891–92 and Konitz, today's Chojnice, Poland, in 1900–1902) and two in Austria-Hungary (Tiszaeszlár, Hungary, in 1882–83 and Polná, today's Czech Republic, in 1899–1900). A central argument of this book is that these proceedings constituted a *new phenomenon* in the long history of the blood libel, as well as a new chapter in Jewish-state relations. These trials are best understood as fundamentally *modern* proceedings, by which I mean that they were grounded in—and rhetorically structured by—methods and assumptions drawn from modern forensic science and criminology.

The people who investigated these cases and those who prosecuted them in court implicitly felt bound to reject—or at least pass over in silence—the epistemological grounds on which the classical accusation had rested. The modern trials also exhibited four important features, which distinguished them from their medieval and early modern precursors: (1) They transpired within legal systems that were structured by modern criminal codes and rules of procedure. (2) In the criminal investigations that preceded the trials, confessions that had been extracted through torture were deemed to be inadmissible. (3) Nearly all of the actors in the cases—investigating magistrates, prosecutors, defense attorneys, victims' families, and the accused—recognized implicitly the new, epistemological rules under which the trials could proceed, in particular the requirement that they be argued in the language of modern forensic science. And (4), scientists, medical practitioners, and academicians played an outsized role in the presentation and evaluation of evidence.

In the Kutaisi case—the early bookend to our investigation—nine Jews from the Caucasus town of Sachkhery were accused of the kidnapping and murder of a Christian girl. Kutaisi was, in the words of John Klier, "the first Blood Libel trial in Russia to be heard in the post-reform courts, in the new confrontational style, before a jury."[6] Following a one-week trial, all of the defendants were acquitted. At the other end of our survey, during the closing years of the Tsarist empire, the more famous trial of the Jewish defendant Mendel Beilis attracted much attention and criticism around the world. In the end, the jury of twelve men—many of peasant background—issued an ambiguous verdict, acquitting Beilis of the murder of Andrei Iushchinskii but agreeing with the prosecution that the murder bore the markings of a ritual crime. Had it been proved, the court wished to know, that the victim, Andrei Iushchinskii, had suffered forty-seven wounds, which caused him "torturous suffering" and resulted in "almost the complete loss of blood"? The jury answered yes.[7]

The Beilis affair, coming as it did on the eve of World War I, might well be viewed as an outlier in some ways, a late example of a trend that already appeared to have exhausted itself in Central Europe. The most intense period for the dissemination of the ritual murder accusation in modern Europe—and, with it, the last of Central Europe's formal trials on this charge—had ended roughly a decade earlier. Indeed, the most sensationalized, public accusations appear to have surfaced from 1882 to 1903, the pace of which quickened from the 1890s to the beginning of the new century. It was during this period of roughly three decades that police investigators, public prosecutors, government officials, and even cabinet ministers changed the traditional approach of the state to such matters, choosing now to place the resources and prestige of the state behind formal, criminal prosecutions—prosecutions, moreover, in which the motive of ritually prescribed murder constituted at least part of the state's theory.

In this new phase, the four major trials occurred in fairly rapid succession: starting in the Hungarian half of the Habsburg monarchy, crossing over to the Prussian Rhineland in the German Empire, moving south to Bohemia (again in the Habsburg monarchy), and coming to rest once more in Prussia, this time in the eastern part of the country. They were public spectacles, attracting large crowds, fame, and, in some circles, infamy in small towns and county seats, in the major urban centers of the countries in question, and abroad. Each case left in its wake a trail of excited newspaper accounts, pamphlets and broadsides, popular traditions, and political debate. And each affair managed somehow to acquire the status of historical precedent for those that followed, shaping their narratives, their discursive construction, and indeed their plausibility.[8]

The spate of ritual murder trials in the late nineteenth and early twentieth centuries came to an end with the onset of World War I. I suspect that the war itself and the violent revolutions that ensued played a part in this development, perhaps because the structure of plausibility on which the trials had rested had long since fallen apart or perhaps because war and revolution had transformed the world beyond recognition, offering a specter of violence that rendered tales of Jewish ritual murder quaint by comparison. All told, the life of the modern trial was something on the order of thirty to thirty-five years, worthy of our attention, both as a phenomenon that seems to be historically misplaced and for its relatively short duration.

For one thing, the modern ritual murder trial offers a rare perspective on the social relations between Jews and Gentiles in the decades following political emancipation in Central Europe. Impinging unexpectedly upon the political and cultural landscape, disrupting the equilibrium of Jewish social and communal life, these confrontations revealed a significant domain of cultural misunderstanding and suspicion and appeared to call into question the liberal assumptions on which Jewish emancipation had rested, that is, the basic humanity of the Jews, their status as Europeans, and the fundamental resemblance of Jews to non-Jews. Moreover, trials against Jews for ritual murder in the modern age raise numerous questions relating to the sociology of knowledge. What, for example, are the means by which *disreputable* knowledge can become reputable, recapturing the imagination of social elites? How is it possible that state officials at the turn of the nineteenth and twentieth centuries, whose ethos was built on a commitment to bureaucratic rationality and scientific method, should commit huge amounts of time, energy, and prestige to such criminal investigations and prosecutions? What would have made the accusation of Jewish ritual murder *meaningful* to self-consciously "modern" individuals? What, in other words, made the modern ritual murder trial *work*?

Figure 1. *Ritual Murder of Simon of Trent*, woodcut illustration, first published in Hartmann Schedel's *Nuremberg Chronicle*, 1493.

Courtesy J. Mabray.

Medieval and Early Modern Precedents

Ritual murder trials were not a constant feature of the European historical landscape: they had a specific origin in time and in place, and they did not flourish continuously. The classical statement of the ritual murder accusation was provided by twelfth- and thirteenth-century England—where the celebrated deaths of William of Norwich (1144) and Little Hugh of Lincoln

(1255) engendered both sites of Christian pilgrimage and well-known literary treatments. Other cases of ritualized execution of Christian boys by Jews were said to have occurred in Gloucester in 1168 and Bristol around 1260. By the 1160s, the accusation had crossed the English Channel into France, where the death of a Christian youth in the French town of Blois in 1171 resulted in the burning of thirty Jews on the orders of the local count. The first recorded accusation in Germany (the Holy Roman Empire) took place in 1235, when thirty-four Jews from the German town of Fulda were executed on the charge of having murdered five Christian boys and drawn their blood, which they later consumed.

In point of fact, Jews were the objects of *three* distinct accusations of religiously inspired crime in medieval Europe: ritual crucifixion (the original ritual murder accusation), in which Jews were charged with periodically reenacting the crucifixion of Christ on the bodies of young Christian boys; Host desecration, according to which Jews (or other malfeasants) would acquire the Eucharistic wafer, already consecrated for the mass—understood, by the thirteenth century, to be the real body of Christ—in order to subject it to various tortures; and, finally, the version most familiar to modern readers: the blood libel, or ritual cannibalism. In this scenario, Jews kidnapped and murdered Christian boys, perhaps out of hatred of the Christian faith, but in particular in order to collect and make use of the blood of their victims. The William of Norwich and Little Hugh of Lincoln narratives were built around the theme of ritual crucifixion, which was by far the dominant motif in the twelfth and thirteenth centuries. Desecration of the Host charges first emerged in France at the close of the thirteenth century. Tales of the Jewish propensity for Christian blood seem to have been articulated most commonly in the Empire, the Fulda case of 1235 being the first known example.[9]

As we know it today, the blood libel implies that Jews feel the need to make use of Christian blood in order to properly perform Jewish ritual. But in its high medieval version, the libel ascribed to Jews a variety of motives—and to Christian blood a range of uses: these included the cosmetic or medicinal benefits of the blood (to cure the widely acknowledged, unpleasant Jewish odor; to stanch the bleeding from the circumcision wound; and to stop Jewish males from menstruating, to name the most common ones), as well as the ritual uses to which it might be put. The fact that the most frequently repeated—hence, preserved—motif in this regard has it that Jews used the blood to prepare Passover unleavened bread (matzah) strongly suggests that it was Christian assumptions concerning the true nature of the elements of the Eucharist (the wine and the wafer) that lent the classical ritual murder accusation much of its plausibility within Christian society.

In the Holy Roman Empire, ritual murder accusations reached a high point in the fifteenth and early sixteenth centuries, often appearing in connection with the consolidation of the political power of city magistrates and town councils. Major cases erupted in Endingen (1470), Trent (1475), Regensburg (1470–76), Freiburg (1504), and elsewhere, ending in most instances in the execution of the accused (or their death under torture), the conversion or expulsion of the remaining Jewish communities, and the consolidation of Christian civic solidarity at home.[10] As R. Po-chia Hsia notes, however, the flood of accusations, trials, and expulsions that swept across southwestern Germany on the eve of the Reformation soon confronted a formidable cultural repudiation. The Reformation's own learned and moral discourses concerning ritual, belief, and religious truth produced what might be called a "disenchantment" of Christian culture in Central and Western Europe, which, in the process, relegated the charge of Jewish ritual murder to the sphere of disreputable knowledge—disdained by learned elites though perpetuated in popular culture. Hsia writes,

> When miracles, pilgrimages, Marian devotion, and the veneration of saints became points of ridicule, manifestations of old superstitions, and fabrications of an unscrupulous Roman clergy, as the Protestants charged; when the eucharistic doctrine of transubstantiation was challenged by the symbolic interpretations of the sacrament . . . when salvation depended on God's grace rather than on human sacrifice, as Luther himself taught; when all forms of magic were attacked . . . the psychological and intellectual foundations of ritual murder discourse also began to disintegrate among the clerical and magisterial elites, although the *popular* discourse on ritual murder was to persist well into the Enlightenment.[11]

Miri Rubin makes a similar claim concerning Christian narratives of Jewish desecration of the Host and the symbolic universe that supported them. This particularly vivid account of Jewish danger and perfidy—embedded in the complex of beliefs concerning the power of the Eucharist—"virtually disappeared" during the first half of the sixteenth century.[12]

Virtually, but not completely. Reformation theology, criticism of Catholic practices and belief, and—eventually—the scientific revolution of the seventeenth century may have pushed "knowledge" of Jewish ritual murder to the fringes of respectable discourse in Western Europe and the Holy Roman Empire, but ritual murder accusations did thrive further to the east in early modern Poland-Lithuania. Both ritual murder and Host desecration accusations had been rare in the medieval Polish kingdom, but their number and frequency rose sharply with the formal introduction of the Counter-Reformation in the 1560s, and over the next two centuries, articulations of the blood libel became a central feature of Jewish-Christian relations.[13] Historians differ as to the precise number of cases that occurred as well as to the ultimate motives that lay behind them. Daniel Tollet has linked them to a conversionary campaign driven by Jesuit priests and bishops; others have emphasized a desire on the part of Catholic clergy to justify Christian theological teachings about the Jews in the face of apparent Jewish success and, in some spheres, dominance in Polish economic life. Recent scholarship by Magda Teter has situated early modern trials against Jews for sacrilege against the Host within the broader context of Counter-Reformation struggles over the meaning of the sacred during a time of religious and political upheaval. As in Western and Central Europe, not all accusations resulted in formal criminal investigations or trials. It appears that between 1540 and 1790, between eighty and one hundred ritual murder accusations were serious enough to have left behind a historical record. The number of formal trials against Jews on this charge was probably in the low twenties for the seventeenth century and the same for the eighteenth century. Church officials appear to have been a good deal more active in these proceedings in the eighteenth century than they had been in the past—there were at least six cases in which bishops were involved—and the number of judicial murders that ensued was also higher. More than one hundred Jews and several non-Jews lost their lives during the eighteenth century as targets of this accusation.[14]

Sandomierz, in the Kingdom of Poland, was the site of two major blood libels at the turn of the seventeenth and eighteenth centuries (1698 and 1710–13). In the latter case, it was Stefan Żuchowski (1666–1716)—parish priest, archdeacon, and town inquisitor—who instigated and organized the criminal investigation. Żuchowski, who had been appointed commissioner for Jewish affairs by the synod of the Cracow diocese in 1711, is thought to have taken a personal interest in the question of Jewish ritual murder in the aftermath of the first Sandomierz trial and went on to publish two books on the subject that proved to be extremely influential in the Kingdom of Poland in later decades. They were read widely, quoted from not only in subsequent literature but in future trials as well, and they formed the basis for a list of ritual murder accusations in Poland that was assembled at the end of the eighteenth century by the Bishop of Kiev, Józef Załuski, and published in Warsaw in 1914. In the 1710–13 Sandomierz case, Jan Serafinowicz, a convert from Judaism who served as a witness for the prosecution, broke from historical precedent in testifying to the court that Jews did, in fact, perform ritual murder on Christian children. He also seems to have been the author of a manuscript filled with "evidence" supporting the blood libel, which became a handbook of sorts for prosecutors and eventually was summarized in the book, *Złość żydowska* (*Jewish Malice*), published in 1758 by Gaudenty Pikulski, a Catholic priest.[15]

The engagement of Bishop Kajetan Sołtyk with followers of the Jewish messianic pretender Jakob Frank provided another, more dramatic occasion in which former or dissenting Jews would step forward to attest to the "truth" of the charge that Jews used Christian blood for ritual purposes. In the aftermath of a public disputation in Kamieniec-Podolski in 1757, Sołtyk sought to exploit the propagandistic potential of the Frankists, who were styling themselves "Contra-Talmudists." He instigated another public disputation, which took place in Lwów in September 1759, in which they asserted that the Talmud teaches that Jews require Christian blood and that whoever believes in the Talmud is bound to follow this teaching.[16] Deeply concerned about the flurry of ritual murder accusations in Poland, the Council of the Four Lands (Va'ad arba aratsot) sent three emissaries to the Vatican between 1754 and 1761 to appeal to the pope for protection. In 1758, Pope Benedict XIV ordered an investigation into the matter and charged Lorenzo Ganganelli, councilor of the Holy Office of the Inquisition—and later Pope Clement XIV—to prepare a report on the commission's work. Ganganelli's report, presented to the congregation of the Inquisition in March 1758, reviewed the major accusations of Jewish ritual murder since the thirteenth century and concluded that the blood libel was indeed a calumny, of which Jews and Judaism were innocent.[17] With the advent of the Polish Enlightenment, interventions by the Holy See against the ritual murder accusation in 1760 and 1763, and the abolition of torture by the Polish Parliament (Sejm) in 1776, the cultural and institutional supports for ritual murder proceedings receded significantly. By the end of the eighteenth century, in the words of Guldon and Wijaczka, "Ritual murder trials had disappeared even from Poland."[18]

To be sure, isolated criminal cases on the charge of ritual murder continued to appear in different parts of Europe. In 1669, Raphaël Lévy stood accused of the kidnapping and murder of a four-year-old boy from a village outside Metz, France, for which he was tortured, tried, and eventually executed.[19] Nearly a century later, in 1764, five-year-old Stefan Balla disappeared from his home in Orkuta near Eperjes in Upper Hungary (today Prešov, Slovakia); his corpse was discovered two days later. In the course of an investigation that lasted for half a year, during which both "mild" and "severe" torture were applied, one of the two Jewish defendants died of his injuries; the second, announcing his willingness to convert to Christianity, managed to survive.[20] But ritual murder trials in post-Reformation and early Enlightenment Europe rested on two shaky and vulnerable legs: one cultural and one juridical.

On the level of high culture, this particular understanding of Jewish criminality and danger was relegated increasingly to the shadows of polite discourse, to be subsumed under the category of superstition and folk belief, and thus beyond the regular institutional practices of the state. From a juridical perspective—as we have seen in the case of Poland-Lithuania—prosecutions for ritual murder could not proceed successfully without confessions of the accused extracted through torture. It is no coincidence, in my view, that the 1764 Orkuta case constituted what Theodor Austerlitz has called the Habsburg monarchy's "*letzte Folterprozedur*" (last torture proceeding). Moses Josefovics, one of the accused in the case, had been subjected to particularly gruesome physical tortures in January 1765 before finally succumbing to his injuries—acts described in excruciating detail in a formal complaint addressed to the Empress Maria Theresa by a Jewish delegation from Pressburg (Pozsony/Bratislava) and in less forthcoming terms in a subsequent justification by the court in Eperjes. Maria Theresa appears to have been disturbed by what she read, and she did eventually intervene in the case, freeing all remaining Jewish suspects. She also moved to ban torture in all criminal proceedings through a rescript issued in 1776, the same year in which the Polish Sejm abolished the practice. The Hungarian law code of 1790 formalized the abolition of torture.[21]

The consensus of respectable opinion in Europe regarding the blood libel, formed in the wake of Reformation critiques of magical thinking and of Enlightenment rationalism, may have begun to crack in 1840 with the playing out of the Damascus affair. At the center of this affair was a ritual murder investigation in the predominantly Muslim Ottoman Empire that began with the disappearance and presumed murder of a Capuchin monk named

Father Thomas but soon mushroomed into a major international incident—involving the governments of France, Britain, Egypt, and Austria—and nearly escalated into a serious military conflict.[22] The theory that a kidnapping and ritual murder had been committed came from within the city's Christian community; the French diplomatic mission in Damascus became involved in the investigation because the Franco-Turkish Concession Treaty of 1740 had put the Ottoman Empire's Roman Catholic clergy under the protection of France. Similar treaties awarded protection rights over Protestant and Orthodox Christians, as well as Sephardi and Ashkenazi Jews, to other European powers. When one adds to these competing interests the challenge to the authority of the sultan posed by Muhammed Ali (Mehmet Ali Pasha), governor of Egypt, who ruled at the time over Syria and was allied with France, one has the makings of an international melodrama, laced with deception, intrigue, and the struggle for power.

The Damascus affair bore characteristics of both the medieval and the modern blood libel. As in premodern times, confessions were extracted from suspects through the use of torture (indeed some of those arrested died as a result); local authorities, including the French consul, appeared to accept the traditional blood accusation at face value as true or at least plausible. At the same time, the imperial protector of the Jews, the Ottoman sultan, responded in the traditional manner, issuing a *firman* (edict) condemning the charge. And, as in most premodern cases, the judicial proceedings did not culminate in a formal trial but rather took the form of prolonged interrogations (again, under torture) punctuated by various delays until higher authorities called an end to them.

The case also exhibited more modern features. These included the dissemination of purportedly neutral—although highly exploitative—coverage of the ritual murder accusation in mass-circulation newspapers in England, France, and Germany (including the *Times* of London); the entanglement of the affair in nineteenth-century international diplomacy and competition; and the political mobilization of Jewish communities across Europe to achieve justice for their coreligionists. Damascus thus occupies a curiously indeterminate position in the history of the ritual murder accusation: it was both a European and a non-European event, a product of medieval religious understandings as well as of nineteenth-century realpolitik, and a marker of both the premodern political status of Jews as a dependent and subservient minority and of the transition to the politics of emancipation. In its investigative and juridical procedures, however, Damascus was a throwback to the past.

A "Horrible Freak" of the Nineteenth Century?

In 1883, Schnitzer Brothers Press in New York, publishers of the *Oesterreichisch-Amerikanische Zeitung*, produced a German transcript of the Tiszaeszlár ritual murder trial that had recently ended in the Hungarian town of Nyíregyháza. By way of introduction, the volume opened with the following declaration:

> In the pages that follow, we offer an account of a trial, which, in its emergence, its course, and the impression that it left behind on the rest of the world, is unparalleled in the history of the nineteenth century. The bloody sacrifice that was evoked in order to be made the object of a judicial proceeding; the throng of accused, whom the mob—inflamed by fanaticism and a merciless, persecuting rage—had already condemned before the day of the verdict and was willing to offer up as atonement; the uproar and sensational reporting, designed to reach and inflame all corners of the world—up to the highest circles—by the machinations of a press that was enraptured of the prosecution—all this allows the trial to appear in a light that stamps it as a trenchant, cosmopolitan question of religion and race.
>
> Every century has its oddities and absurdities. The Tiszaeszlár trial is a baroque monstrosity, a horrible freak of the nineteenth century. One could almost describe it as a bloody mockery, a sickening satire on the powerful progress made in the industrial, political, and scientific realms, of which our era has justly been proud—to wit: that in esteemed Hungary in 1883, under the regime of a progressive and enlightened monarchy, in view of the entire world, such a mean and miserable farce could take place. And yet it is true. A persecution of the Jews was staged; accusations that had once been raised in the barbaric Middle Ages, in the dark times of crassest superstition—and which, one had imagined, lay buried and forgotten beneath deep mud and muck—were now dug up and drawn as a dashing sword against a hunted people; a people whom today's humanity has to thank for many of its most beautiful and noble rights; who believed themselves to be living and working in a close bond with the other peoples in their midst in the light of shining humanity and toleration.[23]

Table 1. Modern Ritual Murder Trials, 1879–1913

Case	*Location*	*Date*	*Summary*
Kutaisi	Russia (Georgia)	1879	Nine Jews accused of the murder of six-year-old Sarra Iosifova Modebadze. All were acquitted.
Tiszaeszlár	Austria-Hungary (Hungary)	1882–83	Salamon Schwarcz, József Scharf, and thirteen other Jewish defendants accused either of the murder of fourteen-year-old Eszter Solymosi or of aiding and abetting. All were acquitted.
Xanten	Germany (Prussian Rhineland)	1891–92	Adolf Buschhoff (Jewish stonecutter and butcher) accused of the ritual murder of five-year-old Johann Hegmann. Acquitted.
Polná	Austria-Hungary (Bohemia)	1899–1900	Leopold Hilsner (unemployed Jewish shoemaker) accused of the aggravated ritual murder of nineteen-year-old Anežka Hrůzová. Convicted and sentenced to death in 1899 and again at retrial in 1900; death sentence commuted by the emperor to life imprisonment.
Konitz; later Chojnice	Germany (West Prussia); later Poland	1900–1902	Adolf Lewy (Jewish butcher) accused of the ritual murder and dismemberment of eighteen-year-old Ernst Winter (never tried). Eventually, his son, Moritz, was convicted not of murder but of perjury for insisting that he did not know the victim.
Kiev	Russia (Ukraine)	1911–13	Mendel Beilis (Jewish brick factory manager) accused of the ritual murder of twelve-year-old Andrei Iushchinskii. Acquitted, but in issuing the verdict, the jury allowed for the possibility that a ritual murder had taken place.

For these Central European immigrants to the United States, the Hungarian ritual murder trial held a kind of grotesque fascination. On the one hand, it had all of the ingredients that sell newspapers: mystery, drama, violence, passion, conspiracy, social and communal conflict, and so on. On the other hand, the entire proceedings were atavistic, a throwback to an age of superstition and intolerance—"a baroque monstrosity"—and, as such, an affront to nineteenth-century liberalism's notions of progress and humanity. Ultimately, then, the Nyíregyháza trial served both as what we might call the "party of humanity's" counterimage and as a warning call to likeminded people, a suggestion of what Western culture might look like if the promoters of reason and progress in human affairs were to cease to be vigilant. To many observers (and partisans) at the turn of the century, what was at stake in the ritual murder trials of the period amounted to nothing less than an epic struggle between enlightenment and obscurantism, rationality and irrationality, science and myth.

Witness another example: the letter writing campaign of Anglican clergy and Cambridge University academics organized by Solomon Mayer Schiller-Szinessy (1820–90), a Hungarian-born Jew who served as the first Jewish reader in Rabbinics at Cambridge, in the wake of the Tiszaeszlár affair. Schiller-Szinessy announced the campaign with a letter to the *Times* of London, later reprinted in the *Jewish Chronicle*, which read in part, "However humiliating it is to me, both as a Jewish theologian and an Hungarian patriot, to have to assist, so near the close of this 'enlightened nineteenth century,' in rebutting so false and cruel a charge, yet it is highly satisfactory to me to have found such ready support from men of such eminence, both for their Christian learning and their Christian virtues."[24]

The letters that were printed in the *Jewish Chronicle* contained a judicious mixture of liberal outrage and Christian charity. One J. B. Dunelm volunteered that not only did he consider the "blood accusations" against the Jews to be "monstrously untrue" but that he was "at a loss to understand how any sane man in this nineteenth century [could] believe them." To adopt such accusations as a ground for persecution, he concluded, was to bring dishonor on the sacred name of Christ.[25] J. J. Stewart Berowne, the dean of Peterborough College, echoed Dunelm's moral outrage, framing his response along the lines of the dichotomy between rationalism and irrationalism, modernity and the "medieval":

> My dear friend, I need scarcely assure you with what feelings of indignation I have heard of the revival, in the recent persecutions

> of the Jews in Hungary, of the cruel and slanderous accusations which have been made against them of using human blood in their Passover feast. One would have thought that in the nineteenth century a charge so gross could hardly have been listened to for a moment. No one who has the slightest acquaintance with Jewish literature, or who knows anything of Jewish belief, could credit it. He must know it to be a malicious lie. But, alas! Bigotry and intolerance and religious fanaticism and hatred are not yet dead.[26]

Letters such as these were grounded in a discourse of modernity, which presumed the progress of rationality in human affairs. They echoed a common refrain of astonishment, mixed with outrage, at the apparent vitality of myth and superstition at the end of the nineteenth century—at the refusal of long-discredited knowledge to stay repressed. At times, the progressive critique of the ritual murder accusation was carried out in an ironic mode, in which the very assumption that theirs was an age of reason and progress was exposed as an exaggeration, if not an outright delusion. The comments of the German Jewish journalist and liberal politician, Paul Nathan, concerning the Xanten trial in 1892 are a case in point:

> The Crusaders slaughtered the Jews of Xanten; that was on 27 June 1096. On 29 June 1891, exactly 795 years and two days later, a poor child whose throat had been slashed was found in the very same Xanten; again fanaticism raged. But this time only one house was demolished, and the guiltless Jewish suspect was dragged no farther than in the vicinity of the scaffold. This is indeed a difference, and who could deny that we have made progress in the course of 795 years. He who would demand more must admit that culture, which stimulates such wonderful blossoming at its heights, does not spread more quickly at the lower levels; and that the struggle against the ever dangerous, ever rampant un-culture must not rest even for a day.[27]

Such efforts to make sense of the ritual murder accusation in modern Europe in terms of a cultural conflict between reason and irrationality functioned on at least two levels. One line of argument viewed the belief in Jewish ritual murder as a holdover from an earlier historical era, benighted in its intellectual gullibility and representing a more primitive stage of human development. In this evolutionary view of culture, irrationality constituted an embarrassing remnant whose presence in a number of European discourses indicated that human development was both an incomplete process and one that required the vigilance of right-thinking people. But another interpretation of the role of irrationality in modern European culture and politics was also implied. Underlying the liberal critique was the sense—perhaps the fear—that the apparent preference for irrational belief constituted not an evolutionary remnant but something new and vital in European culture. From this perspective, narratives of a Jewish thirst for blood might prove to be attractive to Europeans not despite their irrationality but precisely because they could be seen as challenging the intellectual and cultural premises on which a tired and corrupt modernity rested. And the defenders of scientific rationalism sensed as much. Behind their lamentations concerning the tenacity of atavistic beliefs and superstitions—voiced increasingly after 1883—lurked a fear that perhaps the problem lay not so much in the past as in an uncertain future.

Those who bemoaned the renewed articulation of the ritual murder accusation were certainly justified in asking why this cultural trope had not lost its hold on the European imagination. One might well have argued that, from any number of perspectives—law, the liberal institutions and bureaucratic rationality of the modern state, or the high culture of both secular society and the Church—Europeans ought to have given up on this particular narrative, as a compelling explanation for the disappearance and murder of children, long ago. This is not, however, a book about the tenacity of myth and superstition in the modern world. (Historians would be well advised not to transmit uncritically the prejudices of their protagonists, liberal or reactionary, rationalist or romantic.) I have come to believe that obsessive attention to the apparent irrationality of the blood libel simply does not work well as an analytical lens. In addition to reflecting the ideological perspective of one set of actors in the events in question, the argument for the cultural backwardness—the atavism—of the modern ritual murder trials either presumes a regrettable continuity between the medieval accusation and its modern variant—underscoring the incompleteness of Enlightenment education—or suggests that it was precisely the irrational element in the blood libel that its modern protagonists found to be so appealing. Both claims, I think, are incorrect, and each tends to cloud over what I feel are the unique features of the *modern* trials for ritual murder.

My Approach

The ritual murder accusation, as I have argued, was not a constant feature of the Jewish experience of Europe. States outside of Poland and the Russian Empire had indeed chosen—implicitly, at least—not to prosecute criminal cases on the basis of this theory since the mid- to late-sixteenth century, while in Poland and Hungary, such prosecutions ended at the end of the eighteenth century. The trials of the fin de siècle in fact constituted a novelty, a breaking out of one set of cultural and political categories—ones that had essentially confined the blood libel to the margins of polite discourse—to a new set of interpretive possibilities and meanings. And the trials in this period represented something other than simply a "return of the repressed." Certainly, traditional wisdom and popular culture played a role in these trials—particularly in their early stages, in the production of accusations at the local level—and to a certain extent our cases offer compelling, albeit troubling, examples of the convergence of myth, traditional wisdom, rationality, and irrationality in the production of social knowledge. But they also reveal the ways in which different systems of knowledge *compete* for authority and power in modern societies. Ultimately, the modern ritual murder trial rested on the cultural authority of contemporary scientific attitudes and practices, the professionalization and medicalization of the social sciences—especially criminology—and the bureaucratic rationality of the professional civil service.[28]

In the pages that follow, I will be paying close attention to social relations at the local level and to the mechanisms by which narratives of ritual crime emerge: hence, to language and communication as well as the breakdown in communal cohesion; to the social and political settings in which these systems of meaning were created and applied; to the larger, national-political arenas in which our dramas were played out; and—most important, from my perspective—the processes by which local narratives of Jewish conspiracy gained credibility and traction in the eyes of government officials and could be sustained thereafter in modern criminal proceedings. I will be making the argument that what allowed the trials to proceed (and, to a certain extent, succeed) during this period had more to do with their *modernity*—including their ability to appropriate the authority and prestige of scientific culture—than with their irrationality or with appeals to premodern or traditional wisdom. The story of the modern ritual trial is, in my view, not so much that of the lasting power of myth, or irrationality, as a tale of the momentary alliance of high culture and scientific authority with a certain perception of collective Jewish criminality.

The incorporation of ritual murder proceedings against Jews to the business of the state at the turn of the century occurred on the strength of crucial and momentarily intersecting cultural supports. What made it possible for police officials, district magistrates, and state's attorneys in the 1880s and 1890s to take seriously allegations that they would have been more likely to reject out of hand during the previous three centuries might best be described as a "momentum of increasing plausibility." The transition from a politics of deference based on a restricted franchise to mass politics, the corrosive effects of urbanization and industrialization on small-town and village life, the completion of political emancipation for the Jews of Central Europe in the 1870s, the emergence of professional social scientists and criminologists as repositories of expertise and arbiters of social policy, and a crisis over the meaning of female independence and sexuality were all among the factors that combined to produce the impulse to prosecute. Over the course of three decades, however, the temporary consensus that had resulted from the coming together of diverse discourses and their institutional supports will begin to unravel. The accusation of Jewish ritual murder had never constituted undisputed knowledge in Central European societies, and it did not take long for elements of the very constellation of forces that had sustained the accusation—in its modern version—in the first place to dissent, raise doubts, or lose heart. State's attorneys would at times openly criticize the case that had been prepared by investigating magistrates, ministries of justice would order cases retried, individual politicians would call for the overturning of trial verdicts on appeal, and medical faculties would intervene collectively to demand a complete reexamination of a case's forensic evidence. By the time of the Beilis trial in 1913, few elite cultural or political institutions in Europe voiced support for this particular narrative of Jewish criminality; even the Tsarist government may not have believed in its own case.

I have found a number of analytical approaches to the production of knowledge in social settings helpful in my own efforts to reconstruct the cultural foundations of the ritual murder accusation in the modern period, but allow me to signal one in particular. In a classic work in the sociology of knowledge published five decades ago, Peter Berger and Thomas Luckmann explored the cognitive aspects of everyday experience and emphasized the tension that can exist between intersubjective experience and preexisting, received knowledge of the Other. The objects, institutions, and social relations of everyday life, they suggest, reveal themselves to us as an "ordered reality . . . prearranged in patterns that seem to be independent of [our] apprehension of them." Knowledge *of* the world around one, then, precedes and, to a large extent, informs one's experience *in* the world: "The reality of everyday life appears already objectified, that is, constituted by an order of objects that have been designated *as* objects before my appearance on the scene. The language used in everyday life continuously provides me with the necessary objectifications and posits the order within which these make sense and within which everyday life has meaning for me."[29] But reality also makes itself known as "intersubjective" experience. Not only can one not exist in the world without continually interacting with others, but these interactions are predicated on the (mutually held) assumption that the people one encounters "also comprehend the objectifications by which this world is ordered, that they also organize this world around the 'here and now' of *their* being in it."

> I also know, of course, that the others have a perspective on this common world that is not identical with mine. My "here" is their "there." My "now" does not fully overlap with theirs. My projects differ from and may even conflict with theirs. All the same, I know that I live with them in a common world. Most, importantly, I know that there is an ongoing correspondence between *my* meanings and *their* meanings in this world, that we share a common sense about its reality.[30]

Hence, while preexisting knowledge of the world imposes fixed patterns on the ways in which we experience people and phenomena, face-to-face interactions should in theory be highly flexible and open-ended. The expectations that people have when interacting with others, structured or mediated by socially transmitted knowledge and memory, can continually be modified "through the exceedingly variegated and subtle interchange of subjective meanings that goes on."[31] In other words, the individual whom we confront in face-to-face interactions always has the ability to upset or contradict our expectations of his or her characteristics and intentions. Social interactions take place, then, in accordance with what these authors call "typificatory schemes," which are themselves subject to alteration. The closer these interactions are to face-to-face encounters, the more susceptible the patterning is to change; the more distant the interaction, the more dominant the schematic aspects.

This view of social interaction as a *cognitive* process, in which knowledge precedes and directs experience of the world—and is also produced and modified in the course of social encounters—suggests that what is at stake in the interpretation of the modern ritual murder trial is to locate the systems of knowledge that accompanied and sustained the accusation, the social settings in which they were articulated, the network of institutions—national, educational, political, judicial—that could transform an accusation into a formal investigation and trial, as well as the confrontations with Jews, the objects of these ascribed traits, that might have altered, thwarted, or affirmed the cultural assumptions of criminality. The movement is from knowledge to experience and from the local nexus of social interactions to overarching institutions of society and state. But the starting point is the locality: the small town or village, the community, the church, the cluster of families.[32]

* * *

Blood Inscriptions is divided into five chapters, this introduction, and a conclusion. Chapter 1 ("History and Place: Hometown, Local Knowledge, and National Politics") incorporates what I am calling a "cultural geography of place," which focuses on the role of local culture and politics in the production of social knowledge and attempts to reconstruct the nature and quality of Jewish-Gentile cultural exchange and social interaction in the four localities in which our cases transpire: Tiszaeszlár, Xanten, Polná, and Konitz. From a consideration of "the local," it branches out to consider modern historical patterns of Jewish/state and Jewish/society relations in Germany and Austria-Hungary. One of its central arguments is that there is no simple way to correlate the occurrence of a ritual murder trial in a particular locality to the history of antisemitism in that country or to specific patterns of Jewish-Gentile interaction. Moreover, a history of strained or hostile interethnic relations is not necessarily a prerequisite in the production of an accusation of ritual murder. In its final section, the chapter returns to Tiszaeszlár, Xanten, Polná, and Konitz as Jewish "hometowns" and investigates the earliest articulations of the specific accusations of ritual murder that eventually weaved their way to trial.

Chapter 2 ("Hungarian Beginnings: The Tiszaeszlár Affair") offers a narrative reconstruction and analysis of the first of our trials. As in subsequent chapters, the analysis proceeds from the production of a theory of ritual murder to its incorporation by police and judicial officials at various stages in the investigation and eventually to the formal, public trial and the tensions and dramas that it reveals. Special attention is paid to Jewish voices that struggle to make themselves heard—at times with disastrous results—and to the methodological and rhetorical standards imposed upon the proceedings by modern scientific practices and authorities. Chapter 3 ("Roads to Prussia: From Tiszaeszlár to Xanten") surveys a variety of responses to the Tiszaeszlár case in the decade following the trial, from the formation of political parties to riots, from apologetics to polemics to the production of cultural memory. It focuses primarily on the Xanten investigation and trial, emphasizing both the local construction of the ritual murder accusation and efforts on the part of the state to impose order, proper procedure, and healthy skepticism on the investigation and subsequent trial. The twin roles of state authority and scientific, forensic expertise in the Xanten case invite comparison to a similar investigation in the town of Skurz, which produced quite different outcomes. While each of our trials revolved to a certain extant around competing appeals to science and medicine, the events in Xanten and Skurz open up another rhetorical field: the place of Jewish ritual slaughtering (*sheḥitah*) in modern ritual murder discourse and the role of butchers—both Jewish and Christian—in the evolving affairs.

Chapter 4 ("The Hilsner Affair") charts the intertwining of the ritual murder accusation with the antiliberal and nationalist politics of the 1890s in the Bohemian lands, a process that culminates in the Hilsner affair, which transpired in Polná, Kutná Hora, and Písek from 1899 to 1900. The first Hilsner investigation and trial (Kutná Hora, 1899), while carrying forward much of the thematic structure of earlier cases, was also unique in several respects. Hilsner himself was not a functionary of the Jewish community or indeed fluent in Jewish texts and traditions but rather a marginal figure with a somewhat questionable reputation. And, unlike the Jewish defendants of Tiszaeszlár and Xanten, not only was Hilsner not acquitted of the charges, but he was sentenced to death. Hilsner's defenders—including his defense attorney, the then university professor Tomáš G. Masaryk, and the medical faculty of the Czech University in Prague—were just as adamant, however, in challenging the scientific and forensic foundations of the prosecution's case, and the High Court of Appeals in Vienna quashed the verdict, ordering a new trial. The chapter ends with the retrial of Leopold Hilsner in Písek in 1900, his second conviction, and second death sentence. Why did this case break with recent precedent? What happened to the commanding voice of high culture and science?

Chapter 5 ("The Many Trials of Konitz") opens with an examination of the ambiguous role of social science and criminology in the prosecution of ritual murder at the turn of the century. It then explores the Konitz case, the last of the Central Europe's cluster of trials, making note of the indecisiveness and division among investigators, prosecutors, and government officials; the proliferation of minor prosecutions rather than a single trial; and the relatively late, although decisive, intervention of medical and scientific authorities. If Konitz was the end of the line for the modern ritual murder trial in Central Europe, the end was ignominious.

The Conclusion turns its attention at the beginning to the traumatic violence of the Kishinev pogrom of 1903, the Orthodox rabbis' ceremonial oath swearing in Kraków the same year, and the Beilis affair of 1911 to 1913, examining the ways in which these events corresponded to or broke from established patterns. It returns to some of the theoretical underpinnings of the book—the Weberian model of rationality and disenchantment, as well as criticisms of that model—considers the question of science versus bad science versus pseudoscience, and closes with a look at the impoverished narrative meanings attached to "ritual murder" in the modern world.

Chapter 1

History and Place

Hometown, Local Knowledge, and National Politics

Geese, geese, endless geese.
—C. A. Macartney (1934)

Certainly in a place as small as Konitz, one knows with whom one is speaking.
—Presiding judge, Konitz criminal court (1900)

Toward a Cultural Geography of Place

On the morning of 2 June 1891, in the Rhineland town of Xanten, the mother of Johann Hegmann, aged five, sent her son outside to play so that she could attend mass in commemoration of the Feast of Saints Peter and Paul. As one might already have guessed, the boy never returned home, and the tragic discovery that evening of his stabbed and bloodied body set in motion a series of events, which culminated in Germany's first formal trial on the charge of ritual murder since the sixteenth century.[1] Finding himself accused of Johann's murder—presumed to have been carried out for the purposes of violent, anti-Christian Jewish ritual—was Adolf Buschhoff, aged fifty, a native of Xanten and one of the town's eighty-five Jewish inhabitants. A former ritual slaughterer for the Jewish community who more recently had been working as a stonecutter, Buschhoff had enjoyed an impeccable reputation as a friendly and mild-mannered citizen of the town almost up to the moment of his becoming the target of suspicion.[2] The obvious question is, why? Why does an apparently well-adjusted, sociable, and esteemed member of a small urban community become the prime target of a murder investigation? Why was this murder so quickly and easily understood as a crime committed by Jews acting under religious compulsion? And what is the process by which this discursive transformation happened?

Similar questions can be raised with regard to other long-standing and ostensibly well-integrated Jewish citizens of towns and villages in Germany and Austria-Hungary whose lives and sense of belonging were uprooted when they became embroiled in ritual murder proceedings: József Scharf, Salamon Schwarcz, and thirteen others in and around Tiszaeszlár; Adolf and Moritz Lewy in Konitz; and perhaps even Leopold Hilsner, the underemployed ne'er-do-well who spoke German and Czech with equal ease and spent most of his days with likeminded Christian Czechs in Polná.[3] How exactly *did* Jews relate to their local towns and villages in Central Europe during the last decades of the nineteenth century? In what ways were their lives transformed—if at all—by the political emancipation that had become enshrined in law between 1867 and 1871? Was their supposed integration a sham? Did they feel at home in their local environments? What were the means by which intercommunal bonds were shattered?

We got a sense in the Introduction of the many articulations of the renewed blood libel that surfaced in Central Europe's political sphere and mass-market publications. This might suggest that what we are observing is a situation in which a single cultural phenomenon takes root more or less simultaneously across a variety of political and geographic settings. If that is true, then one might argue that any explanation of this phenomenon must necessarily be comparative, giving weight to *common* features and *general* patterns. What do the various settings have in common? What political, economic, or social factors are replicated across discrete borders? Are we dealing with a specific type of Jewish community, a particular pattern of Jewish-Gentile interaction, or a single, generalized, historical crisis?

This would certainly be a valid approach, but it is nevertheless potentially distorting, for it presumes that local conditions and the texture of local experience can adequately be understood as mere instantiations of a general pattern. The universal, in other words, trumps the specific. What I hope to do in this and following chapters, in contrast, is to engage in a type of analysis in which *place*, locality, and the texture of local experience are given equal weight to general, overarching patterns. A cultural geography of place, if you will, is interested in specificity: the physical landscape of a village or a town, local patterns of economic exchange, the distribution of power, and the creation of knowledge. Such an approach embodies the tension between the drive to compare—and hence to emphasize pattern—and the appreciation of uniqueness. It seeks to "enter" the landscape, to uncover the texture of local experience, to capture the perspectives of local actors. It asks of what importance local cultural understandings are to historical processes, or the intrinsic patterns of social relations to political affairs. Finally, it attempts to disengage the modern ritual murder trial, as a cultural phenomenon in which Jews and Gentiles vied with each other and over their own sense of self, from *antisemitism* as an explanatory construct.[4]

At the level of everyday experience, accusations of ritual murder emerged both from social interactions and from the ensuing moral constructions that imbued events with meaning. They were the products of face-to-face encounters—scripted in part by cognitive expectations—each of which added something to the local complex of social knowledge. One could say that the modern ritual murder accusation, whatever else it might have been, was born of, and nurtured by, community. But what kind of community? In virtually every instance, the local setting turns out to have been a village or, more likely, a market town; rarely, a small city. In other words: paradoxically tranquil places whose traditional economic and social structure stood at some remove from the wide-ranging transformations typically associated with the industrial age. Each locality also possessed a long-standing Jewish community, historically rooted to the environment, fully conversant in the surrounding culture, and—by all appearances—on relatively cordial, if not intimate, terms with its Christian neighbors. In each instance, too, the transition from a concrete narrative of Jewish ritual murder to police investigation and trial entangled the town or village in an expansive web of *urban* discourses and political processes (in the form of newspaper coverage, parliamentary interpellations, and the invasion of journalists and national politicians). The present chapter seeks to disentangle this complex relationship when possible, at the very least to give play to the tension inherent in the not always comfortable distinction between the local and the universal.

The places in question, then, were small, of such a scale that social relations usually involved face-to-face interactions. Tiszaeszlár, which lies in the northeastern stretch of Hungary's Great Plain in what was then Szabolcs County (county seat, Nyíregyháza), is arguably the only true village among

Map design courtesy of Tomasz Cebrat, Northwestern University, and Jen Mabray, Washington University in St. Louis.

Figure 2. Modern ritual murder trials and Jewish population centers.

our sample. It sits on the left bank of the Tisza River nestled between two dominating towns: Debrecen to the south and Szatmár (later, Satu Mare in Romania) to the east.[5] It was in villages such as Tiszaeszlár that nationalist historians of the nineteenth century claimed to have discovered the cradle of a nation's values and character. No less a figure than the British historian C. A. Macartney, observing Hungary in the 1930s, went so far as to describe the villages of the Great Hungarian Plain as incorporating "the social and economic ideals of the true Magyar." His portrait stressed the tranquility and banality of the Hungarian village and the predictability of its physical features.

> The village itself is a regular pattern of very wide streets, most of them unpaved, the basking-place of pigs and poultry and geese, geese, endless geese; and bounding the street, rows of little whitewashed, one-storied houses, each with its narrow end turned to the street, while between its verandahed face and its neighbor's back, is a sandy courtyard, a well, a few sunflowers. Behind,

> opening straight onto the fields, are byres, barn, and stable. It is a community which reeks of the soil. Every man in it, from the local magnate downward, lives by, on, and from the soil. The fields stretch up to the very doors, and the fruits of them are scattered in the courtyards. The few craftsmen, who advertise their skill by a painted sign of smock, boot, or scythe, the cobbler, smith, and tailor, are themselves most often peasants who ply their trade in their spare hours.[6]

Midsized market towns served as the setting for subsequent ritual murder accusations as well as for the criminal investigation and trial in the Tiszaeszlár case. In Macartney's view, places such as these amounted to little more than glorified villages in any event. True, their level of economic and administrative activity might have required the presence of a police barracks and a town hall, a few bank branches, and a local doctor (not to mention the ubiquitous inns). But social life in the market towns was structured largely along rural lines. As late as the 1930s, a high proportion of town inhabitants was made up of landowners, many of whom were in fact peasants who went out into the fields during the day; others were owners of estates in the country on which they spent much of their time.[7]

Xanten appears to have been such an "oversized village." Located in Imperial Germany's Lower Rhine Plain in the state of Prussia (the Rheinprovinz), the town was once a Roman river crossing along the main road that ran from Cologne to Cleves and Nijmegen. But Xanten lost much of its economic importance with the subsequent shifting of the course of the river.[8] Between 1875 and 1910, its population grew modestly from 3,292 to just under 4,300; Düsseldorf, in contrast, the seat of the main administrative subdivision (Regierungsbezirk) to which Xanten belonged, had almost 360,000 inhabitants; Cologne, the capital of the neighboring Regierungsbezirk, had a population of 600,000.[9] The Lower Rhineland consisted largely of isolated farmsteads and towns that dated back to the thirteenth century. Robert Dickinson's postwar geographic guide to Germany commented that the only flourishing towns in the region were those that enjoyed both rail transport and direct contact with the Rhine. Xanten was not one of these. With no industry of its own and no direct link to the river's traffic, it remained a local market center and appeared to have preserved much of its medieval flavor.[10]

It was this sense of a town resting in suspended animation that Paul Nathan, sent by the Berlin newspaper *Die Nation* to cover the Xanten trial, tried to convey for his readers back home. The reporter paused on his approach to the town to capture the visual impact of the place as it hovered in the distance, contrasting so starkly from the cityscape of the modern metropolis. The town that lay before him seemed to evoke the German past, entangled in bucolic serenity and stern, medieval, Catholic grandeur.

> Xanten—it lies so beautiful. Lost in greenery, the small, neat houses surround the mighty cathedral, the gothic St. Victor's Church, a towering presence, one of the most serious and memorable medieval constructions on the Lower Rhine. As one stands on the gently rising Fürstenberg and looks over the landscape at the clusters of green trees, the small patches of forest, the farms and villages, the gentle hills and the wide, flat plains, through which the Rhine flows wide and steel gray; and as one's eye is drawn again and again to the powerful mass of the cathedral, it seems as though the ruling power of the Middle Ages stands there as a bodily presence.[11]

Polná, the site of the Hilsner case, offers a variation on the theme of the small town left behind by industrialization. Situated along what was once an important road to Hungary, Polná occupies a corner of the Bohemian-Moravian highlands (Českomoravská vysočina), an extensive, wooded plateau that straddles the border between Bohemia and Moravia, the two major provinces of the Czech lands. Two larger, neighboring towns—Jihlava (Iglau) and Německý (later, Havlíčkův) Brod (Deutschbrod)—achieved fame as centers of silver mining in the thirteenth century, while Polná itself—owned by a succession of noble families—was more closely tied to the organization of feudal property up to the middle of the nineteenth century. The town also felt the tumultuous effects of the revolt of the Czech estates against imperial rule at the start of the Thirty Years War. Its owners from the late sixteenth to the seventeenth centuries had been Protestant, members of the Zejdlič of Šenfeld family, who (as Protestants) had lent their support to the unsuccessful revolt of the Czech estates of 1618 to 1620. They lost their lands with the suppression of the revolt, and in 1623, the Bishop of Olomouc, František (Franz) of Dietrichštejn, acquired the feudal rights to the town from Emperor Ferdinand II for 150,000 zlaty. The Dietrichštejn family ruled Polná (admittedly, from a distance) until 1848 and maintained large tracts of land there until 1922.[12]

Although technically part of Bohemia, Polná lies stubbornly to the east of the closest large town in the region, Jihlava (Iglau), which is in Moravia. This geographic curiosity suggests a remoteness from Prague, the cultural, political, and economic center of Czech life—a remoteness underscored by the mapping of industrialization in the region. In 1871, when the first rail lines connecting Prague, Jihlava, and Znojmo were opened, they bypassed Polná altogether, coursing six kilometers from the outskirts of the town.[13] In 1890, one could find a five-grade lower school (*obecní* škola) for boys and one for girls; one three-grade *měšt'anská* škola (*Bürgerschule*) for each of the two sexes, geared toward trade and commerce; and a two-grade Jewish school. Polná's population at the time stood at 9,102, of whom 8,801 were Catholic, 247 Jewish, 44 Protestant, and 10 "other." The village of Malá Věžnice, which would feature prominently in the events of 1899 to 1900, lay to the northwest of the town. It comprised forty homes, a population of 218, and a one-grade school.[14]

Konitz (Chojnice)—the largest of the towns that produced ritual murder trials around 1900—lies in the formerly German province of West Prussia, to the south and east of Pomerania. This is territory that has alternated between German and Polish political control. Before 1772, it belonged to the Polish-Lithuanian Commonwealth and was administered by the Polish Crown as part of the territory of what was called "Royal Prussia." Following the first partition of Poland-Lithuania, it was attached to the Kingdom of Prussia, and both "Royal Prussia" and its neighbor to the east, the province of "Prussia," were renamed: the former became West Prussia; the latter, East Prussia. From the 1820s to 1878, East and West Prussia were combined administratively; from 1878 to the end of World War I, they were again organized as separate entities, with Danzig (Gdańsk) serving as the West Prussian capital and Königsberg (Kaliningrad) that of East Prussia. After 1918, Konitz/Chojnice was located in the Polish Republic.[15]

Unlike the case in the much smaller Polná, the all-important railway lines did not skirt past this West Prussian town. In fact, Konitz was a stop on two important railway lines: one, which ran from eastern Pomerania toward the southeast, and the other, the main line from Berlin to Danzig (Gdańsk). Not isolated, to be sure, Konitz appears in most other respects to have been completely unremarkable. According to the Baedeker travel guide, the junction of the two rail lines constituted the town's only point of interest.[16] A more distinctive feature of Konitz was its setting in an ethnic and religious borderland. West Prussia comprised a mixed German and Slavic, as well as Protestant and Catholic, population. In 1858, 69.1 percent of its inhabitants were counted (by language) as Germans and 30.9 percent as Slavs. By 1910, the number of Germans had declined somewhat to about 65 percent (equal to 1,100,000 individuals). Of the 35 percent who claimed Slavic ethnicity, 475,000 indicated Polish as their mother tongue and 107,000 Kashubian. About 22,000 people were listed as bilingual.[17] In the city of Konitz itself, there were 10,656 inhabitants in 1895; of these, 4,974 were Catholic, 5,358 Protestant, and 480 (4.5 percent) Jewish. While the surrounding countryside was made up of Germans, Poles, and Kashubians (to the north and east), the town itself was populated overwhelmingly by Germans.[18]

Jews, State, and Society in Germany and Austria-Hungary: Historical Patterns

Despite the lyrical depictions by Nathan and Macartney of an almost timeless village and small-town life in Central Europe, these localities were never frozen in time. Their populations may not have grown appreciably. Their economies may indeed have declined since the onset of industrialization, but they were nevertheless deeply marked by the transformations in social structure, politics, and the economy that had taken place since the last decades of the eighteenth century. They were, in other words, artifacts themselves of modern times. In Hungary, important transformations in politics and the economy dated at least to the Revolution of 1848 and remained in force throughout the period of neoabsolutism (roughly 1851–61). These included the emancipation of the peasants and the cancellation of feudal services and dues, the removal of the landowner's patrimonial rights and police powers, the introduction of the Austrian criminal code and legal procedures, improvements in schooling, reform of the tax system, the removal of internal tariffs, and uniform regulation of banking and commerce. In the countryside, traditional patterns of social life significantly eroded in the 1860s in the face of rapid growth in the agricultural sector; here, too, expansion both preceded and accompanied the political gains of the 1867 Compromise (Ausgleich), which established the dual monarchy of Austria-Hungary.[19]

In the wake of the Ausgleich, new industrial firms, in the words of one historian, "sprang up like mushrooms after a spring rain."[20] Again it was the agricultural sector (mainly grain production) that led the expansion and that encouraged intensive, foreign capital investment in the country. From 1867 to 1868 alone, 170 new industrial corporations and 552 credit institutions were established, and 2,500 miles of new rail lines were built. With increased market-oriented management in agriculture, thousands of new acres of land were devoted to grain production. For several decades, industrial growth complemented developments in agriculture: the milling of flour soon emerged as Hungary's leading large-scale industry. The number of steam-driven mills grew from 146 in 1863 to 1,843 in 1895, and in the 1860s, Hungary exported as much flour as all other European states combined.[21]

Nevertheless, Hungary's economy before World War I also showed signs of structural weakness and vulnerability. The stock market crash of 1873 resulted in a severe curtailment of foreign investment, and a prolonged decline in world grain prices in the 1870s and 1880s induced the government to abandon its previous free-market, laissez-faire policies in favor of increased protectionism.[22] Moreover, while the magnate families—the owners of the largest tracts of land—appeared to thrive in the transition to commercial agriculture, many members of the gentry found it necessary to sell their ancestral holdings. Sons of the lesser nobility, discouraged for cultural and psychological reasons from commercial pursuits, increasingly sought employment in urban professions and the civil service. Thus, the economy and the bureaucracy, although formally bifurcated, were mutually dependent. Andrew Janos has described Hungary's liberal elite of the late nineteenth century as "a political class living off public revenue." It relied on a constantly expanding bureaucracy for its livelihood and so did all it could to encourage economic growth and development. National consolidation, in turn, depended on the state's ability to recruit non-Magyar economic elites and encourage their linguistic and cultural assimilation. It has been estimated that as many as two million nonethnic Hungarians were drawn into the Hungarian cultural and linguistic orbit between 1880 and 1910. This number included not only the country's 700,000 Jews (the population around 1880) but also some 600,000 Germans, 200,000 Slovaks, and 100,000 Croats as well.[23]

The origins of the modern Hungarian Jewish community are to be found in the impressive growth in population—largely the result of immigration—that began in the eighteenth century but saw its most dramatic gains in the nineteenth century. The process began on the heels of simultaneous developments in the areas of military conquest and frankly anti-Jewish administrative retrenchment; it mushroomed following the first Polish partition and the annexation of Galicia to the Habsburg monarchy (1772). The reconquest of Ottoman Hungary by Habsburg forces—begun in 1686 with the capture of Buda and largely completed by 1699 with the signing of the Peace of

Karlowitz—provided the physical space for the rapid expansion of Jewish life into this part of Central Europe, and the repressive Familiants Laws of 1726 and 1727, decreed by Emperor Charles VI—which capped the number of Jewish families allowed to reside legally in Bohemia and Moravia at current levels—provided the raw human material.[24] Since one of the provisions of the Familiants Laws held that only the eldest son from any Jewish household had the right to marry and establish a family of his own, younger sons had to remain officially unmarried or look beyond Bohemia and Moravia to settle; on occasion, they could seek protection in the private estates of the nobility. For many Jews seeking a future that included the prospects for marriage and mobility, Hungary beckoned. The Jewish population of the kingdom grew from approximately 13,000 in 1730 (0.3 percent of the population) to 75,000 in 1785 (a little under 1 percent of the total). Following the annexation of Galicia to the Habsburg monarchy, the pace of Jewish migration to Hungary increased. Its Jewish population grew by 70 percent over twenty years, reaching a total of 128,000 by 1805. Over the course of the nineteenth century, Hungary's Jewish community experienced a demographic explosion: it stood at 369,000 in 1850 (2.8 percent of the population) and 552,000 in 1869 (3.6 percent), and it reached a high water mark of 932,000 in 1910 (4.5 percent). At the beginning of the twentieth century, nearly 10 percent of the world's Jewish population was living in the Kingdom of Hungary, while Jews made up 23 percent of the population of Budapest.[25]

The pace and extent of Jewish social mobility and economic success—while limited largely to acculturating Jews living in urban areas—were equally dramatic. Jews responded enthusiastically to the openness of the country's dominant political class to the recruitment of non-Magyars to business, industry, and the liberal professions. William McCagg has described this state of affairs as a "collaboration" between Hungary's "Jewish capitalists" and the "nobiliary old regime," while Andrew Janos writes of an "ethnic division of labor," in which the Magyar gentry dominated the bureaucracy, parliament, and the judiciary, and Jews monopolized the liberal professions and fed the capitalist economy.[26] In this arrangement, Jews were welcomed to help build the economic infrastructure of what was to become a nobility-dominated, liberal state and—by accepting acculturation to Hungarian linguistic culture and adopting a Hungarian national identity—help the Magyar gentry consolidate its power in this multiethnic kingdom.[27] And help they did. Jews made up much of the middle class of the country, both the business sector and the liberal professions of law, medicine, and engineering. Jews engaged in the marketing and exporting of agricultural produce and invested in the construction of railways; they became directors of banks and industrial enterprises; they even became ennobled. Over three hundred families carried titles of nobility by the early twentieth century—twenty-eight Jews were made barons—and many acquired large estates. On the eve of World War I, one-fifth of Hungary's larger estates were owned by Jews.[28]

There is no simple way to correlate the occurrence of a ritual murder trial in a particular locality to the history of antisemitism in that country or to specific patterns of Jewish-Gentile interaction. One thing does seem certain, however: a history of strained or hostile interethnic relations is not necessarily a prerequisite in the production of an accusation of ritual murder. Hungary is a case in point. As in most parts of Europe, anti-Jewish teachings were a part of the country's cultural and religious heritage, and anti-Jewish sentiments certainly were to be found in its political culture. Additionally, the institutional structures that produced peaceful coexistence between Jews and non-Jewish Hungarians did break apart from time to time, for example, during the popular riots against Jews that broke out during the Hungarian Revolution of 1848 in various localities (e.g., Pressburg/Pozsony, Pécs, Székesfehérvár, and Pest).[29] On the whole, however, relations between Christians and Jews in the Kingdom of Hungary were stable and peaceful throughout the 1860s and 1870s. The Liberal Party's hold on power from 1875 to 1905, moreover, worked to marginalize political voices that were opposed to the *modus vivendi* with Hungary's Jewish middle class.[30]

Some Hungarian politicians, most notably Győző Istóczy (1842–1915), began to articulate a dissident, anti-Jewish ideology during the second half of the 1870s. Istóczy, who represented the district of Rum in Vas County, western Hungary, delivered his first antisemitic speech in parliament in 1875 in the form of a long-winded interpellation of the government, then under the leadership of Baron Béla Wenckheim, in which he complained about the "invasion" of Hungary by foreign Jews. He demanded to know whether the government intended to prevent the naturalization of these Jews and if it opposed the creation of a movement of self-defense against Jewish domination of the country. The prime minister's official response to the house expressed surprise and incomprehension at Istóczy's attack, indicating just how removed from mainstream political culture it was. Yes, the government did intend to regulate immigration and to implement naturalization laws, although not for the reasons that Istóczy had cited; the government would, however, oppose any political movement designed to disturb peaceful social relations among religious communities. Wenckheim took particular notice of the fact that the law of December 1867 had established the principle of Jewish civic equality; as a result, the government did not recognize the existence of a "Jewish Question."[31]

Before the Tiszaeszlár affair, Istóczy's most unusual address to parliament, made in June 1878, urged the government to work toward the restoration of a Jewish state in Palestine, to which Hungary's Jewish population might be encouraged to move, thereby solving the question that the Liberal government of Hungary argued did not exist.[32] Istóczy linked the danger of Jewish presence in Hungary to the country's experience with, and resistance to, occupation by the Ottoman Empire. With an eye to the removal of Ottoman forces from Hungary at the end of the seventeenth century and the more recent retreat of the Muslim state from the Balkans, Istóczy made the following observation:

> With the gradual disappearance of the Mohammedan element, only a single, alien, element remained, from that point on completely isolated in Christian Europe: That alien element is Jewry.
>
> Now that the European nations have rid themselves once and for all of the justified fear of Islamic power, the Jewish people—with feverish excitement and indefatigable activity—strive to realize their bold plan of acquiring control over the peoples of Europe and enslaving them.[33]

Noting that, according to official statistics, the Jewish population of Hungary had grown from some 75,000 in 1785 to over 552,000 in 1870, he surmised that the Jewish community doubled every thirty years and predicted that there would be over a million Jews in Hungary in 1900, over two million by 1930, and 17,600,000 in 2020 (the last remark produced lengthy laughter in the house).[34] The solution to this intolerable state of affairs, Istóczy concluded, "in accordance with the prevailing spirit of our time," was the reestablishment of a Jewish state in Palestine. The Liberal government, now under the premiership of Kálmán Tisza (1830–1902), again responded with disapproval and embarrassment, and Istóczy himself, while he may have managed to win a few converts from the ranks of the Independence Party, seemed to have become something of a laughing-stock in parliament. His speeches in and outside of the legislative chamber hardly constituted a political movement before 1882, and the Tiszaeszlár accusation could not have been manufactured by Hungarian antisemitism, such as it was. It would be more accurate to say that the Tiszaeszlár case and the formation of a self-consciously antisemitic political movement in Hungary occurred more or less at the same time.

In the German Rhineland, the duchies and bishoprics that had made up the region before 1800 were consolidated under Prussian rule in the aftermath of the Revolutionary and Napoleonic wars (and after a period of annexation to France). After 1871 and the formation of the German Empire, the Rhineland—by virtue of its large Catholic population—became one of the sites of the *Kulturkampf*, a prolonged political struggle that pitted imperial centralism and national liberal ideology against regionalism, Catholic culture, and minority rights. German Catholics felt beleaguered by imperial officials in Berlin, who, together with their National Liberal political supporters, introduced legislation designed to remove Catholic influence in public life and questioned the willingness and ability of Catholics to take part in the German national project. Although the conflict was not understood officially to be over until 1887, already by the end of the 1870s, Bismarck was able to forge a long-term alliance with heavy industrialists and large East Elbian landowners. As a result, the state looked less at Catholics as potential enemies and increasingly at Social Democrats and even democratic liberals. During the intervening years, the *Kulturkampf* engendered a deep insecurity among Catholic intellectuals and Church leaders in western and southern Germany as well as a defensive solidarity and strong, antiliberal sentiments.[35] The stock market crash of the 1870s merely increased the tendency on the part of some Catholics to view German unification as a pet project of bankers, industrialists, and National Liberal politicians—a creation of the complementary processes of liberalism, capitalism, and "Jewish" culture. Liberalism, in this critical assessment of contemporary culture and politics, had led to unbridled material interest and the corruption of the social fabric. It had produced demands for the separation of Church and state and for the reduced influence of the Church generally in society.[36]

There is a division of opinion among historians regarding the role of the *Kulturkampf* itself in the development of antisemitism in the Catholic and mixed religious regions of Germany. Olaf Blaschke points to the growth of ultramontanist convictions in the nineteenth century—which urged the creation of a united Catholic front, led by the leaders of the Church, to confront an unremittingly hostile world—as crucial to the formation of the anti-Jewish attitudes and rhetoric of the latter part of the century.[37] Both Blaschke and Barbara Suchy regard the subsequent struggle between Catholicism and the German state as a defining moment in the formation of antisemitism in

Catholic milieux, including the Rhineland. Catholic publicists blamed Jewish politicians such as Eduard Lasker and Ludwig Bamberger—indeed, Jews as a collectivity—for the campaign against the Church and its social values. The entire cultural struggle, Suchy suggests, came to be seen as the cultural-political counterpart to "Jewish" capitalism: "Its single goal was to set aside Christian spirit and ecclesiastical authority, the only obstacle[s] to Jewish power."[38] Ulrich Baumann, in contrast, distinguishing between social attitudes and formal politics, notes that for many Catholics in Baden in southwestern Germany, the confessionalization of politics that occurred in the 1870s and the formation of the Catholic Center Party rendered Catholics less interested in joining or voting for antisemitic political parties when these were established in the following decade. This is not to say that attitudes toward Jews had not hardened during the years of conflict with the state. To the contrary: when candidates from antisemitic parties came to Catholic towns and villages, their criticisms of Germany's Jews often fell on receptive ears and spoke directly to received traditions about Jews. While these speeches may not have changed the voting patterns of the Catholic residents of the region, they left behind, in Baumann's words, "traces of the destruction of place" and, in this sense, also belong to the history of the relations between Jews and Christians.[39]

Suchy's research into anti-Jewish attitudes and policies in the Rhineland during this period attributes much of the hostility toward Jews to the power and influence of the Catholic Church. She points to the role of the Catholic clergy, for example, in implanting in the popular imagination lasting images of Jewish deicide, Host desecration, and the spreading of plague—to say nothing of ritual murder.[40] And we should recall that it was in Münster in neighboring Westphalia that the theology professor August Rohling (1839–1931) had issued his notorious publication *Der Talmudjude* in 1871, a libelous work that claimed to have discovered in the Talmud the prescriptive basis for a wide variety of Jewish criminal behaviors. Rohling's book enjoyed much popularity in the decades leading up to the Xanten affair: it went through six editions by 1878 and was frequently reissued thereafter. In Westphalia alone, 38,000 copies of the book were distributed free of charge by the Bonifacius association.[41]

British and German newspapers covering the Xanten trial in 1892 were quick to pick up on the theme of the nefarious role of the Church in producing a culture of intolerance and suspicion. According to one report, children's readers used in Catholic schools in Germany conveyed narratives of Jewish ritual murders as historical facts.[42] This was especially true of anthologies of the lives of the saints: in one such work, *Katholischer Kindergarten oder Legende für Kinder*—compiled by a Jesuit Priest named Franz Hattler and published under the patronage of local ecclesiastical authorities in Freiburg—among the many saints whose lives were chronicled were three boys said to have been murdered by Jews: Werner of Wesel (1287), Andreas of Rinn (1462), and Simon of Trent (1475). Each of these children had been memorialized—and, eventually, beatified—by the Church as martyrs of Christianity, and the book's Jesuit narrator, in transmitting to schoolchildren the lives of the saints as exempla of holiness, repeated the supposed circumstances of their deaths. It might be argued that no recounting of the lives and deaths of these young saints could have called into question the historicity of the ritual murder charge without, at the same time, raising doubt about the basis for their sainthood. Perhaps Hattler had this dilemma in mind when he introduced the story of Simon of Trent with the observation that "reliable evidence shows that Jews are in the habit of stealing, buying and murdering Christian children."[43]

And yet, I think it would be a mistake to conclude that everyday relations between Jews and Catholics in the Rhineland were structured mainly around such distant discourses as ultramontanism, political Catholicism, the *Kulturkampf*, or Christian martyrology. Baumann's investigations into the everyday interactions of Jews, Protestants, and Catholics in rural Baden from the 1860s into the Nazi period led him to doubt that ideology had much to do with these relations. Occupational differences (and the cultural meanings attached to trade and agriculture), attitudes of mutual support and neighborliness, non-overlapping family lines, and a fairly rigid separation in religious and ritual life appear to have been more important factors in ordering interreligious encounters.[44] Jewish religious life and practices, moreover, while to a certain extent opaque to Christian observers, were hardly hidden from view. In fact, they were carried out in the public sphere, with the result that Jewish practices were understood to be part and parcel of the everyday life of the village. "In communities with a significant percentage of Jews," Baumann writes, "Jewish holidays were as much part of village life as Christian ones. The piety of Jewish men and women was respected."[45] Additionally, at least until 1918, most clergy in southwestern Germany encouraged mutual respect toward members of other religions or Christian denominations. When a synagogue was renovated or built or a Torah scroll obtained, Catholic and Protestant clergy, as well as Christian mayors, would often be present at the dedication ceremonies.[46]

In the eastern parts of the Prussian state (where West Prussia—as we know—was located), the *Kulturkampf* incorporated elements of national as well as religious struggle. Bismarck found that he could quash Polish nationalist activities by applying the legal and political provisions of the *Kulturkampf* against Polish culture in Prussia. Thus, the educational reform of 1871 reduced the influence of Polish Catholic clergy in the schools. By order of the Prussian *Oberpräsident* in 1873, German was declared the sole language of instruction in all schools except for classes in religion and choir at the lower levels. In 1876, German was made the sole commercial language (*Geschäftssprache*) for government officials; the following year, all legal proceedings had to be held in German only.[47] In the 1880s, anti-Polish activity moved in the direction of large-scale land purchases by and for Germans and the establishment of credit and employment associations. The Law for the Promotion of German Colonization in Posen and West Prussia was passed in 1886; its provisions allowed for 100 million marks to be set aside by the Prussian Landtag to assist in the settlement of German peasants and workers.[48] The psychological tone of the anti-Polish campaign may have been more real than the outcome, however. Most of the land purchases in West Prussia, it turns out, came at the expense of other Germans. Poles, moreover, met the challenge of Prussian "colonization" programs by setting up a rival network of banks and credit associations as well as by instituting an economic boycott against German merchants.

In both Konitz and Tiszaeszlár, the local Christian population included Protestants as well as Catholics—a fact that suggests that one must be cautious when assessing the role of religious institutions in general, and the Catholic Church in particular, in the turn-of-the-century trials. And, whereas Prussian policies of anti-Polish repression clearly form a backdrop to the history of West Prussia under the Second German Empire, it is not as certain that the Polish-German conflict strongly influenced the Konitz affair. The Jews of the town identified politically and linguistically with Germany, the murder victim in the case was a German gymnasium student, and the activity of Polish Catholics in the accusation and trial appears to have been minimal. In the Kingdom of Hungary, ethnic conflict and repression were certainly present after 1867, but Szabolcs County was not ethnically mixed, and although the Jews of the high Tisza region tended to be Orthodox in practice, they were also largely Magyar speakers.[49]

In Polná, in contrast, the themes of Catholicism, national conflict, and Jewish culture appear to come together in a significant way. Since the Counter-Reformation of the seventeenth century, Bohemia and Moravia had become overwhelmingly Catholic, and from the mid-nineteenth century, Jews had come to be regarded by many as persistent carriers of German language and culture and as defenders of Austrian centralism.[50] In this understanding of the cultural underpinnings of politics, nationalist Czech writers and publicists could claim to have found a compelling connection between religious difference and ethnic treason, arguing that the "otherness" of Bohemian and Moravian Jews coincided with behaviors that promoted the power and ubiquity of Germans in the region.[51] Thus, we read in a local history of Polná, written by the town's schoolmaster, Břetislav Reyrich, that the Jewish community colluded with the district commissioner (an official of the government in Vienna) in 1874 to convert what had been a privately supported "German Jewish" school attended exclusively by Jewish children into a *public* German elementary school whose doors were opened to the children of Czech-speaking parents. This kind of practice—referred to colloquially by Reyrich and various Czech newspapers as "decanting" or "siphoning off" (from the Czech verb *přelévat/přelít*) had the effect of keeping German-language schools in operation in the face of declining German or Jewish populations and at the expense—in the eyes of Czech nationalists—of an unnatural acculturation of the children of Czech families. Czech publications routinely denounced the practice, and Reyrich accused the former German Jewish (now public German) school of standing as "a symbol of public discord in Polná for a quarter of a century."[52]

Religion alone could never be an unambiguous gauge of national affiliation, however. For one thing, Catholicism itself was deeply implicated in the German power structure in Bohemia and Moravia since the seventeenth-century Counter-Reformation had taken place in concert with an anti-Czech campaign that resulted in the forced exile or execution of scores of noble families. In many respects, to be Catholic was to be loyal to the Habsburg conception of Austria. And this implication was not lost on at least one important faction of Czech nationalist intellectuals—among whom stood Tomáš G. Masaryk—who preferred to equate Czech culture with the Protestant Reformation (remembering that it had been the Protestant Czech estates that rose up in revolt in 1618–20) or with the pre-Reformation Hussite movement.[53] Moreover, the linguistic and national loyalties of Bohemian Jews could not be so easily predicted. The countrywide system of German Jewish elementary schools, which derived from the educational reforms of Joseph II in the 1780s, had to a large extent been imposed on the local Jewish communities. In subsequent decades, Jews used these schools to their advantage in the drive for economic and social advancement and political enfranchisement. From them they entered the classical gymnasia and universities or moved into the economic mainstream. The Jewish graduates more than accomplished the goal of the project's originators—that they become fluent in the high culture of the Habsburg state: they virtually became emblems of the imperial state and its "universal" language.[54]

But the ethnic loyalties of Bohemian Jewry did not remain fixed, nor were they ever free of ambiguity. This is a point on which Czech and German antagonists at the turn of the century often erred. Small-town and village Jews went through the same demographic and cultural transformations that produced middle-class Czech nationalism in general; they were neither immune to historical processes nor blind to the benefits that could accrue to Czech speakers who enjoyed a modicum of cultural and political autonomy. Jews who grew up in provincial cities and towns in the 1860s, 1870s, and 1880s entered Czech gymnasia in increasing numbers and thereby spent their formative years in what might be called the incubator of modern Czech politics. As more and more Jews abandoned the countryside for the cities, especially Prague, fewer and fewer Jewish children remained to fill the German Jewish schools. This demographic imperative, combined with growing political pressure from the Czech national movement, resulted in the gradual elimination of this type of school between 1885 and 1900. Bohemian Jews, moreover, were rarely monolingual. Although they may have sent their children to German schools and found German avenues of mobility to be the most rewarding, they frequently had come from Czech-speaking environments themselves, spoke Czech in the workplace and the market, and interacted constantly with Czech speakers.[55]

Jews could, and did, change declarations of national affiliation depending on political conditions or other circumstances. The census of 1900, for example, recorded what appeared to be a startling "change of heart" for Bohemian Jews. Over 54 percent of both Bohemian Jewry in general and Prague Jewry specifically declared their "language of daily use" (the only indicator of ethnic affiliation recognized by the Austrian census) to be Czech. Only ten years earlier, about two-thirds of Bohemian Jewry—and three-quarters of the Jews of Prague—had indicated German as their language of choice. Were Jews employing simple political expediency? Perhaps. But the more compelling argument, it seems to me, is that the Austrian census did not (or would not) ask the questions that would more accurately capture their sense of ethnic belonging. The census consciously omitted the overt categories of "ethnic group" or "nationality," opting instead for what officials hoped was a more neutral category: "colloquial language." Nor were Austrians given the opportunity to distinguish between political loyalty—citizenship—and ethnic loyalty.[56] And "colloquial language," for a bilingual (if not multilingual) minority group that was often buffeted by political pressures from different directions, was not a good indicator of much of anything. Yet, despite the limitations of the census data, it is worth noting that the Jewish community of Polná had broken with the general pattern of linguistic declaration earlier than had most of Bohemian Jewry. Already in the census of 1890, 198 (approximately 59 percent) of the Jewish respondents declared themselves to be Czech speakers, while 140 (41 percent) indicated German as their primary tongue.[57]

Tiszaeszlár, Xanten, Polná, and Konitz as Jewish Hometowns

It goes without saying that the ritual murder accusations of the late nineteenth century and the ensuing investigations, trials, public debate, and riots revealed fault lines in the relationship between Jewish and non-Jewish Europeans. Yet, while accusations of ritual murder tended to be widely, if not uniformly, distributed across Central Europe, only a handful of trials actually took place. Does this pattern mean that relations between Jews and Gentiles were uniformly in crisis or differentially strained? Were bad relations between the groups at the local level a prerequisite to a formal investigation and trial?

Social relations between Jews and non-Jews in Tiszaeszlár are typically characterized—in both contemporary sources and the historical literature—as "friendly" and "intimate," although defense attorney Károly Eötvös takes pains in his memoir of the affair to add that Christians tended to look down upon the Jews with "a certain old-fashioned, accustomed sense of superiority."[58] The picture offered by Paul Nathan, who completed a book-length study on Tiszaeszlár in 1892 (the same year that he was sent to cover the trial in Xanten), is more nuanced but basically positive. Relations between the two groups appear to have been cordial and cooperative on an everyday level, as would befit life in a village. Tiszaeszlár had no Jewish quarter or ghetto. Jews lived side by side with their Gentile neighbors, and the social contacts seem to have been marked by familiarity and even affection, as well as by jealousy, resentments, and petty conflicts.[59]

The nobleman Géza Ónody, part of whose hereditary estate lay in the vicinity of Tiszaeszlár, articulated the anti-Jewish perspective on interethnic relations. In a polemical tract published in 1883, he described Tiszaeszlár as "a small, modest village . . . with 1,200 to 1,400 inhabitants, among whom are 200 Jews, who with indefatigable diligence and tireless perseverance work toward the exploitation and both the material and moral ruin of the Christian citizenry."[60] Echoes of Istóczy's language and rhetoric are definitely to be heard here. Ónody, moreover, has both underestimated the dimensions of the village and exaggerated the size of the Jewish population in order to achieve the desired effect of depicting "Christian" civilization as a vulnerable island besieged by swarming masses. Andrew Handler, in contrast, has placed the population of Tiszaeszlár at 2,700, including approximately twenty-five Jewish families. If one accepts six as a reasonable multiplier (which may actually be high), the total number of Jews in Tiszaeszlár would have been approximately 150, or 5.5 percent of the general population.[61]

Ónody's polemic drew upon the Galician origins of a large part of Hungarian Jewry to create an image of a fundamentally alien and uncivilized population: "They are the same bigoted fanatics today as [they were] when they migrated in droves to Hungary from the mass warehouse of European Jewry, Galicia. Inspired by the pernicious teachings of Talmudic ethics, they are rigidly separated by dress, mores, life principles, and racial characteristics from the other elements of society—as are their coreligionists and the members of their race on the other side of the Carpathians, the Polish Hasidim."[62] In a similar vein, he described the neighboring town of Tiszalök, the seat of the district rabbi, as "a nest of bigoted, Jewish fanaticism and a genuine Little Jerusalem, where the Christian population is—in the fullest meaning of the word—threatened in its existence."[63]

As a political figure and writer, Ónody was to play a part in creating the vocabulary and iconography of the modern ritual murder accusation, yet his voice was not representative of Hungarian opinion at large. His own "fanaticism" made him an oddity on the national scene, and his particular brand of politics operated at a level that was far removed from the everyday life of the village. Here Jewish-Gentile interactions took place in intimate, face-to-face encounters in which cooperation and mutuality one day might transform into spitefulness and hostility the next—and this for reasons tied more to opportunism and the ambiguities inherent in local culture than as the result of political conviction. Tiszaeszlár resident Eszter Sós, for example, was the type of person who could live contentedly with her Jewish neighbors for years only to become convinced of their nefarious intentions under the right circumstances. Mrs. Sós, who had interacted with and sold geese to the Scharf family in the past, admitted in court that in the aftermath of the disappearance of Eszter Solymosi, she responded to a request from Mrs. Scharf to buy another goose with the taunt, "Neighbor, why do you need a goose anymore? The Jews will be driven out without them; I, too, will drive them out with a stick."[64] The same village, however, contained another Christian resident, Mrs. Gábor Bátori, a neighbor of the Scharfs whom the family also employed to perform household tasks on the Sabbath. On the day of the arrests of the Scharfs and the other Jewish defendants from Tiszaeszlár, Mrs. Bátori brought lunch to their son Móric and cared for him in his parents' absence.[65]

While the historical record of Jewish-Christian interaction in Xanten during the nineteenth century is spotty, anti-Jewish behavior and attitudes seem to have been more continuous than in Hungary. In part, this judgment depends on how far back in time one wishes to reach. Xanten had been the site of a massacre during the First Crusade (1096) in which some sixty Jews were either killed or committed suicide. As recently as 1834, however, anti-Jewish riots broke out in various places in the Lower Rhine, apparently in response to the murder of a boy, Peter Wilhelm Hoenen. Local suspicion for the crime rested on the Jews despite the fact that the investigating magistrate held such views to be groundless. He opposed any discussion of Jewish ritual murder as "a barbarous superstition of centuries long past," but this did not prevent the widespread looting and destruction of Jewish homes and properties. The Prussian government eventually ordered security forces to go into the area to restore order, although not before the riots had spread throughout the countryside and even to Düsseldorf. In Xanten, a crowd of about 200 wound through the town throwing stones, giving the anti-Jewish cry "Hep-Hep" and singing "disreputable" and "threatening" songs. The local police intervened without success, forcing the army and the Royal Hussars to be called in from Koblenz.[66]

The impact of the 1834 riot on relations between Catholics and Jews in Xanten some sixty years later remains an open question. It is difficult to locate the earlier disturbance in the social memory of the actors in the later ritual murder affair, although perhaps indirect traces are to be found in the cautious, decorous behavior of the Jewish community. What we can say is that the Jewish community of Xanten at the close of the nineteenth century was small—some eighty-five people, about 2.5 percent of the population—and that it was both dwarfed by the overwhelming, Catholic majority and fully attuned to the latter's calendar, habits, and daily rhythms.[67]

Such social and psychological integration is attested to in the trial testimony of the accused, Adolph Buschhoff. The date of the disappearance and murder of five-year-old Johann Hegmann, 29 June 1891, corresponded to the Roman Catholic holiday of Saints Peter and Paul—a fact of which Buschhoff and the other Jewish residents of the town were well aware—but also to the anniversary of the death of Buschhoff's father as marked in the Jewish calendar. Buschhoff circumnavigated his immediate neighborhood several times over the course of the day. Starting at the synagogue for morning prayers, he moved on to a pub at the market, where he had a brief conversation concerning a possible business transaction; on his way home around 10 a.m., he met a farmer, from whom he had once bought a cow, and who now invited him to join him for a drink; along the way, they met a third party, and the three sat and talked for a while in Buschhoff's living room; from there, Buschhoff went to see a man named Evers, a Catholic butcher, with whom he had worked for more than a decade. He encountered more acquaintances on this path—a farmer and a merchant—made another stop in a pub, and spoke there with several people. Setting off for home again a little before 1 p.m., he met his neighbor Ullenboom, who accompanied Buschhoff to his house in order to read the *Berliner Abendpost* (to which Buschhoff subscribed) while the latter sat down for lunch. At 3 p.m., Buschhoff left his house to attend a local folk festival (known as Pumpenkirmes)—held every Saints Peter and Paul day—together with two other neighbors. The three men had been drinking together and playing skittles (*kegeln*) when news came later of the discovery of the dead child, breaking the day's restful harmony.[68]

When asked by the presiding judge at his trial to characterize his relations with his neighbors, Buschhoff replied that they had always been good. As someone who knew from personal experience what it was like to lose a child—he and his wife had lost three of their original six—Buschhoff explained that he had made it a point to visit the house of the bereaved family on the very evening that he heard the news. And this was not his first visit to the Hegmann home. During the previous winter, Heinrich Hegmann, the boy's father, had been ill, and members of the Buschhoff family came by to pay their respects. "I thought it was the duty of a neighbor to go there," Buschhoff told the judge. "I said to Hegmann, 'Heinrich, try to be calm for the sake of your wife. I have gone through two tragedies with my wife.' Then we had something to eat, and I left to go to the synagogue."[69]

During the course of the trial, numerous witnesses came forward to testify to the upstanding character of the accused. The mayor of Xanten referred to Buschhoff as "neither hot-tempered nor vindictive, but rather a good-natured man." Wilhelm van de Handt, a Franciscan monk from the nearby monastery in Dorsten, who had been in Xanten on the morning of the murder and who had interacted with Buschhoff on a few occasions, testified that, as far as he knew, Buschhoff was a "good, orderly person."[70] Neither Buschhoff's apparently seamless integration into Xanten's local culture, however, nor the generally favorable impression that his neighbors had of him were sufficient to prevent at least some of the town's residents from rioting against him, destroying his home, and writing on the walls *Mördergrube* (murderer's cell).[71] Indeed, at an early stage in the investigation, Buschhoff had approached Mayor Schleß and requested that he place him in jail for his own safety.[72] It was some consolation, perhaps, that when Xanten residents did riot against Jews and their property in the immediate aftermath of Buschhoff's arrest, the mayor, the district magistrate, and the provincial governor all came down hard against the rioters, threatening swift punishment.[73]

As with most other German towns in "Royal Prussia" before the Polish partitions, Konitz did not have a Jewish population in the early modern period. Jews appear to have taken part in Konitz's trade in textiles with Poland-Lithuania in the late eighteenth century, but the city did not record its first Jewish resident until 1810. Other Jews began to settle in Konitz following Prussia's 1812 Edict of Emancipation, which granted Jews equality before the law, freedom of occupation, and freedom of settlement and subjected them to compulsory military service. Between 1810 and 1850, some eighty Jews received civil rights in Konitz—representing almost 15 percent of the town's new citizens—most of whom had come from surrounding villages and towns in the western and southern parts of West Prussia.[74] The Konitz Jewish community grew at a rapid pace in the following decades, reaching its height of 563 people (equaling 5.6 percent of the population of the town) in 1885. This number represented an increase of close to one-third over the town's 1867 Jewish population (425) and an impressive leap over what it had been in 1829 (163). In contrast to earlier Jewish settlement in Konitz, the more recent growth in population was the result of both internal migration from the West Prussian countryside and immigration from Russian Poland. After the mid-1880s, the Jewish population of Konitz began to decline, following the pattern for West Prussia as a whole: numbers fell as more and more Jews migrated to other parts of the empire, especially to the industrializing cities, and abroad. In 1895, 480 Jews lived in Konitz (4.5 percent of the general population); in 1900, there were 365 Jews (3.4 percent of the population); and by 1910, only 256 Jews (2.1 percent) remained.[75]

The Prussian provinces of Pomerania and West Prussia stood out from other parts of Imperial Germany on a number of counts, not the least of which was the ferocity with which, on occasion, their residents expressed anti-Jewish sentiment. In the summer of 1881, riots against Jews broke out in a dozen or so towns in this region—including Konitz—vaguely mirroring the more extensive and serious outbreak of anti-Jewish violence that had taken place in the Russian empire. The riots followed the same basic pattern: hundreds of demonstrators marched in procession following mass rallies on the streets or in town squares; chanting the traditional anti-Jewish refrain "Hep hep!" or "Out with the Jews," the crowds would throw stones, smashing the windows of stores, private homes, and synagogues. At times, the violence would wind down when the crowd sensed that the Jews had been "taught a lesson"; other times, it would end suddenly when state and local authorities sent in police reinforcements to restore order.[76] The riots originated in the town of Neustettin in Pomerania, where some five months earlier, the synagogue had been burned to the ground. In both the original riot and beyond, the violence appears to have been sparked by a combination of conscious political agitation, popular revelry, and the local settling of interpersonal grievances.

Prussian authorities never made a formal determination as to who had set the Neustettin synagogue on fire on 18 February 1881. Five days earlier, radical antisemitic activist Ernst Henrici had delivered an inflammatory speech against Jews in Neustettin and followed this with another the next day in the neighboring town of Bäwalde. Two months earlier, the local *Norddeutsche Zeitung* had published a feature article entitled "Dr. Martin Luther and the Jewish Question," which reproduced some of Luther's more violent rhetoric regarding Jews, including the exhortation to set fire to their synagogues and schools and to bury under the earth anything that was not destroyed by fire.[77] Remarkably, however, the local *Landrat* and the editors of the *Norddeutsche Zeitung* propounded the theory that the Jews of Neustettin had set fire to their own synagogue, variously, in order to discredit the developing antisemitic movement or to collect the insurance money on the building.[78] The public prosecutor put enough faith in this interpretation of events to institute criminal proceedings against five Jews for having caused the fire. At a trial held in Köslin in October 1883, all of the accused were acquitted of the more serious charge of intentional arson, but one man and his son were convicted of failing to give assistance and not reporting the fire. They received sentences of three and six months, respectively. Another father, a man named Hermann Lesheim, was sentenced to four years' imprisonment for aiding and abetting an alleged conspiracy. His seventeen-year-old son was sent to a state school. The fifth defendant was acquitted and released. Upon appeal, the Reichsgericht ordered a new trial, which was actually held in Konitz in March 1884. This time, the jury acquitted all of the defendants of any involvement in the fire. Lesheim, the only one who was still in custody, was immediately released.[79]

In this overheated atmosphere of Jew-baiting, arson, rabble rousing, and criminal trials, the first riot to break out—in Neustettin on 17 July 1881—had almost comic antecedents. The immediate precipitating event came in the form of a provocation by the president of the Neustettin League of Antisemites, a building contractor by the name of Luttosch, who felt that he had been insulted by an article in the liberal *Neustettiner Zeitung*, edited by the brothers Cohn. Luttosch attempted to attack Adolph Cohn on the street, but as Cohn's brother was nearby at the time, they not only repelled the attack but also succeeded in causing Luttosch to bleed from the head. The bloodied president of the League of Antisemites then rushed around from tavern to tavern calling upon the craftsmen and workers who were having a Sunday drink to drive off the Jews. Some 800 to 1,000 people gathered over the course of the afternoon, chanted the obligatory "Hep, hep!" and proceeded to smash the windows of Jewish shops. The situation escalated that evening when police arrested Luttosch. The mob demanded his release, surrounded the building of the *Neustettiner Zeitung*, wrecked the editorial offices, and damaged the printing presses. Another twenty-one Jewish shops had their windows smashed, and two were totally destroyed.[80] In the end, it took three days and at least two calls for police and government reinforcements to quash the Neustettin riot, by the end of which nearly all of the windows in the houses of Jews had been destroyed, and the Jewish residents were sleeping out in the open. Over the following weeks, the riots spread in concentric circles around Neustettin with the most serious violence taking place in the Pomeranian town of Schivelbein. In Konitz, due east of Neustettin and connected by a direct rail line, riots occurred on 5 and 7 August.[81]

It is certainly fair to ask whether the 1881 riots and the disturbances that ensued in the wake of the 1900 ritual murder accusation epitomized Jewish-Christian relations in Konitz or represented a deviation from normal patterns—irritations to those who continued to trust in the power of the integrationist vision and wake-up calls to those who were growing weary of emancipation's unfulfilled promise. One of Konitz's local newspapers, the *Konitzer Tageszeitung*, frankly attributed the street violence in April and May 1900 to the "drunkenness and uncouthness of adolescent students" but reserved most of its scorn for their more conventional parents who did not hesitate to spread false rumors about civil servants who displayed skepticism toward tales of Jewish ritual murder and who wasted the time of investigators by flooding their offices with false testimonies.[82] It was, however, the second, more pessimistic, message that informed the assessment of the correspondent for the Zionist-oriented newspaper *Die Welt*, who wrote that Jews in the small towns of the Prussian east were generally shut off from all social intercourse with their neighbors; they were effectively excluded from non-Jewish associational life and forced to create bourgeois institutions of their own with such neutral-sounding titles as "Businessman's Association." No Christian businessman, he assured his readers, would ever join such an organization by mistake. The sociability of Jews and Gentiles in these towns, the reader learns, was as modest and tame as it could be in any ghetto.[83]

Last, the Bohemian lands. In Polná, the ability of the Jewish community to enjoy relative stability and security depended on a combination of factors: the noble origins of the town, the impact of Catholic symbol and ritual on popular emotions, economic development, and the political tensions associated with the nationality struggle in the Czech lands. Polná's status as a noble town insulated the Jewish population from the burgher-instigated expulsions that had taken place in the Crown cities of Bohemia and Moravia in the fifteenth and sixteenth centuries. Jews who lived on noble domains could also often evade the effects of Counter-Reformation imperial legislation, which sought to impose strict limits on Jewish family size, residence, and mobility.[84] Jews could and did seek guarantees of protection from powerful noble families in return for economic services and the payment of fees and taxes. It was under such circumstances in 1682 that Count Dietrichstejn laid the foundations for the growth of the modern Jewish community of the town, when he set aside sixteen buildings behind Polná's Upper Gate for permanent Jewish settlement.[85] Dietrichstejn's action had come about at the request of Polná's existing Jewish community, whose medieval settlement had been at the foot of the town's Calvary hill. The hilltop, on which the eighteenth-century Church of St. Barbara now stands, had been the destination point of the annual Easter procession that commemorated Christ's crucifixion. The pageant typically ended with the hanging of an effigy of Judas.[86] I do not know to what extent, if any, Jews sought new living conditions in order to remove themselves from proximity to this annual—and potentially dangerous—symbolic degradation. But the fact that they succeeded in finding both new quarters and long-term security through the agency of the Dietrichstejns points to a convergence of those political, economic, and religious factors that helped to shape local Jewish destiny.

Fifty-two Jewish families lived in Polná in 1724; by 1830, the number had grown to 128—or almost 770 individuals—despite the fact that Familiants Laws, in effect since the 1720s, had, in theory, rendered such growth impossible.[87] The revolutionary upheavals of 1848 spelled the end of noble influence in the town, the removal of some of the restrictions that had been placed on Jewish social and economic life, and the beginning of a political process that would lead eventually to full emancipation in 1867. In June 1848, the town organized a company of the National Guard—supported to a large extent by individual contributions from the Polná Jewish community—and sent it to Vienna to help reinforce the barricades defending the revolution. And while it appears that Jews were not allowed officially to serve in this company, some managed, nevertheless, to fight alongside it on the barricades. Historians have even located one Jew from Polná who fought in Vienna on the side of the imperial government.[88] Over the last three decades of the nineteenth century, Jews from Polná did what most of their coreligionists in the Bohemian and Moravian countryside were doing: they left, leaving behind their village and small-town origins for the likes of Prague, Vienna, Brno, and New York. By 1890, as I have mentioned, the Jewish population stood at 247 (2.7 percent of the general population). Polná's last rabbi left the town in 1920; by 1930, only fifty-one Jews remained.[89]

Toward a Conclusion: The Unmaking of Hometowns

During the 1880s and 1890s, both the Kutná Hora regional court (Krajský soud Kutná Hora) and the Prague criminal court (Zemský soud trestní—Praha) heard numerous cases alleging various forms of anti-Jewish behavior. The prosecutions dealt with libel, defamation of religion, disturbances of the peace, and "provocation" (*popuzování*) against a religious community—all punishable under Austrian law. Most of the charges related in some way to the larger political discourse of Czech-German national struggle, some were directed at newspaper editors who violated government censorship regulations, and some emerged from the day-to-day interactions of Jews and non-Jews in the Czech lands. As a whole, these cases yield valuable information concerning the texture of daily life at the local level and offer a rare glimpse into the complex, highly symbolic, world of Jewish-Gentile interaction.[90]

Two prosecutions from the 1890s warrant special attention: one originated in Polná, the other in east central Bohemia. While both involved humorous, if somewhat bizarre, expressions of interpersonal antagonisms, the two cases point to the boundaries of "acceptable" defamation in Habsburg political culture and highlight the available institutional avenues of redress. The first concerns an indictment brought by public prosecutor Schneider-Svoboda in October 1892 against a thirty-two-year-old resident of Polná, the horse butcher Jan Chalupa.[91] Chalupa was accused of disturbing the practice of religion (*rušení náboženství*) by publicly ridiculing a recognized faith—in this case, Judaism—repeatedly over a period of time between 1891 and 1892. On one level, this was a totally mundane case, one of countless examples of the Habsburg state's monitoring of—and intrusion in—the daily lives of its citizens, part and parcel of what Marc Raeff has called "the well-ordered police state."[92] It serves as a reminder, nevertheless, that Habsburg officials regularly, if inconsistently, prosecuted individuals and institutions for making inflammatory statements about Jews and Judaism, inciting to violence, or, simply, making public ridicule of the Jewish religion.

The prosecution of Jan Chalupa offers intriguing details about daily life in small-town Bohemia and begins to uncover the intricate social context of Jewish-Gentile interaction. The main witness against the accused, interestingly, was not himself a Jew but a Catholic named Josef Skála, who had been employed for the past six years by the Polná synagogue while, at the same time, serving as sexton (*kostelník*) of the Catholic Church—fascinating in and of itself. Skála testified that for nearly two years, whenever Chalupa came upon him on the street, he would set about taunting Skála verbally, saying such things as, "What's that Jewish calf doing? What is he fed with? Is he given hay, dried grass, and water?" Later, Chalupa would admonish Skála, saying that he should *not* feed the calf grass because it would burst! As if in a fit of madness, he would then call upon Skála to "go feed the calf," adding that the Jews would make what the court papers referred to as "*machalabeis*."[93]

It appears that Chalupa's exact words varied from incident to incident, but the gist of his taunts of the uncomprehending synagogue employee and church sexton had to do with what Chalupa took to be the farcical feeding of a "calf" on behalf of the Jews. Chalupa's bantering was as unrelenting as it was mysterious, and he, at least, considered it to be highly amusing. Significantly for the prosecution's case, the teasing always occurred in public. As for the church sexton and erstwhile animal feeder, one thing we can be certain of is that he judged Chalupa's words to be slanderous. Skála himself did not issue a formal complaint, but he spoke about the incidents to one Hermann Aufrecht (presumably Jewish), who in turn brought the matter to the attention of the court.

Aufrecht gave investigators his own account of the exchanges as told to him by Skála: "Skála, go fetch some hay and go the Jewish synagogue; go feed the calf there, and the Jews will make '*machalabeis*' over it" or, alternatively, "Bring straw and water; who will feed the Jewish calf, your wife or you?" After conferring with other members of the Jewish community, he issued a formal complaint to the court on the grounds that Chalupa's taunting constituted an insult to a recognized religion of the state. Three eyewitnesses offered testimony against Chalupa: a shop assistant named Julius Aufrecht, an acquaintance of Chalupa's named Karel Korotvicka, and Skála's wife, Kateřina. Mrs. Skála described an incident in which she and her husband were pulling grass in the vicinity of Chalupa's house. He bounded out of the house and called to her, asking if she was pulling grass for the calf and who was feeding the calf, she or her husband? She told the court that she "immediately understood" what he was talking about, because her husband frequently had relayed word of his teasing in the past. Chalupa's references to "feeding the calf," she explained, had to do with the fact that her husband worked for the synagogue; in her view, the remarks were defamatory.[94]

Schneider-Svoboda, the state's attorney, claimed in the writ of indictment that it was "as plain as day" that Chalupa's utterances constituted evidence of the belittling of a state religion. Just to be sure, however, he solicited the opinions of two rabbis: Philipp Polatschek, rabbi of Polná, and Dr. Nathan Ehrenfeld, chief rabbi of Prague. They appear to have concurred, although neither ventured an interpretation of just what Chalupa may have meant. The accused was sentenced in December 1892 to two months of imprisonment with a mandatory fast day every two weeks.[95]

As a document of social history, this case is remarkable on several counts. We learn, for example, not only that at least one Christian was in the employ of the Polná Jewish community but also that the Catholic Church and the synagogue shared a sexton. This feature of small-town life testified to a certain degree of intimacy between Jews and Gentiles. At the same time, however, it was received by at least one Polná resident as a provocation worthy of almost daily condemnation. Also, while the Christian synagogue employee may not have taken the initiative to issue a formal complaint against Chalupa, he did sense that both his honor and that of his employers were at stake, and he did not take the insults with equanimity. Later, neither he nor his wife hesitated to testify in court against his tormentor. Finally, we see evidence of a well-integrated Jewish community that "knows its rights" and does not shy away from bringing charges against one who would diminish them. And the state, represented by the prosecutor's office, sees it to be in its interest to defend the good name of the Jewish religion.

Chalupa's taunts themselves are fascinating if only because they are so obscure. Why should he have presumed that Skála and his wife were picking grass in order to feed a "calf" that belonged to the Jewish community? Is the implication that Skála was abetting the Jews— "fattening their calf"— by working for them? Perhaps, but in this case, I think one would be well advised to read literally rather than figuratively. We know from early modern ethnographies of Central European Jewish communities, described by Jews as well as non-Jews, that some Jewish communities were in the practice of maintaining an ox in their cemetery from birth to death in symbolic remembrance of the first-born animals that were consecrated to the priests when the Temple was in existence. Among the sources that mention this custom was Yuspah Shammash (Joseph the Sexton, 1604–78) of Worms, who noted that it was customary to give this ox to the Gentile who lived on the cemetery grounds and who was responsible for its upkeep. It was this person's responsibility to "raise him on the grass and weeds of the cemetery."[96] What we may have, then, in the confrontation between Jan Chalupa and Josef Skála is evidence of the maintenance of this custom in Polná, of the Jewish community's engagement of Skála as the person in charge of the ox's (or calf's) feeding and care, and of Chalupa's semiamused, semihostile response to this relationship.

Chalupa also implied that the Jews were making plans to slaughter the animal in some sort of ritual, preparing it for a ceremony or meal, which he calls *machalabeis*. No one involved in the case seems to know what the word means; it is simply transcribed as heard by the several witnesses. At the same time, all concerned are convinced that this image, like that of the fatted calf, is defamatory. It may be the case that Chalupa has simply fitted together Jewish-sounding words or syllables, which may have seemed genuine to him by reason of his relative proximity to Jewish life and speech but amounted to little more than Hebrew or Yiddish phonemes. My best approximation would be that Chalupa was saying something like the Yiddish *maykhl eppis*, which means "something to eat." The allusion, then, was to a tasty treat.[97] On the other hand, it may have been nothing more than a farcical verbal play that bore witness to Chalupa's simultaneous proximity to, and distance from, the Jewish world that lay outside his door—a bit of manic humor, the point of which was to poke fun at Jewish practices and humiliate Skála. The state's attorney unintentionally added to the joke by trying to get to the bottom of it; he needed precise definitions if he was to prove defamation—hence the

Figure 3. Postcard of the Hrůza family (mother and brother are second and third from the left). Březina woods by Polná. Handwritten message: "Good beer / pretty girls / these are the gifts / of the Czech lands."

Courtesy M. Frankl and J. Mabray.

official consultations with the two rabbis. They weren't of much help, but they agreed with all of the principals that there was an insult there somewhere.

If the case of Jan Chalupa reveals fissures in the Jewish-Christian relationship in Bohemia, it nevertheless portrays a conflict that was relatively benign in its social and cultural repercussions, a far cry from the wrenching controversy over alleged Jewish ritual murder that would engulf the country less than seven years later. In 1897, a very different type of libel action took place, in which the image of Jewish ritual murder not only was present but also functioned as a rhetorical device in a political argument. The case involved Anna Vokřálová, the fifty-year-old wife of a stove-fitter who lived in the Bohemian town of Kolín, some 55 kilometers east of Prague. She was accused of having publicly insulted the emperor following the elections of 22 February 1897, in which representatives to the Imperial Diet from the Fifth Curia were chosen.[98] The winning party in the city was the Young Czechs, or National Liberals; in the suburbs, the Social Democrats prevailed. Around 1 p.m. on the day of the elections, Anna Finková (a forty-four-year-old Jewish woman, the wife of a peddler) and Marie Veselá (Catholic, aged sixty-two, and wife of a gravedigger) were walking through the main square in Kolín when they passed a pharmacy next to the Grand Hotel. There they happened upon Anna Vokřálová, who had just emerged from the hotel; a brief conversation ensued, followed about a week later by a tip to the police and the arrest and trial of the unfortunate Mrs. Vokřálová.[99]

According to the formal indictment and confirmed generally by witnesses' statements, Anna Vokřálová had joined the two women and said, in a voice loud enough for them and others to hear, "We won, we won!" "Who won," Marie Veselá asked? Vokřálová responded with the first of two statements that were to get her in deep trouble with the authorities: "Not the Jews; they drink Christian blood, and the Emperor chases Jewish girls (*Císař si namlouvá židovky*)."[100] When Veselá admonished the other woman that she should not say such things, that it was, after all, "our lord and Emperor (*nás Císař Pán*)" that she was talking about, Vokřálová is said to have answered, "He gives you shit, he gives you shit. He shits on you (*hovno vám dá, hovno vám dá, nasere vám*)." At her trial on 15 March 1897, Vokřálová received a guilty verdict and a sentence of four months' imprisonment with a mandatory fast day every two weeks.[101]

As with the Chalupa case, the arrest and trial of Anna Vokřálová contain surprising bits of information and lend a unique perspective to the local dynamic of Jewish-Christian interaction in the Czech small town. The offended pair (excluding, of course, the emperor) comprised a Catholic and a Jew, both Czech speakers, who apparently had been attending the same funeral and who were at least friendly enough to enjoy one another's company on a leisurely stroll home. They, in turn, both knew the accused, who, on her own initiative, greeted the two in the town square. From Marie Veselá's sworn testimony, we learn that Anna Vokřálová lived on the "Jewish street" in Kolín and that she worked as a domestic in Jewish households. We also learn that neither Veselá nor Finková denounced Vokřálová to the police. Veselá kept the incident to herself, she explains, except to tell a shopkeeper named Kantorová (religion not given, but the name may well be Jewish). Could it be true, she wanted to know, what Vokřálová said about the emperor? It is not clear whether or not Veselá needed to be enlightened regarding the description of Jewish culinary habits. The shopkeeper, nevertheless, pronounced on both parts of the statement and assured Mrs. Veselá that what the accused had to say about both the emperor and the Jews was "ugly." Anna Finková revealed that at noon on the day in question, she had been to a burial in the neighboring village of Zálobí and that she had walked back to town with Marie Veselá. She also identified the accused as a domestic worker who lived on the Jewish street. Vokřálová apparently came out of the hotel and accompanied the two women as far as the fountain. She then turned to them and shouted the incriminating sentences.[102]

A state police supervisor named Jan Musil testified that he was approached on 1 March (the day of an annual market fair in Kolín) by a youth of about twenty who identified himself only as a shop assistant in the town (Veselá, meanwhile, claimed that Mrs. Kantorová had no assistant). The youth told Musil that Anna Vokřálová had insulted the emperor on 22 February and that he could get more information from the two female witnesses. Musil interviewed Veselá and Finková, and what he claims to have heard from the two differs in subtle ways from signed testimony of both women. According to the police supervisor's reconstruction, Vokřálová did not preface her remarks with the happy observation, "We won, we won," but with the more ironic "the elections sure came off nicely" (*to to pěkně dopadlo, ty volby*), followed immediately by "the Jews drink Christian blood and the Emperor chases Jewish girls" (according to Veselá) or "the Jews drink Christian blood and the Emperor *keeps* Jewish girls (*drží se židovkama*)," according to Finková. Because he understood Vokřálová's introductory words to be ironic, he concluded that she was, in fact, disappointed with the results of the elections—allegedly she harbored socialist sympathies—and verbally had equated one sorry state of affairs with another.[103]

That fact that Anna Vokřálová was charged only with insulting the emperor and not with defaming Jews is also intriguing. We cannot necessarily conclude from this, however, that accusations of Jewish ritual murder were held by the state to fall under the category of legitimate political discourse. Jan Chalupa learned that one could go to prison for a lot less. And the records of the Kutná Hora court alone reveal numerous criminal cases against newspaper publishers and editors on the charge of defaming a religious group or inciting to violence. What we may have in the Vokřálová case is a decision to prosecute what was considered the graver of two offenses. And if the honor of the Jews meant less than the honor of the emperor, was there much cause for complaint?

There is little doubt from the overall tenor of the proceedings—as well as from witness accounts—that Vokřálová's outburst disturbed a sense of local order and propriety. In both the Chalupa and the Vokřálová case, non-Jews displayed a proprietary concern for Jewish sensibilities and collaborated successfully with Jewish residents to raise the alarm when the peace was disturbed.

A final observation concerning the two cases: the public prosecutor in each was Dr. Antonín Schneider-Svoboda; Dr. Zdenko Auředníček served as the defense attorney for Anna Vokřálová. The same two individuals would face one another again in 1899 in the first ritual murder trial against Leopold Hilsner: Schneider-Svoboda would again occupy the prosecutor's chair, while Auředníček would again act as defense attorney. Yet there is irony in this apparent resumption of roles. One man spends a good part of his career defending the state *and* its Jewish community against antisemitic provocations and libels and proceeds to devote a year of his life to proving in a court of law that a Jewish defendant has committed aggravated, ritualized murder, possibly in order to make use of the victim's blood for religious purposes. Another is a civil libertarian laboring in the courts defending people, whose public political diatribes are laced with anti-Jewish invectives, including images of ritual murder, and who suddenly—barely two years later—strives against all odds for the acquittal of Central Europe's most famous defendant on the charge of ritual murder. What has happened in the meantime to cause such a profound shift in roles?

I suspect that both attorneys might have protested that their roles, to the contrary, had not changed at all. As public prosecutor, Schneider-Svoboda may simply have felt obliged to accept whatever criminal cases were assigned to him. In his view, putting the Chalupas, the Vokřálovás, and the Hilsners of the world on trial may have seemed all of a piece, consistent with his own sense of professionalism. In the Polná case, his job was to prosecute a murder. The larger political discourse that surrounded it was of no interest to him, only a distraction. Similarly, Auředníček's task was to defend those people who had the misfortune to be on the wrong end of a criminal indictment: rich or poor, Gentile or Jew, it made no difference.

Protests of continuity and consistency, however, fail fully to convince. For one thing, Schneider-Svoboda did not just take a completed case file and argue its merits before the court. He oversaw the entire investigation, interviewed scores of witnesses, handled irritating questions from the chief prosecutor's office in Prague, and defended both the manner in which he was proceeding and the cogency of his case against Leopold Hilsner.[104] Together with his counterparts in Hungary and Imperial Germany, Schneider-Svoboda epitomized the sea change that was taking place in the attitude of Central European governments toward the advisability of taking on purported cases of Jewish ritual murder, perhaps toward the cogency of the accusation itself. This chapter has not tried to argue that Jewish-Christian relations in the small towns of Central Europe were free of conflict or that the challenge to emancipation posed by political antisemitism did not spill over to them. My claim, rather, is that the Jewish residents of Tiszaeszlár, Xanten, Polná, and Konitz were rooted in their communities, had a strong sense of place, and felt entitled to the protection of the state when the peace was broken and their security threatened.

And the fact is that, in such instances, the state *did* step in. Most of the time, Schneider-Svoboda and his colleagues both within and outside of Bohemia maintained social order, protected the Jewish religion against defamation, and, when necessary, put the Chalupas and the Vokřálovás, the radical newspaper editors and the street brawlers, in jail. Schneider-Svoboda's crossing of the barricades in this instance stood for that point at which the pursuit of respectability and the defense of order no longer worked in tandem with Jewish interests. From this perspective, the modern ritual murder trial may have marked the beginning of a general criminalization of the Jews in modern European consciousness. Under the shadow of these proceedings, the Jews of Central Europe were transformed from an *embodiment* of the social order to a source of danger and threat. Finally, Auředníček's shift from defender of rabble rousers—and the rabble—to defender of Hilsner symbolized, if you will, the loss in political and social status that Jews suffered as a result of the revived ritual murder accusation. The world had not suddenly turned upside down, yet something had changed to make the accusation appear more compelling than in centuries past and the Jews less worthy of the presumption of innocence. Figuring out why an accusation of Jewish "ritual murder" at the turn of the twentieth century could break apart the social fabric of small-town and village life, as well as why criminal prosecutions of such charges no longer seemed incompatible with a commitment to modernity, order, rationality, and justice, is precisely the puzzle the needs to be solved.

Chapter 2

Hungarian Beginnings

The Tiszaeszlár Affair

In the year 1882, when the Jews had the great Sabbath before Easter, all the Jews of Tiszaeszlár appeared in the synagogue, and there were also strangers.

—Móric Scharf, testimony before the court at Nyíregyháza, June 1883

It may have been rash on my part, but it just came to me. Would that I had never allowed such foolishness to pass through my lips.

—József Scharf, testimony before the court at Nyíregyháza, June 1883

This absurd offspring of medieval superstition, this stupid subject of fairy tales and the conversation of old village women. . . . In the name of national justice, I solemnly protest against the fact that superstition has been smuggled into its majestic circle.

—Ede Szeyffert, Hungarian state prosecutor, before the court at Nyíregyháza, July 1883

Implicit Knowledge, Rumor, and Officialdom

On 1 April 1882, Eszter Solymosi, from the Hungarian village of Tiszaeszlár, failed to return home after running an errand in a neighboring town. Eszter was a fourteen-year-old orphan who lived with her mother (her father having died before she was born) and who for the past two years had been in the employ of a number of different families in or near Tiszaeszlár as a domestic servant. On this fateful day—the Saturday before Easter—her current employer, Mrs. András Huri, of the Újfalu section of Tiszaeszlár—for whom Eszter had been working for about a month—sent her on an errand to buy paint for the spring housecleaning. The mission required that Eszter walk for an hour to a general store in nearby Ófalu. Witnesses later recounted having seen her on the way to the store; she did not return home from her journey. Mrs. Huri was known as an impatient and possibly abusive woman (the police noticed a thick reed switch hanging from the crossbeam in her house); later that afternoon, she made her way to the Solymosi home to ask about Eszter. Had Mária—Eszter's mother—sent her on errands of her own perhaps? When Eszter failed to return that evening, a sense of panic set in. Mária Solymosi and her sister began to canvas the village for any information about the girl's whereabouts.[1]

For Tiszaeszlár's small Jewish community, 1 April was *shabbat ha-gadol*—the Sabbath preceding the holiday of Passover. It was also unusual in another sense, as the community was hosting three visitors, candidates for the position of ritual slaughterer (*shoḥet*) who also were expected to chant from the Torah and lead the congregation in prayer. During their stay in Tiszaeszlár, the three men (Ábrahám Buxbaum, Lipót Braun, and Salamon Schwarcz) were housed with local families, two with the outgoing *shoḥet* and one with the tavernkeeper (and assistant sexton), Emánuel Taub. Saturday morning prayers ended around 11 a.m., after which the candidates went to their hosts' homes for the midday meal. Four indigent Jews (a family of three and a single woman) also found shelter in Tiszaeszlár on that Sabbath in the home of József Scharf—caretaker of the synagogue, cobbler, and part-time laborer—who lived in a modest house adjacent to the synagogue and the ritual bath (*mikvah*).[2] Scharf, who grew up in the nearby town of Hajdúnánás (some thirty kilometers south), was forty-three years old and had lived in Tiszaeszlár with his wife and three children for four years when his Christian neighbor disappeared.[3] Although native to Hungary and intimately tied to the region around Tiszaeszlár, Scharf was relatively new to the village itself and did not personally know all of its residents. He could not recall if he had ever met the young Eszter Solymosi, he testified at trial, but he was acquainted with her mother, and when the latter approached his house that Saturday night in search of news about her daughter, Scharf was eager to greet her with words of comfort.

According to Scharf, the encounter with Mrs. Solymosi took place on the evening of 1 April outside of his house.[4] It was Scharf's wife who first went out to speak with Eszter's mother. When she went back inside, she announced that she had heard some news, that someone had sent a child to Ófalu, but the child had not yet returned. Scharf then went out of the house himself, accompanied by his wife, at which point the grieving mother tearfully repeated her complaint.[5] Scharf now proceeded to do something, which he would come deeply to regret, and to which would be attributed major significance by both the Solymosi family and, eventually, the investigating magistrate. In an effort to allay their worries, he related to the women the story of a similar situation that had taken place in his home town of Hajdúnánás, which he had heard from his mother. Eszter's aunt, Mrs. Gábor Solymosi, testified to what she heard him say during her trial testimony:

> The sun did not go down until after I had gone with my sister to the village, after we had looked for Eszter without finding her, and after we had set out in the direction of Ujfalu. And, as we reached the edge of the graves of the old cemetery, the woman Scharf, the wife of "Six Bushels," approached us. "What's the problem," she asked? "Is Eszter lost?" "Yes," I said. She said: "She's not lost. Perhaps she had a fever and is lying down somewhere." "That cannot be," I said, "She is not that type of child." Her husband also approached us and started up, saying: "When I was still a child, I heard from my mother that in Nánás a child had gone missing, and people also said that the Jews had killed the child. They even searched the ovens of the Jews, and finally the child was found in the meadow."[6]

Two days earlier, Mária Solymosi had related in court more or less the same version of events: "He came up to me on the street and asked me what the matter was. I didn't say anything, but my sister told him that the Huri woman had sent the girl to the village and that since then she can't be found. Thereupon he said that one mustn't be upset, that a similar case happened in Nánás when he was still a boy: then, too, the Jews were suspected; even their ovens were searched; and in the end the missing child was found in the meadow."[7]

Two days later, on Monday, 3 April, Mrs. Solymosi appeared before Gábor Farkas, the village head (*bíró*), to request that he initiate a formal search for her daughter. She saw him later the same day, during which time she relayed her suspicion that the Jews of Tiszaeszlár had had a hand in Eszter's disappearance. Farkas apparently felt that these requests went beyond his formal authority, and he advised her to go to Vencsellő, the district seat, where she might appeal to the district magistrate/justice of the peace (*szolgabíró*). Eszter's mother duly complied, arriving in Vencsellő the next day. Here, however, she encountered a resistant official. The district magistrate reacted with incredulity to Solymosi's claims about the Jews and advised her, in the words of Andrew Handler, to "put such thoughts out of her mind and refrain from giving credence to those who should spread such rumors." Disinclined by virtue of historical practice and self-image to take seriously the ranting of an uneducated woman regarding Jewish ritual murder, the judge did nevertheless dispatch a messenger to Tiszaeszlár instructing the village head to initiate a search for the missing girl.[8]

One wonders what exactly transpired between Saturday evening and Sunday or Monday to make Mária Solymosi resolute in her conviction that Eszter had been the victim of a Jewish conspiracy to kidnap and murder. Contemporary observers, such as the British churchman and scholar Charles H. H. Wright or the American editors of the trial proceedings *Der Blut-Prozeß von Tisza Eszlár in Ungarn*, assigned much of the blame to the production and spread of rumor at the village level. The introduction to *Der Blut-Prozeß* carried the title "The Origins of the Rumor" and informed the reader early on that "before the arrest and investigation of Josef Scharf, his wife, his 14-year-old-son, and the thirteen other accused . . . the wildest rumors concerning the disappearance of the girl began to surface in Tisza-Eszlár and in all of Szabolcs county."[9] Wright, who covered the trial for the periodical *Nineteenth Century*, suggested that what had set the rumor of a ritual murder in motion were the interpersonal communications that Mrs. Solymosi had had with her neighbors. He surmised that she had repeated Scharf's remarks to her friends, "who regarded it at once as the utterance of a man with a guilty conscience. Thus Widow Solymosi became fully persuaded that Esther must have been kidnapped by the Jews. . . . The suspicion that the Jews had a hand in the affair, when once ventilated, rapidly gained a footing among a people imbued with prejudices against their Jewish neighbours. Every circumstance was now looked upon with suspicion."[10] Andrew Handler, writing only a few decades ago, placed similar weight on the importance of speech itself (or, what people in an earlier age might have called "wagging tongues") in the production of local knowledge: "Mrs. Solymosi repeated Scharf's story and conveyed her own fears to a steadily growing audience of neighbors and friends. The hidden meaning of the words uttered in the spirit of compassion and commiseration gradually took on the ring of reality. The willingness of her sympathetic listeners to give ready credence to the possibility of the Jews having something to do with Eszter's disappearance prompted Mrs. Solymosi to turn to the local authorities for help."[11] According to these views, then, local knowledge of a crime of ritual murder was produced not all at once but in the course of verbal interactions between Mária Solymosi and her Christian neighbors as well as among the neighbors themselves. It was socially constructed knowledge, informed by conventional wisdom and resting on solid communal foundations.

Since Mária Solymosi and her sister claimed that József Scharf had unintentionally blurted out what amounted to an indirect confession of wrongdoing (or, at least, knowledge of a crime), efforts were made in the course of the trial to establish Scharf's ostensible motives in recounting his mother's memory of a ritual murder accusation in Hajdúnánás. How did it occur to you to tell the story in the first place, Ede Szeyffert, the public prosecutor, wanted to know? Scharf responded—perhaps testily—that he was moved to tell the story of Hajdúnánás for the same reason that Szeyffert himself had brought up the case of a false accusation of Jewish ritual murder in the town of Tiszaszentimre in his opening statement to the court: presumably, although Scharf never articulates this, to demonstrate how easy it is for dangerous, unfounded rumors to spread.[12] When the presiding judge stepped in to ask the defendant virtually the same question that had been put to him shortly before, Scharf replied in a different manner: "It may have been rash on my part, but it just came to me. Would that I had never allowed such foolishness to pass through my lips."[13] In fact, Mrs. Solymosi's appearance outside of his house, her emotional state, and her frantic searching for her daughter made him uneasy. His action, while certainly unplanned, was as much an unconscious expression of fear as it was an effort to console a grieving mother. When Scharf went back into the house after speaking with the Solymosi sisters, he turned to the charity recipient who had been staying with him over the Sabbath and said, "Nothing good will come out of this. . . . Someone will concoct an accusation against the Jews." During the trial, Szeyffert claimed to be surprised at Scharf's expression of foreboding. Why should he have reacted so pessimistically? Certainly it was natural for a mother to look for her child. "She looked for it [the child]," Scharf responded, "but where it would lead, God only knew."[14]

One question that was never put to Mária Solymosi, but might well have been, also concerned motivation: how was it that she happened to be standing outside the home of József Scharf on the evening of 1 April? Was it a chance encounter, as she often said? In suggesting an answer to this question, I would first point out that Solymosi offered conflicting versions of exactly when she came to suspect (or know) that the answer to Eszter's disappearance lay with Tiszaeszlár's Jews. At one point in the trial, she responded to just such a question by the presiding judge with the statement, "I dreamt it. God revealed it to me," referring apparently to the night of April 1, after her meeting with Scharf. Solymosi later said, "The next morning I sent my son out to look for the grave, because God let it be known to me that during the night my child had been killed; in the meantime the only other person to tell me that was József Scharf, who told me the story of that case."[15] Still later in the trial, Mrs. Solymosi responded ambiguously to questioning by one of the defense attorneys, one moment suggesting that she became suspicious immediately upon hearing József Scharf's story and, the next moment, that this conviction did not come to her until later that night, from God. Not before, the attorney wished to know? Did she not think that the Jews might have killed her daughter on the very evening on which she was searching for her? At this point, Mária Solymosi hedged: "I had thought about it earlier, but I began to believe it more from the moment that József Scharf told me the story."[16] This implicit admission explains, I think, what Solymosi and her sister were doing outside the Scharfs' home in the first place: they had gone there, that is, to the synagogue and surrounding homes, purposefully—to see if "the Jews" knew something about Eszter's disappearance. It was hardly a chance encounter.

Paul Nathan, the Berlin-based correspondent who had been sent by his magazine to Tiszaeszlár to cover the trial, published a monograph on the affair ten years later, in which he scoffed at what he considered to be Mária Solymosi's gullibility and superstition. She was a "believer," he wrote, well before Eszter's disappearance; her "superstitious mind" was well acquainted with the image of Jewish "ritual murder."[17] True enough. But one does not need to resort to condescension to make the case that the implicit memory of many of Tiszaeszlár's residents comprised, among other things, narratives of Jewish ritual murder.[18] More illuminating of the historical moment, I believe, is a different observation, partially articulated by Nathan. This is that in their uncomfortable encounter, both József Scharf and Mária Solymosi revealed much about the shared cultural universe in which they had grown up, a world in which such stories were not only known but keenly felt, albeit differently by Jews and by Christians. The unspoken subtext of the otherwise friendly encounter between these two individuals was fear. Mrs. Solymosi was drawn to the vicinity of the synagogue by a sense of dread that perhaps her daughter had fallen victim to a Jewish conspiracy—a crime that she may never have witnessed before in her own life but knew was within the realm of possibility. Scharf, in contrast, read the silence that lay behind Mrs. Solymosi's tears with foreboding. He blurted out his own poorly chosen words in an effort to ward off an ill wind, to disarm an accusation—which he hoped never to hear—before it had a chance to be uttered.[19]

Over the next five weeks, a stalemate emerged between the Solymosi family and county-level Hungarian officials over the proper steps to take in response to the mystery of Eszter's disappearance. Jenő Jármy, the district magistrate in Vencsellő, had dismissed Mária Solymosi's assertion of a Jewish ritual crime out of hand on 4 April, rejecting her interpretation of Eszter's disappearance in favor of any number of alternative scenarios of a more naturalistic order. Solymosi, for her part, was not one to give up easily and eventually found a compelling reason to make her way back to Vencsellő four weeks later. One way to understand this contest of wills is to view it from the perspective of "rumor" versus official knowledge or information. Rumors, as Jean-Noël Kapferer argues, do not arise out of a reality, which, in their transmission, they proceed to distort. Rather, to use Kapferer's language, they spring from "raw, confused facts." The purpose of rumors is not to describe reality but to explain troubling or mysterious facts, to posit a scenario in the form of a particular narrative.[20] Rumors also work parallel to, or in the absence of, official investigations and explanations; they "seek out a reality that does not await the verdict of official investigations." This does not mean that rumors and official information cannot eventually converge. There is no a priori or theoretical reason why the interpretation provided by a rumor will necessarily differ from the "reality" that might eventually emerge from a complete investigation.[21] Kapferer argues finally that, contrary to the claims of earlier, classic experiments in social psychology, the transmission of rumors does not involve a linear, progressive relaying of information from an original source. Rumors arise in the context of social interactions and conversations—collective deliberations—which work to produce a consensus of sorts on the content of a "convincing, encompassing explanation."[22]

In the case of Tiszaeszlár, Mária Solymosi's rebuff by the county magistrate forced her to return to the village dissatisfied, while Hungarian officials—despite organizing a local search for the girl—failed to offer an official explanation for the event in question. In this unsettling state of affairs, Solymosi and her neighbors did not simply wait patiently for the state to provide an

LE PROCÈS DE TISZA-ESZLAR. — Vue de la place du village — Vue de la synagogue. — Types de juifs et de jeunes filles du pays. — (Dessin de M. Paul Merwart.

Figure 4. Paul Merwart, *Le Procès de Tisza-Eszlar*. Print.

Courtesy H. Kieval and J. Mabray.

answer. They continued to engage in conversation, to forge a more complete picture of what they now took to be a crime.[23] And they appear to have done so in such a way as to anticipate the objections of Hungarian officials, to address the bureaucrats on their own terms by fulfilling the requirements of evidence and eyewitness testimony. Sometime after the first week in April, two women came forward to offer testimony that on the day of Eszter's disappearance, they had seen and heard strange happenings coming from the vicinity of the synagogue, including the muffled sounds of a child's shouts or cries.[24] Toward the end of the month, Eszter Farkas (the sister of Tiszaeszlár's village head), two other women, and a twelve-year-old girl insinuated themselves into the company of József Scharf's younger son, Samu—not yet five years old—apparently through games and candy. On 30 April, Farkas announced to others that she had heard Samu say to some village children that his father had enticed Eszter into the synagogue, bound and washed her, and that a *shoḥet* had cut her. The twelve-year-old neighbor Erzsébet Sós soon revealed that Samu had told her that Móric, his older brother, had held Eszter's hands and his father, her head, while the *shoḥet* cut her feet. On 2 May, yet another woman reported that when she had upbraided the young Samu for dispersing her geese, he warned her, "Just for that I won't tell you what my father did to that Magyar girl!"[25]

Armed with the collected revelations of the past few weeks, Mária Solymosi made a second trip to the district magistrate on 4 May, and this time Jármy could not simply dismiss her contentions out of hand. He proceeded cautiously, instructing Gábor Farkas to begin an investigation into the alleged criminal act. Farkas questioned a number of individuals two days later and prepared a report of his findings, which he dispatched to the court in Nyíregyháza, a former market town and noble domain that had grown into the seat of Szabolcs County. Jármy himself made a personal visit to Tiszaeszlár on 12 May 1882, during which he was unable to locate any physical evidence of a crime. On the same day, however—and on the recommendation of the assistant royal prosecutor, László Egressy Nagy—the president of the Nyíregyháza court, Ferenc Korniss, ordered a formal investigation into the disappearance of Eszter Solymosi. Assuming the case to be of minor consequence, however, Korniss appointed a relatively inexperienced but ambitious twenty-four-year-old notary named József Bary to head the inquiry as investigating magistrate (*vizsgálóbíró*).[26] Bary arrived in Tiszaeszlár one week later, accompanied by Egressy Nagy and Kálmán Péczely, a court clerk. He interviewed scores of people, including little Samu Scharf; examined the synagogue for physical evidence; and detained the members of the Scharf family: the affair had begun.

With the arrival of Bary in Tiszaeszlár, the standoff between the county and state officials and Mrs. Solymosi also ended, revealing more of the close, if complicated, relationship between rumor and official knowledge. Clearly, it is not only the case that rumor exists in the absence of official information or even that it can persist in defiance of official word (what Kapferer calls "a counter-power" or a "check on power"): rumor also can engage official knowledge and seek to alter it. The unofficial information culled by Mrs. Solymosi and presented to the district magistrate was designed to move him to action. In this case, rumor functioned not only to provide an explanation to a traumatic event when such was not forthcoming from the authorities but also to draw the authorities into its own conversation, to elicit a fundamental change in the nature of the official response. Government officials, for their part, actively engaged the local rumor, at first by seeking to discredit and silence it, but later by accepting aspects of its claims (based on the formal criteria of official knowledge), initiating formal inquiries, and, eventually, pushing those inquiries in the direction of the rumor's assumptions and conclusions.

The Testimony of Children and the Floating Corpse

In the transition from local mystery to full-fledged investigation and trial, all roads led through the state. Magistrates, police officials, and government ministers had to make a conscious decision to accept the burdens of the case, investing the state's time, resources, and prestige in its investigation and prosecution. For Jews in Tiszaeszlár and the rest of Hungary, the chance occurrence that József Bary was named to direct the formal investigation into the disappearance of Eszter Solymosi was of signal importance. Another person might have made a perfunctory appearance in Tiszaeszlár, conducted a few interviews, repeated the as-yet unsuccessful search for physical evidence of a crime, issued a report, and returned to the court in Nyíregyháza hopeful that he would be assigned a more promising case the next time. But this was not how the inexperienced but ambitious young court clerk approached his task. He seems to have taken as his starting point the position that he was there to investigate a crime for which substantial incriminating evidence existed. He may or may not have believed in the ritual murder accusation as it pertained to all Jews at all times—he does not admit to this in his memoir of the case—but he was confident that, at this time and in this place, a group of fanatical Jews had engaged in a criminal conspiracy to kidnap and murder a Christian child.[27]

The first truly dramatic turning point in the Tiszaeszlár investigation occurred when the investigators claimed to have produced, in the person of Móric Scharf (József Scharf's fourteen-year-old son), an eyewitness to the murder of Eszter Solymosi. To arrive at this point, Bary and the other investigating officers had first to remove Móric from the category of suspect (he had been named, after all, as a participant in the reported remarks of his little brother Samu to the women of the village) to that of potential witness; more difficult, still, they had to convince him to confess to what he had "seen." The first hurdle was overcome fairly quickly thanks to a bit of intuitive ingenuity on Bary's part. When he began his investigation in Tiszaeszlár on 19 May, Bary did briefly question Samu Scharf but decided, sensibly, that he could not make use of the boy's testimony in court.[28] Just what induced Bary to focus instead on the older brother, Móric, as an alternative source of first-hand information is difficult to say. It seems likely that there was a kind of associative logic at play, which worked in tandem with the folk wisdom that children were fundamentally guileless and, hence, a conduit to truth. Samu may have been an impossible witness from the point of view of the law—and his story may have contained improbabilities and inconsistencies—but he was a child, and he had access to the inner life of the Jewish community. Móric, by this reasoning, would make a more believable witness. Although he had, in fact, been implicated in the earlier telling of Eszter's murder, what was more important to the investigators was his status as *child*. The task at hand, then, was to get him to talk.

The first interview with Móric Scharf proved to be problematic, as his testimony stuck fairly close to that of the other Jewish witnesses who had been examined before him. At the second interrogation, which took place on 21 May, the chief of the district gendarmerie, András Recsky, took part and appears to have applied the requisite pressure to get the boy to lose his composure.[29] In the course of the questioning, Recsky threatened to have Móric taken to Nyíregyháza, the county seat, presumably to jail. At this, he broke into tears. At the conclusion of the interrogation, Recsky, with Bary's approval, headed out with Móric toward Nyíregyháza; the pair stopped, however, at the policeman's house in Nagyfalu. It was here, in Recsky's home—possibly under the pressure of threats from his jailors, possibly under the influence of hunger and fatigue—that Móric began to lose his will to resist. Károly Eötvös, who represented the Jewish defendants at their eventual trial, and others have insisted that Recsky applied physical abuse during this part of the interrogation.[30]

Recsky and a court clerk who had been present during the interrogation drew up a protocol of the testimony and had it signed by Móric. According to the protocol, Eszter Solymosi entered József Scharf's house at his invitation on 1 April at which time he asked her to remove a candelabrum from the table. The testimony then provided a description of Eszter Solymosi's dress, small jacket, and scarf and went on to claim that a "Jewish beggar" brought Eszter from the house to the synagogue under some kind of false pretense. In the courtyard of the synagogue, another Jewish beggar grabbed her and threw her to the ground, at which point she was undressed. As two of the *shoḥet* candidates held her, the third, Salamon Schwarcz, slashed her throat. Her blood was then collected in a pot, and finally, the dead girl was dressed. Móric claimed to have witnessed the event, watching it through the keyhole of the door to the synagogue. He said that he informed his parents of the murder but that they told him to keep quiet about it. The young Scharf closed his statement by attesting to the fact that his confession was made without coercion. The document in hand, the two men sent another gendarme off to inform József Bary that the witness was now ready to talk and to request that Bary come to Nagyfalu to decide on the next step to be taken.[31] This he did in the company of the assistant royal prosecutor, Egressy Nagy. Bary listened to the boy's testimony a second time and prepared his own protocol, which confirmed the contents of the first report.[32]

Móric was brought to Tiszaeszlár on 22 May, where he identified the three candidates for the position of ritual slaughterer, Schwarcz, Buxbaum and Braun, and pointed out Schwarcz as the one who had "cut" Eszter's neck. (The three vigorously denied the charges.) Móric was brought the same day to the Nyíregyháza court, where a closed session under the presidency of Ferenc Korniss met to authenticate his testimony. Remarkably, the Hungarian justice system did not thereafter release the boy from its supervision. The royal prosecutor in Budapest at first ordered Móric kept in custody as a material witness. On 27 May, Bary informed the sheriff of Szabolcs County of his decision to end Móric's arrest and to grant him his freedom. In view of the fact that the boy refused to return to his parents, however (according to Bary), and out of consideration for his well-being and protection, the investigating magistrate recommended that Móric be allowed to exercise this freedom in Bary's custody—physically, however, within the confines of the Nyíregyháza jail![33]

Within the first two weeks of his arrival in Tiszaeszlár, magistrate Bary had managed to conduct two physical searches of the synagogue and its grounds, interview scores of witnesses and suspects, dredge the bottom of the Tisza River, and bring charges against ten Jews on suspicion of kidnapping and murder.[34] But the state's case rested on fragile foundations consisting of apparent inconsistencies in the statements of detained Jews, information from witnesses who claimed to have heard muffled cries coming from the vicinity of the synagogue, and, above all, the prized testimony of Móric Scharf. There was, however, *no body*—no sign of the missing girl and no physical evidence of a violent crime. In the absence of a body, the investigating magistrate's interrogation protocols *might* have been sufficient to bring a case to trial, but the state would have had to convince the court that Eszter Solymosi was not merely missing but dead. This indeterminate state of affairs formed the backdrop to the sensational discovery on 18 June 1882 of the corpse of a woman floating on the Tisza River near the town of Tiszadada by a small flotilla of raftsmen.

Four rafts in all had been floating downstream with a load of lumber and other products from the Carpathian Mountains. They were owned by a company in Máramarossziget (in today's Romania) and sailed under the stewardship of a forty-seven-year-old observant Jew (who, according to some accounts at least, dressed in Hasidic garb) named Dávid Herskó. The sixteen men who accompanied the primitive rafts included both Jews—one steward to each raft—and Christians: both Hungarians and ethnic Ukrainians.[35] Anchored for repairs at Csonkafüzes, less than twenty kilometers downstream from Tiszaeszlár, between Tiszalök and Tiszadada, one of the sailors noticed the body of a woman floating in the water. News of the raftsmen's discovery, spread by local youth and foresters, produced a good deal of excitement in the neighboring towns and villages and beyond because the body appeared to be dressed in the clothing that had been worn by Eszter Solymosi on the day of her disappearance. Indeed, the earliest reports of the sighting indicated that Eszter's body had been discovered *and* that the Jews had *not* in fact killed her, as there did not appear to be any obvious wounds on her body.[36]

The raftsmen's discovery spurred local officials to action as well. The first to arrive on the scene were Dr. Jenő Kiss, the district medical officer; a young medical student named Géza Horváth Kéri; a pharmacist named Kálmán Zurányi; a gendarme; and a small landowner. Well after dark on the 18th, the small group disinterred the corpse from a shallow grave that the raftsmen had dug, and Dr. Kiss conducted—by candlelight—a preliminary examination of the body. He indicated that it was about fifteen years old and of average development, although the hair on the head and body was missing; the teeth were healthy; and tied to the girl's left wrist was a small tin of blue paint wrapped in yellow paper.[37] It was not until the following day that Bary, the chief constable of Tizsalök, and a variety of other officials arrived to take charge of the proceedings. The first order of business was the official identification of the corpse, referred to in Austrian legal parlance as the *Agnoszierung*. Local villagers were called upon to help identify the body, a difficult task under the best of circumstances that was made more shocking for the witnesses because Bary—not wanting them to be "influenced" by the dress in which the body had been found—ordered that the corpse be viewed naked. This action presented two problems immediately: it was difficult for people in this cultural setting to view, let alone recognize, the naked body of a nonintimate; more important, the body may have been under water for an undetermined length of time and, in any event, had undergone various stages of decomposition. As it turned out, at least two people identified the corpse as that of Eszter Solymosi: the pharmacist Zurányi and Eszter's best friend, and both on the basis of a scar that was still visible at the base of the big toe on the right foot (the result of a kick that she had received from a cow). Eszter's mother and her aunt, however, denied that the body could be that of her missing girl.[38]

On the second day following the discovery of the body—outdoors, on the banks of the river in Tiszaeszlár—a court-appointed medical commission, made up of three physicians assisted by a medical student, conducted two forensic examinations on the corpse: an external examination—*Leichenschau* in German—followed by an autopsy (*Obduktion*).[39] In their official report, the doctors made a number of observations and deductions regarding the identity of the corpse, the condition in which it was found, and the probable cause of death. Notice was taken of the absence of head and pubic hair; of the apparent softness and smoothness of the skin on the hands, feet, and soles; of the apparently well-groomed nails; of a waxy substance on the body; and of reddish stains on the dress. These details were recorded in calm and detached language, mirroring the disciplined method with which they were assumed to have been produced. But the neutral affect belied the tense atmosphere of anticipation that surrounded the physicians' work. The judge magistrate had already begun to produce a theory of the crime based on a selection of, often inconsistent, witness narratives; anti-Jewish deputies had already interpellated the government in parliament claiming that a ritual murder had been committed in Tiszaeszlár; and newspapers had already begun to run series of stories on the case. Any one of the physicians' measurements or conclusions could have had the effect potentially of bolstering—or undermining—one or more theories of the prosecution.

In dispatching the physicians to Tiszadada, then, the investigating magistrate was acknowledging, at least formally, the need to make his case in conjunction with medical science. But there is a question as to whether the acknowledgment of form also entailed a commitment to substance. Bary and the Nyíregyháza court consistently preferred the services of local physicians, for example, to those of urban practitioners. Yet the physicians who were selected to conduct the Tiszaeszlár autopsy may have been out of their depth. They had little experience dissecting bodies, let alone bodies that had been under water for long periods of time. And this particular case presented them with a number of technical challenges in the form of biological processes that occur in or on a body that has been submerged under water for a long period of time, the ignorance of which could produce misdiagnosis.[40] Defense attorneys, judges, and expert witnesses sparred with one another over the identification and understanding of these processes during the prolonged investigation and trial. And it would not be an exaggeration to say that the fate of the fifteen Jewish defendants in Nyíregyháza hinged on the outcome of these debates.

The original team of physicians produced a report that appeared to accommodate Bary's working theory of the case but was also vulnerable to attack from other scientists. From the relatively well-preserved condition of the body, the doctors concluded that death could not have occurred earlier than ten days from the date of the postmortem exam. From the delicate nature of the skin on the hands and feet and the seemingly well-manicured nails (actually the empty nail bed) that they observed: this woman had come from the upper social classes and could not have been a peasant servant girl. They only mentioned, but did not investigate, the absence of hair on the head. Judge Bary and local officials who observed the proceedings, however, drew the inference that the body in question belonged to a married Jewish woman who followed the Orthodox custom of shaving her head.[41] The investigating magistrate and police officials did not have a straightforward explanation for the absence of pubic hair—also noted but not explained by the examining physicians. Did they suspect that this, too, was related to Jewish marriage custom? To sexual promiscuity, perhaps? In any event, the doctors concluded—although on the basis of what, precisely, it is unclear—that not only was the corpse *not* that of a virgin but that it belonged to a woman who "had engaged in sexual intercourse in an excessive manner." As to the cause of death, the doctors ruled out drowning and pointed instead to "pneumonic anemia," along with other illnesses, because the lungs, the right heart chamber, and the veins contained only small amounts of blood.[42]

Bary seems to have been determined to turn the potentially exculpatory implications of the discovery of the Tiszadada corpse into supporting evidence for his already formed theory of the case. Now, armed with the results of the forensic examinations, he took the formal position that the corpse from the river was *not* that of Eszter Solymosi. Yet the clothing that covered the body appeared to have been hers. To resolve this contradiction, Bary argued that the very discovery of the Tiszadada corpse had been part of a conspiracy to hinder the investigation into Eszter's murder. He ordered the rearrest and interrogation of the raftsmen (who originally had been allowed to proceed on their voyage) on suspicion of having conspired with unnamed persons to switch Eszter's body with that of a recently deceased Jewish woman, place it in the river, and later discover it, all in an effort to gain the release of the imprisoned Tiszaeszlár Jews. Bary also ordered that the corpse be reburied, as it was—this time in a pinewood box, curled up like a fetus.[43] Several of the unlucky sailors, including Herskó, György Csepkanics, Amsel Vogel, and Ignác Matej, were subjected to brutal questioning by the chief constable of Tiszalök, György Vaj, and the prison guard József Karanczay. These methods included whipping of the feet and forced feeding of large quantities of water until the prisoner had the sensation of drowning. At least one of the rafts-men—Amsel Vogel—was required to spend many hours locked in a small chicken coop together with the chickens.[44]

The Fury Before the Storm: Mobilizations and Interventions Before the Trial

As June 1882 drew to a close, the criminal investigation into the disappearance of Eszter Solymosi had crystallized around a complicated theory of murder and conspiracy after the fact. The original mystery surrounding Eszter's where-abouts had long assumed the form of an accusation of ritual murder and was being transmitted far beyond the borders of Szabolcs County, carried initially by letters to the editors of national newspapers and interpellations in parliament, and eventually by regular newspaper coverage (both in Hungary and abroad), publicity campaigns (both for and against the accusation), the publication and distribution of popular books and pamphlets, political gatherings, and even riots.[45] Győző Istóczy, who for the better part of a decade had been one of the few antisemitic voices to be heard in the Chamber of Deputies (although technically a member of the Liberal Party), and Géza Ónody, a noble land-owner of parcels in and around Tiszaeszlár, introduced the Tiszaeszlár affair to the national political debate: Ónody, on 23 May, in an ad hoc reference in the course of a debate on an unrelated matter, and Istóczy, one day later, through a pointed interpellation of the government. He asked the prime minister whether he had received any information to the effect that the local magistrate had refused to inquire into the matter and that "the Jews" were attempting to hush up the crime by bribing officials. The same day, Hungary's main antisemitic newspaper, *Függetlenség* (*Independence*), published a feature article regarding Bary's investigation, written by the paper's editor, Gyula Verhovay, based on information passed to him by Ónody.[46] Political interventions such as these in all likelihood provided the first occasion for Kálmán Tisza and members of his government to learn of the events in Tiszaeszlár. Indeed, this was the first time that most people in Hungary—including the large and well-established Jewish community of Budapest—had heard of the affair. Istóczy's interpellation caused such a stir among Hungarian Jews that it was commented on at length by the Budapest correspondent to the London *Jewish Chronicle*.[47]

During the initial months of Bary's investigation, the sole legal repre-sentation available to the Tiszaeszlár Jews came from the court-appointed defender and Nyíregyháza resident, Ignác Heumann, himself Jewish. A provincial lawyer without a national reputation, Heumann found himself excoriated by the antiliberal press, attacked on the streets of Nyíregyháza by angry townspeople, and hampered at every step by the investigating magistrate from mounting an effective defense and even meeting with his clients. He was even accused by *Függetlenség* of being the mastermind behind the presumed smuggling of corpses. By the end of June, he had prepared a letter of resignation for the court, although he ultimately stayed on as defense attorney.[48] Officials of the Budapest Jewish community, meanwhile—represented chiefly by the National Bureau of Israelites (Országos Izraelita Iroda)—were coming to the conclusion that the Jews who were imprisoned in Nyíregyháza needed a more visible and effective defense, preferably from non-Jewish attorneys. The organization's secretary, József Simon, paid a visit around the middle of June to Károly Eötvös (1842–1916), a former journalist and current representative to Hungary's Chamber of Deputies for the opposition Independence Party (the same party to which Géza Ónody belonged), who also had some experience as a public prosecutor. He requested of Eötvös that he travel to Nyíregyháza to interview the young Móric Scharf and give his "impartial" opinion on the merits of the boy's testimony.

The meeting between Eötvös and young Móric (accompanied by the assistant royal prosecutor, a police sergeant, and a guard) took place on 18 June, the same day on which the female corpse washed ashore near Tiszadada. According to Eötvös's memoir, he was not allowed to ask any direct questions concerning the boy's testimony, so Eötvös contented himself with observing his general demeanor (he appeared healthy but visibly frightened) and asked him only one question: his age. When Móric looked first to the sergeant and then to the assistant royal prosecutor before answering, the interview, for all intents and purposes, was over. Eötvös had his answer and proceeded to report his findings to both Simon and the chief royal prosecutor, Sándor Kozma. Shortly thereafter, he agreed to head up the defense of the Tiszaeszlár Jews.[49]

Eötvös sought to immerse himself in the intricacies of the forensic evidence of the case soon after his appointment as lead defense attorney. He was not unfamiliar with forensic techniques, having served as a public prosecutor himself, and he knew that much of the state's case against his clients hinged on establishing the identity of the so-called Tiszadada corpse, its probable age, and the cause of death. He also had a strong feeling that the original medical team's official report contained numerous scientific errors. Over the course of the summer, Eötvös made repeated requests to the Nyíregyháza court to have access to the autopsy report on the discovered corpse, but Bary refused Eötvös's entreaties on the grounds that the investigation had not yet been concluded. In contrast, László Egressy Nagy, the assistant prosecutor, and Ferenc Korniss, the presiding judge of the Nyíregyháza court, advocated giving the report to Eötvös. The dispute between the judge magistrate and the public prosecutor dragged on for weeks, ultimately drawing in both the Hungarian minister of justice, Tivadar Pauler, and the prime minister, Kálmán Tisza, in attempts to resolve the quarrel.[50] Toward the end of September, Bary—who was facing pressure over accusations of torture during the interrogation of the raftsmen—finally relented and allowed Eötvös to examine the autopsy report along with other documents from the criminal investigation.[51] Documents in hand, Eötvös formally petitioned the district court in Nyíregyháza in November 1882, challenging the methods and conclusions of the medical procedure and calling for an entirely new forensic examination of the body.[52]

Eötvös's petition to the court reviewed all of the forensic procedures taken—from the brief, so-called police examination to the identification of the body to the original autopsy—point by point, underscoring every legal and medical error that he claimed had been made along the way. While the tone of the petition was critical throughout, questioning both the motives and the procedures of the investigating magistrate, it reserved particularly harsh judgment for the court-appointed medical commission. Neither the external exam nor the autopsy, it charged, rose to the level of accepted forensic medical science, nor were they conducted in such a way as to be able to provide reasonable answers to the many questions surrounding the Tiszadada corpse.[53] To take a few of the most egregious examples, the physicians had noted the absence of hair on the head but had failed to investigate further to determine if this was the result of the decomposition of the body or removal by shaving. They made note of the absence of pubic hair without further comment and without considering the possibility that the person had not yet reached puberty. They offered no description at all of the size or condition of the uterus, the presence of eggs, the condition of the hymen, vagina, and vulva, and yet, they had the *nerve* (Eötvös's term) to render a judgment on the victim's sexual history.[54] Contrary to the conclusions of the medical examiners, Eötvös argued that there was ample evidence to suggest that the corpse found at Tiszadada was, in fact, that of Eszter Solymosi. Any remaining doubt could be removed by the performance of a second, proper autopsy.[55]

At this point, I should alert the reader to some technical terminology that relates to several chemical and biological processes and around which a fair amount of scientific argument turned. One of these was *maceration*, the softening effects of water or some other liquid on a body that is immersed in it; this could include the pulling away of the epidermis, leaving behind only the inner skin (dermis), as well as the breaking off of the hair on the head and body. A related process was the production of *adipocere*, so-called corpse or mortuary wax—insoluble fatty acids that formed on the dermis in very moist conditions and that could leave behind red stains on the clothing. A third concerned *ossification* or, more precisely, *endochondral ossification*: the transformation of cartilage cells into bone in the epiphyseal plate, which is necessary for growth, particularly of the long bones.[56] These terms turn up frequently in the published and oral statements of the expert witnesses; each pointed to crucial procedures in determining the likely identity of the Tiszadada corpse, its age, and the cause of its demise.

The new autopsy was performed by candlelight in an unheated cotter's house at the edge of Tiszaeszlár by a very different team of physicians: three distinguished pathologists from the medical faculty at the University of Budapest (Gusztáv Scheuthauer, Géza Mihálkovics, and János Belky).[57] By now, almost six months had elapsed since the first autopsy; that exam, moreover, had been conducted on a body that was essentially in the same condition in which it had been found. In the intervening months, however, during which time the bent body rested in a pine box underground, it had atrophied considerably. When the pathologists attempted to straighten it, it broke in two.[58] The second autopsy found ample traces of adipocere on the body, suggesting that the corpse must have been immersed in moisture for at least two weeks, more likely considerably longer. The doctors observed an absence of underarm hair, possibly disproving the earlier report's claim that the corpse was that of a sexually mature woman. They conducted a frantic but futile search for the nails, which according to the first report had been well manicured. And they also pointed out a refining, or smoothing, process caused by prolonged friction between water and the surface of an object immersed in it that might have accounted for the first doctors' observation of smooth, well-cared-for skin (implying the regular use of shoes and gloves).[59] After working all day and the next morning, however, the second team of physicians was obliged to leave one question unresolved: the age of the corpse. The pathologists argued in their written report to the court that in order to make an accurate estimate of the age of the corpse, they would need to bring it to Budapest to a properly lit, heated, and equipped dissection room. The new public prosecutor, Szeyffert, and the defense attorney, Eötvös, concurred.

Although doubtless annoyed, the court once more acceded (at least partially) to this request for further examination, but—citing concern for the integrity of the state's evidence—it only permitted parts of the body to be taken to Budapest; the rest had to stay behind.[60]

Estimating the age of the corpse (by this time little more than partially mummified skin and bones) proved to be a tremendous challenge for the pathologists even in the more comfortable conditions of their Budapest laboratory. One question that they faced was what to use as a baseline for comparison. Dr. Mihálkovics had at his disposal the bones of a recently deceased seventeen-year-old boy, which he estimated to be less developed than those of the Tiszadada corpse based on a comparative analysis of the ossification of the connecting joints on the ribs. His first inclination therefore was to agree with the initial autopsy report, which had put the age at between eighteen and twenty.[61] None of the doctors, however, had actually seen the fully intact skeleton of a fourteen-year-old girl, which, they agreed—at Eötvös's suggestion—would make a better basis for comparison. And so they wrote urgent letters to colleagues at the universities of Graz, Vienna, and Prague asking for help in locating a suitable skeleton. They managed to receive a positive response from Dr. Carl Toldt in Prague, where, sure enough, there was a skeleton of a fourteen-year-old girl. Over the course of several communications back and forth, Gusztáv Scheuthauer—the most senior of the Budapest pathologists—gave an exhaustive description of the ossification process as he observed it in the Tiszadada corpse. Toldt replied that these descriptions made him more convinced than ever that there was no perceptible difference between the body discovered at Tiszadada and the skeleton in Prague.[62]

In the end, the findings of the second autopsy report, completed on 9 January 1883, stood in stark contrast to those of the first. On the question of age, it ruled—in accordance with Toldt—that the corpse was not younger than fourteen and not older than seventeen.[63] It attributed the absence of hair on the skull and body to prolonged exposure to water, not to forcible removal. It also directly refuted a number of points in the original autopsy report. These included the apparent condition of the hands and feet (the original doctors had missed or ignored the macerating effects of water on the skin), the length of time during which the body had been immersed in water (at least six weeks, more likely eleven or twelve), the cause of death (undetermined, but there was nothing to rule out drowning), and the sexual history of the victim (the condition in which the body was found could not have allowed for any determination in this regard). But the pathologists' report went even further, offering an opinion on one or more theories of the prosecution. On the question of the identity of the corpse, it argued that there was no physical evidence from either the first or the second autopsy that would corroborate the theory that the Tiszadada corpse was *not* that of Eszter Solymosi. Finally, it deemed the theory that the raftsmen had exchanged the corpse of Eszter Solymosi with that of another female, who had been dead for around the same length of time and who bore a close physical resemblance to her, and then of placing it in Eszter's clothes and floating it in the river to be very unlikely.[64]

Faced now with two conflicting autopsy reports, the president of the Nyíregyháza court chose not to accept one over the other but rather to seek a third opinion. He was at a loss, however, as to whom to approach to resolve the dispute between the two sets of physicians. In a letter to the minister of justice, Tivadar Pauler, he explained that he could not turn the matter over to the medical faculty of the University of Budapest since that was the home institution of the three pathologists. The University of Kolozsvár was out, as far as he could tell, because it would most likely defer to Budapest's academic standing and prestige. And he hesitated to approach the University of Vienna because he feared that it would accord preferential treatment toward its counterpart in Budapest, as the two institutions and their staffs maintained very close ties. Finally, in a revelation indicative of the very thin line that separated judicial impartiality from residual prejudice, Korniss admitted that he also worried that a certain "philosemitic mentality" prevailed in the Vienna Medical School.

The minister of justice suggested that Korniss seek out the advice of Hungary's National Council on Public Health, which he did.[65] This scientific body seems to have been decidedly reluctant, however, to judge one report correct and the other in error, preferring in some instances simply to split the difference between the two opinions. Issuing what it understood to be a summary of the scientific findings in the case, the panel concluded that (1) the age of the corpse was between sixteen and eighteen, (2) the available evidence could not confirm either suggested cause of death (anemia or drowning), (3) there was not enough evidence to determine the amount of time that had lapsed between death and discovery of the corpse, (4) it was unlikely that the corpse had been immersed in water longer than fourteen days, and (5) no more light could be shed on other issues, such as participation in sexual intercourse, the cause of the loss of hair, the presence or absence of nails, or the probable lifestyle and occupation of the victim (based on the condition of the skin).[66]

Needless to say, this was not to be the final word on the matter; in fact, there would not be a last word. To counter the ambivalent response of the Public Health Council, Eötvös would seek out other, even more distinguished, voices from the highest levels of the European medical establishment, including Eduard Hofmann in Vienna and Rudolph Virchow in Berlin. But, by this point in the legal proceedings, too many scientific pronouncements had been delivered for any single one to be accepted by the Nyíregyháza court as definitive. Even Eduard Hofmann could not completely satisfy Eötvös's hopes for a vindication of the conclusions of the Budapest medical team. While he estimated the age of the corpse to be only slightly older than fourteen and refuted the theories that its hair had been shaved off and that the unusually smooth skin of the hands and feet and the finely shaped fingernails had been receiving regular care, he *also* argued that the violent death that the victim had endured could have been induced by force, for example, from a blunt instrument, after which the body was thrown into the water to create the impression of drowning.[67] The Budapest pathologists would get the opportunity to repeat their objections to the original autopsy in open court and even to confront the local physicians directly, at times with stinging criticism. But their expert opinion and academic stature did not carry the power of a "knockout" punch.

The Nyíregyháza Trial, 13 June to 3 August 1883

Nearly a year elapsed between Eötvös's appointment as lead attorney for the Tiszaeszlár defendants and the opening of the criminal trial in Nyíregyháza. The intervening time was taken up with the interrogation of witnesses and suspects, defense petitions to the court to exhume and reexamine the Tiszadada corpse, a second autopsy of the body, the soliciting of expert testimony on the same, and—it must be said—a certain degree of bureaucratic inertia on the part of the Nyíregyháza court itself. The raftsmen Herskó, Vogel, and Smilovics were released from detention following their confessions, only to retract their statements and file petitions against their jailors for illegal mistreatment.[68] But the core group of accused Jews—including the sexton József Scharf; the ritual slaughterers Salamon Schwarcz, Lipót Braun, and Ábrahám Buxbaum; and the "Jewish beggar" Hermann Vollner—languished in prison for thirteen months awaiting trial. József Scharf's son Móric, now almost fourteen years old, had spent the past year in protective custody under the watchful care of Antal Henter, the constable of Szabolcs County.[69]

The Nyíregyháza trial finally opened on 19 June 1883 and did not conclude until six and a half weeks later. After the many months of procedural wrangling, opportunistic politics, and bureaucratic immobility, the delayed start of the trial produced an atmosphere of tense anticipation. Austrian, German, and French newspapers sent correspondents to this modest Hungarian city (where they waited impatiently for daily, on-the-spot translations of the court proceedings); Istóczy, Ónody, and Verhovay made appearances representing the nascent antisemitic movement; and local dignitaries vied with shopkeepers, housewives, and professionals for seats at the event.[70] And event it was. The head of the Nyíregyháza court realized well before the start of the trial that the county courthouse would be much too small to accommodate the proceedings and prevailed upon officials to make the more spacious council room of the county hall available.[71] When the doors opened on the morning of the first day, 240 spectators filed in to occupy the benches reserved for ticket holders; an additional thirty or so places had been reserved for the judges, prosecutors, defense attorneys, defendants, and expert witnesses.[72]

Along several rows facing the judges and attorneys sat fifteen individual defendants. Salamon Schwarcz, Ábrahám Buxbaum, Lipót Braun, and Hermann Vollner had been charged with murder; József Scharf, Adolf Junger, Ábrahám Braun (alias Brenner), Sámuel Lusztig, Lázár Weiszstein, and Emánuel Taub with being accomplices to murder; and Amsel Vogel, Jankel Smilovics, Dávid Herskó, Ignác Klein, and Márton Grosz with aiding and abetting.[73] The case was heard by a three-judge panel made up Ferenc Korniss, who continued to occupy the position of president of the Nyíregyháza court, and two subsidiary justices, Ernő Gruden and Gusztáv Russu. Ede Szeyffert, the deputy chief prosecutor, had the responsibility of presenting the state's case against the accused. Following an introductory statement by Korniss, Szeyffert took the floor and began methodically to describe both the state's theory of the crime and the criminal investigation that had taken place over the preceding months. This investigation, it will be recalled, had fallen under the jurisdiction of a judge magistrate, József Bary, appointed by the Nyíregyháza court. Szeyffert did not "inherit" the case, as it were, until Bary's investigation had ended and indictments had been handed down. This took place during the late fall or winter of 1882, and both Szeyffert and Eötvös had been present at the second exhumation and autopsy of the Tiszadada corpse. Reading the testimony of witnesses, reviewing the scientific reexamination of the physical evidence, and learning the formal accusations of physical torture made by some of the raftsmen, Szeyffert had probably become skeptical of the state's case even before the start of the trial. He chose in his long opening to follow a subtle line of argumentation, hewing a narrow path between promotion and rejection of the state's narrative of events.

Formally, as both Korniss and Szeyffert explained, the purpose of the trial was to determine the fate of a missing fourteen-year-old girl since it remained an open question—still to be resolved by the court—as to whether or not the body that had been recovered, apparently wearing Eszter Solymosi's clothes, was in fact she. Szeyffert embarked on a detailed narrative of events that began with the day of Eszter's disappearance and proceeded to touch upon every ensuing event, including among its many turning points the earliest suspicions of the family that she had fallen victim to a crime of violence perpetrated by Jews of the village, the fateful encounter between József Scharf and Eszter's mother and aunt, the appointment of József Bary as investigating magistrate, the interrogation and testimony of young Móric Scharf, and the discovery of the Tiszadada corpse.[74] Szeyffert seems to have been a reluctant prosecutor in this case. Andrew Handler contends that "only the most ignorant and fanatical people could fail to detect the thinly concealed phrases of contempt and ridicule" in his remarks to the court.[75] Indeed, less than a week after the opening of the trial, a group of attorneys from Nyíregyháza petitioned the Ministry of Justice to replace the deputy chief prosecutor on the grounds that he was deliberately undermining the state's case and acting as an advocate for the defense. The petition failed.[76]

If Szeyffert did intend for his opening statement to undermine the very case he was arguing, he did so subtly and through both rhetorical and tactical means. He punctuated his long narrative of the events of the previous fourteen months with language that was uncomplimentary toward some of the key actors in the investigation and that had the effect of distancing himself from its conclusions. Szeyffert spoke, for example, of the "lively rumor" that began to spread in Tiszaeszlár, in which "women and children" repeated "a few disjointed words" of little five-year-old Samu Scharf. When referring to the sensational testimony of Móric Scharf, he first pointed out that, in earlier testimony to magistrate Bary, Móric had denied knowledge of Eszter Solymosi or of her whereabouts. Implicitly critical of the conditions under which the boy was subsequently held and interrogated, Szeyffert went on to characterize Bary's entire investigation as having been carried out "with feverish enthusiasm."[77] It was, however, Szeyffert's tactical decision to make explicit reference to the ritual murder accusation in presenting the state's theory of the crime—even though the official indictment made no mention of it—that was most damaging. And the printed transcripts of the trial make clear that the deputy chief prosecutor intended by this move to suggest the untenable nature of the indictment itself.[78]

"Let us assume as established," Szeyffert interjected near the end of his remarks, "that a terrible crime has been committed." Yet, he wanted to know, what was the alleged motive for the crime? The indictment itself did not explicitly discuss motive, but Szeyffert insisted on reintroducing the question as a way of bringing to the surface the underlying assumptions of state actors as well as the Christian residents of Tiszaeszlár.

> Therefore I will answer this question and explain that the suspicion of ritual murder was at work against the accused. I mentioned at the beginning of my remarks that at the start of April 1882 the Jews had their Passover—about which I know that the Jews at that time celebrate the liberation of their ancestors from Pharaoh, the oppressive king of Egypt, with prayers of thanksgiving; and that, in remembrance of the fact that because of their sudden departure the refugees were instructed to prepare unleavened bread, their religious descendants eat for seven days Passover crackers known as "Mazzes." According to popular belief, however, the Jews also require Christian blood for Passover. Not only is this popular belief circulated among the lower orders of society; we also come across it among those who count themselves among the educated class. Salamon Schwarz and his three associates sit on the defendants' bench on suspicion of having committed murder for religious purposes.[79]

In thinking about Ede Szeyffert's personal motivations in introducing the theme of Jewish ritual murder in his formal presentation to the court, one would do well to remember that he did not have to say anything. Whatever the underlying assumptions and attitudes of Hungarian officials—local as well as national—might have been, the Ministry of Justice (through the offices of the judge magistrate) had prepared a writ of indictment that elided this very point, choosing instead to base its charges on forensic evidence and witness testimony alone. At this relatively early stage in the proliferation of modern ritual murder trials, the traditional accusation of ritual murder—and the folk beliefs that undergird it—still carried an odor of disrepute. Szeyffert clearly was aware of this fact. And his decision to tie the state's case against Salamon Schwarcz and his fourteen codefendants not only to evidence and to witness accounts but also to the cultural underpinnings of the suspicions that had been directed at the Jewish defendants in the first place was calculated to make it more difficult for the trial to proceed as though it had no connection to the long history of the blood libel. In essence, then, there were two voices of liberal skepticism represented at the Nyíregyháza trial: that of Károly Eötvös and his defense team and that of the prosecuting attorney. Judge Korniss, on the other hand, responded to Szeyffert's opening by denying that the court had considered the ritual murder accusation in the course of its investigations or that it wished to present this as a theory in the trial.[80]

The long parade of witnesses that followed the opening statements of the prosecutor and the defense attorneys featured the mother and aunt of Eszter Solymosi, physicians and other forensic scientists, and individuals who had come forward during the course of the investigation to offer eyewitness testimony. The proceedings themselves eventually coalesced around three central themes: the question of whether the presumed murder also involved a larger conspiracy to obstruct justice (here the validity of the original confessions of the raftsmen was partly at issue), the identity of the body that was found floating in the Tisza River near Tiszadada, and the reliability of Móric Scharf's potentially damning testimony. Three pathologists from the University of Budapest Medical School—Géza Mihálkovics, Gusztáv Scheuthauer, and János Belky—who, at the behest of Eötvös and with the approval of the Nyíregyháza court, had conducted a second autopsy on the Tiszadada corpse (as it had become known), argued strenuously against the findings of the preliminary forensic examinations, thereby throwing into question the state's theory of body switching and obstruction of justice. They were joined in this challenge by the pharmacist Kálmán Zurányi from Tiszalök, who had been present at the initial identification of the body and who consistently maintained that it was that of Eszter.[81] Scheuthauer, the most senior of the Budapest pathologists, who testified to having performed thousands of autopsies, provided the courtroom with colorful outbursts of indignation and sighs of exasperation at what he viewed as faulty methodology or general scientific ignorance. He could be cruel during the time in which he was allowed to cross-examine the local physicians who had performed the first forensic examinations on the body—one of whom, Soma Trajtler, had in fact been a medical student of his—prompting Presiding Judge Korniss on occasion to intervene on the witnesses' behalf.[82]

While the conflicting accounts of witnesses—expert and other—and the testy exchanges that erupted on occasion among attorneys, witnesses, and the presiding judge occupied much of the time, for pure drama, nothing could match the occasions in which young Móric Scharf was brought before the court to repeat his account of the alleged abduction and murder of Eszter Solymosi. On the first day of the trial, under questioning by Judge Korniss, Móric acknowledged that when he was first questioned by József Bary in Tiszaeszlár, he claimed not to have had any knowledge regarding the disappearance of Eszter Solymosi. Later, after he was taken to Nagyfalu by the police officer Recsky, he changed his story. Why, the judge asked? The boy replied that Recsky had told him that if he did not tell all that he knew, he would be put in prison forever. "And so I freely confessed."[83] To what did you confess, the judge countered? At this point, Móric uttered a short monologue, which he would repeat—with slight variations—at various points in the trial:

> In the year 1882, as the Tiszaeszlár Jews gathered—and among them were strangers: the Tiszalök ritual slaughterer Salamon Schwarcz and the ritual slaughterer from Téglás, whose name I don't know—services began around 8–8:30 and lasted until a little after 11. At this time the Jews departed, but Salamon Schwarcz and the ritual slaughterer from Téglás remained and said that they wanted to stay in the synagogue to pray. I left and went to my father's house. Later a Jewish beggar with a three- or four-year-old boy came in. The beggar had come to us on Friday night and stayed there until Saturday. My father called a girl in, but the Jewish beggar led Eszter Solymosi into the Temple, telling her there that he wanted her to fetch something. Later, after a quarter of an hour, I heard a scream. I ran to the door [of the synagogue] and since I was not able to open it, I looked through the keyhole and saw as the Tarczal and Téglás slaughterers held Eszter Solymosi down and Salamon Schwarcz cut across her neck, drew her blood, and poured it into some sort of vessel. Then these four—Lázár Weiszstein, Sámuel Lusztig, Adolf Junger, and Ábrahám Braun—went into the synagogue. I moved away from the door; I don't know what they had done with the key. But after they had murdered Eszter Solymosi in the synagogue, I found the key in a window in the foyer and I locked the outer door. I don't know where they took the body.[84]

József Scharf, Móric's father—who had been implicated, although not directly accused, in the boy's narrative—interrupted a brief follow-up question by Judge Korniss to ask his son if he had been reading from a text that he

Figure 5. Zoltán Csörgey, *The Ritual Murder of Eszter Solymosi* (1882), *Füstölő*, 1 November 1882. The heading reads In the Fifty-Seventh Century (According to the Jewish Calendar)

Courtesy D. Véri.

had written down. This caused much stirring in the courtroom. While the presiding judge attempted to restore order, the father continued, "I humbly request of the honored court: I cannot remain silent if my son seeks to destroy me." When the judge replied that Scharf had not been accused of anything by the witness, Scharf noted that he was, in fact, sitting among the defendants (hence *did* stand accused), and he demanded that Móric tell the court who had coached him "in these lies." Again, commotion erupted in the courtroom.[85]

At issue was whether or not József Scharf had the standing in this instance to confront his accuser; was Móric in fact testifying against him or only against those who allegedly lured Eszter into the synagogue and those who were said to have done the actual killing? Remarkably, the presiding judge chose instead to question the boy regarding the integrity of his overall testimony and his knowledge of biblical commandments.

Korniss, turning to Móric: Do you know the Ten Commandments, which say: Thou shalt not bear false witness against thy neighbor?
Móric: I know them.
Korniss: And do you also know from the Holy Bible what punishment is meted out to one who gives false testimony?
Móric: Yes, I do.
Korniss: You have learned all of this. Is what you have brought before the Royal Court true and factual?
Móric: Yes![86]

Apparently unconvinced—and eager to bring the discussion back to József Scharf's earlier challenge—Károly Eötvös rose and asked "whether he [Móric] could not also give his deposition—in verse." The published transcript recorded "loud noise and stirring in the auditorium" followed by a stern reproach by Korniss: "I shall not allow the seriousness of the proceedings to be profaned in this way. That is the only answer that I can transmit to this question."[87]

The provision whereby defendants were given the opportunity to respond to witnesses who gave incriminating testimony produced moments of tense confrontation. It also revealed the degree to which the Jewish defendants were willing to defend themselves against the charge of ritual murder, as well as the contempt in which they held witnesses such as young Móric Scharf. Judge Korniss first addressed the butcher Salamon Schwarcz, asking him if he had heard the charges that the witness had made. Schwarcz replied that he heard them but had "not understood a word." His reference was not to the Hungarian language in which the testimony was given—although, as we will soon see, language would play a role in witness-defendant confrontations—but to the incomprehensibility of the accusation itself. Nevertheless, Korniss gave Móric a chance to repeat the gist of his testimony, after which Salamon Schwarcz called the boy a scoundrel and told the judge, "I say that all of this is not true. I will prove that it is impossible": "I will prove it through sacred scripture. (Laughter in the auditorium.) I will prove it through world history; I will prove it through my experiences: that it is impossible that a Jew would commit and carry out a murder out of religious motives. Everyone sees that the boy has been coached. He spoke as though he were telling a fairy tale."[88]

The exchange that ensued between Móric and the Galician *shoḥet*, Ábrahám Buxbaum, was particularly interesting as it showcased the place of language and linguistic acculturation in the shaping of modern Jewish identity in East Central Europe. Buxbaum was the one defendant who did not know much Hungarian (he had only begun to learn it in prison). During the course of the trial, he relied upon the German translator whom the court had installed, and when he addressed the court, he did so in German. When given the opportunity by Judge Korniss to confront his accuser, Buxbaum chose to make a virtue of his handicap, emphasizing the linguistic divide between the witness and himself and suggesting that the language in which Móric had chosen to give his testimony provided further evidence of its fabricated origins. He insisted that Móric look him in the eye and repeat his charges—but in German.[89] Móric refused, insisting on speaking in Hungarian only. At one point in the encounter, after Móric repeated his contention that the Galician *shoḥet* was present in the synagogue when the alleged murder took place, Buxbaum actually spat in the boy's face. Móric's father stood up and attempted to approach his son, but a guard blocked his way and dragged him back to his seat. With the proceedings verging on chaos, Judge Korniss threatened to empty the courtroom if order could not be restored.[90]

Móric Scharf responded to repeated attempts by the defense team to get him to give his testimony in German with a combination of formality and defiance. He would launch periodically into a retelling of his story—always in Hungarian and always using the same formulaic phrases: "In the year 1882, when the Jews had their Passover," "when the Jews had their Sabbath before Passover," "when they had their Great Sabbath of Passover," and so on.[91] Scenes transpired that can only be described as comical, one of which pitted the third *shoḥet*, Lipót Braun, against the fourteen-year-old. Braun was teasing the witness, trying to goad him into speaking German.

Móric: If you don't know Hungarian, well it is the only language I know. You were present in Tiszaeszlár [using the Hungarian word *jelen* for present].

Braun: What does that mean, *jelen*?

Móric: Yes, you were present in Tiszaeszlár.

Korniss, to Braun: Why do you ask this?

Braun: Because I definitely know that he did not learn the word "*jelen*" at his house and that he does not even know what the word means.

Móric: If you do not know Hungarian—I know what it means.

József Scharf: You don't know Hungarian well.
Braun: His father was a poor man; he couldn't afford to have him educated.
Móric: I always went to school and am still learning.[92]

Even the royal prosecutor got into the act. Toward the end of the day's proceedings, Ede Szeyffert picked away at Móric's claim that Eszter had been lured into the Scharf home (and then the synagogue) under the pretense that she was needed to perform certain labors that Jews could not do on the Sabbath. In other words, Eszter was asked to assume the role of *shabbes goy* (Sabbath Gentile; *goy shel shabbat*). People who were well versed in Jewish law (*halakhah*) would have known that it was highly problematic, if not illegal, to ask someone on the Sabbath itself to perform a task that was forbidden to Jews to do on that day. Perhaps Szeyffert was aware of this fact, although there is no indication in the printed transcript that he was. What he did seem to know was that it would have been highly unlikely for anyone in the Scharf household to ask someone on the spot to do work on the Sabbath because the family already had an agreement with someone to do this on an ongoing basis. "Tell me," he asked Móric, "didn't someone come every Saturday to take care of household chores? And if so, who was that?" Móric answered that that person was a neighbor, Mrs. Gábor Bátori. Her main job was to remove the candlesticks from the dining table, where they had been placed before Friday night, and put them on the cupboard. He claimed, however, that she did not come to work on the Saturday before Easter. "Perhaps she was also there that day?" the prosecutor pressed. Móric held firm: she was not there. "Since she lived in the neighborhood, why did you not go out and get her? I did not go, because no one sent me."[93]

At the end of the first day of the trial and into the second, the court took up the question of whether or not Móric understood that the decision to testify against his father was his alone to make. He was not required to do so. Getting the boy to respond to this question proved to be difficult. His first response to Judge Korniss was that he would "tell everything," if that was the court's wish. Korniss tried to impress upon Móric that the court's wishes were not at issue but his; did he wish to testify against his father? Móric answered, "I do not."[94] This answer raised numerous difficulties, one of the defense attorneys pointed out, because, while the law did not require a person to testify against a close relative, it also did not permit "partial testimonies," in which a person would agree to talk about some—but not all—of what he or she knew about the case. Moreover, as the prosecutor pointed out, on the previous day, the boy had said that he *was* ready to testify against his father. Clearly, he was confused, as was, it seems, the presiding judge, who allowed the testimony to continue nevertheless.[95] On this day, when asked by Korniss what he did after having witnessed the abduction and murder of Eszter Solymosi, Móric explained that the family sat down for lunch! And what did people talk about around the lunch table? "I told them about what I had seen." And what response did you get? "My mother told me that I should be quiet." And what did you do? "I kept quiet."[96]

A new and longer confrontation between father and son ensued on this second day of testimony after the presiding judge asked József Scharf to comment on Móric's claims. "It is *not* true!" Scharf exploded, "He lies! He's been coached. Why do you ask things about which one can give no answer?" Károly Eötvös rose at this point to urge, owing to the unprecedented nature of the case—but also on the grounds of legal practice—that the accused be allowed to direct questions at the witness and that the presiding judge assure the accused that he could ask these questions not only as a defendant to a witness but also as a father to a son. Korniss agreed to permit Scharf to address questions to the witness in this fashion but warned him to preserve the dignity of the court and to pose his questions in a respectful and not insulting manner.[97] What ensued was a remarkable and moving encounter between a father who stood accused of participation in a horrendous crime by a son whom he clearly loved—and who could not help but reprimand the son on several counts—and a fourteen-year-old, whose attitude alternated between defiance, bordering on disdain, and a desire to protect the father from the fate toward which he was leading the other defendants.

Taking a cue from the presiding judge, who earlier had asked Móric if he knew the Ten Commandments and their prohibition against bearing false witness, József Scharf now posed the same question to his son in order to highlight the command to honor one's father and mother. József Scharf began by asking simply, "Do you know me? Who am I?" "My father." He then tried to get his son to identify the fifth commandment, but without much success. "Thou shalt not lie," offered the boy. "That is not correct; then you don't know the Ten Commandments." At this point, Korniss intervened, objecting that he could not allow such cruelty in the courtroom. A member of the defense team urged the judge to allow the questioning to go on in light of the unusual nature of the case.[98]

József Scharf: Come stand beside me, and look me in the face as though I were not the grotesque figure [*Schreckbild/maskara*] you have made me out to be.
Presiding Judge, to Móric: Don't allow yourself to become confused. Answer what you know; do not answer what you don't know.
Móric Scharf: I know that no one harmed me.
József Scharf: I asked you what the fifth commandment was.
Móric Scharf: Thou shalt not take the name of God in vain.
József: That is not it! How do you know the Ten Commandments?
Móric: When I learn the Bible, then I'll know them.
József: You have studied the Bible. I spent forty forints on your education. I brought your lunch to you in school myself, so you would not have to go home, but would learn. So tell me, does it say there: Honor thy Father and Mother?
Presiding Judge: That is not the fifth commandment either! (Lively laughter in the audience.)[99]

Much of the confrontation between József and Móric Scharf revolved around the father's efforts to draw the son back from his yearlong association with his Hungarian guardians—his simultaneous acculturation to both the Hungarian language and Christian norms and concepts—and to get him to identify once again with his Jewish family. When cajoling did not work, József Scharf resorted to browbeating and reprimand, and both father and son were quick to throw sarcasm into the mix. Language and religion frequently served as notes meant to signal authentic communal affiliation. Lipót Braun's earlier teasing regarding the use of the Hungarian idiom *jelen* to indicate being present was complemented by József Scharf's chuckling at his son's interjection of the Hungarian *igenis* to stand in for the German *Jawohl*—"When you were home, you didn't even know what the word '*igenis*' meant; now you have learned it very well. Tell me all about it."[100] And when the father pressed Móric regarding his change of stories to the authorities—threatening to have his mother called in to testify—the boy revealed another piece of linguistic information. His mother, who had sat in on his interview with Bary's assistant, had spoken to her son in Yiddish. She was warned by the investigator not to do this, that is, speak in a language that he did not understand, but she persisted in doing so a second time.[101]

From time to time, Scharf and some of his codefendants tried to get Móric to admit that his testimony contradicted basic tenets of Jewish law and, hence, was impossible. "Is a slaughterer allowed to take a knife in his hand on the Sabbath?" József asked. "Is he allowed to cut something on the Sabbath?" "I don't know," the son replied, "I haven't studied those many, big Bibles" (a reference to the Talmud, perhaps). Buxbaum tried next. "Do you know that on the Sabbath one may not even slaughter a chicken?" Móric: "I don't know." József: "You don't know? May heaven strike you down, you animal!"[102] Told by his father that he had tried mightily to intervene with the Hungarian authorities to provide his son with Passover food, Móric responded, "I didn't need your unleavened bread; I had better to eat."[103] Was this a full-fledged rebellion? It is difficult to measure the degree of Móric's alienation from Judaism and the Jewish community. He was capable of expressing extreme positions, as when asked by Ábrahám Lusztig, another of the defendants, whether it was true that he had said that he no longer wished to be a Jew. "I said that," he replied. "Why not," József Scharf asked? "Because I don't want to be a Jew anymore."[104] Later on the same day, an exasperated father turned to his son and asked, "Tell me, do you pray every day?" "I pray." "Show me if you are wearing your *tzitzis* [fringed undergarment]." In his memoir of the trial, Károly Eötvös reports a response by Móric that is not included in the printed German transcript: "I'm not a horse that I should have to wear a collar."[105]

The Unraveling

The personal confrontations between the state's key witness and the defendants (including, of course, the boy's father)—emotionally turbulent to be sure and rich in insight into language, customs, and family life among the Jews of the Tiszaeszlár region—produced no major effect on the outcome of the trial. More important were the defense and prosecutorial strategies of Eötvös and Szeyffert, respectively (which tended to reinforce rather than contradict each other), and the struggle over how to interpret the scientific evidence in the case. After all, most of the six and a half weeks of deliberations in the makeshift courtroom in the Nyíregyháza County Hall was taken up with two key questions: the identity of the corpse that floated to the surface of the Tisza River six weeks after Eszter Solymosi's disappearance and the medical plausibility of Móric's account of the killing of the girl in the synagogue and the collection of her blood. Ultimately, in the opinion of the judges, neither question could be determined unequivocally. As we have seen, the case had featured a duel of experts pitting the prestige and authority of the medical institutions of Budapest, the capital, against the stubborn insistence of local physicians that they, too, could claim the mantle of competence in scientific examination. In the end, the judges chose not to accept one body of opinion over the other.

What proved much more difficult to sustain was Móric Scharf's eyewitness testimony. It began to unravel as early as the second day of the trial under the polite but insistent cross-examination of the state's attorney. Szeyffert did nothing fancy; he did not trot out experts—at least not at first—but simply engaged in the tried-and-true method of asking for more specificity from Móric on each point of his somewhat perfunctory account. How much time had elapsed between the cries for help and his arrival at the door to the synagogue? What did he see through the keyhole? Was Eszter still dressed or undressed? Where were her clothes? What position was the body in? Was the girl resting or struggling? How was she held, by the head or the feet? How was she lying when her throat was cut? How many cuts? Where did the blood go? (Into two plates, the witness responded, from which it was poured it into a pot.) How is that possible? How were the plates held? Was the girl still on the ground? Was she moving? Did the blood flow upward or downward? (It flowed into the plate.) But how? Were only two plates of blood collected? How many men were doing the collecting? (Only one, Móric claimed.) Had he ever seen a corpse before? Had he ever seen a person being killed?[106]

Implicit in the questioner's skepticism lay the strong suspicion that, if the butcher Schwarcz had indeed sliced open the girl's neck, his knife would have hit an artery, and blood would not have flowed cooperatively downward into waiting plates but would have gushed forward and splattered across the room. Yet a thorough search through the synagogue had revealed no residual bloodstains. Hours of testimony would be taken from six expert witnesses (the three local doctors and three members of the Budapest medical faculty) during the last week of trial on just this question: was it conceivable that a cut across the neck could produce a flow of blood slow enough to collect calmly in shallow vessels while still causing the death of the victim?[107] As I mentioned above, consensus on this point was difficult to reach. In theory, if one were careful not to pierce the carotid artery, the flow of blood could be moderated, and the victim would die from asphyxiation. But what was the likelihood?

Remarkably, considering the amount of time and energy spent on battles over scientific procedure and authority, the state's case decisively collapsed over a simple, unsophisticated test. Toward the end of his questioning of

Móric regarding exactly what he saw, Szeyffert asked, "Tell me, was the keyhole open? Could you see through it?"

> *Móric:* Yes.
> *Szeyffert:* During this entire time, was there anything that hindered your sight? Were you always able to see?
> *Móric:* Yes.[108]

This testimony, together with the contradictory accounts of the medical examiners and scientific experts, provided the defense team with the opportunity to request that the court make a special trip to Tiszaeszlár for a physical inspection of the alleged scene of the crime. On 17 July 1883, the judges, defendants, defense attorneys, prosecutor, court reporters, and Móric set out for the now vandalized and largely desolate Jewish quarter of the village.[109] Móric was asked once again to give a detailed description of what he saw, where the acts had taken place, and who had been engaged in doing what. The actual murder, he claimed, had taken place in the entry hall, outside the door to the sanctuary. At one point, all but four individuals left the outer chamber of the synagogue, and Móric was asked to demonstrate how he had observed the events through the keyhole and to describe what he could see. The keyhole stood much lower to the ground than he had recalled, forcing him to kneel in order to try to see through its opening. The view that this position did accord Móric was limited to a very small area of the courtyard, dimly lit, and not near the alleged scene of the crime.[110] His credibility damaged, the entourage returned to Nyíregyháza.

According to Hungarian criminal procedure of the time, witnesses who gave testimony at trial were not sworn in until their testimony was judged by the court to be credible.[111] One week after the excursion to Tiszaeszlár, on the twenty-ninth day of the trial, prosecutor Szeyffert and defense attorneys Eötvös, Funták, and Heumann indicated to the court their strong conviction that Móric Scharf did not have credibility as a witness and should not be sworn in. His testimony was rejected.[112] In the wake of a criminal investigation that lasted thirteen months and a trial of some six and a half weeks—which featured accusations of torture and prosecutorial misconduct, as well as struggles over the reading and interpretation of scientific data—the supposed eyewitness testimony of a fourteen-year-old boy had assumed enormous significance. His was to have been a voice that cut through village prejudice and rumormongering, the mendacity of police officials, and the squabbling of experts. Whether or not the Jews of Tiszaeszlár had conspired with the raftsmen to switch bodies, whether or not the rust-colored stains on the clothes of the Tiszadada corpse indicated human blood, whether or not the body was in fact that of Eszter Solymosi—young Móric, the son of one of the defendants, had come forward as an eyewitness to murder. His account had the potential to tip the balance in favor of the state's case, but the story broke down under the weight of its own improbabilities and contradictions.

Closing Arguments and Verdict

The state had the first word. When Ede Szeyffert rose to address the three-judge panel on 27 July 1883, he had already become a controversial figure, castigated in some circles for having cast doubt on his own case early on. His first words to the court on that day were meant to defend himself against the insinuation that he had acted unprofessionally during his opening statement—appearing to have taken on the role of defense attorney rather than prosecutor—and that he had impugned the competence of the investigating magistrate. Szeyffert countered that he had done no such thing; he had simply quoted from the protocols of the investigation itself; under ordinary circumstances, he continued, the case would never have made it to trial.[113]

> Indeed, we are facing a special and unique opportunity. It is not the case that there was insufficient formal evidence at hand; the problem lay in the fact that the trustworthiness of this evidence and its inner value proved to be highly questionable. Under other circumstances, such doubt would have led the public prosecutor to drop the charges and discontinue the proceedings. In the case before you, however, the public prosecutor, considering the prevailing circumstances—in the interests of the accused as well as in order to reassure the public—wished to have this case heard in open session. People who suspected—or who expected—that I would be a "criminal hunter" were quite wrong. The modern state aspires to punish justly, and therefore requires of its prosecutorial organs, as state functionaries and, on the strength of this qualification, as a legal duty, to avoid carefully anything that could lead this punishing power to commit an injustice.[114]

Szeyffert's remarks underscored the tension that lay at the heart of modern ritual murder prosecutions: the desire on the part of the state to structure the proceedings according to modern criminal procedure and to admit into evidence only that which had been examined forensically, countered by the nagging suspicion—indeed the knowledge—that the entire investigation had been contaminated by a priori assumptions based on discredited narratives of Jewish criminal compulsion. The presiding judge had hoped to avoid any explicit mention of the blood libel during the trial proceedings and had chided Szeyffert when he introduced the subject in his opening remarks. Yet it was precisely the contamination of the state's case with prejudicial knowledge that, in the prosecutor's view, could not be avoided. "I followed every single instance of tedious testimony with the most zealous attention and exactness," Szeyffert noted, and the only conclusion he could draw "was that the idea of ritual murder had extended through the entire investigation up to the beginning of the trial."[115] "One cannot find the slightest hint in the investigation files to indicate that another basis for the alleged crime was pursued or that another reason for the disappearance of Eszter Solymosi was considered."[116] The state would be more than happy, Szeyffert remarked, to endorse Judge Korniss's wish to discard the accusation of ritual murder. By all means, he urged, let go of the idea of ritual murder, "this absurd offspring of medieval superstition, this stupid subject of fairy tales and the conversation of old village women. . . . In the name of national justice, I solemnly protest against the fact that superstition has been smuggled into its majestic circle."[117]

The prosecutor patiently reviewed the evidence and testimony that was presented at trial. Concerning the Tiszadada corpse, he suggested that its discovery ought to have resolved once and for all the riddle of Eszter's disappearance, that it was only the existing prejudice against the Jews that overruled the presumptions of the law, as he put it. "Now, after the conclusion of all the testimony, I venture to say with certainty . . . that the remains of a female corpse that lie here under judicial seal are those of fourteen-year-old Eszter Solymosi who disappeared on April 1 of last year."[118] Again he leveled sharp criticism at the behavior of the investigating magistrate, not only because he insisted on showing the naked body to the family and friends of the missing girl but also—just as importantly—because he had kept the clothing in which it had been found hidden from view. He moved on to the testimony of Jankel Smilovics and Dávid Herskó, two of the raftsmen who discovered the body at Tiszadada, who had admitted at one point in the investigation to having agreed to transport a body along the length of the Tisza and to having deposited it at the site of its discovery. Both retracted this testimony—during the investigation itself—and complained of having been tortured in order to induce a confession. Szeyffert explained to the court that, as a result, under Hungary's legal principles, their previous testimony was void. He nevertheless elaborated on the fact that it would have been impossible—on account of the odor alone—to transport a decaying corpse without arousing notice, not to mention the fact that the raftsmen then would have had to dress the body in Eszter's clothes once they had gotten to the vicinity of Tiszaeszlár.[119]

Turning finally to the testimony of Móric Scharf, Szeyffert emphasized the fact that the state's case hinged fundamentally on this sole "eyewitness" to the killing. But the facts of the case contradicted the teenager's testimony at every turn. Móric claimed, among other things, that the cut to the girl's throat had been deep but that the blood flowed gently into the bowls that had been held to catch it—an impossible scenario according to the expert medical witnesses. "All of the circumstances and facts have completely destroyed the strained testimony of Móric Scharf and robbed it of all credibility."[120]

> Eszter Solymosi went missing and is no longer among the living; but she was not brought down under the knife of a ritual slaughterer; her disappearance and death must in reality be attributed to an unfathomable accident or an as yet undetermined cause. The belief in a ritual sacrifice, begun and spread by Mrs. János Solymosi, also found other converts—and, through the incorrect measures of the investigating magistrate and the state prosecutor's office, has been inserted, finally, into this trial.[121]

"At this moment," he observed, playing perhaps to dramatic effect, "the eyes of the entire country—yes, of the entire educated world—are aimed at me." He urged the court ("all of us") to do what duty required, to have the courage to accept the responsibility that they had taken on—"the responsibility before God and the world, before the tribunal of posterity and one's own conscience." Szeyffert's recommendation was given twice in quick succession: "I hold the accused to be not guilty and respectfully move that they be acquitted of the charges and their consequences."[122]

Each of the remaining attorneys, individually—the defense team of Funták, Friedmann, Heumann, Székely, and Eötvös but also Károly Szalay, the private attorney for the Solymosi family—was given the opportunity to speak as well. Szalay was the first to follow Szeyffert, and the two summations could not have been more distant from each other. It was as if the prosecutor's words had landed on the dark side of the moon, never to be heard from. Complaining of the cynicism that the court had had to endure on the part of both the prosecutor and the defense attorneys, Szalay made certain that both the mother's narrative and the ritual murder accusation were heard once again. He replayed the circumstances of Eszter's disappearance and demise from the family's perspective, including the vision that the mother had received of the scene of the murder and the sound of the girl's last cry. (At this, Mrs. Solymosi broke into tears.)[123] Szalay, who was affiliated with the Hungarian antisemitic movement, appealed to no less an authority than Josephus Flavius to prove that Jews resorted to murder in order to acquire Christian blood. The unnamed reporter who produced this transcript noted elliptically, "He cited the titles of Jewish books in the original language. The speaker then began passionately to attack all of Jewry, who had united to cover up this unmistakable crime and to save the institution of kosher slaughtering (*die Schächter-Institution*)."[124] By this time, Korniss was at his wit's end. Szalay had managed to inject into the proceedings everything that the judge had wanted desperately to keep out. He chided Szalay for wandering from the matter at hand: "At times your words involve hatred against a religion; at times you wish to prove ritual murder. I can allow neither the former nor the latter." Scattered applause and whispering broke out among the spectators, and Korniss threatened to clear the court.[125]

By the time Károly Eötvös rose to speak, on 30 July 1883, before a packed and hushed courtroom, each of the four other defense attorneys had already given their summations. These included, in addition to points of law and the review of trial testimony, impassioned refutations of the historical ritual murder accusation by Sándor Funták and Bernát Friedmann.[126] Technically, Eötvös was speaking only on behalf his particular clients—Scharf, Buxbaum, and Vollner—but it was clear to all that he and Szeyffert were the main events, and he played his celebrity role with relish, blending disingenuous modesty, humor, and outrage to great effect. At one point, Eötvös announced that he would not touch upon the ritual murder accusation "as a proposition," since his colleagues on the defense had already effectively dealt with it, but he did wish to remark (hence reversing himself!) that until he became a parliamentary deputy, he had never heard of the accusation: "The blood libel is a fairy tale for children. If an educated man says that he believes in it, he is slandering himself and wishes to slander others. It is fashionable today to raise this accusation! [But] it is tragic to see educated people follow this absurd trend."[127]

After reintroducing the forbidden narrative backdrop to the affair, Eötvös proceeded to defend his clients from a minimalist position, focusing on narrow questions: What is the crime? Who are the perpetrators? What were supposed to have been their motives in committing this crime? It has not even been established, he argued, that a crime has been committed. No one can agree on the facts of the case. All that the court has before it is that Eszter Solymosi disappeared on 1 April 1882; beyond that, nothing. Personally, Eötvös assured the courtroom, he was convinced that on the day she disappeared, Eszter also lost her life. But how and why she lost her life "has in no way been determined . . . Yet so-called public opinion was convinced that the Jews collectively were answerable. The Jews, and only the Jews, were asked the question: 'Where is Eszter Solymosi? Give her here, you Jews.'"[128]

Eötvös's closing played heavily on the determining value of scientific expertise in legal proceedings but also on the importance of common sense untainted by ideology and preconceived notions. Along these lines, he contrasted the behavior and judgment of József Bary, the investigating magistrate, with both the assessments of the medical experts from Budapest and the naive reactions of townsfolk and witnesses, who easily recognized the body pulled from the Tisza River as that of Eszter Solymosi. In a disarming move, Eötvös claimed that he, like Bary, suspected at first that there may have been body smuggling involved. After consulting with experts, however, he became convinced that the original medical examination contained numerous frivolous and unscientific errors, and he made an official request to have the body exhumed. And the results of the exhumation proved him right! "One cannot change the facts," he exclaimed, "not even through the testimony of a Matej and a Móric. One can produce witnesses, but one cannot deceive men of science!"[129]

In closing, Eötvös turned to the inflammatory remarks of the Solymosi family's private attorney, Szalay.

> The private attorney referred to the God of the Christians. I, too, am a Christian, but I did not hear the voice of my God coming from his mouth. It was not the voice of any God, neither of the Jews nor of the Christians; I heard only the voice of hatred, which knows no God, but in fact demands the death of those whose guilt he cannot prove. It is a crime to preach religious war under the sign of the cross

> against those who sit among us in Parliament, in the university, and in school, and who are good citizens of this country.[130]

With this, the Nyíregyháza court adjourned. It would be called back into session on the third of August—the thirty-first meeting of the trial—for the reading of the verdict.

Judge Korniss began by once again listing all of the accused by name, age, occupation, religion, family status, whether they had ever been convicted of a crime, and the crimes for which they had been charged. He then proceeded quickly to the judges' decision: the acquittal of all fifteen: "The accused . . . are acquitted and are to be set free immediately; the costs are to be borne by the state." The longest part of the proceedings was taken up by a detailed reading of the grounds for the verdict: the inconsistency and unreliability of testimony—including the hateful accusations of Móric Scharf against his father—had severely undermined the state's case; Matej's testimony concerning the supposed plot to smuggle bodies was not believable; moreover, since there had been no crime to begin with, there could not have been any assistance in carrying it out or covering it up. Korniss continued to push back against the claims made by both the prosecution and the defense that belief in the blood libel had served as a backdrop to the criminal investigation. In once again rejecting that assertion, he concluded that "such a possibility had never been entertained, and no trace of it is to be found in the investigation protocols or any other official document."[131]

Finally, Korniss turned to the fifteen defendants:

> You are relieved of the charges and given back to your families and to society. You will be returning to the world and to your Christian fellow citizens. I urge you to comport yourselves calmly and peacefully and not to appear provocative, lest the irritated passions be released against you disturbing peace and tranquility. The judges are not responsible for the many sufferings and tribulations that you have endured; it was only the tragic circumstances, which brought you disaster. Accept your fate without anger. This is the message that I give to you as you go on life's path.[132]

Chapter 3

Roads to Prussia

From Tiszaeszlár to Xanten

The worst of it is that this revival of the Blood Accusation in Germany is not, like the Tisza-Eszlar case, the blowing into a flame of certain embers of mediaeval superstition, which a lingering ignorance had preserved and banked up. The anti-Semites themselves would be the first to resent the suggestion. As a matter of fact, they have revived the wicked charge of malice aforethought, and the authors of it are almost all men of education and position in the world. It is no longer the unthinking peasant who repeats the fanciful legend which has been handed down to him through generations of brutalizing ignorance. The Xanten case originated in the mind of a medical student; it was taken up and expounded by responsible newspapers; and Herr Stoecker and Baron von Wackerbarth-Linderode championed it in the Prussian Parliament amid the cheers of the extreme wing of the Conservative party. The reason of this success is easily explained in the same way that the anti-Semites have revived the old-fashioned Rishuth on a pseudo-scientific foundation, they have attempted to rationalize the legendary Fee Fi Fo Fum which dates from the days of Apion.

—*The Jewish Chronicle*, 22 July 1892

From Riots to Rhetoric: Responses to the Verdict at Nyíregyháza

The collapse of the state's case against the fifteen Jewish defendants, followed by their acquittal and release from long-term imprisonment, provoked a violent response on the part of some Hungarians. Disturbances broke out in Budapest on 7 August in anticipation of the arrival in the capital city of József Scharf and his family. Crowds of people gathered outside the hotel where the Scharfs were rumored to be staying; demonstrators attacked the hotel, broke windows in its tavern, and looted nearby stores. Policemen and soldiers dispersed the demonstrators and put up barricades; the crowds fought back, while skirmishes broke out in other parts of the city; in the end, it took five days to restore order.[1] Eventually, the unrest spread to no fewer than thirty-two counties, distributed throughout the country—including the westernmost parts of Hungary, far from the actual scene of events—and touched both cities and towns.[2] Across western Hungary, Robert Nemes notes, "Sizeable crowds broke windows, looted shops, carried antisemitic signs, and sang antisemitic songs." In Somogy County alone, riots broke out in nearly twenty locations. In one of these, Gyékényes—a town of just over 2,000 inhabitants—eyewitnesses estimated the crowds to have been between 300 and 400 people, many of whom broke into the homes of Jewish residents, stole money and alcohol, and caused more than 20,000 forints in damage.[3]

For the most part, the central government tried to contain the disturbances, in the provinces as well as the capital. Prime Minister Kálmán Tisza took a hard line against the rioters, not hesitating to dispatch troops to affected regions; Lajos Kossuth—the hero of the 1848 Hungarian Revolution—denounced the riots from his exile in Turin in pronouncements that were printed in the Hungarian press.[4] Provincial and town authorities, for their part, did manage to restore order—with aid from the state—but it usually took several days to do so and came about through the cooperative efforts of local police, armed landowners, and outside troops.[5] As a popular response to the Tiszaeszlár affair, the demonstrations of 1883 were, in Nemes's view, "more widespread, varied, and purposeful than most scholars have allowed."[6] Shaped in part by well-established local antagonisms—including resentment toward the central state as well as religious and social prejudice—the disturbances transpired in what was also a highly politicized, national context and exposed the vulnerability of Jews in postemancipatory Hungarian society. For many provincial Hungarians, Nemes points out, Tiszaeszlár served as a "formative political experience," which produced a language of intolerance and illiberalism whose effects would be felt for decades to come.[7]

Publicists, newspaper editors, and politicians had begun in fact to lay the rhetorical groundwork for a modern account of Jewish ritual murder months before the opening of the Nyíregyháza trial, and Géza Ónody, the nobleman who represented the Tiszaeszlár district in parliament, was one of the more active players in this process. Following Bary's appointment to head the criminal investigation, Ónody took it upon himself occasionally to escort magistrates and police investigators around Tiszaeszlár, then to feed reports of what were supposed to have been secret investigative proceedings of the Nyíregyháza court to the main Hungarian antisemitic newspaper, *Függetlenség*.[8] *Függetlenség*, for its part, as the first major paper to disseminate news of the criminal investigation, was able to dictate for a period of time the type of knowledge that the Hungarian public had of the affair. Ónody thus mediated in an important way among fragmented strands of knowledge, opinion, and expertise. His public status was simultaneously complex and authoritative: nobleman, local resident, and parliamentary deputy; self-proclaimed student of Jewish customs; adviser to Istóczy—who would become a leader of the Hungarian antisemitic party, founded in 1883—and occasional confidant of the investigating team headed by Bary.[9] He could observe and appropriate local cultural negotiations over the meaning of Eszter Solymosi's disappearance, translate these meanings into the idiom of parliamentary life and party politics, and exert control, for a period of time, over public opinion.

The first International Congress of Antisemites, meeting in Dresden in September 1882, reserved much of its closing evening for a solemn commemoration of the events in Tiszaeszlár. Most of the leading figures of the fledgling antisemitic movement in Germany, Austria, and Hungary attended the meeting, as did representatives from France and the Russian Empire: Adolf Stöcker, Ernst Henrici, and Alexander Pinkert, from Germany; Karl von Zerboni, editor of the *Österreichischer Volksfreund*; and the Hungarians Iván Simonyi, Géza Ónody, and Győző Istóczy were in attendance at the two-day gathering, in which the Hungarian delegation was particularly active.[10] Simonyi, who had been appointed one of the chairmen of the event, delivered an address on "Antisemitism and the Laws of Human Society," which was later published in Pressburg/Pozsony. Istóczy authored the meeting's major programmatic statement, *Manifesto to the Governments and Peoples of the*

Christian States Threatened by Jewry.[11] But it was Ónody who dominated the proceedings at the meeting's close. Approaching the podium, he announced in somewhat halting German that he wanted to read from a soon to be published, "genuine" account of the Tiszaeszlár "murder affair."[12] The rest of his talk—delivered by a colleague of his who was more at home in the German language—conjured up images of Jews emigrating by the thousands from Galicia ("the central warehouse of Jews") and lording it over the Hungarian peasantry, whose spiritual impulses and strivings they suppressed. It spoke of the "Talmud Jews" of Tiszaeszlár who, in the name of holiness, maintained a steady solidarity with "Galicia" and who routinely shirked their military obligations, and it called for restrictions on civil rights and the imposition of special laws (*Ausnahmegesetze*) for Jews.[13]

Ónody's speech comprised several elements in an emerging, anti-Jewish interpretation of the unfolding investigation into the possible murder. In this narrative, Jews conspired to kill for ritual purposes, harmed the moral fabric of traditional Hungarian society, and obstructed justice at all costs. Even at this point in time—less than one-third of the way through the official investigation—Ónody claimed that numerous "sins of omission" had been committed by Hungarian officials; that the Pest branch of the Alliance Israélite Universelle had attempted to suppress evidence by substituting a phony corpse for that of the real Eszter Solymosi; that, in fact, Eszter's body had been burned by her killers; and that attempts had been made to bribe the victim's mother (presumably so that she would identify the corpse in question as that of her missing daughter).[14] Ónody's next words signaled an important step in the politicization of Tiszaeszlár and its usurpation by the nascent antisemitic movement: "The case is no longer the affair of a village, a county, or the land of Hungary alone, but rather of all mankind. The butcher's knife (*das Schächtermesser*) has struck simultaneously through the heart of humanity's spirit."[15]

For dramatic effect, Ónody had carried to the podium a large picture frame draped with a curtain. Waiting through a chorus of "bravos" and pleas to remove the cover, he finally pulled the curtain to reveal an oil painting of a girl, in Hungarian peasant dress, barefoot, her head covered by a scarf. The painting, he announced, had been executed "true to life" by the "young and talented artist" Ludwig (Lajos) Ábrányi "through the living spirit of memory."[16] It stood, he told his audience, as a symbol of the "fanatical racial hatred" of Jews toward outsiders: "See, here before us stands the figure of that unfortunate girl! . . . Here before us she stands, that girl, whose guiltless soul breathed its last sigh in the dark, criminally insane circle of

Figure 6. Drawing by Zoltán Csörgey of what purports to be Eszter Solymosi, 1882, based on a painting by Lajos Ábrányi. Published in Géza von Ónody, *Tisza-Eszlár in der Vergangenheit und Gegenwart*. Budapest, 1883.

Courtesy J. Mabray.

vengeance-breathing, ritual-murder butchers; that poor girl, whose body neither the priest of her faith nor the love of her relatives has been able to follow [in mourning]; that guiltless creature, whose corpse has perhaps been brutally dismembered by semitic fanaticism."[17]

"Long live freedom!" Ónody concluded. "May all the nations of Europe soon be freed from the cancer of Jewry."[18] Other speakers at the Antisemitic

Figure 7. Géza Ónody at the Dresden Antisemitic Congress, unknown caricaturist. *Borsszem Jankó*, 17 September 1882.

Courtesy D. Véri.

Congress had alluded to the Tiszaeszlár murder investigation before Ónody's dramatic address. During the previous session, Simonyi had highlighted the affair, stressing that it undoubtedly concerned a ritual murder. And the Congress itself had passed a resolution that called upon the Hungarian judiciary "to fulfill its highest obligations" in this matter.[19] But it was Ónody's speech that introduced the specialized vocabulary of late-nineteenth-century ritual murder discourse to the proceedings of an international political gathering and that tied the imagery of the modern ritual murder accusation to the programmatic concerns of political antisemitism. To paraphrase the words of Robert Nemes, it was not antisemitism that produced the Tiszaeszlár affair but, rather, Tiszaeszlár that helped to galvanize modern antisemitism.[20]

Eszter's "portrait" became an icon of sorts of the young antisemitic movement, even as it occasioned controversy among liberal journalists and politicians. Four days after the close of the Dresden Congress, Vienna's *Neue Freie Presse* reported that Istóczy and Simonyi had attended a second antisemitic gathering in Berlin at which the famous painting was displayed for an entrance fee of fifty pfennigs. It went on to be exhibited in Hamburg and later in Budapest. *Neue Freie Presse*'s correspondent railed against the "swindle" that had been played so cynically on "the most naive and gullible minds." Assuring his readers that no one, in fact, would ever have bothered to take a photograph, let alone paint the portrait, of a poor peasant girl from the Great Hungarian Plain, he dismissed Ábrányi's creation as a "figment of the imagination."[21] When Paul Nathan, who had covered the Nyíregyháza trial for *Die Nation* in Berlin, published his book-length study of the case a decade later, he, too, took pains to discredit Ónody's account of the iconic portrait. He did so by offering a counterversion of the painting's provenance. Far from being a faithful rendition of the innocent Eszter, he claimed, produced "through the living spirit of memory," the portrait was in fact that of a young prostitute from Nyíregyháza, and he went so far as to provide the name of the woman who served as the model for the Ábrányi painting.[22]

Nathan seemed to revel in the simple irony of mistaken identity: here was an artistic rendering of a small-town prostitute, placed in Dresden alongside the busts of three reigning monarchs, mourned and adulated by religious and political leaders alike. From our vantage point, it is impossible to know exactly who served as the model for the painting—or from what social class and occupation she hailed. But it is clear that the liberal retelling of the event, in addition to underscoring the cynicism and gullibility said to be characteristic of antisemitism as a political phenomenon, implicitly juxtaposed all that Eszter was understood to represent with its opposite. Even her status as victim—blameless, virginal, and pure—was inverted by the insinuation that one was standing in front of the portrait of a woman of easy virtue.

If Paul Nathan's goal was to undercut the antisemites by subjecting their icon to ridicule, he nevertheless recognized that the newly found imagery of ritual murder held enormous potential for mass politics. The Hungarian representatives at Dresden, he argued, had accomplished two major objectives. Their discourse on Jewish ritual murder, offered in the name of people who had an intimate connection to the place and events in question, replaced what up to then had been a vague narrative with a concrete image—a *feste Gestalt*, as he put it. The events in Hungary also provided the antisemitic movement in Central Europe with an important morale boost. In Nathan's view, the Russian pogroms of the spring and summer of 1881 had put political antisemitism on the defensive, as Jews appeared to be the victims of outrageous barbarism. The dissemination of the Tiszaeszlár affair allowed for the events in Russia to be pushed into the background, as it were, while the Jews' ontological status as victims could be replaced with that of violent criminality.[23] "The murdering butcher (*der mordende Schächter*), like the usurer who slaughters the nation in its time of need (*der den Nationalnotstand schächtende Wucherer*), belonged now to the official apparatus of the Party. An occurrence in a remote village along the Tisza had become a world-famous event. Tiszaeszlár was on everyone's tongue and thousands believed the ritual murder accusation. For the wide multitudes ritual murder had become a conceivable possibility after all."[24]

These initial steps in the production of a renewed discourse of Jewish ritual murder were met with—and eventually overshadowed by—a wide array of interventions and appropriations, ranging from academic treatises to public theater.[25] August Rohling, the author of the 1871 tract *Der Talmudjude* who was appointed five years later to a professorship in the Catholic Theological Faculty at the University of Prague, placed himself in the middle of a public debate that was raging in Vienna over the meaning of the Talmud for Jewish-Christian relations. He began by offering testimony on behalf of one Franz Holubek, an anti-Jewish agitator who had gone on trial in April 1882 for disturbing the public order. When, in response to Holubek's eventual acquittal, Vienna's two leading rabbis—Moritz Güdemann and Adolf Jellinek—printed a public statement in defense of the Talmud, declaring that its writings contained nothing that was hostile to Christianity, Rohling countered with a five-piece series in the Vienna *Tribüne* in which he famously branded the rabbis' intervention "utter roguishness" (*arge Schelmerei*).[26]

The articles soon were printed in a freestanding brochure—in both German and Czech editions—under the title "My Answers to the Rabbis, or: Five Letters Concerning the Talmud and Jewish Ritual Murder."[27] The German edition quickly went through four printings, the Czech edition, two, and at least 20,000 copies had been distributed before the public prosecutor and the Bohemian governor's office ordered the work confiscated in May 1883.[28] Seeking to have the decision reversed, Rohling later testified in court under oath—and on his oath as a public servant—that he had not intended his assertions regarding rabbinic writings to provoke hostility toward Jews. He was simply conveying the results of dispassionate, scientific research. What standing had the court to judge whether or not the Talmud contained the incriminating passages that he, a professor of ancient Hebrew, appointed by the emperor, claimed it did?

During the proceedings, Rohling spoke for an hour and a half, defending his positions and quoting from what he presented as the "original text" of the Talmud as well as from French, German, and Latin authors. Why should it be forbidden, he asked, to publish translated passages from the Talmud? No such restrictions applied to translating the Quran, he noted; why should it be different for the Talmud? "We know what the Turks believe," Rohling argued, "Christians would like to know what the Jews living next to them believe. . . . I have taken in this hall an oath to speak the truth and have written only the truth."[29] The confiscation order remained in place.

On 19 June 1883, the day on which the Tiszaeszlár trial opened in Nyíregyháza, Rohling wrote to Ónody offering his services as an expert witness on the Jewish religion and remarking that he would like to have the opportunity to testify at the trial.[30] In the letter, which was soon disseminated in German and Hungarian newspapers, Rohling reiterated a point that he had made in his *Answers to the Rabbis*, namely, that the printed editions of the Talmud no longer contained any reference to ritual murder—the Jews having been careful to expunge the printed text of any direct teachings in this regard. Now that another such case was to be heard in the halls of justice, he explained, he regarded it as his duty to inform Ónody (and, through him, the court) that he has since come into the possession of more recent Jewish literature, which directly advocates spilling the blood of non-Jewish maidens. Specifically, Rohling claimed to have found incriminating passages in the thirteenth-century mystical text, the *Zohar*, and in *Sefer ha-likutim* (*Book of Gatherings*) of Hayim Vital (1542–1620), an important disseminator of what has come to be known as Lurianic Kabbalah.[31] In the end, Rohling's testimony was never requested by the Nyíregyháza court, and he would soon become entangled in a major libel case of his own—directed at the Galician-born, Viennese rabbi, Joseph Samuel Bloch (1850–1923)—which, along with his professorship in Prague, Rohling would lose.[32]

The events in Hungary in 1882 and 1883 presented a significant psychological challenge to Jews throughout Central Europe as well as to non-Jewish supporters of Jewish emancipation. Religious leaders, scholars, and politicians who condemned the ritual murder accusation on both moral and intellectual grounds sensed that the rumors in Tiszaeszlár and the judicial proceedings in Nyíregyháza represented a fundamental challenge to modernity and required a commensurate rhetorical response, a final, powerful refutation that reflected the highest achievements of scholarship. To that end, an assembly of Hungarian rabbis met in Budapest in July 1882 and solemnly declared that, "having searched, investigated, and examined all categories of Jewish literature, Jewish works from all the ages, we guarantee before God and the world that there is not the slightest hint in the above [sources] that might give occasion to this malicious accusation."[33] The rabbinical assembly also delegated its secretary, Leopold (Lipót) Lipschitz, rabbi of Abaújszántó, to canvass Christian scholars of Judaism at leading European universities in order to elicit their opinion concerning the ritual murder accusation. Lipschitz and his colleagues received replies from at least sixteen professors, two Catholic bishops, and three Protestant theological faculties. These were assembled and published later that year under the title *Christian Testimonies Against the Blood Accusation of the Jews*.[34]

Some truly distinguished figures in academic Jewish studies in Germany and Austria—at a time when the field was represented solely by Christian practitioners—came forward to condemn the ritual murder accusation: Franz Delitzsch (Leipzig), Adalbert Merx (Heidelberg), Theodor Nöldecke (Strasbourg), Hermann L. Strack (Berlin), and August Wünsche (Dresden), among others. One name in the group of professors whom Lipschitz approached seems, however, to have been an odd choice: Paul de Lagarde, from the University of Göttingen. Lagarde (1827–91), a biblical scholar and orientalist, was known for his radical positions on both Christianity and Judaism. In the first edition of his well-known work of cultural criticism, *Deutsche Schriften*, published in 1878, he famously had insisted that Jews were an unassimilable, foreign element in German society and had no role to play in German cultural creativity. Toward the end of his life, he would engage in ad hominem attacks on the Jewish scholars Abraham Berliner, David Kaufmann, and Leopold Zunz (on whom Lagarde gleefully bestowed the first name Lipman).[35] In Lagarde's response to the rabbinical assembly, he protested that he did not have the time to prepare a historical exposition of the ritual murder accusation. He would, nevertheless, be prepared to testify in court that it was his "strong conviction" that Judaism—as characterized by its officially recognized texts—has never employed human blood for religious purposes. "The superstition of individual Jews," he equivocated, "to the extent that this exists—and I am not in a position to judge—should not be held against Judaism any more than the superstition of individual Christians, against Christianity."[36]

In the wake of the general success of the *Christian Testimonies* project, the Budapest rabbinical board approached a Hungarian-born British Jew, Solomon Mayer Schiller-Szinessy (1820–90), who was serving at the time as the first Jewish reader in Rabbinics at the University of Cambridge, with the request that he conduct a similar canvassing campaign in the United

Kingdom, beginning with his own university. In January 1883, the *Times* of London published a letter to the editor from Schiller-Szinessy describing the request and his subsequent mission. Chagrined by the apparent need to embark on such a campaign in the first place, Schiller-Szinessy was pleased, nevertheless, to report to the readers of the *Times* that his efforts had met with great success: "However humiliating it is to me, both as a Jewish theologian and an Hungarian patriot, to have to assist, so near the close of this 'enlightened nineteenth century,' in rebutting so false and cruel a charge, yet it is highly satisfactory to me to have found such ready support from men of such eminence, both for their Christian learning and their Christian virtues. If you can see your way to inserting these letters you will be rendering a real service to many innocent sufferers."[37]

As it turned out, the *Times* chose to print only one of the replies that Schiller-Szinessy had received, a brief expression of sympathy from one J. B. Dunelm, who wrote, "I have no hesitation in saying that I consider the 'blood-accusations' against the Jews as monstrously untrue as they are cruel, and I am at a loss to understand how any sane man in this nineteenth century can believe them." The *Times* editors closed the column with the following remark: "Letters to the same effect are given from the Dean of Peterborough, the Master of Queen's College, Cambridge, the Master of Christ's, Professor Westcott, and Dr. Lumby."[38] It was left to the *Jewish Chronicle* to print these learned responses.

The letters that were printed in the *Jewish Chronicle* blended a judicious mixture of liberal outrage and Christian charity. Dunelm concluded his answer with the observation that to adopt such accusations as a grounds for persecution was to bring dishonor upon the sacred name of Christ.[39] J. J. Stewart Berowne, the dean of Peterborough, framed his response to Schiller-Szinessy along the lines of a dichotomy between rationalism and irrationalism, modernity and the "medieval":

> My Dear Friend,—I need scarcely assure you with what feelings of indignation I have heard of the revival, in the recent persecutions of the Jews in Hungary, of the cruel and slanderous accusations which have been made against them of using human blood in their Passover feast. One would have thought that in the nineteenth century a charge so gross could hardly have been listened to for a moment. No one who has the slightest acquaintance with Jewish literature, or who knows anything of Jewish belief, could credit it.

> He must know it to be a malicious lie. But, alas! Bigotry and intolerance and religious fanaticism and hatred are not yet dead.[40]

The oft-repeated refrain that the ritual murder accusation constituted a "depth of ignorance which is a disgrace to the age in which we live" (to quote from another letter) revealed the extent of Central European Jewry's reliance on the presumptive power of reason to ensure emancipation.[41] At the same time, the very repetition of expressions of outrage pointed to the vulnerability of their position. In a few months' time, the editors of the *Jewish Chronicle* would be able to greet the "not guilty" verdict that was handed down in Nyíregyháza as a complete vindication, a sign that the "last of the 'blood-accusations' has been completely disproved in the face of Europe."[42] But how long would the protectors of the liberal order be able to keep the unwanted guests of "barbarism" and "irrationality" at the door?

For the better part of a decade, Tiszaeszlár would stand in the European Jewish imagination as both turning point and temporal boundary marker, indicating a true transition to modernity. In August 1883, the *Jewish Chronicle* trumpeted the conviction that "henceforth we shall always be able to point to a crucial instance of the charge being fully refuted."[43] In a similar vein, the *Nationalzeitung* of Berlin could write that the conclusion of the Tiszaeszlár trial rendered any future accusation of ritual murder "juridically and scientifically impossible."[44] Law and science, then, were to act as the guarantors of a new age of reason. The optimism, however, could not be sustained, as accusations of Jewish ritual murder continued to be publicized into the next decade and beyond, twinned rhetorically to the political program of antisemitic parties and newspapers and bolstered, as much as thwarted, by claims to scientific corroboration.

After Tiszaeszlár, it becomes increasingly difficult to disentangle locally constructed knowledge of Jewish criminality and "ritual murder" from either Central European politics writ large or urban interventions of various kinds. Political party interests and the authoritative, structuring voice of urban bureaucracies were always to be found, offering behind-the-scenes direction punctuated by direct, periodic interventions. Thus, when the *Jewish Chronicle* mentioned the Xanten accusation for the first time—in late July 1891, about a month after the discovery of the body of a young boy—it did so in the context of a report on the general diffusion of ritual murder claims by German antisemitic newspapers.[45] From its perspective, the events in the Rhineland town merely represented the most recent manifestation of a large-scale campaign in Europe and the Middle East to defame Jews. And when the Xanten trial opened in Kleve in July 1892, editors felt obliged, finally, to admit to their own diminished optimism in the liberal order.

> The anti-Semites in Germany have made so much progress that they are enabled to offer a home in the midst of German culture to that Red Spectre of Judaism, as the Blood Accusation has been called, which ten years ago was thought to have made its last appearance in Europe among the rude peasants of Tiszaeszlár. Ten years ago, almost on the spot where Hunyadi finally thrust back the tide of Musulman conquest, this ghastly survival of daemonic Paganism was said to have been exorcised once and for all. Europe, it was complacently declared, was no longer a possible abiding place for the morbid figments of a mediaeval fancy. They might linger in the Grecian Archipelago, where Christianity is still in the stage of compromise, and they might venture occasionally into the ruder recesses of the Balkans, where time has stood still since the days of the Crusades, but in Western Europe the air had become too rarified for them to breathe.[46]

Of Butchers, Neighbors, and Young Lads: Xanten and Skurz

On the morning of 29 June 1891, the mother of little Johann Hegmann sent her son out to play so that she could attend mass in celebration of the Feast of Saints Peter and Paul. He did not show up when the family sat down to morning coffee at 10:30 a.m., nor was he seen the rest of the day; sometime in the afternoon, Johann's mother sent family members and friends to look for the child. The boy's body was found around 6:30 p.m. in the barn of the innkeeper and town councilor Wilhelm Küppers by a maid who had gone in to milk and feed the cows.[47] Xanten's local physician, Joseph Steiner, arrived shortly after 7 p.m., pronounced the child dead, and proceeded to inform both the police and the court in Kleve. Steiner remained at the scene where, sometime after 9 p.m., he began a formal postmortem examination (*Leichenschau*) consisting largely of a visual description of the condition of the corpse in the place where it lay in the Küppers' barn.[48] The doctor observed a 13-centimeter-long wound on the front of the boy's neck; the wound extended on the right side to 4 centimeters behind the mastoid process, where it ended in a sharp angle, and it appeared to have cut sharply through all of the soft tissue, the major vessels, and the windpipe (at the height of the Adam's apple) up to the cervical vertebra, stretching left to 1 centimeter before the mastoid process, where it also ended in a sharp angle. A pool of blood—about 30 centimeters long and 18 to 19 centimeters wide—lay on the straw beneath the body, apparently, the report read, "from exsanguination" (*Nachblutung*). Steiner reported that the boy's clothing around the upper part of the body was stuck to his jacket from coagulated blood, and he also noted that "straw and some chaff, a grain of oats, sweet pea, and poppy-head" had been balled up in the boy's clenched fist.[49]

Journalists in the 1890s, as well as historians subsequently, have had a tendency to *naturalize*, if you will, the production of accusations of Jewish ritual murder. Start with a disappearance or mysterious, violent death; blend with village naïveté and superstition; sprinkle in a dose of antisemitism; and bake for an hour. But not every kidnapping of a small child, not every unsettling murder, led in the direction of a ritual murder charge. How was it, then, that Adolf Buschhoff should have become a suspect in Xanten? As Bernd Kölling has so aptly put the question: what does it mean, in concrete terms, when one writes, as one historian did, "immediately after the discovery of the corpse, the rumor arose" that the Jews had killed the child for ritual purposes? How does a rumor *arise*? What does it mean when one says (as another historian has written) that the "idea of ritual murder" was brought into circulation in a given society?[50] What are the actual means by which these phenomena take shape?

As Kölling suggests, they do not just take shape; they are *given* shape by purposeful individuals. One of the local residents who arrived early on the scene on 29 June, and who made himself conspicuous by his presence, was a cattle dealer and former butcher by the name of Heinrich Junkermann. Junkermann engaged directly in the examination of the corpse and issued opinions on the preliminary findings, which he wished to be taken as expert and authoritative. One of these had to do with the nature of the wound on the boy's neck. It was, he assured his audience, a Jewish butcher's cut (*Schächtschnitt*). Calling upon his own experience as a butcher, Junkermann was also quick to claim that the boy could not have been killed in the barn. There was simply not enough blood on hand, he explained, to accept the theory of an exsanguination on the spot.[51] He appealed, finally, to an unimpeachable scientific authority: his son, who was a medical student in Berlin! Newspapers covering the 1892 trial in Kleve quoted Junkermann as having said incongruously that "the Jews make use of the blood of Christian children for their Passover bread; I know this from my son, who is a medical student."[52] The next morning, Junkermann paid a visit to the mayor of Xanten and gave him his version of the motive for the crime; afterward, he spread his story in the town's taverns.

Junkermann was not alone, however, in issuing "expert" pronouncements on the murder of Johann Hegmann; the Xanten physician Joseph Steiner seems to have had a hand in promoting a theory of ritual murder as well. Nowhere in the official postmortem, dictated that evening, did Steiner comment on an apparent *paucity* of blood on the corpse or in its vicinity. Nor did he raise the question of where the murder might have taken place. Later, however—during both the criminal investigation and the subsequent trial—he elaborated significantly on just these points. "In my opinion," Steiner told the presiding judge at the trial, "I did not find at the scene all of the blood that could have flowed out of the body. I consider it [the amount that was found] to have been blood that left the body after the first outpouring of blood, and after death had occurred." Was it his opinion, the judge asked, that the murder had taken place somewhere else, and the body had been taken to the barn? "Yes."[53]

County physicians Ferdinand Bauer and Julius Nünninghoff, who conducted an official autopsy (*Obduktion*) on the body the day after its discovery, contradicted Steiner on most key points but produced, in the end, a report that allowed for some ambiguity in its conclusions. The two emphasized at every step in their examination the copious amounts of blood that they found on the face, hands, body, and clothing of the boy, as well as in the straw on which it lay, while the bulk of their dictated report focused on determining the cause of death ("exsanguination . . . as the result of a tremendous cut on the neck, which was carried out with significant strength using a large and sharp knife in at least two strokes").[54] Already at this early stage, however, information and rumor impinged on the medical examination. Unsatisfied with the narrow focus of the autopsy, the district court judge who was in attendance felt that the county physicians had failed to address one important question, and he sought to rectify the situation by adding a short notice as a postscript to the report the following day.

> Considering the importance for the investigation of determining whether the child was killed where it was found, at the conclusion of the above protocol the undersigned directed a question to the [medical] expert, county physician Dr. Bauer: Is it possible to

> establish whether or not the amount of blood that was found in the clothing, under the neck of the corpse, or on the ground was *all the blood that had to have been in the body*? The question was answered by the expert in the negative.
>
> Xanten, 1 July 1891. (Signed) Risbroeck, District Judge.[55]

Risbroeck's postscript served to muddy what the county medical officers had intended to be a cut-and-dry report and left the state prosecutor's office with no alternative but to pursue the matter further. On 15 July, Bauer received a telegram from District Attorney (*Erster Staatsanwalt*) Baumgard asking the doctor to reply to two questions: "1. Whether and why, from the medical point of view, one was to conclude that the child had been killed where his body was found. 2. Whether in fact the corpse of the child was noticeably empty of blood, and whether the traces of blood at the discovery site were unusually small, such that one would have to conclude that an intentional drawing of blood had occurred."[56] In his reply, Bauer expressed surprise at the questions, claiming to have addressed them adequately in the autopsy report. Nevertheless, he reviewed his earlier findings that a "considerable amount" of blood had made its way into the straw, chaff, and earthen matter or was stuck to the surface of the straw and chaff, confirmed without a doubt by visual observation. Beyond this, a "considerable amount" of blood had been found to have dried to the child's clothing, so that the outer shirt, the undershirt, the vest, and the pants were heavily stained with blood, not to mention the face and chest, on which large amounts of dried blood were found; in addition, both ears were filled with blood. Finally, he reminded the district attorney that a small bundle of straw and chaff was found in the tightly balled right hand of the child, which was exactly of the same quality as that which lay at the discovery site. This material was held so tightly that it could only be removed with effort, and, since both the hand and the bundle were stained with dried blood, "apparently the boy had grabbed at the straw in the death struggle."[57]

The three points taken together, Bauer argued, added up to the conclusion that the child had bled heavily at the discovery site and that, during the death struggle, he had grasped at the (blood-stained) straw with his right hand, which remained clenched after rigor had set in. Moreover, if one added these to the other major findings—the colossal wound to the neck and the strength and thoroughness with which it had been executed, which resulted in the opening up of the major veins and arteries—one would have to conclude that exsanguination occurred in a very short amount of time, a

Figure 8. Crime scene photograph with the body of Johann Hegmann (wounds covered).

Courtesy Hans-Martin Scheibner.

few minutes at most, perhaps within one minute. In short, it was physically impossible that the boy was killed (in the manner in which he was killed) somewhere else and the body then transported to the barn.[58]

While Bauer rejected the characterization that an "unusually small amount of blood spatter" was found at the discovery site, he appears to have been sensitive to the cultural-political atmosphere in which the scientific investigations were being carried out. Although the prosecutor had not asked him to comment on the theory that a "ritual murder" had been performed on Johann Hegmann, Bauer chose deliberately to comment on this point. Adopting a position of agnostic neutrality, he proclaimed that, whether the murderer was a Jew or a Christian, he slaughtered the boy *there* in the barn. On what grounds, to what purpose, the autopsy and site examination could not determine. Similarly, whether any blood could have been captured in some sort of vessel at the scene of the crime could not be determined scientifically; it had to remain an open question.[59] Bauer conceded (again, without having been asked) that the method in which the cut was carried out suggested the way in which a butcher handled his knife, and he surmised that the murder weapon was long, strong, and sharp. He repeated his earlier answer that he found no evidence, from either the autopsy or the on-site examination, to suggest a Jewish ritual murder. Anyone who wished to raise this charge, Bauer surmised, would have to base it on other grounds.[60]

Adolf Buschhoff and the Image of Kosher Slaughtering

Three elements coalesced in Adolf Buschhoff's life story to allow him to emerge as a prime suspect in Johann Hegmann's murder. They were, in ascending order of importance, the location of his property—directly in back of Küppers's barn; his status as a Jew; and the years that he had spent as a butcher. In the overheated atmosphere that followed the discovery of the body, it was this last piece of information that weighed most heavily against Buschhoff—emphasized by investigators and prosecutors—because it appeared to corroborate the theory that had already gained traction in the minds of local residents and officials, not only that the crime had been carried out with anatomical expertise but that it had incorporated an important feature of Jewish ritual slaughtering, the so-called butcher's cut.

The combined images of Jewish butchering and Jewish ritual murder had begun to be deployed at least as far back as the Dresden Antisemitic Congress of 1882. During the Tiszaeszlár affair, the rhetoric of Jewish butchering necessarily took on a more nuanced tone, since it could not be established that Eszter Solymosi had in fact come to a violent end. And yet three Jewish butchers (Salamon Schwarcz, Ábrahám Buxbaum, and Lipót Braun) were nevertheless swept up in the maelstrom that followed her disappearance, having had the misfortune to be present in Tiszaeszlár on that fateful Sabbath in order to audition for the newly vacant position of community *shoḥet*. Following the Nyíregyháza verdict, the image of the "murdering butcher" peppered discourses of Jewish danger, and in formal accusations of ritual murder, Jewish butchers and ritual slaughterers played central, dramatic roles as objects of suspicion.

A criminal proceeding that took place in the village of Skurz in West Prussia from 1884 to 1885 provides an illustrative example of the ways in which images of Jewish ritual slaughtering entered—and eventually came to dominate—the modern discourse of ritual murder. The Skurz case also offers variations on other features of the Xanten affair of the next decade, and even though, technically, it did not culminate in a ritual murder trial, it certainly warrants recounting.[61] The narrative begins in the early morning hours of 22 January 1884, when passersby discover parts of a dismembered body while crossing a bridge in the vicinity of Skurz. The victim was identified as Onophrius Cybulla, known in the village as Onophri: a fourteen-year-old working lad, son of the tailor from Skurz. The boy had last been seen the previous evening at the establishment of the innkeeper Japa, where he had been rinsing glasses.

The district attorney soon entered the scene to run the criminal investigation, while two physicians were assigned the task of conducting a postmortem exam on the incomplete corpse. The postmortem came up with a number of "highly important facts" (to quote from the *National-Zeitung* of 25 April 1885): (1) The neck of the victim had been slashed almost to the spinal column. (2) The thighs had been "expertly" separated from both the torso and the lower legs at the pelvis and the knees. (3) There were seven cuts to the head. (4) The stomach had been ripped open. (5) The entire "operation" must have lasted for hours. (6) Numerous wounds and contusions on the victim's hands, back, and head indicated that he must have put up a defensive struggle. (7) There were no signs of a sexual crime having been committed. The attending physicians also noted that it was curious that this "very strong and full-blooded" body (of the victim) was empty of blood ("*blutleer*").[62]

As in the Xanten case, most narrative accounts of Skurz propose that, some time after the discovery of the body and the ensuing medical examination, a "local rumor" spread that Jews had killed the boy and collected his blood for ritual purposes. The missing body parts (thighs) seem to have played a role in this construction of the crime, as well as the doctors' observation that the existing torso was lacking blood; even the seven cuts to the head were said to be significant in this regard, as they supposedly alluded to the significance of the number seven in Jewish culture.[63] As in the Xanten case, the one individual who was most vociferous in his accusations against the Jews was a Christian butcher, this one by the name of Josef Behrendt. The way in which the boy's body had been dissected led the district attorney to conclude that the crime had been committed by someone with good anatomical knowledge, either a doctor or a butcher. And, since there was neither much blood nor signs of struggle at the scene of the discovery of the body, he presumed that the actual murder and dismemberment had occurred somewhere else.[64]

With their sights set on someone who was a butcher—and possibly influenced themselves by the local dissemination of "news" of a ritual murder—investigators first interrogated the Jewish ritual slaughterer, Blumenheim. It turned out, however, that he had been out of town on the night of the murder. Suspicion then fell on a horse trader and former butcher by the name of Hermann Josephsohn. A laborer named Johann Mankowski had come forward and told police that he had seen Josephsohn in the early morning hours of 22 January 1884, in the vicinity of the place where the body parts were found, with a heavy sack on his back. Another witness claimed that she had seen Josephsohn in the vicinity of the bridge around 6 a.m. on that day dragging a heavy load in a bright cloth. Someone else brought testimony against a Jewish dealer in manufactured goods named Heymann Boß and his seventy-three-year-old father Rochem Boß. This witness claimed to have seen the victim lured into the Boß household by someone speaking with a "Jewish accent."[65]

Heymann Boß's house was searched in early February. In the cellar, police discovered what appeared to be a pot with blood in it, which Boß claimed was oxblood. Again, Josef Behrendt appeared on the spot as an expert and declared that the blood in question was "unquestionably human blood." When one of the officials who were present expressed doubt, Behrendt is said to have replied, "I as a butcher ought to know what human blood is and what oxblood is."[66] Josephsohn and his "associates" were then imprisoned while an investigating magistrate from Danzig conducted what was officially a preliminary investigation into the three men. Various witnesses started to come forward to testify that they saw Jews from the area gathering on the ground floor of the Boß house, carrying on late into the night, with a lot of "hustle and bustle" (*Leben und Treiben*). In the course of the investigation, the blood that had been found in the Boß's basement was sent to Berlin for chemical analysis. The results came back on 15 February: it was indeed oxblood. Investigators also determined that in the stable of the Jewish family, there was a beef slaughtering facility, which may have accounted for the presence of blood stains and residue.[67]

The results of the preliminary investigation, however unnerving for the Jews under suspicion, did not warrant the issuing of a criminal charge against the three. For the time being, the crime remained a mystery, but local opinion clamored for an indictment. The officials who were heading the investigation turned at this point to the Prussian Ministry of the Interior with the request that it send a qualified detective to conduct more inquiries. The minister of the interior concurred and, in consultation with the minister of justice, decided to send in a detective superintendent (*Kriminalkomissar*) from Berlin by the name of Höft. This second intervention of urban officials into a small-town murder investigation moved it in an unanticipated and, ultimately, decisive direction. Höft arrived in Skurz highly skeptical of the theory of a Jewish ritual murder and turned his attention instead to the Catholic butcher, Behrendt.[68] More than anything else, the very fact that Behrendt had expended so much energy agitating against the Jews of the village and in favor of his own theory of the crime aroused Höft's suspicion. Behrendt's own alibi was that he had been at home in bed on the night of 21–22 January, but Höft determined that this was untrue; he had in fact been with the innkeeper Stenzel.[69]

Johann Mankowski, under questioning by the detective, changed his earlier testimony, admitting that it was Behrendt and not Josephsohn whom he had seen in the vicinity of the bridge. Apparently, Behrendt and a friend of his had approached Mankowski several times to try to influence his testimony; the friend promised Mankowski a reward if he testified that it was Josephsohn whom he had seen. Höft reported his findings in April 1884 to the district attorney, who ordered that an official investigation be opened against the Christian butcher Behrendt. Shortly thereafter, the *Voruntersuchung* against Josephsohn and the two Boßs was closed. This reversal of fortune did nothing to ease tensions in Skurz, however, where the Jews continued to be threatened and where *Kriminalkomissar* Höft was accused of having been biased in their favor.[70] Nevertheless, when the criminal trial in the Skurz affair took place on 22–27 April 1885, before a jury in Danzig, it was Behrendt who sat in the defendant's chair.

Four key elements seem to have been central to the "butcher's cut" discourses of both Skurz and Xanten: (1) a deep cut to the neck as the apparent cause of death; (2) the presumed skill with which the murder had been accomplished or the body dismembered, suggesting a person who understood human anatomy and who knew how to wield a butcher's implements; (3) the widely disseminated image of Jewish ritual slaughtering as unusually violent and cruel (the opposite, if you will, of the image that the same institution holds among observant Jews), and (4) a general knowledge that one of the main functions of the *Schächtschnitt* in kosher ritual was to drain the animal of its blood. Thus, the separate observations—claims, really—of both Behrendt and Junkermann that the wound across the neck was a genuine *Schächtschnitt*, that the victims had bled out, *and* that there was not enough blood at the scene to suggest that the physical act of murder had taken place there achieved the intended effect of pointing investigators in the direction of a Jewish ritual crime. Underlying the last point was the unarticulated assumption that the actual collection of blood had been accomplished somewhere else, in a private, domestic location and out of sight.[71]

Charges that Jewish ritual slaughtering constituted a form of cruelty toward animals have shadowed this particular institution for the past century and a half, but no less noisily than at the turn of the twentieth century. In fact, as Robin Judd has shown, kosher butchering frequently was paired with (and mirrored against) ritual circumcision as singular markers of incivility—bordering on inhumanity—that called into question the suitability of Jews to assume the role of citizens of the German Empire.[72] Between 1880 and 1890, eleven German municipalities considered the question of kosher butchering; that number grew exponentially after 1890. Germany's Bundesrat and Reichstag debated the possibility of instituting a ban on kosher slaughtering three times during the decades preceding World War I, while seven state parliaments and ministries dealt with the question of whether or not to regulate kosher butchering. Animal protection groups, some of which advocated a general reform of all slaughterhouse practices and focused specifically on Jewish ritual practices, constituted the largest single participant in this growing debate.[73]

The *Schächtfrage* narrowly conceived had nothing to do with the butcher's implements or even with the actual act of killing through a single cut across the neck. In its rough outline, this method did not differ measurably from non-Jewish forms of animal slaughtering. At issue, rather, during the last decades of the nineteenth century was the refusal of Jewish authorities to adopt the increasingly popular practice of stunning before slaughter (accomplished in a variety of ways, including shooting a bullet or hammering a stake or mallet into the animal's head), because this would have violated the provision in Jewish law that required that the animal be conscious up to the moment of slaughter.[74] On a formal level, then, the debate revolved around a technical innovation, which, in the eyes of animal protection societies, spelled the difference between unnecessary suffering and humane killing but could not be accepted by religiously observant Jews, because Jewish law considered animals in an unconscious state to be ill or otherwise unfit to eat. A few indicators suggest that many German Christians felt the same way. In the town of Rheydt in the Rhineland, Jews constituted only 0.8 percent of the population, but more than 50 percent of the meat slaughtered in the local slaughterhouse was produced by the so-called *Schächten* method (no stunning was used). In Bütow, where Jews made up less than 1 percent of the population, it was alleged that 95 percent of the meat produced in the public slaughterhouses was killed by kosher slaughterers. Even the German army was implicated in this practice. During the first decade of the twentieth century, it was accused of purchasing a good portion of its meat from cattle that had been slaughtered without having been stunned first. Some military spokesmen insisted that the meat from animals that had been killed while conscious stayed fresher longer.[75]

If the formal debate on Jewish ritual slaughtering centered on the question of the application of a technological innovation to an ancient practice, the popular imagination was captivated by a more basic, yet menacing, set of images: bearded *shoḥets*; long, sharp knives; deep neck wounds; and blood. These were, moreover, transportable images, which could easily be dislodged from one set of referents (ritual slaughtering) and applied to—or imagined in relation to—another (ritual murder). And since the two phenomena (real or imagined) shared a set of images, their social messages could be mutually reinforcing. Again, Robin Judd: "Imagining the Jewish butcher or circumciser as a Jewish murderer, detractors used the libel charge to condemn Jewish rites while simultaneously pointing to Jewish ritual behavior as proof of the blood libel's existence. As such, when blood libel charges were laid, officials and townspeople often blamed local ritual practitioners."[76] This complex of associations, less visible in the Tiszaeszlár affair, clearly was at play in Skurz and in Xanten, producing a cultural backdrop against which conventional methods of criminal investigation and prosecution inevitably operated.

In the Skurz case, as we have seen, when the detective superintendent from Berlin became involved in the investigation, attention shifted from potential Jewish suspects to the Christian butcher who had aggressively promoted the ritual murder accusation. A similar pattern of urban intervention occurred in Xanten but with very different results. Heinrich Junkermann—the Christian butcher who commented vocally on the evidence in Xanten—was never indicted for the crime, nor was any other non-Jewish person, despite the fact that over the course of 1891 and 1892, at least four individuals in addition to Buschhoff and Junkermann came under suspicion at one point or another. There was the "insane brother-in-law" of Johann Hegmann's father, for one, who apparently had threatened the father immediately before the murder, and a wood lathe operator from Xanten, who was seen on the morning of the day in question with bloody hands and sleeves. Dora Moll, the maid who discovered Johann's body in the barn, had a reputation for piety, but one theory held that she might have been caught with a lover, and the pair had decided to get rid of an irksome witness. Finally, the brother of one of the most important prosecution witnesses against Buschhoff made himself an object of suspicion when, long after the Kleve trial, he demonstrated "conspicuous behavior" whenever the murder was brought up.[77]

But it is Junkermann and his relative by marriage, Wesendrup—a stonecutter by occupation—who stand out as the most likely perpetrators in a recent study by Bernd Kölling. It seems that the cattleman Junkermann's main competitor was a leader of the local Jewish community by the name of Oster, whose business was a good deal more successful than his. The immediate context for the crime concerned a public auction for the leasing of some pastureland. Junkermann had tendered the highest bid, but during an eight-day ratification period, Oster's son added to his father's offer and, in doing so, garnered the lease for him. The turn of events so enraged Junkermann that he reportedly told another cattle dealer from the nearby town of Rees that he would like to get back at the Jews of Xanten, particularly Osten. Why, then, implicate Buschhoff? Kölling speculates that he was conveniently positioned to take the fall; the larger goal was to discredit the Xanten Jewish community.[78]

Kölling cautions, however, that even if Junkermann could have been behind the murder, it was Wesendrup—by all accounts a morally dissolute man, who also owed Buschhoff money—who carried out the crime.[79] The relationship among Buschhoff, Junkermann, and Wesendrup, simultaneously intimate and conflictual, bore many of the qualities of small-town social life. Junkermann, it seems, avoided most contact with Wesendrup—despite their family ties—in fact rarely spoke with him until shortly before the murder. Buschhoff, in contrast, paid a visit to Wesendrup's home about six months prior to the murder and—upset by the depth of poverty that he found there—took up a collection for the family, to which Junkermann agreed to contribute under strong protest. Two weeks before the Hegmann murder, Junkermann and Wesendrup mysteriously resumed their relationship. By this time, Wesendrup was working for Buschhoff preparing gravestones and receiving visits from both Junkermann and his son, the medical student in Berlin.[80] Continuing in a prosecutorial mode, Kölling underscores the fact that Junkermann had worked for thirty years as a butcher, suggesting that Wesendrup would thus have had access to butcher's knives and would have known how to make a deep cut in the manner of an animal slaughterer. He knew the barn in which the boy's body was found and was careful not to hide the body but rather put it "on display," as it were, wishing for the boy to be discovered there. Last, according to the

State Prosecutor's Office in Cologne, people who had sat with Wesendrup in two different bars in November 1892 reported that Wesendrup had told them (remorsefully) that *he*, and not Buschhoff, had killed the child.[81]

Yet neither Junkermann nor Wesendrup was ever indicted. Despite the similarities between the Skurz and the Xanten affairs, in Xanten, only the Jewish suspect eventually went on trial. The reason for this, I think, has less to do with differences in rates of antisemitism or in the strength of beliefs about Jewish ritual murder and more to do with chance—specifically, with the unpredictable consequences of state intervention. Prussian officials engaged with the local investigations in Skurz and in Xanten in similar ways, but the results of these interactions could not have been more different. The backdrop to the decisive intervention of the state in the Xanten affair involved a heightening of tensions in July 1891, when some of Xanten's population took to the streets attacking property and threatening Jewish residents. The situation became so precarious for Buschhoff and his family that he went so far as to ask the mayor of the town to place him in prison until the atmosphere calmed down and his innocence could be proved. The mayor declined to do this, but he did appeal to county officials in Moers to help restore order in the town.[82] By August, life had become unbearable for Buschhoff, and he felt obliged to relocate with his family to the relative security and anonymity of Cologne. On 15 September 1891, the head of Xanten's Jewish community, together with Rabbi Jakob Horowitz of Krefeld, wrote to the Prussian minister of the interior and requested—in light of the lack of progress in the investigation as well as the growing antisemitic agitation—that a detective superintendent be dispatched to help break the investigative stalemate. The Jewish community even offered to assume the costs.[83] Enter detective superintendent Wolff, charged with taking over the investigation on 24 September, who in less than two weeks produced a report of his findings for the police superintendent in Berlin.[84]

The Modern Detective and the Investigation into Ritual Murder

To say that Wolff's investigation and report did not produce the effects that Rabbi Horowitz had hoped for would be a gross understatement. Like his counterpart Höft, Wolff claimed to have found no grounds for the theory of a ritual murder, and he expressed criticism in his report for those residents of Xanten who spread such talk, as well as for those who engaged in street demonstrations and public disturbances against Jews. He also rejected, however, the counterclaim that the boy had been murdered in a plot, motivated by economic envy and competition, to frame the Jews. He followed leads in both directions, he wrote, but all that he heard was "empty speech and absurd suspicions." Interestingly, Wolff contended that both popular versions of the crime had the effect of making people overlook or cover up simple, obvious facts, and both made it appear (for different reasons, of course) that Buschhoff was in fact *not* the killer.[85] But Wolff prided himself on not allowing rhetorical positions to sway what he saw as his objectivity. And he never wavered from his conviction that Adolf Buschhoff was, in fact, a murderer.

What Wolff did was to offer an alternative theory as to motive and a revised narrative of the crime itself. The "plain facts" that he considered relevant were that the Hegmann boy had disappeared sometime around 10 a.m. on the day in question and (based on testimony from one adult and two of the boy's playmates) that he was last seen alive being pulled by someone into the Buschhoff home.[86] The rest required some narrative reconstruction. In the days before his death, Wolff contended, Buschhoff had become convinced—mistakenly, perhaps—that Johann Hegmann had damaged some gravestones that were being prepared for the Jewish community and that it was for this reason that he had been forced into the Buschhoff home. Wolff did not think it likely that the murder had been premeditated: the act of pulling the boy into the house had been done pretty much in the open, after all. Initially, perhaps, Buschhoff had intended merely to give the boy a verbal dressing down, but he ended up beating him and rendering him unconscious.[87] In the ensuing panic, and in fear that the now missing boy would be discovered in their home, Wolff surmised, the Buschhoffs moved him in the afternoon into Küppers's barn, where Adolf Buschhoff proceeded to kill him "with the appropriate knife and an expert hand."[88]

As incriminating evidence, the detective superintendent briefly mentioned the "suspicious behavior" of the Buschhoff family upon hearing of the disappearance and, later, the death of Johann. You will recall from an earlier chapter that Buschhoff visited the Hegmann home on the night of the tragedy and urged Heinrich to be strong for the sake of his wife. More significant in Wolff's eyes, however, was a statement that Mrs. Buschhoff reportedly made to none other than stone cutter Wesendrup the next morning, in which she expressed happiness and relief that the boy had not been found "with her" (*bei ihr*) because of the fact that she was a Jew. "From this statement,"

Wolff allusively interjected, "the thought, which apparently must have moved the Buschhoff family to bring the act to completion, is illuminated." Taken most plainly, the thought that was "illuminated" by Mrs. Buschhoff's communication was the desire not to be discovered. The boy had to be killed so that he could not report what the Jewish family had done to him or so that his unconscious body would not be discovered in their house.[89] On a deeper level, however, Wolff's interest in the woman's words pointed to a different set of associations.

Let us accept for the moment the truthfulness of Wesendrup's account. Mrs. Buschhoff's words recall, uncannily, the fateful encounter between József Scharf and the mother of Eszter Solymosi following her disappearance in Tiszaeszlár. Small events such as these, which came to assume an importance totally out of proportion to their intent at the time, remind one just how dangerous it was to say *anything* in response to the disappearance of a Christian child. Any sentiment that a Jewish resident of Tiszaeszlár or Xanten might have expressed by way of sympathy or support, anxiety or relief, ran the risk of exposing that person to the danger of self-incrimination. What accounted for this communicative trap in the first place, it seems to me, was the knowledge shared by Jewish and Christian neighbors of the ubiquity of the ritual murder accusation, but it was knowledge whose implications for the two communities differed in critical ways. Jews understandably felt the urge to remove themselves from suspicion, but it was this very impulse that rendered them, at times, even more suspicious in the eyes of their neighbors. And *Kriminalkomissar* Wolff, who prided himself on his deductive methods and claimed to be led only by considerations of evidence, apparently could not see that these very deductions emerged in no small measure from a culture of accusation.

On the strength of Wolff's report, District Attorney Baumgard simultaneously ordered the opening of the official judicial investigation against Adolf Buschhoff, his wife Sibilla, and daughter Hermine and their imprisonment in Kleve, the district capital.[90] District judge Brixius, an official of the Kleve court, was given the task of conducting the judicial investigation. At the same time, the Prussian government in Berlin began to take a more active interest in the case, disturbed by the prominence that it was receiving in the national press and concerned that prosecutors and the court in Kleve might be letting matters get out of hand. Indeed, the case was becoming more and more unpredictable. Traveling to Xanten in October and November 1891 to interview witnesses, *Landgerichtsrat* Brixius came to the conclusion that the charges against the Buschhoffs were untenable—the product, in his words, of "child's babble (*Kindergeschwätz*) and fantasy." With the apparent approval of both Baumgard and senior prosecutor Hamm in Cologne, Brixius ordered the release of the prisoners, on 23 December 1891, a move that set off a new storm of protest at home and a tug of war with the Justice Ministry in Berlin, which preferred that the family remain in custody.[91]

With an interest in reopening the formal investigation, the Justice Ministry now sent a representative of its own (Bietsch), together with Baumgard and Hamm, back to Xanten to ascertain the reliability of the central witness against the Buschhoffs (the gardener Mölders). Apparently satisfied that the testimony was credible, at least in its broad outlines if not all of its details, Justice Minister Ludwig von Schelling moved that the investigation be reopened.[92] Berlin also seems to have wanted Buschhoff to be returned to prison, but judge Brixius—still nominally in charge of the investigation—was not likely to comply in the absence of any new evidence against the accused. Brixius's continued involvement in the case was becoming increasingly tenuous, however. He faced accusations in both the local and the national press that he was demonstrating bias *on behalf* of the Jewish suspects, a charge that rested partly on the fact that his son-in-law had been named to Buschhoff's defense team. When Brixius turned to the criminal division of the Justice Ministry for a determination as to whether or not he was fit to continue to serve as investigating magistrate, he may not have been aware that Bietsch had been actively lobbying for his removal. The *Strafkammer* replied to Brixius that it found no reason why he should not continue, but he was forced nevertheless—under the weight of public opinion—to withdraw from the case.[93]

A number of developments converged during the first week of February 1892 to ensure that the state's case against Adolf Buschhoff would go forward. Asked by the state prosecutor to examine one of the butcher's knives that had been found in Buschhoff's possession, district physician Bauer now claimed to have discovered evidence suggesting that it was very likely to have been the murder weapon. The investigation was officially reopened on 6 February 1892, three days before the Prussian House of Deputies opened a formal debate on the Xanten case. Brixius's withdrawal from the investigation had taken effect the previous day.[94] His replacement, Judge Birk, took additional testimony from Bauer but also directed a series of questions to the Royal Medical College in Koblenz, which delivered its report in early April. The public prosecutor issued a formal indictment later that month.

The Kleve Trial

The text of the indictment, issued by Baumgard on 20 April 1892, not only outlined the state's case against Buschhoff and his family in the months leading up to the trial. It also revealed a political strategy that sought to follow a middle course between accommodation to the increasingly vocal calls for prosecution on the basis of the ritual murder accusation and the dismissal of the case against Buschhoff on essentially the same grounds. We know from the archival record—analyzed admirably by Johannes T. Groß—that the decision to bring the case to trial (reversing, after the fact, Brixius's attempts to have the case dismissed) came from the Ministry of Justice in Berlin.[95] Less clear are the motives for insisting that the case go forward or the degree of confidence that the state had in its case. It is certainly possible that the ministry wished to see the case reach a legal conclusion—with or without a conviction—if only to defuse the local and national tensions that had been building steadily for nearly a year. If this were in fact the strategy emanating from Berlin, it would help to explain the prosecution's subsequent behavior over the course of the trial.

The overall approach of the district attorney in the indictment was to accept, in its rough outline, the reconstruction of the crime offered by detective superintendent Wolff while explicitly rejecting some findings and innuendos that suggested or alluded to an argument for Jewish ritual murder. At this stage in the criminal proceedings, Adolf Buschhoff was charged with premeditated murder; his wife, Sibilla, and their daughter, Hermine, with aiding and abetting in the commission of the crime.[96] By the time the trial opened in Kleve in July 1892, Sibilla and Hermine were dropped from the indictment (for reasons that will be explained in this chapter), and the proceedings were directed at Adolf Buschhoff alone. The charge sheet regarded the testimony of Mölders and two of Johann Hegmann's young playmates that the boy was pulled into the Buschhoff house on the morning of 29 June by "an arm" as compelling. It noted that this was the last time that Johann was seen before his body was discovered that evening and suggested that it was up to the Buschhoffs to account for the boy's whereabouts after ten o'clock that morning.[97]

Also "weighing heavily" (to quote from the language of the indictment) against Buschhoff and family was the testimony of the neighbor Küppers, who claimed to have walked past the slaughterhouse alongside the Buschhoff home (by way of the courtyard) and to have seen and heard—through the open door—several men talking. It was not the presence of people conversing that aroused suspicion but the fact that the door was open, because Buschhoff had apparently nailed it shut the previous Friday evening, with the help of a neighbor, in order to prevent his employee Wesendrup—who had threatened Buschhoff before the weekend that he would not be enjoying "any more *shabbeses*"—from entering the house. Finally, there was the testimony of the carpenter Hermann Brands: he claimed to have run into Buschhoff on Klevestraße, coming from Kirchstraße, at about 10:30 a.m., moving very fast, acting strangely, trying to avoid Brands, and saying, finally, that he was on his way home.[98]

It was Wolff's report that provided the narrative structure to the indictment. It also suggested a likely motive for the crime (which, Baumgard acknowledged, was not proved): a hastily constructed effort to conceal another misdeed, the beating of the boy in their own home. The indictment repeated the account concerning damage to some gravestones that Buschhoff had been working on, as well as Wolff's surmise that the Hegmann boy had been pulled into the house in order to be "disciplined," in the course of which he was subjected to a beating and may have lost consciousness. Terrified that he might wake up and scream for help or, worse yet, be discovered unconscious in their home, the family moved the boy to the Küppers's barn, where, sometime later, Adolf Buschhoff finished the deed.[99] Baumgard also consciously weighed in on the conflict among the various forensic medical opinions that were delivered in the course of the investigation. He rejected out of hand the first physician's contention that the amount of blood on hand at the site of the discovery of the body was somehow "insufficient," a suggestion that the murder had been committed somewhere else and the body then moved to the barn. He also dismissed—in line with the special commission of the Royal Medical College in Koblenz—the contention that the boy had been killed by means of a kosher butcher's cut.

The committee of experts in Koblenz, it turns out, had taken its charge quite seriously. In order to answer whether or not the wound on the boy's neck corresponded to the method of slaughtering employed by Jewish *shoḥetim* (ignoring the obvious fact that ritual slaughtering was only employed on animals fit for consumption), the commission decided actually to learn about the procedure, and the response that it delivered was both sophisticated and technical. The wound on the victim, the medical experts concluded, was *not* to be identified as a "so-called slaughterers cut, as it is practiced in the Jewish slaughtering of animals." Johann Hegmann's killer in fact violated Jewish practice because the cut was not positioned *below*, but rather on the upper edge of, the larynx; because it had not cut through the trachea and gullet but only the pharynx; because the knife had not been held at a right angle to the front of neck, and the neck was not cut through evenly on both sides; and, finally, because the cut was executed from front to back and under the clothing of the child.[100]

Baumgard invoked the report of the Koblenz medical faculty to the extent that it undergirded the state's rejection of a theory of ritual murder, but he did not view it as having exonerated the accused. The indictment in fact put great stress on the fact that Buschhoff's profession as a butcher and ritual slaughterer—and the fact that "various very large and sharp slaughtering, and ritual slaughtering, knives" were found in his possession—constituted important circumstantial evidence against him. Even the medical commission had arrived at the conclusion that "a sharp-cutting, knife-like, not particularly small instrument must have been used, and that the wound could have been caused by any of the knives found in Buschhoff's possession."[101] On the eve of the Kleve trial, the state seems to have wanted to "have it both ways," to reject popular claims that a Jew had committed a ritual murder while emphasizing the connection between this killing and the implements of kosher slaughtering, as well as to adopt the "just the facts" attitude of detective superintendent Wolff but to enhance those facts with powerful symbolic allusion.

The trial against Adolf Buschhoff on the charge of premeditated murder was held in the criminal division (*Schwurgericht*) of the district court in Kleve from 4 to 14 July 1892. Unsurprisingly, public interest in the proceedings was enormous: the trial was held in a courtroom that accommodated 150 people, and every seat was taken. By the end of the first week, soldiers had to clear a passage in the crowd of onlookers in order for the attorneys, judges, and members of the jury to make their way into the building. Many journalists from within the German Empire and abroad covered the trial daily; of these, however, only sixteen were allotted places inside the courtroom. Three judges and twelve jurors ultimately heard testimony from 164 witnesses over eight and a half days, while the last day and a half were taken up with closing statements by the prosecution and the defense (there were five addresses in all), instructions to the jury by the presiding judge, and the jury's deliberation and verdict. Reflecting the seriousness of the case in the eyes of the Ministry of Justice, the prosecution was conducted by two men: the *Oberstaatsanwalt* from Cologne, Hamm, and the Kleve district attorney, Baumgard. A team of three attorneys headed up the defense.[102]

In determining to go forward with the trial, the Kleve court (presided over by district court director Kluth) decided to dismiss the charges against Sibilla and Hermine Buschhoff for lack of actual, incriminating evidence against them.[103] It seems clear that there was also some doubt in the mind of the court as to the strength of the case against Buschhoff himself, but the judges and prosecutors decided to move the case to trial in any event. Judge Kluth, writing to the president of the superior court in Cologne at the close of the trial, explained that he felt it was in the interest of the public at large—as well of Buschhoff—to give the case a full and open hearing. Only a public trial had any hope of silencing the angry voices that were complaining of a coverup of Jewish crimes.[104] Offered as justification after the fact, Kluth's argument does exude a certain self-righteousness. But, when read in conjunction with the curious behavior of the prosecution and the rapid verdict of not guilty that the jury delivered, the court's special pleading deserves at least some suspension of disbelief.

In their lengthy and impassioned closing remarks, Hamm and Baumgard aggressively attacked any suggestion that the death of Johann Hegmann involved a ritual murder. The chief prosecutor bemoaned the fact that the legal case against Buschhoff had been forced to play out—long before the trial—in an atmosphere of political agitation and provocation, and he expressed dismay that the guilt of the accused had already been proclaimed in the press. Even at this late point in the trial, he noted, when the court was trying to determine the relative weight of incriminating and exculpatory evidence, the agitation had not stopped; he urged the jury not to allow itself to be influenced by the noise around it.[105] Hamm was extremely critical of the local doctor, Steiner, for his comment that there was too little blood at the site where the body lay. Stressing more than once that Steiner's contention had been definitively refuted by the autopsy of the following day and the later report of the Koblenz medical commission, Hamm expressed strong displeasure at Steiner's careless remark to the contrary, because it had played a crucial role in the formation of the local knowledge of ritual murder. In the prosecutor's words, "The completely mistaken popular understanding (*die ganz irrtümliche Volks-Instruktion*) on the spot rested on an error: they believed—led on by the statement of Dr. Steiner—that not all of the blood was there." To the contrary, what is certain, Hamm underscored, is this: "The place where the body was discovered is the scene of the crime (*der Fundort ist der Tatort*). I'll say it again: The scene of the crime is incontrovertibly certain."[106]

Of course, Hamm and Baumgard went well beyond denying the theory of ritual murder in this crime. Breaking with the state's position in the indictment (which Baumgard himself had written), the prosecution essentially abandoned detective superintendent Wolff's reconstruction of the crime and concluded that Adolf Buschhoff had not killed—could not have killed—Johann Hegmann. The prosecutors urged the jury to acquit. In making his case, Hamm in part followed the well-trodden path of reviewing the physical evidence and the key pieces of testimony, but he also felt that he needed to explain why the state had not simply followed the earlier recommendation of Judge Brixius and dismissed the charges against Buschhoff and, also, why the prosecution no longer considered the testimony of Mölders (who claimed to have seen the boy being pulled into the Buschhoff home) to be credible.

It was on the basis of a site investigation to the town that Brixius originally had come to the conclusion that Mölder could not have seen what he claimed to have seen and so dismissed the testimony as impossible. Hamm explained to the jury that, in his and Baumgard's view, Brixius had acted too hastily. Mölders's testimony had been offered in good faith, they argued, and while it may have been mistaken in some of its details, it reflected what the witness genuinely thought he saw.[107] Mölders's good-faith testimony alone, Hamm submitted, justified the original arrest and detention of the defendant and also justified his being put on trial.[108] Ultimately, however, Mölders had indeed been mistaken. Buschhoff could not have pulled the boy into the house around 10 a.m. on the date in question because he had, as it turned out, a solid alibi. He was in the house at the time discussing business matters with two individuals—Kock and Prang—who testified to this fact during the trial. In Hamm's view, it was impossible to believe that the boy could have been in the house during this time against his will and that no one would have heard him struggling or crying out. Moreover, all of Buschhoff's movements in the morning in question were accounted for.[109] "Where he was every moment of that morning has been clearly demonstrated," Hamm concluded. Thus, Mölders saw some kind of pulling in of a child at the time, but it could not have been the Buschhoff's house into which the child was pulled. I come now to the conclusion: It has been proven that Buschhoff could not have committed the crime, and the prosecutor's office must make the recommendation that the defendant be found not guilty."[110]

Baumgard followed with a summation of his own, which focused in greater detail on the whole range of testimony that was heard at the trial. "You will recall," he said on day ten of the trial, as he resumed his remarks from the previous afternoon, "that, in the end, we heard testimony from witnesses from all over (*von allen Ecken und Kanten*) whom we called to the stand because they had something suspicious to report." Baumgard painstakingly reviewed each incriminating statement, demonstrating "that none of these things, in and of themselves, could be construed as suspicious but were, rather, very natural responses." Additionally, some of the suspicions were simply not believable.[111] At the end of his lengthy summation, Baumgard concluded, "Gentlemen, here you have been presented the whereabouts of the entire Buschhoff family during Saints Peter and Paul's Day on the 29th of June. I must say that in my long career as a criminal prosecutor I have never had a single case in which a clearer, more coherent proof has been put forward than this one that the accused could not have committed the crime."[112] The jury—composed of twelve Christian males and headed by a count—deliberated for an hour and a half before giving its verdict. On the single question of whether Adolf Buschhoff was guilty of the premeditated murder of Johann Hegmann, it answered no. Buschhoff was declared a free man, the costs of the trial to be borne by the state. According to some reports, the reading of the verdict was followed by shouts of "bravo" from spectators in the courtroom.[113]

Conclusion: The Rules of the Game

The Nyíregyháza and Kleve proceedings—like all trials, perhaps—comprised an amalgam of disparate elements: the state's theory of the crime; testimony from numerous witnesses, often contradictory and sometimes directly at odds with testimony given during the criminal investigation; the opinions of expert witnesses; and physical evidence and struggles over its interpretation. These features yielded an at times unwieldy combination of empirical measurement, story, and informed analysis. What is most significant about these trials, however—and those that would follow in the 1890s and 1900s—are the epistemological and procedural structures within which they were required to operate.

These cultural and intellectual boundaries differed markedly from those obtained in medieval and early modern proceedings. Gavin Langmuir's studies of the ritual murder accusations in Norwich and Lincoln in the mid-twelfth and mid-thirteenth centuries, respectively, have underscored both the psychological and theological functions of this phenomenon in the context of religious doubts over the nature and efficacy of the Eucharist.[114] R. Po-chia Hsia's work on the spate of ritual murder trials that erupted in the Holy Roman Empire during the last third of the fifteenth and the first half of the sixteenth centuries has showcased both the cultural-religious effects of ritual murder discourse—in which the lessons of Christian sacrifice and salvific redemption were vindicated—and the political imperatives that propelled these cases—characterized mainly by the consolidation of urban unity and power at the expense of imperial control.[115]

But the accusations, trials, and expulsions that occurred in cities and towns in late medieval Germany were eventually overtaken by the cultural and institutional challenges put up by the Protestant Reformation. To be sure, isolated criminal cases on the charge of ritual murder continued to appear in Central and Western Europe. In the Polish-Lithuanian Commonwealth, meanwhile, trials against Jews for ritual murder—a postmedieval phenomenon—flourished in the seventeenth and eighteenth centuries in conjunction with the Counter-Reformation.[116] For the most part, however, this particular understanding of Jewish criminality and danger was increasingly relegated to the shadows of polite discourse, beyond the regular institutional practices of the state. When ritual murder trials reappeared in Central Europe in the late nineteenth and early twentieth centuries, they could never be articulated again in pre-Reformation language and symbols. Prosecutors, magistrates, trial judges, police investigators, and even journalists and politicians shared an implicit understanding that a new universe of knowledge was in place, in which academic experts and practitioners of science defined the boundaries—linguistic and conceptual—of plausible argument and were to be accorded deference. This does not mean that popular beliefs and understandings of Jewish ritual murder suddenly ceased to be disseminated or no longer influenced courtroom proceedings, or that zealous investigators and prosecutors did not pursue their cases armed with a priori assumptions about likely perpetrators and their motives. But cultural material, psychological predisposition, and even narrative accounts built upon eyewitness testimony would never suffice to move the state to indict or a jury, or panel of judges, to convict. Whatever nonrational thinking or prejudices may have accompanied it, the modern ritual murder trial was to be structured by powerful, if implicit, rules of expression and authority: it could only be articulated through the epistemological categories and idioms of a culture that understood itself to be both rational and scientific.

What commands our attention, then, in the Tiszaeszlár and Xanten cases are the processes whereby ritual murder discourse bended—as it were—to the discipline of modernity, as exemplified by the structures and rules of legal procedure, parliamentary politics, mass circulation journalism, criminology, medicine, and forensic science. In this context, Tiszaeszlár represents *a moment of transition to the modern ritual murder trial*. Up until the discovery of the Tiszadada corpse—that is, for a period of eleven weeks—the case for Jewish "ritual murder" was constructed out of narrative fragments and cultural memories that conformed to the basic patterns of traditional ritual murder discourse. These attitudes also informed the state's theory of the case even as they reverberated in coffee shops and bars, in the headlines of newspapers hawked on the street, and in the halls of parliament. But in seeking to establish the *corpus delicti*, the traditional language of ritual murder struggled—and eventually failed—to keep up with the interventions of physicians, pathologists, and medical faculties and with the scalpels, micrometers, microscopes, and scientific prestige that they wielded. The presumptive superiority of scientific observation and measurement over traditional social knowledge was strong enough to raise the single question of the identity of the corpse to a level of supreme importance. If the body was that of Eszter, the game was over.

In the Xanten case, medical experts oversaw and structured the terms of the criminal investigation from its earliest stages, although from at least three different angles or levels of expertise, reflected in successively distant places of remove from the town itself. Not surprisingly, perhaps, the closer the medical practitioners themselves were physically to the social and cultural universe of the town of Xanten, the more susceptible their analyses were to the cultural assumptions that supported accusations of Jewish ritual murder, and the more closely their "science" appeared to accommodate this particular construction of Jewish criminality. At the same time, the self-conscious rationality and bureaucratic esprit of various regional and national officials—from Berlin detectives to judge magistrates to public prosecutors—encroached further on the state's ability—or even its willingness—to prosecute these murders or disappearances as cases of ritual murder.

True, when a detective superintendent was dispatched to Xanten from Berlin, he upset the expectations of some by becoming convinced of Adolph Buschhoff's guilt. Nevertheless, the big-city detective flatly rejected any scenario of a ritual crime, and his own theory of the murder was itself eventually rejected by the state's attorneys, who had become convinced that Buschhoff could not have murdered Johann Hegmann. Alarmingly, as we shall see, in the Polná case, Leopold Hilsner would not enjoy this kind of support from the prosecutor and would in fact be convicted of aggravated murder both in 1899 and in his retrial in 1900. But even this gloomy outcome emerged at the end of a long legal contest over forensic analyses and judgments, the discursive rules for which had been established over the previous two decades. Most Jewish defendants eventually were freed while a few languished in prison—all, however, under the aura of science.

Chapter 4

The Hilsner Affair

I was so used to the superstition regarding Christian blood that whenever I happened to come across a Jew—I never got close to one on purpose—I used to look at his fingers to see if there was any blood on them. I was in the habit of doing this stupid thing for a long time.

—T. G. Masaryk, "Náš pan Fixl" (Our Little Mr. Fox) in *Dvě povídky* (Prague, 1930)

And now this conclusion: what was the motive of the murder? The ritual murder legend has a powerful and persistent hold on all of public opinion. You fight believing it, you cannot admit that, at the end of the nineteenth century, a race exists whose religion demands, or allows, murder for religious ends. You fight believing it, but the strength and persuasive force of circumstances is overwhelming. Never up 'till now has all the evidence testified [so clearly] for ritual murder. If ritual murder exists, then Polná is a case in point.

—*Vražda v Polné. Otisk článků "Radikálních Listů"* ("Murder in Polná"; reprint of articles from *Radikální Listy*)

I did not write my pamphlet in order to defend Hilsner but to defend Christians from superstition. It pained me that such a dark superstition was possible—admittedly on the basis of views disseminated by physicians and other authorities. I am convinced that I did the right thing, and if ever in my life I have been satisfied with something, certain about my motives, it is this case.

—T. G. Masaryk, speech to the Austrian parliament, 5 December 1907

A Momentum of Growing Expectation: Radical Politics, Economic Nationalism, and Ritual Murder in the Bohemian Lands

The 1890s in the Bohemian lands were marked politically by the ascendancy of the National Liberal, or Young Czech, Party in both the provincial and imperial parliaments but also by challenges to national liberal hegemony on the part of agrarian, Catholic, and radical nationalist constituencies. Expressions of economic nationalism in the form of boycott campaigns directed at both German and Jewish businesses often accompanied the growing challenges to the political status quo.[1] Proponents of economic nationalism in the Czech political camp—many of whom came from the ranks of the Young Czech Party, some from more radical orientations—argued that as long as ethnic Germans occupied a dominant economic position in the country, the political balance of power would never shift in favor of the more numerous, but politically disadvantaged, Czechs. For Czechs to realize the vision of political and cultural autonomy cherished by their national spokespersons, they would have to conquer the marketplace.[2]

In theory, all "Germans" could be targeted for commercial boycott; Jews, however, whose national allegiance could not be measured with certainty, seemed to attract particularly harsh criticism. In fact, they performed a dual role, paralleling the split function of the boycott movement itself. Ostensibly viewed as undifferentiated supporters of German hegemony, Jews constituted a compact, accessible, and politically vulnerable economic target—a reasonable facsimile of Austrian Germans in general, perhaps. But the boycott also worked as a cultural ban, ostracizing from the nation elements that were considered ethnically indistinct, uncertain, or dangerous. The act of ostracism, then, can also be seen as an effort to define, to clarify the boundaries of community, to remove doubt.[3]

In this context, discussions of Jewish ritual murder—which took place with ever greater frequency in the 1890s in newspapers and pamphlets, on street corners and pubs—connected with both the well-worn, liberal nationalist critique of German Jewish acculturation and the more recent political-economic critique of German hegemony and Czech dependency to produce a volatile compound whose repercussions included local riots, extensive destruction of property, and the continued exodus of Jews from the small towns and villages of the Czech countryside.[4] The themes of economic nationalism, linguistic competition, and antisemitism combined frequently in the writings of provincial newspapers; often such articles landed their editors in court and, occasionally, in jail. The editors of two papers that were allied for a time with the Young Czech Party, *Polaban* and *Kolínské listy*, made frequent appearances before a judge and prosecutor at the Kutná Hora/Kuttenberg regional court. *Polaban*'s editor Václav Nevídek was forced to appear on at least six occasions in 1885 alone because of articles that agitated against Jews, Germans, the army, and the state.[5] *Kolínské listy*'s editor, Václav Řezníček, was brought to trial in July 1886 on the charge of making antisemitic statements, which in post-1867 Austria violated the law, as it denigrated an established religion. At issue was an article entitled "The Jews and Our National Struggle," whose characterization of the Jews of Bohemia as "the most fanatic opponents of the Czech nation" constituted, in the opinion of the court, "a general inclination to violate public peace and order."[6]

Such cases were followed by a whole series of prosecutions against *Kolínské listy* and *Polaban* that lasted well into the next decade. By 1891 and 1892, editors for the two papers were making court appearances seemingly every other month, occasionally for circulating articles that had already been confiscated. This pattern continued through much of the 1890s as mass-circulation newspapers, books, and pamphlets in the Bohemian lands published an ongoing stream of accounts of alleged ritual murders. During these years, the docket of the Prague Criminal Court was often taken up with appearances by the editor of *České zájmy* (*Czech Interests*)—Jaromír Hušek—and those of other newspapers, who were cited for incitement, disturbance of the peace, and defamation.[7] In the spring and summer of 1891, word of a ritual murder that was said to have taken place on the Greek island of Corfu was widely reported. The rumors quickly proved to be false—the apparent victim in question had in fact been Jewish—but not before extensive rioting had taken place on the island.[8] Radical Czech newspapers covered the events in Corfu with crude and highly sensationalized reporting. A front-page story in the 23 May 1891 edition of *Naše zájmy* (*Our Interests*)—also edited by Hušek—printed under the banner headline "Murder of a Christian Girl in Corfu," was punctuated with epithets such as "Yid synagogue" (židáčká synagoga) and "Yid" (židák). Purportedly based on the testimony of a Czech sailor from Dalmatia, the account testified, according to the editor's introductory remarks, to "the danger of talmudic teaching and of the entire Jewish nation."[9] The Xanten affair followed closely thereafter, quickly surpassing both Corfu and Tiszaeszlár in notoriety and inspiring a small cottage industry of antisemitic and propagandistic literature. The events in Xanten and Kleve seem also to have had a hand in producing a temporary spike in the number of *local* ritual murder accusations that appeared at the same time in the Czech press.

On the heels of the Kleve trial, a Viennese priest by the name of Josef Deckert published a tract in 1893 that altered the tenor of popular antisemitic literature by moving the discourse surprisingly close to the genre of critical historiography. The work in question, *A Ritual Murder: Documentarily Proven*, was widely distributed throughout Bohemia and Moravia until finally confiscated by the state. Playing the role of historian—pious, to be sure, but historian nonetheless—Deckert countered enlightened dismissals of Jewish ritual murder by appealing to "the archive," as it were—that is, what he claimed to be irrefutable legal and historical evidence.[10] The brochure thus comprised a self-consciously modern defense of the ritual murder accusation. Deckert confronted the charge that the ritual murder accusation was irrational by arguing for the historicity of memorialized events. He upheld the believability of the accusation, in its traditional forms, by appealing to history as a scientific discipline while unquestioningly accepting the sources on which it was built.

In Deckert's view, the case of Simon of Trent (1475)—for whose death six Jews were burned at the stake and two strangled (after converting to Christianity)—provided the most direct, "irrefutable," historical and legal evidence of the Jewish propensity toward this type of criminal behavior.[11] Alternatively quoting from and paraphrasing the interrogation record of the Trent investigation and trial, Deckert characterized the denials of various Jewish defendants as "stubborn lies" but accepted at face value the confessions extracted by means of torture. He thus put forward as a plausible motive for the crime the explanation offered by one defendant: that the dried blood of the Christian child was applied as a powder to heal the circumcision wounds of Jewish boys.[12] When Deckert deviated from his historicist mission to quote at length from the recollections of the court physician Johannes Tiberinus, he revealed what he understood to be the theological and cultural truth that lay at the heart of his enterprise as well as its political implications.

> See here, my fellow Christian, how once again Jesus is crucified between two thieves. See what the Jews would do if they had power over Christians. The glorious, innocent martyr, Simon, hardly weaned from the mother's breast and not yet able to speak, has been crucified by the Jews as an insult to our faith. Listen, you who allow so cruel a race [*eine so grausame Menschenrasse*] to be

tolerated in your cities, how daily they curse the holy Eucharist and the saintly Virgin Mary, uttering scandalous, sinful words, which they follow with expressions of open contempt for the Roman Church.[13]

In the murder of Simon, then, the Jews of Trent not only reenacted the crucifixion of Christ, not only added to their scandalous treatment of the Eucharist and the Virgin Mary, but also were also issuing a warning as to what Christians might expect if the Jews were ever allowed to exercise power in their midst. In his brief conclusion to the tract, Deckert returned to his earlier stance as naive observer of empirical reality. Was this murder in fact a ritual murder, he asked? The question, of course, was rhetorical. When one acknowledged the timing of the act (on the eve of the holiday of Passover), its location (the synagogue), the circumstances under which it was carried out, and the purposes to which the blood of the child was put, what other conclusion could one draw? "One has to admit that this was, indeed, a ritual murder; otherwise, I would not know what meaning to attach to the term." Echoing the ostensibly scholarly opinion offered a decade earlier by August Rohling, Deckert willingly conceded that no explicit, written law of the Talmud commands Jews to commit such a crime. "Rather, it is a question . . . of a secret teaching transmitted orally by the 'sages' of the Jewish people, the traces of which are frequently revealed in the trial records." Most Jews, Deckert conceded—Orthodox as well as Reform, Hasidic Jews as well as Karaites—may know nothing of this esoteric teaching. But those who are guilty of this kind of crime must be called to account.[14]

While Deckert claimed to be acting merely as an honest transmitter of the empirical record, his historical journalism worked precisely to spread the suspicion of guilt by association, and Habsburg officials in Bohemia and Moravia were justly concerned about its impact on public order.[15] Tensions had already been high in the summer of 1892 in places like Kojetín, in Moravia, where the disappearance of a Christian servant employed by a Jewish family gave rise to a rumor that she had been murdered for religious purposes. The town's Jews were physically mistreated as a result, and windows in many Jewish homes were smashed, but apparently, when the girl's body turned up in the river without any marks of violence on it, relations returned to normal.[16]

A more serious case of rumored kidnapping and ritual murder surfaced in the Bohemian city of Kolín in March and April 1893. This, too, involved the disappearance of a young, Czech, female servant who had worked for a Jewish employer, and elements of the case bore an eerie resemblance to those of Tiszaeszlár.[17] According to the report of the district captain (*okresní hejtman*), the victim—Marie Havlinová, identified in this report only by the last name—had "disappeared without a trace" while in the service of a Jew named Reitler. Although the girl's aunt had testified to the fact that Havlinová had been contemplating suicide, the official asked the public prosecutor in Kutná Hora to initiate a criminal investigation, because the word on the street—spread largely by the newspaper *Polaban*, at the time the mouthpiece of the Progressive Party in Kolín—was that this was a case of a "Jewish ritual murder." The judicial investigation, however, was hampered by the absence of physical evidence of an abduction, suicide, or murder. When the body of a young woman eventually was pulled from the river, it was identified as that of the missing girl by her aunt. News of the discovery resulted in renewed popular excitement; again, there was talk of Jewish ritual murder; again, the newspaper *Polaban* took a leading role in spreading this interpretation.[18] The district captain wished to report, however, that a medical examination of the body had demonstrated the rumors to be groundless; the girl had taken her own life.[19]

The following day, the official in Kolín sent another dispatch to Prague. We now learn that the servant girl had been missing for six weeks before the body was recovered and that, unfortunately, the optimism of the previous day had been unwarranted. Popular demonstrations had taken place in response to rumors that the medical team that examined the corpse had found stab wounds on the body! Mobs gathered in the city's Jewish quarter, where they were joined by unemployed textile workers. Fearing that rioting could take place in the vicinity of the Ringplatz, the local police called in reinforcements from the Gendarmerie, and eventually the crowds were dispersed. The official expressed concern that similar disturbances might take place during the girl's funeral and in the nights ahead, and indeed, the telegram that he sent on the third day indicated that rioting had in fact taken place.[20] Here, then, was a case in which local officials confirmed rather than denied that the body of the young woman pulled from the water was that of the missing Marie Havlínová and that she had *not* been the victim of a violent death, yet these alert responses did not in the end prevent continued agitation and, eventually, rioting. Did the message—the results of the medical examination—not get through to the residents of the city? Did the counterfactual narrative of a ritual killing compete, perhaps, with the official version of events and, in the short term, prevail? In this overheated atmosphere, conspiratorial thinking may actually have held greater appeal in the popular imagination than government assurances to the contrary.[21]

Similar allegations of kidnapping and ritual murder played out in Mladá Boleslav and Nové Benátky. On one level, they can perhaps be regarded as "nonevents." In combination with the heightening of national tensions and the bellicose rhetoric of the economic boycott movement, however, such stories helped to produce what might best be described as an atmosphere of growing expectation. Sooner or later, the presumed Jewish propensity to "ritual murder" would be uncovered in the Bohemian lands. And, in the context of increasing political radicalization, in which ethnic mobilization, economic nationalism, and antisemitic symbol and rhetoric fed off one another, even false reports of Jewish ritual murder may have enhanced the plausibility of the accusation itself.[22]

In the three years leading up to the first arrest and trial of Leopold Hilsner of Polná, the tensions that swirled around issues of electoral politics, language choice, economic power, and sovereignty (Bohemian state rights) reached a feverish peak. The first step in this acceleration concerned electoral politics. In 1896, the Austrian prime minister, Count Kazimierz Badeni, met growing demands to expand the vote by creating a fifth electoral curia, which now gave the franchise to all males over the age of twenty-four. In the runup to the imperial elections, scheduled for March 1897, the Young Czech Party—particularly its more radical wing—competed for the votes of newly enfranchised shopkeepers, artisans, and workers with the Christian Social, Social Democratic, and Progressive Parties, adopting in the process increasingly antisemitic positions.[23]

In Prague, the party nominated Václav Březnovský, a person popular with the lower middle classes but also an outspoken antisemite, to be their candidate for several districts in the fifth curia, including the heavily Jewish quarter of Josefov. Jews, as a result—particularly Jews sympathetic to Czech nationalism—faced a difficult political choice: Březnovský; the clerical candidate, Father Josef Šimon (himself fiercely anti-Jewish); or Karel Dědič, a socialist.[24] Even before the elections were completed, Czech newspapers—liberal, Catholic, and radical—were accusing Bohemian Jews of betraying the nation, voting as a bloc for the Social Democrats. Political meetings during the electoral campaign served as forums for the expression of popular distrust of the national loyalties of Jewish constituents. During one election meeting in Prague-Smíchov, the Social Democratic candidate, Alfréd Meissner, urged the audience to remember that Social Democrats, too, were Czechs, only to be answered by a member of the audience, “From the Jordan River.” When Meissner called upon those gathered not to vote for Young Czech candidates, he was met with the call, “A Jew, then.”[25]

Jewish voters were indeed riven by the sudden disappearance of political options. At a meeting of the Czech Jewish Political Union (Politická jednota českožidovksá), which normally aligned with the Young Czechs, Jakub Scharf, a Jewish Young Czech parliamentarian, put on a brave face and defended Březnovský to the 150 or so people in attendance. But others spoke in favor of the Social Democratic candidate, Dědič. Ultimately, the Union decided to leave the choice of whom to support in the fifth curia to its individual members, but the mood of the assembly seemed to have soured on the Young Czechs.[26] Even the more well-to-do German Jewish middle class was preparing to throw in its lot with the Social Democrats. The *Israelitische Gemeindezeitung*, mouthpiece of the German-oriented Centralverein zur Pflege jüdischer Angelegenheiten, raised the possibility in these words: “For the time being we will not discuss the economic program of Social Democracy. Every true liberal, however, can subscribe to its political program; and besides, ‘The enemies of my enemies are my friends!’”[27]

On the day of the fifth curia elections in Prague, *Národní listy*, allied closely with the Young Czechs, published a front-page editorial entitled “Jews in Our National Society,” expressing anger at Jewish support for Social Democracy.

> The Jews repay our people with a bad coin for seeing in them fully equal fellow citizens, for not excluding them from our public life, not despising them or persecuting them as is done—by Germans. . . . If the adherents of Marx and Lasalle, enemies of big business, enemies of the present individualistic production, of the present social system, manage to gain a victory in one of the Czech electoral districts, it would not be a victory for the Social Democratic Party but for Jewish Social Democracy.[28]

In most areas of Bohemia, the Young Czechs did exceptionally well in the elections. In the controversial Prague election, Březnovský, too, was victorious, but only after the second round.

Shortly following the 1897 elections, the Badeni government issued new regulations for Bohemia and Moravia regarding language use in the inner workings of government offices and the courts. The Czech language already enjoyed formal equality with German, and citizens could engage with government officials in either language; the new regulations now required most civil servants in Bohemia and Moravia to be able to conduct business in both German and Czech. Those who were not already bilingual—mainly German speakers—were given a deadline of three years to bring their language abilities up to par.[29] German parties in the Reichsrat responded immediately by introducing emergency legislation to have the regulations repealed and, when that failed, instigating a policy of obstruction. Raucous demonstrations and even fistfights broke out in the lower chamber; public protests were mounted in Vienna and in the predominantly German border regions of Bohemia and Moravia, where riots against Czechs were also reported. As Michal Frankl observes, reports of violence against Czechs in the spring and summer of 1897 contributed to the radicalization of Czech nationalist rhetoric, which now began to call for a linguistic cleansing of Czech regions, including the removal of bilingual signs above stores and businesses and even the refusal to provide restaurant customers with menus in German. Political gatherings in Prague heard calls for the exclusive use of the Czech language in stores, restaurants, and government offices. Národní obrana, a national self-defense league, sent letters to all Jewish religious communities in the Czech regions of Bohemia calling upon them to abolish any remaining German-language schools and to "give up their Teutonism in public life."[30]

In the face of entrenched opposition to his reforms, Badeni resigned as prime minister on 28 November 1897. Now the tables were turned as German politicians, students, and tradespeople organized parades and celebratory gatherings, and Czechs counterdemonstrated. Serious riots broke out in Prague on 29 November, triggered by a procession of jubilant German university students through Wenceslas Square, a physical confrontation between a German Jewish and a Czech student, and the subsequent attack on the Jewish student by a gathering crowd. Czech counterdemonstrations continued the following day, many of which now directed their attention at German and Jewish homes and businesses—stores, coffeehouses, theaters, synagogues, and private houses. By the end of the day on 30 November and into the next, the demonstrations had degenerated into a full-scale anti-Jewish riot—a *pogrom*, if you will; many of the hardest hit were in fact Czech-speaking Jews, who tended not to live in the city's more fashionable and better policed neighborhoods.[31] Finally, on 2 December, the government declared martial law.

The "December Storm," as it came to be known, did not result in the loss of life, but it did have a traumatic effect on Czech Jewish political culture. The carefully constructed plans and cherished hopes of countless Czech-speaking Jews lay strewn along the sidewalks of Prague and tens of smaller communities together with the shards of glass and broken furniture from Jewish homes and shops. Predictably, the national liberal press did nothing to soften the blow. *Národní listy* reminded its readers that the Prague disturbances had been precipitated by German and Jewish provocations, that the coffeehouses from which German students had taunted the Czech population were mainly frequented by Jews, and that "Semitic" faces could be seen through the doors of these establishments.[32] Among Jewish observers, the more charitably inclined could not help but conclude that Czech politicians and institutions had abandoned them in their hour of need. The less sanguine feared much worse.

* * *

In a context of intense political pressure and intimidation, what role, one might ask, did noisy discussions of Jewish ritual murder play? On one level, they functioned to announce, locate, and exemplify the overarching theme of "Jewish danger" in postemancipation Bohemia and Moravia. News of the ritual killing of helpless Czech girls and young women may have provided commentary on contemporary social crises, including sexual crime, female suicide, and the breakdown of social cohesion in small towns, but it also diverted attention from those very real issues by substituting preconceived narratives based on older, received traditions. Stories of ritual murder also functioned as an indictment of the role that Jews purportedly played in the national conflict between Czechs and Germans. The largely indeterminate position of Jews in the national landscape, the fact that they were not easily legible as clearly German or clearly Czech—indeed their very bilingualism—produced among some the suspicion that Jews were unreliable partners in the national struggle. This judgment now merged with new warnings about Jews and ritual killings—thus conflating otherwise discrete blocks of social knowledge—to produce a mixture in which one set of symbolic associations tended to confirm the validity of the other.[33]

Reproducing Ritual Murder

By this point in our study, narratives of individual cases—disappearance, worried family, physical searches for evidence of a crime, discovery (or nondiscovery) of a corpse—must begin to appear repetitive, variations on a common and well-established pattern. Polná comes near the end of almost two decades of precedents, of the accumulation of narrative techniques and symbolic elements, and of rousing political agitation. Thus, I should like to change my own strategy in presenting the details of the case, stepping back, as it were, to underscore features that it shared with earlier investigations and trials as well as significant points of divergence. In Polná, as in Tiszaeszlár and Xanten, the case began with a missing person in a small-town or village setting, although here the missing family member was neither the classic young boy nor a preadolescent girl but a nineteen-year-old woman named Anežka Hrůzová. As in the Hungarian case, the victim lived with her widowed mother (although also with an older brother), and she had been sent to work at the home of another person when she went missing. In all three cases, Jews and Christians lived literally side-by-side, with no physical and few social or economic barriers separating them. In Polná, many Jews continued to live, work, and pray on the streets of what had been in the seventeenth and eighteenth centuries an informal ghetto, but they did so now alongside numerous Christian neighbors, in the words of one historian, "not particularly loved and not particularly hated—not yet."[34]

The Polná case also stands out because of the suspicious behavior displayed by the Hrůza family itself in connection with Anežka's disappearance. On the morning of 29 March 1899, the nineteen-year-old walked the three and a half kilometers from her home in the small Czech village of Malá Věžnice to the neighboring town of Polná, using a path that went alongside the Březina woods, much as she had done nearly every day that month. She recently had taken on work as an assistant to a seamstress, Blandina Prchalová, whose house stood adjacent to Polná's Jewish quarter, in fact next door to the Jewish school. Anežka failed to return home on the evening of 29 March to a cottage that she shared with her widowed mother Marie and her older brother Jan, but it would not be until 31 March (which coincided in 1899 with Good Friday in the Catholic calendar) that Marie Hrůzová decided to contact the authorities. Although Anežka's mother would later testify that her daughter had never before stayed away from home overnight, she made no effort to locate her for a full day and a half.[35]

Eventually, Marie Hrůzová took the same walk to Polná that her daughter had taken so frequently to inquire after her whereabouts. Marie first approached the seamstress, Mrs. Prchalová. According to later testimony, the first thing that Anežka's mother inquired about was the basket that her daughter had been carrying, not Anežka herself. When the employer explained that the young woman had left work at the normal time the previous Wednesday afternoon and had not returned for work the following day, Marie Hrůzová finally paid a visit to the local police constable, Josef Klenovec. True to historical pattern, upon listening to the mother's story, Klenovec's first reaction was skepticism. Why had the mother waited almost two days to report the missing daughter? Moreover, when she did finally present herself to the police, she appeared to be sporting a black eye, suggesting violence in the household. He immediately suspected someone in the Hrůza family itself with having caused harm to the young woman. The brother, for one thing, had a reputation for having a violent temper; he and Anežka had also been seen quarreling not long ago over a small amount of money. Klenovec decided, therefore, to go that afternoon to Malá Věžnice to search the family house for any evidence of foul play. It is important, I think, to emphasize this small detail of everyday police work, because it reminds us how some ritual murder trials start out as simple episodes of local violence before bursting through structures of control. When the police constable could find neither any sign of the missing girl nor any incriminating evidence, he seems not to have pursued the matter of the brother further—at least not for the time being—and instead organized a search for the following morning to be conducted in the area between the village and Polná.[36]

It did not take long for the party searching the Březina woods on Saturday, 1 April, to discover Anežka's body slightly off the footpath, partially concealed beneath freshly cut evergreen branches. Klenovec hastily assembled a judicial commission made up of the local investigating magistrate, two local doctors, and a recording secretary, whose statement of the facts of the case (*Tatbestandsaufnahme*) later would form part of the criminal indictment against the state's chief suspect. According to this report, the dead woman was found lying face-down on the ground, her head resting between her two hands and wrapped in a section of her partially torn, partially cut, and bloodied blouse. The legs were bent at the knee at a sharp angle; the body slightly arched. Anežka was naked from the torso to the left thigh. Preliminary examination revealed numerous wounds around the head, which was "everywhere smeared with blood," and the hair was matted together. The body was covered with spruce branches, which had been cut by a knife and brought to its resting place; the actual scene of the crime was thought to have been a few meters away in a small depression surrounded by young spruce trees about three to four meters in height. While the survey of the crime scene noted that an "insignificant pool of blood, about the size of a small plate," lay underneath the victim's body, there were "clear signs of spilled blood," in one spot still quite fresh, at the actual site of the murder. Also strewn about were pieces of Anežka's clothing and stockings, hair, threads, and a swath of canvas, said by onlookers to be a bricklayer's apron—all spattered with blood; six meters away, a bloodied pine branch had been hidden under some moss.[37]

A violent murder, then, strongly suggestive of sexual assault but also a body staged in repose and covered neatly with branches of spruce, indicating either that the murderer spent a good deal of time with the corpse or that he or she returned—at least once—to the scene of the crime. It is hard to imagine why at this point Jan Hrůza should not still have been a prime suspect, nor is there a strong documentary trail outlining the process by which local opinion should have turned suddenly to Leopold Hilsner—a twenty-two-year-old unemployed shoemaker—as the likely killer. One major problem for historians is that most descriptions of how this knowledge came to be formed emerge from narrative recapitulations produced days or weeks after the events in question. If we are to believe these accounts, people who were gathered at the crime scene came suddenly—and unanimously—to the realization that Anežka's death had been a ritual murder, as if swept up by the shock of recognition. How so? Interestingly, the *Tatbestandsaufnahme* has nothing to say in this regard, only that the body of the victim was transferred with great care to a coffin that had already been brought to the scene by Mrs. Hrůzová and transported—under the watchful eye of Polná's mayor, Rudolf Sadil—directly to the morgue that was attached to the cemetery outside St. Barbara's cathedral. A postmortem examination and autopsy were scheduled for 3 o'clock that afternoon.[38]

A picture of what *might* have transpired to shift the attention of local authorities from a violent, possibly sexual, assault and murder to a ritual murder—and from the Hrůza family to Leopold Hilsner—emerges from other kinds of sources, some of which, as I have noted, are of questionable genesis. A report of the Polná district court to the investigating magistrate in Kutná Hora conveys the statement of the police constable Klenovec that his suspicions regarding Jan Hrůza dissipated the moment Anežka's body was turned over and he saw a large knife wound on her neck (an act not mentioned specifically in the original statement of facts).[39] I will have more to say below about this and other wounds on the head and neck. At this point, I wish only to point out that, in this charged atmosphere, physical marks on the body carried significant symbolic weight. Nearly two decades after the revival of

Figure 9. Postcard. "Commission over the corpse of A. Hrůzová in the Březina woods by Polná, 1 April 1899. Dr. Michálek and Dr. Prokeš make their report."

Courtesy J. Mabray.

the ritual murder accusation in Central Europe, in the wake of two preceding trials and scores of sensational newspaper stories, with politicians and reporters mobilized and waiting, potentially ambiguous or neutral physical evidence could produce predetermined emotional responses. Klenovec's sudden realization that his earlier instinct had been misdirected offers one such response; more dramatic reactions have found their way into a number of narrative reconstructions of the day in question.

Stories of discovery and realization soon began to appear in newspaper reporting beginning around a week after the judicial commission had first come upon Anežka's corpse. Among the newspapers that produced ongoing coverage of events in Polná were a variety of Czech publications—including *České zájmy* (radical nationalist and antisemitic), whose editor Jaromír Hušek arrived on the scene on 13 April; *Katolické listy* (Catholic, antiliberal), which appeared to have a reporter in place even earlier; *Radikální listy* (radical nationalist and antisemitic); and *Národní politika* (Old Czech)—joined by papers from Austria and Germany, including Vienna's leading antisemitic paper, *Deutsches Volksblatt*. To take just one example, one easily can trace the ways in which such reporting began, from its opening coverage, to lay the rhetorical groundwork for a narrative account in which the accusing finger pointed inevitably toward a Jewish culprit. What *Katolické listy* found fascinating about the crime was the combination of *mystery* in which it was shrouded—a favorite headline of the time was "*Tajuplná vražda*," a mysterious murder—and the rumor (let us call it unofficial information), already rife at the local level, that one was dealing here with a case of religiously inspired ritual killing. The mystery consisted of three known "facts": although the crime in question appeared to have been particularly brutal and although the woman's body had been stripped of much of its clothing, the preliminary investigation had ruled out both robbery and rape as motives for the murder. A purse with four crowns still in it was found near the crime site, and the body supposedly showed no evidence of a sexual assault.[40]

Added to the cruelty, violence, and apparent absence of conventional motive was, of course, the coincidence of timing: Anežka Hrůzová was murdered during the holy week preceding Easter. In a seemingly detached fashion, the paper announced that, locally, suspicion had fallen on a Jew named Leopold Hilsner, described as an unemployed person who often wandered about in the woods and who, it was claimed, received support from "Social Democrats in Brno."[41] A period of five days would elapse before *Katolické listy* again reported on the Polná case, but starting with its extended coverage of 16 April, it would devote almost an article a day to the case for the next six weeks. The story that day added several new details to the "mystery," each of which would acquire pride of place in the evolving narrative reconstruction of Anežka's murder. The first involved testimony from the mother of the victim that, although money had not been taken from her daughter, a white rosary with a crucifix attached—which she always carried on her person—was missing. Why would a thief leave behind money but take a rosary and crucifix? The same day's report issued both a new theme and a closely related pictorial image that were to move quickly to the center of all subsequent discourse on the murder. First, local observers—including two examining physicians—now claimed that significant quantities of blood were missing from the body of the victim as well as from the general crime scene. Second, while the most important wound on the body—a deep cut to the throat—might easily account for the absence of blood in the corpse itself, it could not explain why only an "insignificant" amount of blood was found in its immediate vicinity. The wound to the throat was said to be long and deep; according to *Katolické listy*'s Polná correspondent, the victim had been "*zakošerovaná*" (literally, "koshered;" meaning "killed in the kosher manner")![42]

The timing of the paper trail left behind by Czech and German newspaper accounts might give the impression that popular understandings of the Polná crime as a ritual murder emerged only gradually, that they did not begin to take shape until days or weeks after the initial discovery of the body. I think this would be a mistaken conclusion, however. It is, of course, in the nature of oral culture not to produce written documents—at least not right away—and one needs to be cautious when reading interrogation and courtroom testimony about sudden realizations, but there is one major piece of evidence to suggest that talk of a Jewish ritual crime spread quickly among some segments of Polná society: rioting in the Jewish quarter. Anežka Hrůzová was laid to rest three days after the discovery of her corpse. Hers was a formal, somber funeral, which most of the residents of Polná attended. The casket lay on display in the passageway to an inn in the town square; Josef Šímek, the dean of the St. Barbara's cathedral, sprinkled it with holy water and led the slow procession to the cemetery outside the church. Music played; people hung poems to Anežka along the cemetery's walls. As Jiří Kovtun writes, many people sincerely mourned the young woman's fate, but others felt overwhelmed by the need to exact revenge, to "draw the appropriate political conclusions" from the fact that they were burying a Christian martyr. Following the discovery of the body in the Březina woods, it was no longer pleasant to be a Jew in Polná; this was particularly true on the day of Anežka's funeral, as the first acts of violence broke out.[43]

Moreover, communication across genres or forms of knowledge did not move in one direction only. Symbolic language, received tradition, rumor, and forensic medicine not only coexisted in Polná but also could communicate with and influence the content of the other. One striking—and fateful—example of such mutual effect occurred early on in the investigation, spurred by the combination of a flurry of sensationalistic newspaper articles, dissatisfaction on the part of the investigating authorities with the quality of the early medical reports, and their desire to elicit more specific findings from the medical examiners.

Jaromír Hušek, the radical nationalist newspaper editor who had faced criminal charges in the past for anti-Jewish incitement, began to receive reports from Polná shortly after the discovery of the corpse and was quick to insert himself into the ongoing investigation. He had written already on 7 April to Ernst Schneider, a Reichsrat deputy and leading figure in Austria's antisemitic movement, informing him that a nineteen-year-old girl had been murdered by "a Jew" and complaining of the fact that the leading suspect had been released by a "Jewish judge" (incorrectly identifying Bedřich Reichenbach's religion), "who is attempting to silence (*totschweigen*) all of history."[44] Schneider forwarded the letter to the Ministry of Justice in Vienna, which in turn referred it to the state prosecutor's office in Prague, thereby setting in motion a pipeline of questioning, requests for clarification, and self-justifications extending from the imperial capital through Prague to the office of the Kutná Hora regional court.[45] Attached to the court were the two individuals who would assume primary responsibility for the criminal investigation and eventual prosecution: the investigating judge, Otto Baudyš, and the public prosecutor, Antonín Schneider-Svoboda. In their respective attitudes toward the conduct of the investigation and the likely guilt or innocence of the main suspect, Baudyš and Schneider-Svoboda could not have been further apart. We have seen such a situation before in both the Tiszaeszlár and the Xanten affairs, but with Polná, the relationship was reversed: it was Baudyš, the investigating magistrate, who was skeptical of the state's case and Schneider-Svoboda, the prosecutor, who was determined to push ahead with a focus on Hilsner as the most likely suspect. This reversal of roles means that the "skeptic," placed in the position of overseeing the investigation, might seek to challenge it at certain points along the way, while the "believer" felt committed to a prosecution to the end, with obvious consequences for the course of the trial and the ultimate fate of the accused.[46]

Baudyš was bothered by the diffusion of what he considered to be wildly irresponsible newspaper reporting and rumor but also confused by discrepancies that he found in the three forensic reports that had crossed his desk: the original survey of the possible crime scene (*Tatbestandsaufnahme*); the post-mortem examination of 1 April 1899; and the supplement issued on 6 April.[47] The original autopsy report, produced by Drs. Prokeš and Michálek, had noted three types of injury to the body: a deep wound to the front of the neck, about 8 centimeters in length; clear strangulation marks on the right side and middle of the neck; and, once the bloodied and matted-down hair on the head had been rinsed, eight wounds to the back of the head—ranging in length from 2½ to 6 centimeters—all caused by the same blunt instrument. The hymen was unbroken, although the pubic hair appeared to be clumped together in two places by a grayish substance. Five days later, the doctors offered their opinion as to the most likely cause of death. In their view, the fatal wound was the cut to the neck; they rendered the attempted strangulation and the blows to the head "life threatening." And the chief cause of death: exsanguination and sudden loss of breath.[48]

Information from these findings had clearly made its way to the news organizations that were on the scene in Polná, as the stories of 11 through 16 April all accounted for the three types of injury in their reconstructions of the crime. The most common scenario pictured Anežka being disabled by the blows to the head, then pulled from the path to the depression in the woods by a rope around her neck, and finally murdered by the swift and deep cut to the neck. But what bothered Baudyš in particular was another claim found in the rapidly accruing newspaper reportage: the paucity of blood in the body of the victim and its absence from the purported crime scene (by this time, a classic trope of the modern ritual murder accusation), the assumption being that the murderers had either absconded with the blood or hidden it away. Nowhere in any of the three medical reports was there mention of a paucity, or absence, of blood. In fact, the original *Tatbestandsaufnahme*, describing the condition of the body when it was first found, remarked that the head "was everywhere smeared with blood" and the hair matted (*verklebt*), "that is, with blood."[49] Neither the autopsy report of 1 April nor the addendum of 6 April had anything to say about blood at the scene, missing or otherwise. Yet *Katolické listy*'s story of 16 April had made just this claim, citing as sources both local residents and the two examining physicians! Clearly upset by the sudden circulation of sensational accounts of the crime and perplexed that the physicians themselves should have been named as a source for this information, Baudyš sent an official request to the Polná physicians on 17 April to weigh in on the matter, asking them to review the results of their previous examinations.[50]

The doctors responded confidently to the judge's query two days later in an opinion that was to have far-reaching consequences for the conduct of the investigation and the trial. Although other, competing medical authorities would later challenge it, the report made its way almost verbatim into the formal criminal indictment against Hilsner and, for this reason alone, constitutes one of the seminal documents in the turn-of-the-century struggle to establish proper scientific procedures in forensic medicine. Drs. Prokeš and Michálek, despite having said almost nothing on the subject of blood until prompted to do so by Baudyš, wasted no time in responding; quite simply, yes, they agreed with those reports.

> With regard to both external and internal examination we claim that the body of Anežka Hrůzová was almost completely empty of blood (*fast vollständig ausgeblutet war*). The exsanguination had to

> have occurred through the gash to the neck, as the result of which many powerful vessels were cut.
>
> Exsanguination occurred in a short period of time and blood must have flowed in a mighty stream from the body. Blood flowing out from the wound in such quantity would have coagulated when making contact with the air, such that within a few minutes a large coagulated mass of blood (*Blutkuchen*) would have formed. . . .
>
> Additionally, we do not agree that the two days that elapsed before the discovery of the body and the moderate amount of rain that fell on Thursday could have resulted in the complete disappearance of the coagulum.
>
> . . . In light of the fact that the murder apparently occurred in the mentioned hollow by the path, where the escaping blood would have remained, and in light of the fact that the pieces of clothing . . . were only slightly soaked in blood, or rather simply damp, we can conclude with certainty that the traces of blood that were found do not correspond to the amount that we would expect to find in the vicinity of the body in such a murder.[51]

The document thus opens with the acceptance of a line of argument that it had never considered worth mentioning before. Now that it had been mentioned—by the investigating magistrate, of course, but equally importantly by popular communication and the press—Drs. Prokeš and Michálek gave it their seal of approval and added a patina of scientific reasoning. It is hard to escape the conclusion that the Polná physicians were erasing the distinction between their scientific work and local knowledge, vulnerable to the influence of suggestion but also serving as a funnel of information in their own right. What may have begun as unauthorized communication between the forensic examiners and residents of Polná and the press now had the effect of popular narrative modifying expert testimony.

As if to leave no doubt about the power of suggestion in this case, our physicians ended their reply to the Kutná Hora court with a remarkable paragraph, one that might, under other circumstances, have been lifted directly from popular accounts.

> Finally, with regard to the method by which the cut to the neck was carried out [*the investigating magistrate never asked about this*], we must claim with certainty, that the cut to the victim was carried

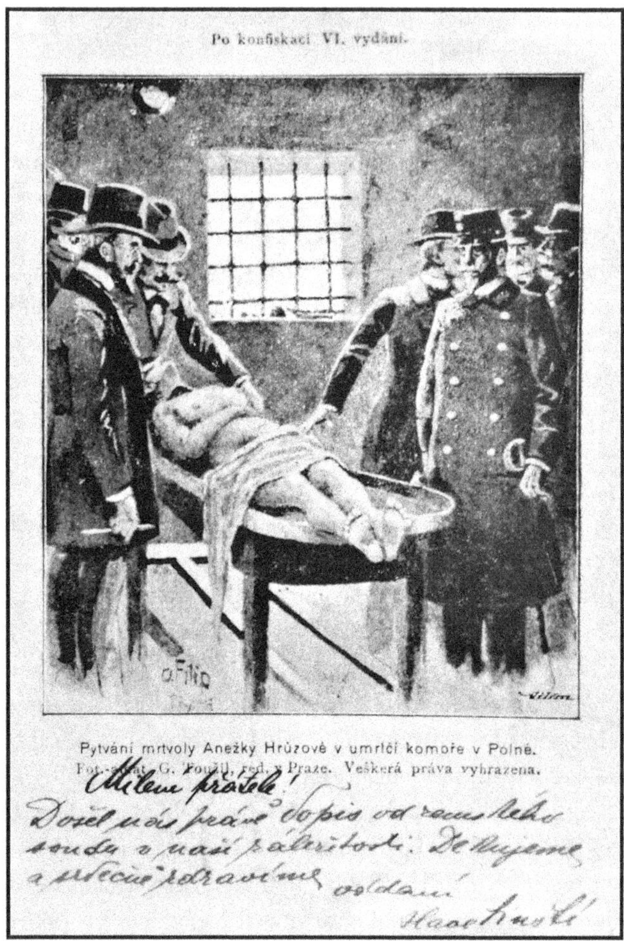

Figure 10. Postcard. "Autopsy on the corpse of Anežka Hrůzová in the Polná morgue." Handwritten message: "Dear Friends, we just received a letter from district court concerning our matter. Thanks and heartfelt greetings, Your devoted, Havelinský's."

Courtesy J. Mabray.

out with the face pointing toward the ground. For if the cut had been made with the back to the ground, the surrounding area and the trees would have been covered with the blood shooting out in all directions, which, in close examination, we did not find; the area marked by blood was small and of limited extension.[52]

Here, the physicians appear to have been making their own contribution to the expanding narrative: science, once again, improving the story. And it did not take long for this version of events to make its way into subsequent newspaper reporting. By the third week in May, *Katolické listy* had sent its "legal correspondent" to Polná for on-the-spot reporting.[53] This reporter described in a series of dispatches to Prague how he sought out the expertise and opinions of local residents and was given guided tours through the topographical landmarks of the crime.[54] *Katolické listy* had long since abandoned whatever critical distance it appeared to show at the start of its coverage, now aligning squarely with generally accepted, local knowledge of the mystery. In a story of 19 May 1899, the correspondent offered readers a step-by-step reconstruction of Anežka's murder, which he claimed to have heard from one of the members of the local judicial commission, certainly a possibility. Note, however, the implicit incorporation of material from the physicians' reports.

> When Anežka got to the top [of the hill], she began to walk slowly. The murderer grabbed her by the arm or by the throat, threw her down to the overgrowth, where a rope was tossed over her neck to prevent her from crying out. Her clothing was stripped down to her knickers, stockings, and shoes, and there in the thicket—six steps from the path—the act of cutting took place. The wound went from one ear to the other, straight and even above the Adam's apple to the vertebrae: precisely the way in which cattle are (kosher-) slaughtered. Whoever cut the throat of Anežka Hrůzová was not performing the act for the first time; he knew what he was doing. The position of the body pointed downhill, the legs, bent at the knees, tumbled uphill. All of the blood, therefore, must have poured out of Anežka Hrůzová. The body when it was found looked like a white scarf, the head resting on the arms. Her face was to the ground. At a quarter to seven people already saw Hilsner in the town below, but the two foreign Yids [who, it was claimed, aided Hilsner in the crime] did not return from Březina.[55]

This dispatch may represent the first relatively complete, imaginative reconstruction of the Polná murder that exists in print. One remarkable feature, given the Catholic affiliation of the newspaper, is the virtual absence of religious symbolism: there is no stand-in for Jesus, no crucifixion, no mocking of God, no martyrdom. In its place stand raw brutality and an anatomically imprecise knowledge of animal slaughtering. As a meditation on blood, this text has lost all connection to Calvary; sacrifice has been transmuted into slaughter, the altar into the cutting block. Similarly, what characterizes the crime as "Jewish" has little or nothing in common with established medieval motifs alluding to the crucifixion or the Eucharist. In classical narratives, the telltale "signs of crucifixion" had identified the sacrifices as Jewish affairs; what defines the Polná case as Jewish can be reduced to blood and brutality, to the imagined butcher's cut of kosher slaughtering. The Jews, themselves, finally, are not religious adversaries, the vanquished recipients of the Old Law; they are Yids.

Journalistic reconstructions, then, constituted the first attempts at coherent narrative in the wake of Polná, but it was Gustav Toužil's sensational publication, *Polná, 29 March 1899*—timed to coincide with the end of Hilsner's trial in Kutná Hora—that constituted the first comprehensive, mass-market portrayal.[56] Roughly crafted as a detective story, it pointed inevitably—when all the "evidence" was sifted—to a Jewish ritual crime. In Toužil's account, the three themes of butcher's cut, absence of blood, and multiple perpetrators continued to serve as the rhetorical core that determined the logic and flow of the story. To this logical knot he added both imaginative detail and dramatic tension, referring repeatedly to on-the-spot reconstructions of the crime by local experts and appealing to the honest sentiments and unshakable convictions of local residents. The reader was invited to revisit the discovery of the corpse, to remark in silence the presence of wounds around the head and neck of the victim, to wait with breathless anticipation as the body—which had been lying face-down—was carefully turned over, and to join in the collective gasp as the horrendous cut on the neck is revealed. "In that moment," Toužil wrote, "suspicion fell away from the Hrůza family, and a single breath emanated from the frozen spectators; this was the verdict: This girl has been koshered (zakošerované)."[57]

Toužil assured his readers that they could pierce the curtain of mystery surrounding the death of Anežka Hrůzová through the use of the senses; all one needed to do was look, listen, and employ common sense: look at the evidence gathered at the scene of the crime, at the manner in which the murder was carried out; listen with empathy to the collective knowledge of the community; and then draw the obvious conclusions. In a section of the book entitled "Where Is the Blood?" he marshaled the scientific testimony of the examining physicians, the resourcefulness of ad hoc detectives, and the commonsense judgments of local residents to arrive at the only possible conclusion. Toužil invoked the independent confirmation of ordinary people to counter any skepticism that the reader might have had concerning the doctors' opinion—late in forming—that the amount of blood found on or by the victim was "insignificant."[58] He introduced his readers to his local guide, a Mr. Došek, and to the game warden, Antonín Dvořák (not to be confused with the famous composer), whose own detective work was a good example of this kind of reciprocal confirmation. Dvořák was said to have shown up with his two English hounds, Lord and Piks (!), and painstakingly scoured the area for two hours, yet found no traces anywhere. Nor could fisherman observing the lakes or detectives from Prague, convinced (big city cynics that they were) that this was a case of necrophilia.[59]

Where, then, did poor Anežka's blood disappear? On this point, Toužil explained, the people of Polná had many particulars and were absolutely convinced. From the simple country bumpkin to the urbanized intellectual, the conclusion was the same: wherever the blood of the murdered girl went, "Leopold Hilsner and his two companions know . . . and this pure, innocent blood cries out to heaven for vengeance."[60] Popular opinion itself had to be seen as an arbiter of the truth, and this opinion, Toužil wrote, "calls out now to the Christian world like a resounding bell."[61]

* * *

In the person of Leopold Hilsner (1876–1928), the proponents of the charge of ritual murder in the death of Anežka Hrůzová had found a useful villain—useful but atypical of the modern pattern of accusation. He was a semiliterate shoemaker's apprentice who never seemed to be employed and typically lived off of the charity of others. Indeed, he lived with his widowed mother and younger brother in the basement of the Jewish community's German-language elementary school (which closed in 1900 for lack of students), where the family received free lodging in return for their willingness to provide shelter and food for other indigent Jews who happened to be traveling through Polná. Bilingual in spoken Czech and German, Hilsner ("Polda" to his Czech friends) tended to socialize with a small group of similarly disadvantaged, and Christian, Czechs and was known to take walks with his friends in the Březina woods nearby. He clearly lived on the margins of respectable society—Jewish as well as Christian—by virtue of his poverty, if nothing else, but also because he and his associates seemed to have an air of disrepute about them and, honestly, too much time on their hands.[62]

There were also other incriminating circumstances. The school in which the Hilsner family lived happened to be next door to the seamstress Prchalová's house, so the chances were good that he had seen Anežka there at least once; perhaps—so the thinking went—he had followed her on her way home from work on the day of her murder, through the Březina woods, which he knew well. True, Hilsner maintained in an early interrogation that he had not been in the woods on the afternoon of 29 March, but several of his friends contradicted him in their testimony to authorities.[63] Schneider-Svoboda's own report to his superiors in Prague, dated 12 April 1899, in which he strongly defended his handling of the case, frames the arrest of Hilsner in just these terms. He describes the most likely suspect as a "23 year old, unemployed Jew . . . who lives with his mother in Polná's Jewish quarter; who, since he is unemployed, used to roam about in the Březina forest nearly every day; and the seamstress Prchalová had her workshop exactly next to the house in which Hilsner lived with his mother, to which the murdered Anežka Hrůzová came nearly every day."[64]

Schneider-Svoboda added other pieces of incriminating evidence to bolster his decision to arrest Hilsner, chief among which was his inability to establish an alibi. Hilsner claimed to have been with a friend, Vincenz Zelinger, on the Ringplatz between the hours of four and six-thirty; from there, he went to the synagogue for prayer. But Zelinger denied that he had been with Hilsner during this time, and none of the other possible witnesses from the synagogue (named by Schneider-Svoboda) could confirm Hilsner's presence. Finally, Hilsner claimed not to have known the victim, an assertion that the prosecuting attorney countered was untrue.[65]

If, in his correspondence to his superiors in Prague, Schneider-Svoboda portrayed himself as a disinterested party acting solely on the basis of physical evidence and credible testimony, one person who was close to the case has offered a dissenting view. Anna Auředníčková, a writer and translator, was the wife of Hilsner's court-appointed defense attorney, Zdenko Auředníček. The daughter of Jewish converts to Catholicism, she would spend three years as a prisoner in Terezín/Theresienstadt during World War II.[66] In 1948 to 1949, following her return to Prague, Auředníčková published a short memoir of the Hilsner case and gave at least one public lecture on the subject.[67] She writes of a train trip that she took in April 1899 from Prague—where she had been visiting her ailing father and before her husband was assigned to the case—to her home in Kutná Hora. It so happened that Schneider-Svoboda boarded the train at the Kolín station and made his way to the first-class car, where he spotted Anna and sat down next to her. (Auředníček and Schneider-Svoboda were both dignitaries of the small provincial city, and the families were well acquainted.) The prosecutor eagerly informed his train companion that he was just returning from Polná to see firsthand the scene of a gruesome crime, a ritual murder. Seeing the puzzled expression on his interlocutor's face, Schneider-Svoboda explained that Jews require the blood of Christian girls and that the chief suspect in the case had received instructions from other Jews to kill this particular victim. Auředníčková could not help but laugh at this, but her response only induced Schneider-Svoboda to insist that it was "well established" that such ritual murders take place throughout the world and assured her that he could provide her with proof of his contention. Upon their arrival in Kutná Hora, Schneider-Svoboda accompanied Anna Auředníčková on foot to her home and bade her farewell with the customary kiss on the hand.[68]

Added, then, to the local suspicion that had fallen so rapidly on Leopold Hilsner as the "obvious" suspect in Anežka Hrůzová's murder, we have this recollection of an unnerving encounter between the prosecutor and the wife of the future defense attorney on a train from Prague to Kutná Hora. Together they reveal a fundamental tension in the prosecution of modern ritual murder cases: the impulse to frame the crime (or supposed crime) as a compulsive, even mysterious, religious ritual versus the trained response to approach the incident in question from a more naturalistic, empirical perspective. We know enough about the imbrication of poverty and social marginalization in criminal prosecutions not to be surprised that the police and citizenry should have felt confident that they had "gotten their man" in this case. Hilsner was just the type of person to get swept up in the criminal justice system regardless of his guilt or innocence. The problem is that he was not a likely candidate for a ritual murder accusation. In contrast to every other case, with the exception of the Beilis affair in Late Imperial Russia (1911–13), the accused was not a functionary of the local Jewish community, not knowledgeable in Jewish law and practice, and not a butcher or ritual slaughterer; in fact, he lived on the margins of the community and socialized almost exclusively with Christians of his own social class.

For this reason, the somewhat fictionalized "moment of realization," when members of the judicial commission and gathered onlookers caught sight of the overturned body with the large slash across the throat, produced a response that was built upon contradictions. The young woman had been "koshered" but seemingly by an ordinary criminal; hers was both a ritual murder and a common act of violence. Faced with a crime, which local knowledge construed as simultaneously mundane and endowed with mystery, state and local authorities seem to have had difficulty deciding what kind of case they wished to prosecute. And it was this indeterminacy, I think, that accounts for the inconsistencies in the proceedings—the shift in tone and direction in the early forensic reports, from neutral descriptions of the crime scene and the condition of the corpse to the addition of ex post facto measurements and surmises concerning exsanguination, and the claim of calm, deliberate, unprejudiced police work in Schneider-Svoboda's reports to Prague belied by clear evidence to the contrary of external, political influence and the power of suggestion. And the problem remained that Hilsner was just not a likely subject for an accusation of religiously inspired, ritual murder—that, and the fact that the case lacked both eyewitnesses and hard forensic evidence.[69]

The hoped-for eyewitnesses eventually came forward, although not before the investigation had already been going on for nearly a month, and the behaviors and circumstances they claimed to have witnessed mainly involved placing the defendant—and two unidentified accomplices—in the vicinity of the spot where Anežka's body had been found. On 24 April, František Cink, a wagon driver, reported to the district court that he had been making a delivery of hay to a house near the Jewish quarter on 29 March around 5 p.m. when, suddenly, Hilsner, in the company of two strangers, came galloping by and headed off in the direction of a stream leading to the Březina woods. All three were smoking cigarettes, Cink observed, and one of the three was slipping an oblong object wrapped in paper into the inner pocket of his coat. Cink knew Hilsner well; the other two men he claimed never to have seen before but described them in terms that were unmistakably "Jewish": the first had a full face, protruding mouth, partially grown black beard, and knock-kneed and gimpy legs (Cink seemed not to want to leave anything to chance). Hilsner himself was wearing the telltale gray suit that would be found in his mother's house—without overcoat.[70]

Cink's testimony accomplished several objectives, purposefully or not: it placed Hilsner around the scene of the crime at the appropriate time; the recollection of the long, oblong-shaped object being slipped into the inside of an overcoat suggested that the three were about to undertake a nefarious act; and the involvement of the two, unknown Jews helped to resolve doubts about whether Hilsner would have had either the knowledge or the strength to carry out such a crime on his own. In the succeeding weeks, other Polná residents came forward to bolster Cink's account, but the prosecution's case still lacked an eyewitness who could place Hilsner at the scene of the crime (presuming that the discovery place was also where the crime occurred).[71] Such a witness finally came forward late in the investigation, long after an indictment had already been handed down (which was on 17 June 1899). In August 1899—four months after Anežka's corpse was discovered—Petr Pešák, age forty-nine, who worked as a locksmith and in a variety of other jobs, came forward with new testimony: he claimed that around 5:45 on the evening of Anežka's disappearance, as he paused to relieve himself while looking in the direction of the Březina woods, he spotted a man with a slim build, dressed in a gray suit, and holding a white stick looking back toward the town. He assured his interrogators that he definitely recognized this individual as Hilsner; moreover, as the man with the white stick turned around to head toward the saplings, Pešák could make out the figures of two men dressed in hats and dark clothing. They appeared to be stockier than Hilsner and also older.[72]

There is much to be skeptical about in this testimony: its lateness, for one thing; the fact that it managed to fill the most gaping hole in the prosecution's circumstantial case; and the physical distance separating the witness from the forest. Expert witnesses in Hilsner's second trial in Písek sparred over the question of just how much one could accurately see from a distance of approximately 676 meters. Two court doctors from Písek judged Pešák's eyesight to be normal; two eye doctors from Prague rated it as somewhat above normal; in any event, the Vienna ophthalmologist, Schnabel, testified at the same trial that he had tested experimentally whether or not one could make a positive identification from a distance of 676 meters and concluded that it was not possible.[73]

Clouded as it was, Pešák's testimony proved to be a crucial weapon in the state's case against Hilsner; Pešák himself, in the words of Jiří Kovtun, "soon became a fateful figure in the Polná case and the principal agent of the tragedy of Leopold Hilsner."[74] Principal agent, perhaps. But it is important to keep in mind that, in addition to witness testimony (however suspect), the state was also building a case around forensic evidence and medicine, and it was in this sphere that Schneider-Svoboda felt that his scientific experts had made a major discovery. On one of their many searches through the home of Hilsner's mother, first in Polná and then, following Hilsner's arrest, in Velké Meziříčí (Gross-Meseritsch), the authorities found a pair of men's gray trousers, presumed to have belonged to Leopold, on which there were stains. Schneider-Svoboda had the stains examined using chemical, microscopic, and spectroscopic analyses and reported to his superiors in Prague on 25 May 1899 that the tests demonstrated, "with greatest probability," that the stains were from blood; that, "according to the bulk of the isolated elements," they were from human blood; and, finally, that efforts had been made to wash the stains clean.[75] Game on.

The Trials of Leopold Hilsner

The first of what, ultimately, would be two trials took place in Kutná Hora, the district capital, over the course of five days, 12 to 16 September 1899. As with the Kleve trial (Xanten affair), the case was argued before a jury. Schneider-Svoboda—true to his protestations to the chief prosecutor's office in Prague—did not make overt reference to the ritual murder accusation in his questioning of witnesses or his remarks to the jury; in fact, he addressed many fewer questions to witnesses than did the presiding judge, Ježek. Nor did the state offer a theory of religious compulsion in its presentation of the case. Schneider-Svoboda preferred to be deliberately vague on the question of Hilsner's purported motive, insisting that only physical evidence, alibis, and the testimony of credible witnesses interested him. "Motive is beside the point," he stressed to the jurors during his summation. "The only question is whether Leopold Hilsner committed the crime for which he has been indicted."[76]

Schneider-Svoboda was not averse, however, to introducing the theme of ritual murder through the back door, as it were, indirectly and by way of suggestion. Again, in his address to the jury shortly before the verdict was delivered, he drew attention to the fact that the victim had been hit on the head with a rock numerous times (eight to be exact), yet none of the blows had been strong enough to kill her. Why not, he wondered? "It is obvious to me that, if he had wanted to kill her immediately, among the eight wounds, *one* would have been delivered in such a way as to kill her. It appears, however, that the goal was to stun her."[77] To stun the victim, then—to keep her alive temporarily for some other purpose. The state's attorney also played to the jurors' prejudices through his tactical choice of language, at times using the neutral designation "accomplices" (*spolupachatelé*) when referring to Hilsner's presumed co-perpetrators and at other times the much more charged "these Jewish pals" (*ti druzi židé*).[78] And, in an effort to demolish Hilsner's own credibility (he had claimed throughout the criminal investigation "that he did not know Anežka Hrůzová, that he did not see her, and that he did not want to hear anything about her"), Schneider-Svoboda made sure to repeat before the jury the words of Anežka's mother, who reported that her daughter had complained of being pursued (*pronásledovat*) by an "ugly Jew" who "stared at her."[79]

Schneider-Svoboda seemed perfectly content to leave the more incendiary references to ritual murder to the private attorney representing Mrs. Hrůzová: the former defense attorney for radical Czech students charged with treason at the Omladina trial of 1894 and the future mayor of Prague, Karel Baxa.[80] Baxa expanded the state's inquiry into the reasons why the victim might have been stunned (or rendered unconscious) before she ultimately was murdered in such a way as to leave no room for doubt in the minds of the jurors. The issue, to his mind, was blood—and its reported absence at the crime scene: "With the first murder in the world, the blood of the victim called out for revenge. Here, however, blood did not call out for revenge, because there was no blood in her. Rather her entire corpse called out for revenge."[81] Then, claiming to want to deal not in myth but in the testimony of experts, Baxa continued, "Only a small amount of blood was found in the corpse, and that amount that was found, did not correspond in the least with the amount of blood that every person has to have, to say nothing of a healthy, strong, woman like Anežka Hrůzová."[82] Finally, lest the members of the jury not be able to anticipate the end point of his argument, Baxa removed all ambiguity. Re-creating for his audience the last moments of Anežka Hrůzová's life in vivid, almost pornographic detail, he concluded, "Whoever considers those [last] moments has to acknowledge that Anežka Hrůzová was a martyr in the proper sense of the word. To what end was this carried out, that no blood was to be found? . . . They wanted to murder a Christian person, an innocent girl, in order to obtain her blood. All of this changing the subject is to no avail. This is what the purpose of the murder was."[83]

Thus, the Kutná Hora trial proceeded in several different registers. None was more fascinating or significant, in my view, than the relatively brief skirmishes that took place over expert testimony and the nature of scientific argument. One such battle was fought on the fourth day of the trial and featured the testimony and cross-examination of Dr. Alois Prokeš, the Polná physician whose postmortem examination of Anežka Hrůzová and subsequent reports had been influential in the arrest and eventual indictment of Hilsner. Leading off the questioning, Karel Baxa, the family's attorney, worked to elicit the doctor's professional endorsement of his own theory of the case, to confirm—using medical language and categories—a narrative of ritual murder. To get this endorsement, Baxa circled carefully, focusing on secondary details of the condition in which the corpse was found.

Dr. Baxa: It appears that the dress on the deceased was torn violently. If someone wished to slit someone's throat, would he have to strip the clothes to the waist?

Expert: That would not be necessary.

Dr. Baxa: The dress was ripped off. When did this take place, during the murder or after?

Expert: During the murder.

Dr. Baxa: In your opinion, when blood was not found at the scene of the crime, what happened to it?

Expert: I couldn't say.

Dr. Baxa: You say that, when someone cuts through the neck, blood spurts out from it swiftly. Did the amount of blood that was found correspond to the amount a person has?

Expert: One thirteenth of the body is comprised of blood. If Hrůzová weighed 70 kg, she could have had five kg of blood, or five to six liters.

Dr. Baxa: Show the gentlemen of the jury how large a pool of blood would have been left at the place.

Expert: It would have left behind an enormous coagulum. (Demonstrates on the ground.)

Dr. Baxa: There were impressions from pine needles on the breasts. Blood would have to have splattered the breasts, the abdomen. Was there blood there?

Expert: None at all, just the pine needles.

Dr. Baxa: Is it possible that the blood was deliberately collected?

Expert: I grant you that.

Dr. Baxa: What do you think about the possibility that the blood was trampled down [into the ground]?

Expert: That's not possible. People would not have trodden on the blood [presumably people at the crime scene], and drops of blood would still be found.

Dr. Baxa: We believe that she was wearing a dress. She had on knickers, an underskirt, etc. If she had been killed when (fully) clothed, would more blood have been found on her lower parts?

Expert: Yes.

Dr. Baxa: The perpetrators removed her clothes so that she would bleed out?

Expert: Yes.[84]

Note how, in this line of questioning, Baxa focused precisely on those details that might have led the police and prosecutors to see the murder of Anežka Hrůzová as a sex crime: the stripping of the clothing from the top half of the body. At first, he seemed to be interested only in the apparent absence of blood from the victim's breasts as confirmation of the claim that the blood had been drawn away from her body, but he quickly maneuvered the physician (without any resistance on the latter's part) to attribute Anežka's nakedness to the physical requirements of a ritual murder. ("The perpetrators removed her clothes so that she would bleed out?") This was an inspired move on Baxa's part, to manipulate supposedly expert, scientific testimony not only to corroborate his theory of ritual murder but also to neutralize the most compelling counternarrative.

But the fight over expert testimony—its nature, methods, and requirements—was not over. There was equally as much at stake for the defense in Prokeš's testimony, and Zdenko Auředníček pressed the witness repeatedly over the distinction between demonstrated, scientific conclusion and unsubstantiated opinion. At issue here was the meaning behind the three types of injuries that the victim had sustained, only one of which proved to be fatal.

Dr. Auředníček: You mentioned the order of the injuries: first to the head, [then] strangulation, and then the cut. You maintain that [it was] carried out in this manner in order to render her unconscious. How do you substantiate this? What serves as the basis of your claim that he wanted to stun and not kill her?

Expert: If he had wanted to kill her, the injuries would have to have been carried out with greater strength.

Dr. A: What if he did not have that strength, if it had been unsuccessful?

E: He would have hit her with greater force where the bone was smaller.

Dr. A: Yes, if he were a physician.

Expert: He would have known.

Dr. A: I wouldn't have known that right away. The injuries were carried out from the back?

Expert: Yes.

Dr. A: You testified that she had on two dresses and had very thick hair. It must have taken a lot of force to kill her.

Expert: It appears so. [*Přijde na to.*]

Dr. A: Someone would have to have been very strong?

Expert: It is not the same for everyone.

Dr. A: You say that he only wanted to stun her.

Expert: We said that he hit her with a rock then tossed a cord around her and pulled.

Dr. A: But I am asking for you to substantiate your claim that he only wished to render her unconscious.

Expert: I don't know how I could prove it.

Dr. A: I say that he did not have the necessary strength. And the proof of this, perhaps, is in the fact that he did not kill her, that he was not able to smash her skull, because she had on two dresses.

Presiding Judge: That she was able to endure a heavy blow?

Dr. A: Yes. And from that you conclude that the as yet unknown perpetrators did not want to kill her?

Expert: I believe that he wanted to stun her so that she would be unconscious and he would be able to work on her. I cannot know what the intention of the perpetrator was; I maintain that he wanted to stun her.

Dr. A: If you do not know, then don't assert it. Now please demonstrate it. It is not a demonstration to say, "Because she had those strangulation marks, the perpetrator did not wish to kill her." Rather, it is precisely because he might have strangled her that [we must conclude that] he failed in killing her. You are claiming that he did not *intend* to kill her.

Pres. Judge: The blows to the head?

Expert: I maintain that he wanted to render her unconscious.

Dr. A: I want you to demonstrate that scientifically. Dr. Baxa, please don't prompt him all of the time. It is like in school! I would like you to demonstrate this scientifically.

Pres. Judge: Can it be demonstrated scientifically?

Dr. A: Then he should not maintain it.

Pres. Judge: The expert deduces that when he sees a wound to the neck and strangulation marks, wounds to the head, which, in and of themselves, are lightly injurious, he forms the conclusion that this was in preparation for the main act, the cut to the throat.

Dr. A: But this is not a scientific conclusion.

Pres. Judge: I believe that, on the basis of observation, it is not possible to say whether the blows to the head were made before, that it has to be assessed as a whole.

Dr. A: That is something for the court to determine. But an expert witness has to demonstrate it.[85]

What is most remarkable in this exchange is the unwillingness, or inability, of Dr. Prokeš to understand Auředníček's objection to the characterization of his surmise that the blows to the head and the strangulation marks indicated deliberate attempts to render the victim unconscious, that the killer, or killers, had intended only for the cut to the neck to produce the victim's death. Could the witness establish this claim scientifically, the defense attorney wanted to know? Prokeš seemed to be taken aback by the question. He was offering an opinion by virtue of his status as a medical expert, hence an expert opinion. Auředníček countered that, if it could not be substantiated scientifically, the court had no business presenting it as scientific testimony. It was simply an opinion reflecting one possibility among several—and not a very compelling one at that. All one could know for certain, Auředníček implied, is that the victim suffered three different types of injury and that one of these appears to have been determinative in causing her death. There is nothing in the evidence itself that would lead one to conclude that the attacker wished first to stun the victim, to render her unconscious, and only then to kill her. This was a crucial point, since, intentionally or not, Prokeš's opinion conformed to the underlying assumptions of a ritual murder narrative. It spelled the difference between a simple murder and a mysterious one.[86]

As the trial wound down, the court presented the jury with two questions: a main question and an alternative, should the first not be responded to affirmatively. The first question read as follows: "Is Leopold Hilsner guilty of having acted in such a manner—on 29 March 1899, around six o'clock in the evening, in the Březina woods in Polná, together with as-yet-unknown perpetrators, against Anežka Hrůzová, daughter of the widow M. Hrůzová of Malá Věžnice, with the intention of killing her—so as to have caused her [Anežka Hrůzová's] death, and that this murder was carried out in a malicious manner [*způsobem potutelně*]?"[87]

The question's convoluted and legalistic phrasing comes through in the Czech original as well as in my English translation. Two points stand out, however. The first involves the effect of Hilsner's actions: did he act in such a way as to cause the victim's death? The second point is subtler and concerns the number of persons attached to the verb "to kill" (or to intend to kill). In this question, the verb is expressed in the third person singular, which means that Hilsner intended to kill the victim and acted in such a way (although with accomplices) that death was the result. The jurors returned one vote of yes and eleven votes of no to question number one, suggesting that they were not convinced that Hilsner himself had done the killing or had intended to kill the victim. They were next asked to consider an equally dense alternative question: "Is Leopold Hilsner guilty of laying his hands on [Anežka Hrůzová] or of taking part in an active manner when Anežka Hrůzová, daughter of the widow M. Hrůzová from Malá Věžnice, was attacked in a malicious manner by additional perpetrators with the intention of killing her, so that her death resulted directly from this, through the completion of said murder?"[88] In this version of the charge, the intent to murder is rendered in the third person plural and Hilsner's complicity is described in indirect terms—guilty of "laying on of hands" or of "taking part in an active manner" in an assault by several individuals, which resulted in the victim's death. On this question, the jury returned a unanimous verdict: twelve votes of yes and zero votes of no. Hilsner was found guilty of murder and sentenced to death.[89]

* * *

Here we must pause. The Kutná Hora trial took place a full sixteen years after the first of the modern ritual murder prosecutions, the Nyíregyháza trial, which brought the Tiszaeszlár affair to a close in 1883, and seven years after the Kleve trial (the Xanten affair), yet it was only now—at the very close of the nineteenth century—that the ritual murder accusation produced a guilty verdict and a death sentence. Mention has already been made of the conflict between the investigating magistrate and the public prosecutor in this case, as well as of the reversal of the roles of skeptic and believer that had obtained in the earlier trials. Attention has also been drawn to the political turmoil that plagued the Bohemian lands in the 1890s, including the bellicose national campaigns of Czech and German activists and of the uneasy, and often involuntary, involvement of Jews in this struggle. But something else was at play as well, a sense that the ritual murder accusation was gaining rather than losing strength as the century wound down.

One begins to see expressions of resignation and weariness in Jewish speeches and editorials during the Hilsner affair. As the editors of *Českožidovské listy* wrote during the week of the trial, "Whether Hilsner is guilty or innocent, the fact is that he has already been convicted in large segments of our society as a foregone conclusion."[90] Even Jews who knew that Hilsner had been victimized by a biased police investigation and an unfair trial wished at times that he could just have been an ordinary criminal. In an address delivered to a gathering of the National Union of Czech Jews (Národní jednota českožidovská) a week after the verdict, Ignát Arnstein suggested almost wistfully, "If Hilsner were to have been found guilty on the basis of clear, direct evidence for simple murder, we would not be concerned with this issue. And if the antisemites reproached us for Hilsner, we could certainly say calmly, 'Why should only you have the privilege of having criminals [in your midst]? Why couldn't murderers also be found among us?'"[91] Hilsner, of course, was not convicted of "simple murder" on the basis of clear evidence, but rather, in the words of Arnstein, "as the result of the conviction of lay judges [the twelve jurors? public opinion?] that murder for the purpose of Jewish ritual exists."[92]

But the Kutná Hora verdict evinced other responses as well, including strident protest. And one of the strongest and most consistent expressions of dissent came not from the Jewish world but from Tomáš G. Masaryk, then a young sociology professor at Prague's Czech University.[93] Masaryk was drawn initially into the growing debate over Hilsner's guilt or innocence through the intervention of a former student of his when he taught at the University of Vienna. This individual, identified by Masaryk as Sigmund Münz, was, like Masaryk, Moravian born; he had been a contributing editor to the *Neue Freie Presse* since 1891.[94] It seems that Münz wrote to his former professor for his thoughts regarding the fact that both the liberal and the radical press in the Bohemian lands had come out so passionately against Hilsner—as well as against Alfred Dreyfus, whose retrial at Rennes on the charge of treason had ended less than a week before the start of the Kutná Hora proceedings. Masaryk's response appeared, with permission, in the 29 September 1899 edition of Vienna's *Neue Freie Presse*.[95] It read in part as follows:

> I find your amazement at the behavior of the Czech press in the Dreyfus matter and in the Kutná Hora trial unfortunately very understandable. But you are confusing Young Czech and radical with liberal and progressive, and you do not take note of the fact that our organs of truly progressive orientations have spoken out from the very beginning for Dreyfus and against the ritual murder superstition. . . .

There is no need to waste any more words regarding the Dreyfus judgment. I myself am happy now that the unfortunate Captain will carry the trial forward without consideration of pardon. The malicious behavior of his opponents deserves no pardon. France itself can only win if the antisemitic and clerical anarchism of the generals is openly crushed. . . .

Rather it is a question of blocking up the source of this moral scourge. This is all the more important as it has become—as the Polná situation demonstrates—a European sickness. Dreyfus and his brave friends will have performed a service to civilized humanity if they lead this disgraceful trial *usque ad finem*. . . .

Regarding the Kutná Hora trial, I shall not expound on "ritual murder" in general. The cultural history sources for this are closed. But allow me to offer the following observations with regard to this special case.

The antisemites never tire of presenting the Jews as the *non plus ultra* of cunning and slyness. How do these qualities fit with the brutally stupid crime in Polná? Today if some kind of apparently secret society or sect wished to acquire human blood, it would look for the unknown and still living victim of its insane criminal mind in the larger cities and not in the countryside. It is from this perspective that I judge all recent cases purported to be ritual murders. The Polná murder, too, contradicts all of the conditions, which the antisemites themselves attach to secret—and secretly carried out—ritual murder. And if there should somewhere be found some unlucky person who succumbed to antisemitic suggestion, even this case would have to be charged to antisemitism and its provocative propaganda.

As far as I can see, the antisemitic ritual murder superstition at present has a predominantly economic meaning. The antisemites pretend that they want to free the people from the economic vampires; but a people—or, rather, social strata—that has been raised in economic fetishism will *de facto* only remember the distinction between Jewish and Christian vampires.

Obviously this antisemitic superstition is general, is international; to oppose it, therefore, requires the common effort of all who disagree. If my statement can help in any way in this task, you are free to publish it.[96]

The publication of the letter triggered a series of events that would quickly lead to Masaryk's direct engagement with the Kutná Hora proceedings—in particular with the forensic methods used in the case—his call for a judicial review of the trial, and his very public campaign against the myth of Jewish ritual murder. That Masaryk should have found himself under attack in the conservative, Catholic press in both the Bohemian lands and in Vienna did not surprise the professor; he frequently laid much of the blame for the persistence of ritual murder belief in popular culture at the feet of what he liked to call "the clerical party." One encounter that he had with a fellow liberal—a university professor and "baptized Jew," with whom Masaryk was well acquainted—caught him by surprise. Masaryk described the encounter in an address he made to the Reichsrat in December 1907:

> He said to me: "You should not have come out so publicly in the affair. You know, I myself am a Jew and do not believe that the ritual murder legend is true; it is only a legend. But this case demonstrates that one cannot exclude the possibility that there is some kind of secret sect, which might have ritual murder in its laws."
>
> I admit that I was not a little surprised to hear an educated person talking this way. I said to him, "It is not possible to believe such a thing."
>
> "No, the case is very suspicious."
>
> I went out and bought the entire stenographic protocol of the trial, and the first thing I did was to read over the medical reports.[97]

This early engagement with the medical and forensic record resulted in the publication of a short pamphlet, *The Need to Review the Polná Trial*, which comprised a pointed critique of the Polná investigation, its forensic mistakes, and the trial itself—and which was quickly confiscated by the Austrian authorities. The booklet's suppression occurred on 6 November 1899. Three days later, however, Ferdinand Kronawetter—a liberal democratic deputy from Vienna—managed to read the entire pamphlet into the record of the House of Deputies (Abgeordnetenhaus) in the Reichsrat (in a hastily produced German translation) during an interpellation addressed to the minister of justice, an act that effectively rendered the confiscation useless. Both the German and the Czech editions were immediately published and distributed.[98]

Figure 11. Political cartoon from *Humoristické listy* (December 1, 1899). "From the most recent repertory: *Brothers, a Chinese Play*, by Julius Zeyer."

Courtesy J. Mabray.

Over the next several months, Masaryk threw himself into all aspects of the case, paying close attention to what he took to be highly questionable methods and conclusions on the part of the forensic investigators—the imprecision of their language, the clumsy way in which they handled the examination of the area in which the body was found, their presumptions regarding the positioning of the body, their determination that the Březina woods was the place where the murder took place (Masaryk felt that the murder had been committed elsewhere and the body later brought to Březina), the overly facile dismissal of sexual gratification as a motive in the case, and the certainty with which they estimated the speed with which the blood must have escaped the body, as well as the amount that one would expect to find at the scene of the crime—but, equally importantly, to the intrusive role played by the antisemitic discourse of ritual murder in the scientific reports themselves. Masaryk argued that there was nothing in the trail of physical evidence to lead one to conclude that anything other than an "ordinary" crime of violence had occurred. Were it not for the insistent cultural noise that kept hammering home the theme of Jewish ritual murder, he was convinced, there would have been no Hilsner affair. Masaryk published the results of his study in the early months of 1900, in Berlin, thus evading the Austrian censors once again. The title of this, much longer, pamphlet, *The Meaning of the Polná Crime for the Ritual Murder Superstition*, belied its ironic intent, as he explained in his foreword. "The antisemites see in the Polná crime the strongest confirmation of the belief in ritual murder. This has moved me to examine the Polná affair carefully from all sides, and the result of this examination is: the Polná crime is not a ritual murder. On the contrary, it is striking proof of the fact that the ritual murder accusation is, in the fullest sense of the word, a superstition."[99]

Masaryk paid a high personal price for his vocal defense of what was a decidedly unpopular cause in Czech nationalist circles. The London-based *Jewish Chronicle* (which had been following his activities with great admiration for over a year) caught up with Masaryk at the Kingsley Hotel in Bloomsbury in May 1901, where the Czech leader had been visiting his daughter. In the course of a published interview, Masaryk touched upon the difficulties that he and his family had been facing for more than a year and a half.

> My students were stirred up to riot against me, physical force was introduced into the lecture room, and I had to stop my lectures. Even my children were insulted with cries of "Hilsner," and were consequently compelled to cease their attendance at school. My daughter, whom you see there, was no longer able to pursue her studies in history at the University. Indeed, every kind of persecution was leveled at me and my family. Till now I have been sentenced four times for commenting on the Hilsner trial, and each occasion have paid the fine to which I was condemned for "contempt of court."[100]

Masaryk's recollections in his later conversations with the writer Karel Čapek were more vivid.

> Vienna's anti-Semites set the Czech nationalist and clerical press on me, and when they attacked, well, I was forced to defend myself, wasn't I? And having taken the first step, I had to go on. That meant studying criminology and physiology, all of which I wrote about in great detail. When I traveled to Polná to inspect the scene of the crime and its surroundings, they said I'd been bribed by the Jews. A group of non-students came to my lectures to shout me down. While they shouted, I wrote a protest against their stupid calumnies on the blackboard, calling upon them to give me the reasons for their demonstration. (Only one of them did so; he came to see me that afternoon, a slender, decent young man who

> later became the poet Otakar Theer.) To make certain the demonstrators did not think I was afraid of them, I walked all around the lecture hall, challenging them to argue their points; no one dared. And how did the University react? Instead of taking a strong stand and restoring order, it suspended my lectures for a fortnight.[101]

Other individuals worked independently of Masaryk during the fall of 1899 and the winter of 1900, appealing either to the chief prosecutor's office in Prague or to the Court of Appeals in Vienna for a rehearing of the Kutná Hora trial. One of the first to challenge the proceedings against Hilsner on the basis of faulty scientific procedure was Josef Bulova, a physician and chief medical officer in Karlín on the outskirts of Prague. Bulova submitted his own analysis of the Polná crime—including a sharp critique of the methods and conclusions of Drs. Prokeš and Michálek—to the Prague police headquarters just two days after the conclusion of the proceedings in Kutná Hora. Later in the month, he and his wife paid a visit to Otto Baudyš, the investigating magistrate who had expressed his own misgivings about the investigation the previous spring, and requested permission to examine the evidence from the case. Dr. Bulova contended that the cause of death may have been strangulation, not a cut to the throat, and that the actual murder most likely was committed in some location other than the Březina woods. His wife, a professional seamstress, upon examining the clothing of the victim, pointed out that the tear in her blouse had been made by scissors, not by hand.[102]

Spurred on, perhaps, by the Bulovas' visit, Baudyš intervened once more in the case, submitting a letter in early October to the chief prosecutor's office in Prague, which undoubtedly made its way to the Ministry of Justice in Vienna. In it, Baudyš urged that the case be reopened, echoing a number of Bulova's contentions: that the murder had been committed somewhere else and the body moved to Březina; that Anežka Hrůzová had died from asphyxiation, not exsanguination; and that Jan Hrůza had fought with his sister shortly before the murder and that he was said to have had to use his left hand to shake hands with people at the funeral. Now, however, no one in Polná was willing to step forward to speak out against Jan Hrůza, his mother, or any of the individuals who had offered false testimony—so convinced was the town of Hilsner's guilt. Baudyš closed his letter by appealing to the chief prosecutor to hear his request, to protect him in hostile circumstances, and to help him overcome the tremendous obstacles he faced in achieving justice.

Finally, if possible, he wished to request a face-to-face meeting in which he could add information, which he preferred not to give in writing.[103]

A third front was opened by Adolf Stein, a Moravian-born Vienna attorney who began to represent the interests of the Hilsner family in November 1899. Stein had some experience in criminal cases that bore a resemblance to the ritual murder accusation, having represented Moses and Gittel Ritter before the Vienna Court of Appeals in an infamous murder case that took place in Galicia from 1883 to 1886. It was he—joined, I should think, by Auředníček—who spearheaded the effort before the Court of Appeals now to have the case either overturned or retried.[104] What united each of these separate endeavors was their fierce criticism of the forensic procedures, assumptions, and conclusions of the court physicians in Polná. And, while the Court of Appeals chose not to respond to Judge Baudyš's letter (or to defend him from attacks by Karel Baxa and others), the court did concede that a formal, expert evaluation was called for. For this review, it turned to the Czech Medical Faculty in Prague.[105]

The lengthy report of the Czech Medical Faculty, dated 27 March 1900, took the form of an exhaustive review of all forensic procedures that had been performed on the body of Anežka Hrůzová and the evidence collected (such as Leopold Hilsner's gray trousers).[106] The findings did not support all of the contentions of Baudyš, Masaryk, or Bulova—with regard to the cause of death, the location of the murder, or the sexual nature of the crime, for example—but they raised serious enough doubts concerning the quality of the earlier examinations, the procedures employed, and the unspoken assumptions that lay behind them so as to provide the Court of Appeals in Vienna with sufficient grounds to nullify the Kutná Hora verdict. The medical faculty averred that it was impossible to determine with certainty whether or not the faint stains on Hilsner's trousers were from blood and that it was unable to find sperm either on Anežka's clothing or in her pubic hair. On the more difficult question of cause of death, here the faculty came down on the side of exsanguination caused by the cutting of the carotid artery and concluded that the wound to the neck had been produced while the victim was still alive—thus potentially bolstering the prosecution's case. At the same time, the Prague faculty pointedly challenged the earlier medical opinion on at least four crucial points: (1) The bleeding out was produced by blows to the head as well as by the cut to the neck. (2) The neck wound was not particularly wide and could have been produced by any ordinary pocket knife. (3) The murder could have been carried out by one person. (4) There was no evidence to suggest that the amount of blood found in the victim's body, on her hair and clothing, and in the general vicinity where the body was found was anything *other* than what one would expect to find from a normal, healthy woman. Indeed, the earlier investigators had overestimated how much blood Anežka would have carried while alive. Finally, the faculty experts had no opinion to offer on why some of the victim's clothing had been removed and/or torn, some pieces buried, and some hung on branches. They would not rule out the possibility that the murderer suffered from some kind of sexual perversity.[107]

Four weeks later, on 25 April 1900, the High Court (Oberster Gerischtshof) in Vienna overturned the September 16 verdict and ordered a new trial to be held in the district court in Písek in southern Bohemia.[108] The court referred in its decision numerous times to the report of the Czech Medical Faculty, particularly when it contradicted the earlier findings of Prokeš and Michálek or the statement of facts as laid out in the original indictment. It made note of the fact that numerous aspects of the indictment had relied directly on the accuracy of the Polná physicians' findings and flowed from their narrative reconstruction of the crime. When these facts were called into question, the narrative scaffolding of the indictment collapsed. To begin, the High Court dismissed the presumption of multiple perpetrators—the notion that the murder had to have been committed by several individuals. In so doing, it also rejected the Kutná Hora court's determination of *malicious manner* (*Tückigkeit* or *způsobem potutelně*), since the lower court had tied the definition of malice in this case to the scenario of the crime as imagined by Dr. Prokeš (and doggedly challenged by Auředníček), in which several individuals lay in wait for an unsuspecting Hrůzová, then lassoed her with a rope and hit her with a rock to render her unconscious.

The High Court seems to have been well aware of the fact that both of these elements of the state's case—multiple perpetrators and malicious intent—carried implicit assumptions regarding the question of motive. Both were building blocks in the construction of a prosecution for a crime of ritual murder: the state presumed that on his own, Hilsner lacked both the expertise and the physical strength to carry out such an act, and the forensic analysis of the crime had posited that the injuries that had been caused by strangulation and blows to the head had been designed to render the victim unconscious in preparation for the subsequent fatal assault, the act that effected exsanguination. The court appeared to mock Schneider-Svoboda's formal claim to the jury that motive in this case was irrelevant, implying that this was just so much posturing, and noting that the indictment in fact suggested motive when it repeated the claim of the Polná physicians that Anežka Hrůzová appeared to have been completely emptied of blood. The prosecutor, then, was trying to have it both ways: maintaining the image of neutral skeptic while promoting through suggestion the charge of ritual murder. But the High Court would have none of it. The report of the Prague medical faculty, it concluded, has "absolutely eliminated the removal of the victim's blood for whatever use as a motive for the crime." Look instead to "the sexual sphere."[109]

* * *

Jiří Kovtun has observed that the decision of the High Court in Vienna to overturn the Kutná Hora verdict signaled the defeat of the ritual murder accusation "in the contest of facts, well-founded opinion, and verified argument," that is to say, in the realm of modern legal procedure and argumentation.[110] After more than a year of criminal investigation, changing and evolving testimony, contested forensic examination, dueling expert opinions, and political provocation, the ship of state appeared to have righted itself. It would have been understandable to presume that the new trial in Písek, which opened on 25 October 1900, would lay the matter of ritual murder to rest once and for all. The court had ordered that the case be retried as a sexually motivated murder and that Hilsner be considered a sole perpetrator. A new prosecutor and new investigating magistrate were to be assigned to the case; Auředníček would continue to represent the accused. If Hilsner were to be convicted again, it would have to be as an "ordinary" murderer and sexual predator.

But the Vienna court could not foresee all eventualities, such as the fact that, before the start of the new trial, an additional murder charge would be added to the indictment against Hilsner (the remains of a woman, the victim of an earlier crime, having been discovered in the meantime). Nor could the High Court control the ongoing politicization of the ritual murder accusation in the Bohemian lands—or its symbolic importance in the increasingly heated contest between Czech and German nationalists. In the short term, the court's decision did little to quash the appeal of ritual murder narratives in popular culture. At the end of a three-week trial, four questions were put to the jury in Písek, two for each case. To the first set of questions, whether Hilsner undertook specific actions that led to the death of the victim, the jury responded no. To the second set of questions, whether Hilsner *participated* in acts that led to the death of the victim, the jury's response was yes. Thus, while the breakdown of the verdict might seem to have expressed equivocation on the question of Hilsner's guilt, the presumption of multiple perpetrators—and the implication of conspiratorial behavior of one type or another—in fact returned the symbolism and imagery of the blood libel to center stage. Hilsner once again was sentenced to death by hanging. To borrow from monarchical discourse, the ritual murder accusation was dead: long live the ritual murder accusation.[111]

Chapter 5

The Many Trials of Konitz

Along the way from Berlin to Russia lies the city of Konitz. A murder took place here, a bestial murder of an innocent, eighteen-year-old youth, who was forced to bleed out under the knife of a cruel murderer. We are filled with horror at the beast who could commit such an act, and with sympathy for the poor parents, who are unable to pray at his grave. And yet it is nothing more than a murder, like the hundreds, indeed thousands, before it, which have found only partial atonement, or none at all; for the police are made up of men who are neither omniscient nor omnipresent.

—*Dr. Bloch's Oesterreichische Wochenschrift*, 4 May 1900

The "Ritual Murder" Myth Officially Exploded

Berlin, 15th September

I have just learnt that high medical experts have given their opinions as to the character of the crime by which the student Winter met his death at Konitz, and which the anti-Semites have exploited against the Jews as one of "Ritual Murder." This opinion of medical experts puts quite another construction on the murder.

As the medical witnesses at the trial disagreed as to the cause of the death, the Crown Prosecutor referred the whole matter to the Royal Medical College at Danzig. This Faculty has now given its opinion, which contains the following important points:

1. Winter died from suffocation (therefore not from loss of blood).
2. The cut in the throat was inflicted only after death, as part of the mutilation of the body. Moreover, the cut was not made with a butcher's knife.
3. Winter was killed while committing an immoral offense or immediately afterwards.
4. The corpse was not bloodless; several parts were full of blood. The bloodlessness of certain portions of a body is caused either by suffocation or by long immersion in water.

The medical opinion has been supplemented by a letter from the Crown Prosecutor to the Counsel who defended the members of the Levy family charged with complicity in the murder.

The Crown Prosecutor affirms:

1. The not the slightest foundation exists for suspicion against any Jews.
2. That the allegation of a Blood or Ritual Murder has not been proved; but, on the contrary, has been disproved by the condition of the body and the expert opinions of the Danzig Medical College.

—*The Jewish Chronicle*, 18 October 1901

The Psychopathology of Superstition: A New Take

Writing in 1902 for his journal *Archiv für Kriminal-Anthropologie und Kriminalistik*, the criminologist Hans Gross (1847–1915) reviewed a hefty tome refuting the ritual murder accusation, written by the Russian orientalist Daniil Khvol'son (Daniel Chwolson). Khvol'son (1819–1911), a native of Vilnius (Wilno, Vilna) in the Russian Empire, had been born to a Jewish family and had received traditional rabbinic training in his youth before leaving Russia for university studies in Breslau, where he received his PhD in 1850. He converted to Orthodox Christianity in 1855 and soon thereafter assumed a professorship at the University of Saint Petersburg. Appointed in 1857 by Tsar Alexander II to a commission of experts charged with investigating the ritual murder accusation (as well as purported references in Jewish literature to the use of

Christian blood for ritual purposes), Khvol'son ended up devoting decades of his life to a passionate campaign to refute the accusation in all its forms.[1] The book under review was a German translation of the second, revised edition of his Russian-language opus, *The Blood Libel and Other Medieval Accusations Against the Jews: A Historical Investigation Based on Sources.*[2] The reviewer, who at the time was teaching criminal law at the German University in Prague, had spent the early decades of his career as an examining magistrate, and then public prosecutor, in his native Styria and other parts of Austria, where he had built a reputation for advocating the systematizing and rationalizing of criminal investigation. He was, together with Cesare Lombroso (1835–1909) and Franz von Liszt (1851–1919), one of the creators of the emerging field of criminology, which applied methods from several disciplines—notably medicine, psychology, anthropology, and forensic science—to impose order, rationality, and empirical method on the study of criminal behavior.[3]

In addition to promoting the new discipline in their own countries, each of the pioneers of criminology had things to say about the connections—real or imagined—between Jews and criminal behavior.[4] It was Hans Gross, however, who engaged most directly with the ritual murder trials of his day, as well as with the question of crime and ritualized behavior. He followed the criminal investigations and trial proceedings of the Central European ritual murder cases with much interest and reviewed many of the publications that grew out of them in his journal.[5] His review of Khvol'son's work was the second to appear on the theme of ritual murder and was relatively brief compared to one that he had written in 1900 on a book that addressed an ongoing investigation in Konitz (Chojnice) in West Prussia. It did not take more than a few pages to drive home his major criticisms.

"This book, too," Gross began—indicating that he and his readers had been down this path before— "seeks to demonstrate that the Jews are innocent of the suspicion that they make use of Christian blood for various purposes." And it does so, he added, noting that Khvol'son had studied some 20,000 volumes of Hebrew writings, with "an immense expenditure of erudition."[6] Gross then delivered a brief, but cutting, criticism: all this scholarship, while important, perhaps, from a historical and bibliographical perspective, was essentially wasted effort. Useless. The average person is not going to read, or put his or her faith in, such a book. And educated people had long since ceased to believe that either Judaism or a book of Jewish religious ritual "explicitly prescribed the use of Christian blood." Thus, to fight the ritual murder accusation as a cultural trope or as an item of belief was completely beside the point; more important, such apologetics ignored the crucial issue: blood superstition (*Blutaberglaube*), Gross argued, was endemic to human societies; it has always existed and would continue to exist. To charge that only the Jews had succumbed to "blood belief" (*Blutglaube*) was certainly unjust, but it was also senseless to try to prove that only the Jews were *free* of such superstition. "Blood belief today is still pandemic; all peoples have it; the Jews included."[7]

Earlier, Gross had delivered much the same verdict, using some of the same language but in more elaborate detail. In his review of an early book on the Konitz case, Gross admitted to being angered by the temerity of the author, who—in his eagerness to demonstrate that the murder in question was not a ritual killing committed by Jews—found nothing wrong with the fact that he was intervening in an investigation that had not yet been completed. But whom, Gross wondered, was the author trying to convince? Knowledgeable people now acknowledged that "blood belief," that is, the use of human blood for superstitious ends, "has always existed, and among all peoples; it exists today and will not likely disappear for a long time to come." Jews were no more immune from such superstitious practices than anyone else. Certainly, the contention that Jews were instructed by their religion to hold such beliefs about blood—in teachings known to Jews but not to Christians—was childish. It is well known, he added, that the Talmud—considering its encyclopedic nature—contained all sorts of superstitious rubbish (*Zeug*), but no educated person believes that, therefore, the Jewish religion commands the murder of Christians.[8]

This much for the blood libel in its traditional formulation. If Gross at times expressed exasperation at the numerous apologetic tomes that came across his desk, this, it seems to me, was for two reasons: (1) Direct refutations of this belief would never convince those who held it to change their minds. (No amount of scientific refutation, Gross opined, would be likely to succeed in changing the mind of a person who was convinced that thirteen was an unlucky number.[9]) (2) More important, from Gross's perspective, such apologetics ignored a crucial fact, which judges and criminal investigators needed to bear in mind: individual criminals might indeed act under the influence of superstitious beliefs regarding blood and its magical effects. In such cases, they would leave clues as to their identity at the scene of the crime.

For Gross, understanding the psychopathology of criminals, especially murderers, was both a theoretical pursuit and a prerequisite to solving violent crimes. And the tendency of violent criminals to engage in compulsive, ritualized behavior provoked by superstitious belief constituted an important feature of their psychopathology. From this position, he chided those well-meaning people who would dismiss out of hand the prosecution's contention, for example, that Leopold Hilsner had committed murder. To the contrary, he argued, in a two-part article that he wrote for his *Archiv* in 1902 to 1903 and that was reprinted in his *Collected Essays on Criminalistics* in 1908. He expressed support for the decision of the public prosecutor following the quashing of the original Kutná Hora verdict by the High Court in Vienna not simply to retry Hilsner but to charge him now for two murders: that of Marie Klímová in 1898 as well as that of Anežka Hruzová in 1899.[10] In both cases, Gross claimed, the killer had demonstrated the same kind of compulsive, ritualized behavior: the victim had been found naked to the waist with her clothing partly torn, partly cut, and lightly covered with evergreen branches. Pieces of clothing had been scattered about the corpse, some hanging from branches, some tied together with string. The immediate motive for the murders—robbery, sexual gratification, or whatever—did not matter.

In any event, Gross suggested, the distribution of the victim's clothing could not be explained by the act of murder itself; it had to be examined closely on its own terms. If such patterned behavior were to appear more than once, one could derive from it much epistemological information regarding the criminal psyche; on a practical level, one could be certain that one was looking for a single killer.[11] Recall that even the Czech Medical Faculty in Prague had agreed on this point. In its report to the court, it concluded, "If the two murders had been committed by different people, who had no knowledge of one another, how could such a striking correspondence between the circumstances of the two murders be explained? The only possible explanation to be found is that it the perpetrators were the same, and that when they saw how well they were able to keep the murder of Klímová secret, they killed Anežka Hruzová in the same manner."[12] Gross fully concurred. There could be no other explanation. The same person or persons had committed both crimes. And Hilsner's denials of his own guilt failed to convince.[13]

Gross intended his analysis of the relationship between superstitious belief and violent crime to be applied narrowly to the field of criminalistics, that is, to detecting the identity of the perpetrator of a crime based on a close examination of the modus operandi. In principle, the ritualized behavior of a killer—the staging of the crime scene, the physical clues left behind—could lead to the identification of the perpetrator independent of other questions, such as the motive behind the murder or even the methods used to carry it out. Narrowly conceived, then, Gross's concept of "psychopathic superstition" had no direct bearing on the rhetoric surrounding the ritual murder accusation. The superstitious beliefs that interested Gross and his colleagues could relate to almost anything: compulsive actions meant to ensure good fortune, for example, or to ward off the evil eye. In the chapter on "Superstition" in his widely distributed *Handbook for Examining Magistrates*—which went through five editions between 1893 and 1908, was translated into several languages, and continued to be published in the interwar period—Jews appeared only twice and the blood accusation only once, and then only to indicate that it continued to be believed by many.[14]

The language of criminal psychopathology, however—incorporating such terms as "superstition," "religious compulsion," "ritual," and "belief"—was both highly suggestive and steeped in ambiguity. And the claim that a connection could be drawn linking superstitious belief to violent crime troubled many who had hoped to subdue the ritual murder accusation through the discipline of science. Gross's pursuit of the criminal through the patterns of his or her own ritualized behavior seemed to suggest that the blood libel could, in fact, be scientifically rehabilitated. One person who voiced such concern was the Berlin attorney, and later professor of law, Arthur Nussbaum (1877–1964), who had been a postgraduate student of Franz von Liszt, who, at the time, was conducting experiments regarding the reliability of witness testimony concerning things they claimed to have observed. Aware of his work in this area of psychology and law, representatives of the Österreichisch-Israelitische Union (Austrian Jewish Union) appealed to Liszt in 1904 to reexamine the two Hilsner trials. The Berlin professor pleaded lack of time and suggested that Nussbaum take up the cudgel in his place. The result was Nussbaum's 1906 book *Der Polnaer Ritualmordprozess: Eine kriminalpsychologische Untersuchung auf aktenmässiger Grundlage* (*The Polná Ritual Murder Trial: A Criminological-Psychological Examination on the Basis of Documents*), with a preface by Liszt.[15]

Following the work of his mentor, and in contrast to Gross, Nussbaum directed *his* criminological analysis at the prejudicial social and cultural backdrop to the affair, as well as at the unreliability of certain kinds of witness testimony, *not* at the defendant himself. He strongly objected, in fact, to the very concept of "psychopathic superstition," labeling it ill-defined, highly biased, and unscientific, as it claimed to be able to deduce not only the state of mind of violent criminals but also their motives for killing on the basis of clues left behind at the scene of the crime. "Evidently," he wrote, some forty years later, "we are confronted with a scientific version of popular prejudice and party agitation."[16] On to Konitz.

The Crime, the Many Trials

Eighteen-year-old Ernst Winter was older, taller, and more physically developed than the other *Obertertianeren* at the Konitz Gymnasium in West Prussia.[17] A native of the nearby town of Prechlau, where his father was in the building trades, Winter had taken several years off from school to work as a carpenter's apprentice before resuming his education. On March 11, 1900, he sat down for his regular Sunday lunch with the Lange family, with whom he took room and board; got up from the table at 1:30 p.m.; collected his hat and coat; and went for a walk on what was a bright and sunny afternoon. He did not return for afternoon coffee. Nor did he show up for supper. At first, Winter's absence did not cause much worry for the Lange family; they knew that he had relatives in Konitz whom he often visited on Sundays. The Langes became concerned, however, when he did not return overnight, did not come down for morning coffee, and did not pick up his schoolbooks. Lange, a baker, sent word to Winter's relatives to inquire if he had gone there on Sunday and perhaps spent the night. The relatives replied that they had not seen him. Lange reported Winter's absence that morning to the gymnasium director as well as to the police. He also sent a telegram to Ernst's parents, who came to Konitz the same day. The rest of Monday proceeded with unsuccessful searches for the young man.[18]

Ernst Winter's tragic demise announced itself on Tuesday, March 13. Lange met the young man's father at the home of his relatives. Together with Lange's daughter, they headed for the local lake, the Mönchsee, as a rumor apparently had already begun to spread that Winter, known as an excellent ice skater, may have attempted to skate on the lake, fallen through the thin ice, and drowned. The party proceeded toward the Mönchsee, which they surveyed from a high point, but saw no signs of broken ice. They then made their way to a raft made of wooden planks floating by the shore in an unfrozen part of the lake. It was here that they spotted a package floating in the water and, struggling with its size and heavy weight, managed to bring it over to the raft and investigate it. What they found was shocking: the top half of a human torso with no arms or head. Lange's daughter was sent to summon the police while the two fathers continued to scour the lake around the raft.

A short while later, they came upon another package, which contained the lower half of the torso. Most of the internal organs were missing, but the genitalia and the buttocks were intact. Winter's father declared the torso to be that of his son, perhaps based on its general size and strength. The missing arms and legs appeared to have been artfully severed from the body.[19]

A macabre turn of events, to be sure, yet body parts kept appearing over the next days and weeks. On 15 March, a boy found the right arm of a man on the gate to the courtyard of the Evangelical church; it did not appear to have been there long, and it attached neatly to the upper torso that had been found in the lake. On 20 March the left thigh was found, once again in the Mönchsee, and it, too, had been neatly severed from the lower torso. On Easter Sunday, which fell on 15 April in 1900, another boy found the head of a man lying in a ditch on the outskirts of town by the shooting club. By now there could be no doubt that the scattered remains had come from one body, which was that of Ernst Winter.[20] For months, however, no piece of his clothing was found. Suddenly, in January 1901—ten months after the discovery of the first body parts and the start of the criminal investigation and months after three separate trials had already taken place—pieces of Ernst Winter's clothing turned up. His jacket and vest and the remains of a handkerchief were discovered in some woods on 8 January by members of the local watch command; five days later, his trousers turned up in a public garden and his overcoat, in the yard of the girls' school, on 15 January.[21]

As the reader has doubtless already surmised, the Konitz affair—the last of Central Europe's major ritual murder investigations and trials—departed significantly from earlier patterns on several levels. The first pertained to the victim's age and sex, when taken together: Ernst Winter was neither a young boy nor a vulnerable adolescent female or young woman; he was eighteen years old and male, by all accounts healthy, vibrant, and strong. Second, as we have seen, the body had been dismembered and subsequently dispersed, at different points in time, across the town—a development, it should be noted, that not only complicated the criminal investigation but also made forensic medical examinations quite challenging and their results often tentative.

A third major difference had to do with the Konitz case's underlying instability: its unfinished quality and its constant wavering between a straightforward—although gruesome—murder investigation and a sensational affair. Despite an intense criminal investigation that lasted for approximately two years, the Konitz prosecutors never managed to indict or try any individual for the murder of Ernst Winter. This does not mean that there was no trial

Figure 12. Postcard. "Memorial Card for Ernst Winter, murdered in Konitz on 11 March 1900." Top right: "Murder in Konitz. 20,000 mark reward is being offered by the Minister of the Interior to any private person who gives decisive information concerning the murderers of the upper gymnasium student, Ernst Winter. The minister reserves the right to decide on the payment of the reward."

Courtesy J. Mabray.

relating to the Konitz crime; in fact, five separate trials took place between September 1900 and October 1902: one on the charge of aiding and abetting, three for perjury, and one for libel.

Each of the Konitz trials offered advocates for the theory of Jewish ritual murder ample opportunity to insert their claims into the proceedings—either directly or by way of suggestion—and in each trial, both prosecutors and defense attorneys needed to factor into their questioning of witnesses and summations to the jury the degree to which any intervention either promoted or challenged such a theory. Instability and uncertainty also permeated the field of forensic examination and analysis. By this point in the story, we would expect to see competing claims to competence and authority, pitting the locality against the center and small-town medical officers against the state's top medical examiners—or the faculty of elite medical schools—as we have seen such scenarios play out in each of the three previous cases. But in the Konitz affair, the number of separate medical reports and autopsies—completed, supplemented, repeated, reviewed, and challenged—is quite extraordinary.

Table 2. Konitz Trials

	Konitz Trials	
Defendant(s)	*Dates*	*Charges*
Wolf Israelski	8 September 1900	Aiding and abetting
Richard Speisinger	5–6 October 1900	Perjury
Bernhard Masloff, Anna Ross, and two other defendants	25 October–10 November 1900	Perjury
Moritz Lewy	13–16 February 1901	Perjury
Paul Bötticher and Wilhelm Bruhn, editor and publisher, respectively, of the *Staatsbürgerzeitung*	30 September–11 October 1902	Libel

In 1903, the major Jewish civil rights association in Germany, the Centralverein deutscher Staatsbürger jüdischen Glaubens (hereafter: Centralverein), collected the numerous medical reports that were now part of the official record—stretching from the external examination of the body parts found at the Mönchsee (March 1900) to the extensive review of the entire investigation (referred to as an *Obergutachten*, a higher, or superior, opinion) by the Royal Scientific Deputation for Medical Affairs in Berlin in January 1902—and published them in a single volume.[22] This eighty-seven-page-long publication included the protocols of three separate autopsies; a forensic chemist's examination of partially digested food and fibers following the recovery of Winter's head and neck; a follow-up report on the earlier autopsies responding to specific questions posed by the state prosecutor; trial testimony from several forensic physicians, including testimony from a veterinary medical inspector regarding Jewish ritual slaughtering practices; the oral testimony of a forensic physician from Berlin (hired by the defense in one of the trials), which contradicted the conclusions of some of the earlier reports; a full review of the various medical examinations to date, prepared by the Royal Medical College of West Prussia, in Danzig (Gdańsk); and the higher opinion of the Royal Scientific Deputation mentioned above. This collection of documents does not easily reveal a linear progression from preliminary conclusions to a final judgment. It is built, rather, around assessments that are often at war with one other, with the most compelling analyses of the evidence hidden in the maze of contradictory, and sometimes supporting, positions.[23] A perusal through the volume and much of the other archival material of the affair leaves one with the impression that the Prussian state—buffeted between a proliferation of sensational, often unreliable witness statements from Konitz residents and the more measured, skeptical assessments of its own criminal investigators, as well as between the active intervention of political antisemites and the forensic examinations of its own scientists—had no clear strategy of how to bring the investigation into Ernst Winter's murder to a successful conclusion.[24]

But Konitz also shared much in common with previous ritual murder investigations and trials. It featured local medical examiners who, in their naïveté and their closeness to local knowledge, proved to be susceptible in their medical reports to cultural suggestion; higher state officials—criminal investigators, prosecutors, and forensic physicians, often attached to elite medical faculties—who were determined to discipline the local investigation to the strictures of modern criminal procedure and critical forensic analysis; and, again at the local level, the dissemination of a theory of ritual murder—in the form of powerful rumor—which filled the information void created by a hamstrung investigation.

Body Parts, Rumor, and Forensics

If for Hans Gross the telltale sign of a psychopathic personality operating in the Polná case was the scattering of clothing, what did he make of the delayed scattering of body parts in the Konitz affair, which was as yet unsolved at the time that he wrote "Psychopathic Superstition"? Gross paused near the end of his 1902 study to consider the murder of Ernst Winter. The characteristic feature of both Polná and Konitz, he suggested (as well as in a few others that he examined), lay in the obsessive behaviors of the murderers, that is, the "carrying about" (*Herumschleppen*) of items belonging to the victim: "To be emphasized here is the well-known criminal-psychological finding that similarity between different events consists not in objects but in action. And so here one emphasizes the fact that, in all of our cases, partly the clothing and partly the body parts of the victim were spread around. What is characteristic is the carrying around; whether it is clothing, or body parts is unimportant."[25] "Whether it was clothes or body parts," then, it made no difference. It was the patterned behavior itself, "the curious similarity in such mysterious incidents," that captured his attention and, he urged, called for closer examination, "for the possibility that one can find a singular type and the same motive in these murders is not out of the question."[26] Thus, even though the identity of the killer in the Konitz case remained unknown, there was much to learn from the similarity in the behavior of the killers in such situations.

What is the "singular type" and "motive" that he is referring to? By way of conclusion, Gross returns to the theme of compulsive behavior driven by superstition and, in so doing, moves well beyond the careful empiricism that he seemed to employ earlier in the article. Superstitions of various types, he reminds the reader, are much more widespread in human societies than one generally likes to admit. Most people, however, are able to balance such universal impulses with more conventionally rational choices. In any event, they do not, for the most part, act on these inclinations in a criminal manner. That is, unless and until something goes wrong in their lives or they come to a psychological breaking point: "This is the only explanation for a long line of so-called 'gruesome' crimes, which cannot be explained by normal feeling: the killing of children, purposeless or gruesome killings of adults without discernable motive, terrible maltreatments and mutilations, etc.; many crimes that can be traced back to religious hysteria, religious madness, belong here."[27] This brings Gross to what he calls his final assumption: "If we can say that a series of homicides share noticeable similarities, and that in each of them some unclear event is perceived (the scattering of clothing or of the body parts of victims); and if we can say with regard to at least one of these cases, that this occurrence can be explained by the growing superstition of a psychopathic individual, then the supposition that the other homicides lead back to similar situations is permitted."[28]

It is not difficult in hindsight to see the weaknesses in Gross's methodology: the promiscuous blending of assumption and empiricism (is it, in fact, permitted?), the questionable appeal to supposedly universal human proclivities, the arbitrary limitation in the number of hypotheses to be entertained, and the false conclusion that findings from one criminal pattern necessarily apply to a different, although similarly patterned, case. Most glaringly, Gross seems deliberately to have opted for an unnecessarily complicated solution to the riddle of the dispersal (over time) of body parts and clothing when a more obvious answer could easily have been reached. For it is certainly conceivable that Ernst Winter's killer or killers, in dismembering the body and scattering the remains and clothing over a period of ten months, were acting rationally and not under superstitious compulsion. The object was to divert attention and protect themselves from discovery or perhaps also to direct suspicion toward other potential suspects.[29]

It was, moreover, a strategy that was remarkably attuned to the cultural landscape of turn-of-the-century ritual murder discourse. The discoveries in March and April 1900 of upper and lower torsos floating in a frozen lake, a right arm lying in the Evangelical cemetery, and a head lodged in a wooded ditch produced the desired effect of generating public excitement and dismay and setting in motion various rumors and theories of the crime. There was nothing in the dispersal of evidence that ought to have suggested a ritual killing other than the larger cultural context in which the crime occurred. Debates over, and claims of, Jewish ritual murder constituted one of the key points of reference in discussions of crime and criminality in Central Europe at the time, and it was almost inevitable that the murder of Ernst Winter would be held up as a prime example. Again, not because shocking murders had not occurred in the past, but because the field of reference was overdetermined.

The Konitz affair swirled about like a slow-moving atmospheric disturbance held aloft by four simultaneous and seemingly endless events: the sensational series of discoveries of body parts and clothing; the production and dissemination of rumor, some of which was locally produced, some generously provided from other parts of Germany; a long line of, at times, mutually contradictory forensic medical examinations and reports; and not one but five separate trials emerging from the investigations into the events in Konitz, none of which included an indictment for murder—ritual or otherwise—but all of which provided ample space for further articulations of the blood libel. In the first days following the discovery of body parts on the Mönchsee, "the Konitz rumor soup," to borrow from the language of Christoph Nonn, "was still simmering on a low flame."[30] These were days when people exchanged questions and theories concerning Ernst Winter's disappearance and apparently gruesome end in informal settings—in pubs, at market stands, across garden fences.

One might well suppose that rumors of ritual murder were part of these communications. At this point, however, whatever isolated accusations were leveled at Jews did not amount to much. While prosecutors and the police may have been "virtually drowning in a flood of generally worthless tips from the local population," residents and investigators appeared at this point still to be working cooperatively.[31] In Nonn's analysis, this relatively calm state of affairs came to an end when the official investigation failed to produce a break in the case—after approximately ten days to two weeks—at which point the local population lost confidence in the police investigation. What had up to now been a flood of tips dried to a rivulet. In the absence of a compelling official version of events, people resorted to communication among themselves. Rumor, in this context, substituted for official information and became, in Nonn's words (and similarly to what transpired eighteen years earlier in Tiszaeszlár), a "*Gegenöffentlichkeit*" (a counter public sphere, or discourse), while local knowledge established itself as "an alternative forum for the investigation of the murder": "Since official explanation was lacking, rumors of ritual murder and other theories concerning the identity of the perpetrators began to blossom. The residents of Konitz filled the holes left by the investigators with their own stories."[32]

The sequence of medical examinations conducted on Ernst Winter's torso, limbs, and head between March and June 1900 did little to dislodge rumors that he had fallen victim to a ritual murder. From the earliest external examination of the body parts to the autopsy on the head in April to the "post-postmortems" of May and June, the two local forensic physicians (Drs. Müller and Bleske) maintained that the body had undergone a near-total emptying of blood, thereby signaling a potent, if not very original, motif in the modern discourse of ritual murder. After the first autopsy, they determined that the cause of death was exsanguination (*Verblutung*), most likely caused by the cutting through of the blood vessels in the neck. At the time of these medical procedures, the public prosecutor instructed Dr. Müller to inspect the kosher butchering facilities of the local Jewish community, from which he removed the remnants of blood—partly coagulated, partly frozen—from a large container. A chemist was asked to examine the knife and other objects belonging to a Rabbi Hamburger from Charlottenburg, presumably the community's *shoḥet*. Müller went so far as to look up the records of the Skurz murder case of 1884, which he found to be similar in many respects to the Winter murder. (You will recall, however, that in that case, the state decided to charge a Christian butcher with having framed a Jewish butcher for the crime.) Yet another conclusion drawn by the medical examiners concerned the manner in which the body itself was dismembered. Müller and Bleske at times noted that the operation had been performed by a "skilled hand" ("von kündiger Hand"); on at least one occasion, it was described as having been carried out "mit grosser Kunstfertigkeit," with great artistry, suggesting a person whose profession it was to cut up a body or butcher an animal. In a less charged environment, these two depictions—exsanguination and skilled cutting—might have suggested any number of scenarios, but in

Central Europe in 1900, they inevitably conjured powerful and widely held images of the Jewish ritual murder accusation.[33]

Two forensic physicians from Berlin, Drs. Mittenzweig and Störmer, were sent to Konitz in May 1900 at the request of the public prosecutor to conduct further autopsies on Winter. It was at this point that elite expert opinion began to question some of Müller's and Bleske's findings, setting in motion a process of revision that would go on for another year.[34] In reviewing the original autopsy reports, Mittenzweig and Störmer wrote respectfully of the examining physicians while offering, at first, subtle and eventually substantial corrections. The dismemberment of the body, they noted, was at times clumsy, the technique "nothing special." They conceded, nevertheless, that it betrayed "the hand of an expert," thus corroborating the original opinion.[35] More important, the Berlin physicians found petechiae on Winter's head, lungs, and heart, strongly suggesting that his killer(s) either suffocated or attempted to suffocate him.[36] But did this discovery change, in their view, the cause of death? Here, too, Mittenzweig and Störmer showed deference to the local medical authorities, admitting that the most likely cause of death was exsanguination produced by a cut across the neck, but that this act was carried out immediately following an attempted strangulation or suffocation that had probably rendered Winter partially or fully unconscious. Finally, there was no evidence that the victim had been poisoned or drugged prior to his murder, although too many internal organs were missing to be certain.[37]

What difference did these seemingly fine distinctions make? The answer, I think, lay in the symbolic associations—the signs, if you will—of the ritual murder discourse within which the scientific work took place. The meanings attached to blood, absence of blood, cutting, and kosher slaughtering are clear enough. But where did the matter of suffocation or the hunt for drugs or poison come into play? One obvious answer is that if exsanguination was *not* in fact the cause of death, the presumption of ritual murder would have been greatly weakened. (I recognize, of course, the obvious fact that every year, many killings and accidental deaths are caused by exsanguination and no one ever suggests in these cases "ritual murder.") Beyond this, however, I would suggest that these two questions were understood implicitly to explain how an apparently healthy and strong eighteen-year-old might have been overpowered long enough for his throat to be slashed and how many people would have been needed to carry out the crime. If evidence of chloroform or a similar drug had been found by the body, one might conclude that a single perpetrator would have been sufficient. And, to the contrary, the fact that none was found might have suggested to investigators and prosecutors that one was looking for multiple killers, another popular image of the blood libel.

Thus, the petechiae on the surface of the skin, the lungs, and the heart could have suggested two different outcomes: either that suffocation was the cause of death or that it functioned to render the victim sufficiently unconscious in order to carry out a cutting and exsanguination. In this second case, more than one perpetrator would have been needed, one to hold down and suffocate the victim and one to wield the knife. Therefore, in suggesting that the act of suffocation was not carried out to completion and occurred immediately prior to the knife wound to the neck, Drs. Mittenzweig and Störmer were guilty of more than mere timidity—being willing only to offer a qualified disapproval of the previous medical examinations. In fact, they suggested a sequence of events that neatly accommodated a theory of murder for the purposes of religious ritual. Their commissioned report of August 6, 1900, did not depart significantly from the main conclusions arrived at in May. The body was found to be emptied of blood, the cause of death was exsanguination effected by the slicing of the throat, and the dismemberment of the corpse was accomplished with a sharp instrument and a "knowledgeable hand." Reviewing a chemist's analysis of the partial stomach contents that had been lodged in Winter's larynx and esophagus (a regurgitation occasioned by the suffocation), the physicians estimated the time of death to have been anywhere between 1 and 7 p.m., but 7 p.m. at the latest.[38]

The accommodation of scientific expertise to popular narratives of Jewish ritual murder continued into the following year. In one of the more unusual examples of such collaboration, a veterinarian named Friedrich Wendt, who had served for more than a decade as the local slaughterhouse inspector, provided sworn testimony regarding the techniques involved in Jewish kosher slaughtering. Explaining that he was often present on occasions when this kind of operation took place, Wendt described in much detail the characteristics of the ritual slaughterer's knife, how the slaughtering (and then the butchering) took place, the removal of the head from the animal, and, finally, how the slaughterer inspected the lungs and other internal organs for defects.[39]

Following some back and forth, in which Drs. Müller and Bleske offered their own assessments of the similarities between Dr. Wendt's descriptions and the dissection of Ernst Winter's body and removal of most of its internal organs, Wendt went on the explain that, while the two doctors testified publicly that they had found only a small amount of clotted blood in the heart of the victim, in his experience, one would have found a larger blood clot.

Finally, from what he heard in court proceedings from the two doctors, it is possible that the cut to Winter's neck was a *Schächtschnitt*, a butcher's cut. Dr. Müller concurred. After hearing Dr. Wendt's testimony, "one can find a similarity between the cut to the neck found on Winter and the butchers' cuts applied to the necks of animals as described by the expert Wendt."[40]

It was a forensic physician from Berlin by the name of Georg Puppe who began the slow demolition of the scientific scaffolding surrounding the state's investigation into the Konitz murder. Puppe (1867–1925), who habilitated in forensic medicine at the University of Berlin in 1898, was working at the time as a university lecturer and forensic investigator.[41] Exactly how he came to be interested in the Konitz affair is unclear, but by September 1900, he had reviewed all of the medical reports issued to date and testified as a witness for the defense in the first of the long series of Konitz trials—this one against Wolf Israelski, an itinerant dealer in old clothes who was charged with aiding and abetting. (Numerous people had come forward to say that they had seen Israelski carrying a sack on his back with what looked like a large round object inside three days before Ernst Winter's head was discovered in a ditch.[42]) Puppe's major claim, based on his assessment of the significance of the petechiae that had been highlighted by Mittenzweig and Störmer, was that violent suffocation caused Winter's death, not exsanguination. The dissection of the lungs did not, he argued, suggest that the body bled out; nor did the neck wound, which failed to indicate suffusion to the surrounding area. There was nothing new, nothing unusual in the case of the gymnasium student's murder. Most important, he added, "We have no right to attach a different meaning to a knife wound to the neck than a knife wound to any other part of the body."[43]

A second, important blow to the months-long alliance of forensic science and suspicions of ritual murder occurred in January 1901, when, you will recall, pieces of Ernst Winter's clothing suddenly appeared—first his jacket, vest, and the remains of a handkerchief, followed by his trousers and, finally, his overcoat. The pieces of clothing contained two elements that rendered one working theory of the crime highly questionable while suggesting a likely mise en scène for the murder itself: a light amount of dried blood on the underside of the vest (and none on the outside) and semen residue on the vest, the jacket, and the outside of the pants near the fly.[44] Both types of evidence would be given quite a bit of play by yet another scientific body that was called to provide expert testimony, the Royal Medical College of the Province of West Prussia, in Danzig (today Gdańsk), whose report—based largely on new, microscopic analysis of tissue from the victim and chemical analysis of his clothing—was submitted to the public prosecutor's office on September 7, 1901.[45] A year earlier, Georg Puppe had taken a lonely stand, a stubborn intervention by a determined individual (and one who had not even conducted his own medical examination on Winter's body). Now, with the report of the Danzig medical faculty, Puppe found that all of his central conclusions had been confirmed. In fact, the report specifically framed its conclusions as agreeing with and upholding Puppe's earlier analysis.[46]

The medical faculty's report methodically reviewed the earlier autopsies, examinations, and chemical analyses, noting that the petechiae on the body could only have been produced if suffocation itself had led to death; that Puppe was indeed correct to say that, in such cases, the heart keeps beating even after a person stops breathing (thus causing continued blood flow in the body); and that microscopic analysis confirmed that the tissues in the lungs and other parts of the body were, in fact, dark red in color, hence full of blood. Moreover, as Puppe had argued, if the neck wound had been the fatal injury, one ought to have been able to observe suffusion of blood throughout the tissues alongside it. Rather, the neck had been cut in the context of the dismemberment of the body, and it took place while the body was unclothed; otherwise, the outside of the shirt, vest, and trousers would have been soaked in blood.[47]

Not to leave a stone unturned, regarding the cut across the neck, the Danzig faculty asked, was it a so-called *Schächtschnitt*? (One might be forgiven for assuming that this question had been resolved a decade earlier in Xanten.) The physicians replied with confidence that the cutting did *not* resemble a kosher butcher's procedure. Such action would have proceeded in a transverse direction across the front of the neck beneath the larynx in order to sever both arteries and the windpipe at the same time. Definitely, then, not a "butcher's cut."[48] The semen stains on the outside of the trousers and vest were determined to have occurred while the victim was still wearing them. The most likely explanation, then, for the setting in which the murder took place was that Winter was surprised while having—or attempting to have—sex while fully clothed.[49] Finally, one could not conclude much from the contents of the esophagus other than that Winter was killed sometime within the first six hours after having had lunch.[50]

Thus, by the middle of September 1901, the temporary alliance of science, the crown prosecutor, and ritual murder theory in Konitz had come to an end. From here on out, there would be little to no chance that the state would continue to investigate Moritz Lewy, or any other member of the Konitz Jewish community for that matter, as suspects in the murder of Ernst Winter. Indeed, according to a correspondent's report in the London *Jewish Chronicle*, the prosecutor's office had said as much in a letter that it sent to the attorney who had defended Lewy at his trial in February.

> The Crown Prosecutor affirms:
>
> 1. That not the slightest foundation exists for suspicion against any Jew.
> 2. That the allegation of a Blood or Ritual Murder has not been proved; but, on the contrary, has been disproved by the condition of the body and the expert opinions of the Danzig Medical College.[51]

Producing Social Exclusion

At this point, the Prussian state essentially gave up trying to solve the case. It would bring two more people to trial in connection with the affair a full year later—Paul Bötticher, the editor of the antisemitic *Staatsbürgerzeitung*, and Wilhelm Bruhn, its publisher—but on a libel charge, not as suspects in the murder. Otherwise, the case was closed. What must stand out in the reader's mind, I would think, is the amount of time it took for the royal prosecutor and the courts to arrive at the realization that the whole investigation up to this point had been misguided—led astray by explicit and implicit bias, rumor, the power of suggestion, and, finally, by confidence in a scientific methodology, which, while rigorous up to a point, was proven to be seriously flawed. In the weeks and months that elapsed between March 1900 and September 1901, ruined lives, demolished property, and badly (perhaps irreversibly) damaged relations between Jewish and Christian neighbors lay scattered.[52]

In fact, Christian residents of Konitz and its vicinity did not wait to the end of the criminal investigation to express rage against the Jewish population; violent demonstrations were held on three different occasions within the first five months—well before the opening trial was called to order in September. The first riots broke out in Konitz, as well as in several nearby communities, over the weekend of April 20 to 22 following the discovery the previous Sunday (Easter Sunday in 1900) of the severed head of Ernst

Winter, days of rumormongering and accusations, and, finally, the arrest of Wolf Israelski.[53] The second outbreak coincided with Winter's funeral on May 27 and the arrival in Konitz of a second police inspector from Berlin (Johann Braun), who, determined to solve the case, focused on a Christian butcher named Gustav Hoffmann as a person of interest.

The funeral itself attracted thousands of onlookers who had streamed into Konitz from nearby villages and towns.[54] Many individuals accompanied the funeral procession by shouting antisemitic slogans and beating on the doors and windows of Jewish shops as the procession wound its way down Danzigerstraße, Konitz's main street, on which both the Lewy and the Hoffmann families lived. At the cemetery, Pastor Hammer of the Protestant church delivered the funeral oration, which, while not mentioning Jews specifically, did suggest that the murder must have been planned.[55] Two days later, on 29 May, word spread quickly of the interrogation of Gustav Hoffmann by the police inspector Braun; rumors started to circulate that Hoffmann would be arrested at 1 a.m. the next morning.[56] At the same time, Wilhelm Bruhn, publisher of the *Staatsbürgerzeitung*, did his best to try to influence the course of the investigation by publishing a new version of purportedly eyewitness testimony offered by Bernhard Masloff, a local resident and worker, who would himself be put on trial six months later on perjury charges.[57] Masloff was now claiming that he had been lying in wait in the alley behind Lewy's house hoping to steal a slab of meat when he observed Adolf Lewy and two other men walking toward the Mönchsee carrying a heavy package. On the night of 29 May, crowds began to assemble outside the hotel where Bruhn was staying as the rumor began to spread that Hoffmann was about to be arrested. The crowd grew to about 1,000 people; some tried to storm Lewy's house; others tried to break into Jewish homes along the side streets. Helmut Smith describes what occurred next: "Most contented themselves with yelling anti-Semitic epithets and tossing stones, first at Jewish houses and shops, then at local officials. The mayor tried to calm the people; when he could not, the gendarmes—eight men on horses, two on foot—drew their swords and, around three o'clock in the morning, dispersed the crowd."[58] The county official, Baron Gottlieb von Zedlitz, would later get word that a group of men had assembled, armed with sticks and clubs, and was preparing to liberate Hoffmann in the event of an arrest. "No one doubts," Zedlitz reported, that "lynch justice against the Lewy family would have followed."[59] No longer confident that local gendarmes could maintain order, Zedlitz requested that the 35th Division of the Prussian army (stationed in nearby Graudenz) send a company to Konitz to keep the peace. Disregarding pleas to stay in their homes after sunset, large crowds continued to assemble throughout the day and into the evening on May 30.

Konitz police received warnings that they were going to go after the mayor, Deditius, who was criticized for being overly protective of the Jews, and that they would also drag Adolf Lewy from his house. The *Staatsbürgerzeitung* further inflamed the public mood with an erroneous report that the police had ordered a medical examination of Hoffmann's daughter, Anna (presumed to have been involved in a relationship with Winter), to determine whether or not she was still a virgin.[60] The crowds confronted soldiers later that evening, and although they were able to clear the streets without any shots being fired, the situation remined very tense. Zedlitz lamented in a report to the Prussian minister of the interior, "For three months the population has been roused against the Jews with all the weapons of fanaticism. Many really believe that they are doing a good deed and protecting their children from the fate of Winter if they beat a Jew to death."[61]

The third and most destructive phase of the rioting took place in early June following the arrest by Inspector Braun of Bernhard Masloff and his mother-in-law, Anna Ross, on the charge of having supplied perjured testimony against the Jewish butcher Adolf Lewy and his family. The local *Konitzer Tageblatt* pushed tensions beyond the boiling point when it reported on June 7 that the police intended to pursue its investigation into Gustav Hoffmann "with renewed vigor." That night, a group of people began to set fires to the fence that sealed off the synagogue, as well as a number of nearby sheds (including one belonging in Gustav Hoffmann). The fires spread quickly, and people resisted efforts of the fire department to put out the flames, pelting the firefighters with stones. The next day, the *Staatsbürgerzeitung* reported that the Jews had started the fires themselves in order to destroy inculpatory evidence of their crimes.[62] On June 9, a crowd gathered on Danzigerstraße shouting epithets and demanding that Masloff and his mother-in-law be released; stones and bricks were hurled at the houses of the Jews; the police, charging through the streets six men abreast, dispersed the demonstrators.[63]

The next morning, people from Konitz went by train and bicycle into the countryside recruiting farmers and rural laborers to join the protest. And people came—according to one report, not only from the region around Konitz but also from surrounding counties. The demonstrations continued into Sunday, when a throng of people approached the town hall and threated the mayor, who had to barricade himself inside the building. The police and gendarmes drew

Synagoge,
davor die Trümmer des abgebrannten jüdischen sogenannten Waschhauses. Die Entstehung des Brandes ist noch nicht aufgeklärt.

Figure 13. Konitz synagogue. Ruins of the Jewish Ritual Bath in the foreground. From *Der Blutmord in Konitz* (Berlin, 1901).

Courtesy J. Mabray.

their swords, but this did not seem to have much effect. Zedlitz considered giving the order to present rifles and shoot, but he was loath to fire on women and children. He also worried that a violent response would unleash, as he said, a "storm against Jewish houses, especially in the side streets," and that the authorities could not offer the Jews sufficient protection.[64] Later in the afternoon, a group made up of men, women, and children made their way to the synagogue, where they smashed pews, yanked down lamps, ripped apart drapes, and tore pages out of prayer books and Torah readers (*ḥumashim*). The Torah scrolls had already been moved to a safe place and so were spared. But the destruction was thorough; according to the *Danziger-Zeitung*, the Konitz synagogue now "resembled a ruin."[65]

Zedlitz once more appealed to the Prussian authorities to send in troops, which they did. Traveling by train from their garrison in Graudenz, the infantry marched into town that night, as Helmut Smith writes, "with rifles loaded and bayonets fixed." No shots were fired, but some people were struck by rifle butts or cut by bayonets. The violence in Konitz was so serious that the

Prussian minister of the interior met with Emperor Wilhelm II to apprise him of the situation. This time, the emperor sent in not just a company but a battalion (some 650 men), thereby ending the riots with what amounted to a military occupation of Konitz. From the perspective of the Prussian government, both Nonn and Smith argue, the entire region of Konitz and its environs was in revolt.[66] And the soldiers remained. Some five hundred troops were quartered in Konitz into the next year, where they patrolled the streets day and night in squads of twenty.[67]

Demonstrations, riots, and the general atmosphere of threat altered the conditions of Jewish life in Konitz definitively. Adolf Lewy had begun to lose business at his butcher shop soon after Winter's killing. Within a month, he was forced to close. By the end of April 1900, all of the windows in the Lewy house on Danzigerstraße had been broken and covered over with wooden planks. This did not prevent more stones from being hurled against the house following Winter's burial on 27 May, although there was no more glass to break. In the aftermath of the June riots, a guard stood posted at the Lewy house around the clock, while a chain of men surrounded the largely destroyed synagogue.[68] Konitz's newly appointed rabbi, Benzion Kellermann, had only been in the town for a month when news first broke of Ernst Winter's disappearance and death, and he was not fortunate enough to escape the whirlwind. Kellermann found himself the target of various rumors and accusations of "mysterious behavior." More than mere insults were hurled at him during the spring rioting, when a rock went through his window as he was sitting in his home. Kellermann kept it for the rest of his life as a reminder of the events of his first rabbinical posting.[69] Technically still a student at the liberal Hochschule für die Wissenschaft des Judentums when he took up the position, Kellermann decided to return to Berlin in the fall of 1901; he never spoke or wrote about either Konitz or the ritual murder accusation.[70]

The events in Konitz should remind us that modern ritual murder trials were more than legal proceedings designed to adjudicate crimes—more than the social and political expression of a dangerous accusation. They were also occasions for social exclusion, for the migration under pressure of entire Jewish communities. At the start of 1900, the Jewish population of Konitz stood at 480 (out of a total population of some 10,000); by the time the last trial got under way, in September/October 1902, only 350 Jews remained. And the population continued to decline. In 1913, it stood at 257; by 1920, after the town had been annexed to newly independent Poland, it had fallen to 110.[71] Very similar patterns can be observed in Tiszaeszlár (and Nyíregyháza),

Xanten, and Polná. And, while it is true that Jews at this time were leaving smaller towns and villages throughout Central Europe for larger urban centers, most of that migration occurred gradually, if decidedly. Jews were not pushed out as a rule; they were not attacked in the streets; their homes and synagogues were not first destroyed. One might, then, call this demographic collapse "ritualized social exclusion," a series of violent performances, which accelerated but did not change the direction of long-term demographic trends. The immediate effect on Jews was primarily psychological. As Helmut Smith writes, "The murder of Ernst Winter was an event that unleashed a process whose consequence was to render the Jews of Konitz strangers in their own home-town."[72] The same was true of Tiszaeszlár, Xanten, Polná, and other "Jewish hometowns" in Central Europe at the turn of the century.

Perjury, Not Ritual Murder? The Masloff and Lewy Trials

To understand how twenty-nine-year-old Moritz Lewy found himself in the accused's box in criminal court in February 1901, we need to look first at the perjury trial of Bernhard Masloff, his mother-in-law Anna Ross, his wife, and his sister-in-law, which took place the previous October. What had gotten Masloff and the other family members into trouble was a series of shifting, inconsistent stories that were meant to implicate the Lewy household in Winter's murder. Masloff first came forward with testimony on 24 March, two weeks after Winter's disappearance, which he then repeated under oath to investigators on 2 May 1900.[73] He reported that on the night of 11 March, at around 10 p.m., when he was on his way home from a pub walking along Danzigerstraße, the stopper from his snuff tobacco pouch fell out in front of a house. Bending down to look for it, he noticed that there was a light on in the cellar, and he could hear several men speaking. The cellar window was covered by a curtain, but light shone through a narrow opening. He went around to the alley in back of the house to hear better, got on the ground, and looked through a crack in the door. He could see into the courtyard as a small man came out from another door, looked around, and went back inside. He then said, "There is nothing out there!" The door remained open, however, and inside Masloff could see two heads; the door was then closed. He listened for a while longer and went home around 2 a.m. because, he explained, there was nothing more to hear. Later he showed his mother-in-law, Mrs. Ross, the house, and she told him it belonged to the Lewys.[74]

After Masloff's initial testimony, Konitz officials conducted a thorough search of the Lewy house, the courtyard, and the cellar and found no evidence to suggest that a crime had been committed there. But things were about to get worse. On 18 April, after a significant reward had been offered for information leading to the identification of Winter's killer or killers, Anna Ross appeared before the police with the first of her own set of stories.[75] A young farmhand from out of town, who had come to Konitz to look for work, allegedly told her that he had been walking by the back door of the Lewy house on the night of the murder when he spotted three people carrying a package to the raft on the Mönchsee. She could not remember the name of the farmhand, but he told her he would come back. The police asked her to let them know as soon he returned.

She did not come back, however, so the police summoned her for more questioning. This time she gave the following account: she herself had been in the Lewy house on the afternoon of 11 March to consult about a servant girl. When she entered the house, she heard muffled whispering (*dumpfes Geflüster*), which seemed to be coming from the cellar, from which Helene Lewy, Adolf's niece, soon came out. Frau Ross was once again at the Lewy house the week before Easter—this time to pick up washing that she was to do. She noticed a handkerchief among the clothes to be washed, which did not appear to be very soiled. When she got home, she mentioned to her daughter that the handkerchief had the stitched monogram E. W. on it. Yet another search of the Lewys' house turned up no such article of clothing. Anna Ross's two daughters added bits and pieces to the story: one, that she had found a watch chain on the oven at the Lewys' house and had picked it up; Mrs. Lewy then demanded it back, saying that it belonged to her son Moritz. The other, that when she was doing washing at the Lewys, she found a photograph of Ernst Winter on the laundry locker. The three female witnesses again gave their testimony under oath before the Konitz district court on 28 April.[76]

All four witnesses were examined by the investigating magistrate in early June, after Masloff had been persuaded by the *Staatsbürgerzeitung* to submit a more elaborate report of what he had seen to the local "citizen's committee," a self-appointed body determined to solve the crime once and for all.[77] The new account contained more extensive, sensational details and also offered a new explanation for why he had been loitering in back of the Lewys' house. On the night on which he was lying behind the back door to the house, he heard, in addition to voices, a throaty, groaning sound, and he was certain that the man who had come out of the cellar into the courtyard was Adolf Lewy. Two other men had come out and conferred with Lewy in the courtyard. The door opened, and Masloff slipped back into the darkness. The three people then came through the open door and headed off toward the raft on the Mönchsee. They were hauling a package wrapped in canvas packaging material. Once they had passed, Masloff went into the courtyard, where he heard a noise, as though the cellar were being scrubbed. At the same time, his foot hit against a piece of meat weighing about five pounds; Masloff made up his mind to steal it, took it, and headed home. It was for this reason that he never said anything about men hauling a package to the Mönchsee in his first story.[78]

This was not the first time, of course, that Moritz Lewy had come under suspicion. Numerous Konitz residents had come forward even before the Masloff trial to claim that they had seen Moritz Lewy in Ernst Winter's company, standing together on the street and also talking to him. A line of these witnesses was called to testify by the defense during the Masloff trial, where they repeated, now quite publicly, their claims. Moritz Lewy himself steadfastly denied that he knew Winter—throughout his police interviews, during the Masloff trial, and throughout his own perjury trial the following February. At the Masloff trial, Moritz was the last member of the Lewy family to be called to the witness stand. His alibi for 11 March was solid and had already been verified by police investigators. But he now denied again, under oath, having known Ernst Winter personally, even though quite a few witnesses had said the opposite.[79] The presiding judge pressed him on this point.

> *Judge:* Now, answer, did you know the deceased Ernst Winter while he was alive?
>
> *Witness:* As far as I know I did not know him.
>
> *Judge:* Did you perhaps speak with him without knowing that it was Ernst Winter?
>
> *Witness:* As far as I was aware, I did not know that it was Ernst Winter.[80]

Apparently unmoved by the various witnesses who claimed to have seen Winter together with Moritz Lewy in town, Lewy remained steadfast in his denial; meanwhile, the courtroom spectators became increasingly agitated. As in the Israelski trial eight weeks earlier, the Masloff proceedings featured a repetition of all of the forensic evidence gathered and medical examinations conducted to date. In other words, both trials seem to have been structured not only to adjudicate the narrow question of perjured testimony but also, in the process, to put forward the state's best theory of the murder itself. It is not hard to reconstruct the motivations behind this strategy: in the Israelski trial, on the charge of aiding and abetting, the coherence of the charge itself depended at least in part on the persuasiveness of a particular narrative of the murder and subsequent scattering of the victim's remains. In the Masloff trial, the main impetus to reintroduce all of this material—to say nothing of the various individuals who claimed under oath to have heard Jewish residents of Konitz talk about the need to acquire Christian blood—lay with the defense team. After all, the lawyers representing Masloff and family did not need to demonstrate the truthfulness of their clients' statements so much as to put doubt in the minds of the jury that the state had made its case. From this perspective, the defense had a strong interest in suggesting, if not the likelihood, then at least the *possibility* that the murder of Ernst Winter had taken place in the Lewys' home. (The prosecutors, in contrast, ridiculed the idea that Winter had been the victim of a ritual murder and explicitly ruled out the Lewy family as having been complicit in such a crime.)[81] And even if the first tactic failed to convince, another option at their disposal was to suggest that the Lewy family, if not guilty of the murder themselves, at the very least might be suspected of knowing something about it. Hence the significance of the eyewitnesses who came forward to report having seen Moritz Lewy and Ernst Winter in each other's company—and of Lewy's steadfast denial of having known him. It would appear, Masloff's lawyers argued, that he did not have a clean conscience.[82]

In his summation, Masloff's lead attorney assured the jury that neither he nor the other members of the defense team believed that Adolf Lewy or his son Moritz had *personally* taken part in Ernst Winter's murder. They may have provided the locale for the killing, however. Admittedly, he considered the assertion that the Jewish religion mandated killing for the purposes of blood ritual to be a legend. But, he suggested, there could be morally depraved individuals among the Jews—or those who, as the result of a false interpretation of the religion—might engage in ritual murder. "That is the background to the deed at hand; what we have is not merely the possibility, but the likelihood, of a ritual murder."[83] The jury, after deliberating for an hour and a half, found Masloff guilty of one count of perjury, concerning his first narrative to the police and the district court in May, but not guilty on the second count—his more elaborate and damning story of June. In essence, his crime was that he had not been forthcoming about why he found himself in back of the Lewy house in the first place (i.e., to steal meat). Anna Ross was found guilty on both of the counts that she faced; the other two women were set free.[84] Moritz Lewy, who had already been under active investigation for perjury, was indicted soon thereafter. His criminal trial was set for February 1901, to be presided over by the same judge as in the Masloff trial, *Landgerichtsdirektor* Schwedowitz.[85]

One might well ask what the state was hoping to accomplish in bringing Moritz Lewy to trial since neither he nor his father were considered suspects any longer. The most obvious answer would be that since it was actively prosecuting other cases of possible perjury (Richard Speisinger, on 5–6 October 1900; Bernhard Masloff and company, 25 October to 10 November 1900) and since Lewy had steadfastly refused to recant his statements from the Masloff investigation and trial, there was really no way the state could *not* indict and prosecute Lewy. To this, however, one needs to add two additional factors: first, public opinion—inflamed by sensational newspaper coverage and local agitators—was clamoring for a trial, suspecting that the Lewy family was continuing to hide what it knew about the murder, and second, the personnel in the prosecutor's office had changed, with attorney Schweigger having replaced Settegast as chief prosecutor (*Erste Staatsanwalt*). Schweigger, as we shall see, did not necessarily share Settegast's conclusion that one needed to look elsewhere to find Winter's killer.

Some twenty-five witnesses gave testimony over the course of the four-day trial, claiming to have seen Moritz Lewy and Ernst Winter together on Danzigerstraße either standing among a group of people or acknowledging and greeting each other.[86] Through it all, Lewy hardly budged in his denial. At the trial's opening, he replied to Judge Schwedowitz's various questions: "I did not know him"; "I believe, to the best of my knowledge, that I did not know Ernst Winter"; and "It is possible that he greeted me [on the street] and knew my friends, perhaps even spoke to me; but, to my knowledge, I did not know Ernst Winter." At the very close of the trial, when asked if he had any final statement to make, Lewy said simply, "I wish to deny the accusation that I knowingly gave false testimony under oath, so help me God."[87] Just why Lewy stubbornly insisted that he did not know Ernst Winter personally has troubled journalists and historians down to the present. With so many individuals having come forward to offer eyewitness testimony to the contrary, is it really possible that Lewy did not know the victim? What would have motivated him steadfastly to deny such knowledge? The prosecution argued that Lewy committed perjury out of fear that, if he had admitted to knowing Winter, he would have been dragged into the investigation himself as a suspect.[88] Writing in the 1950s, Otto Steiner—himself a retired chief prosecutor—feels that this does not make much sense as a motive since Lewy's stubborn denials had the effect of making him appear to be more, not less, guilty. In the end, Steiner throws up his hands and declares Lewy's behavior to have been inexplicable.[89]

I think that the most likely answer to Moritz Lewy's consistent answers to judges and investigators is that he, in fact, did *not* know Ernst Winter. Admittedly, the prosecution was able to trot out twenty-five eyewitnesses who testified to having seen Winter and Lewy in each other's company, but the defense called to the stand the two police investigators from Berlin who had worked on the case earlier, Inspectors Braun and Weyn, who testified to being skeptical of much of this supposedly firsthand knowledge.[90] Two specific categories of witnesses tended to confirm Lewy's account: people who knew him well and teachers at the Konitz gymnasium who had taught both young men. To a question from defense attorney Sonnenfeld, detective Wehn testified to the fact that the gymnasium director, Tomaszewski, had surveyed his students to see if any had seen Winter and Lewy together. The students all responded in the negative. One Dr. Stöwer, a member of the senior faculty, testified to the fact that he had known the accused for five years as a member of the Turnverein (gymnastics association). He had never heard anything detrimental about the accused. To the contrary, Lewy had been very much liked up to the moment that the "antisemitic current" (*antisemitische Strömung*) set in.[91]

To have accepted Lewy's denials at face value would have required a defense strategy of attacking the credibility of the eyewitnesses, suggesting that they had been solicited and coached. This would have been challenging given the number of people who came forward to testify, but the Berlin detectives had already begun to lay the groundwork for such a defense. And one member of the defense team, attorney Appelbaum from Konitz, pursued this line of argument himself on day three of the trial when he asked that a journalist named Georg Zimmer, who was observing the proceedings as a spectator, be removed from the courtroom so that Appelbaum could address the court. Appelbaum then proceeded to brief the court on a bizarre incident in which Zimmer—well known as a correspondent and editor for the antisemitic newspaper the *Staatsbürgerzeitung*—approached Appelbaum to report that people were working hard to discredit Moritz Lewy and offered, for a price, to, as it were, work for the other side. He had it in his power, Zimmer told Appelbaum, to see to it that nothing happened to Lewy; otherwise, he would definitely be lost. Soon thereafter, however, as the first of the Konitz perjury trials was drawing near, Zimmer returned to Appelbaum to declare that it was too late; now he would not help the attorney for 20,000 marks! He ended by declaring, "Lewy's fate is sealed."[92]

In reading the examination and testimony of Georg Zimmer, several things become clear. To be sure, Zimmer had no genuine ideological convictions; he would write for anyone who paid him. He was, however, well ensconced in the Konitz social milieu—which he, himself, was helping to radicalize through his reporting for both the *Staatsbürgerzeitung* and the *Konitzer Tageblatt*—and he was aware of a quiet campaign to recruit "eyewitnesses," who might impugn the credibility of Moritz Lewy and direct attention away from other suspects. Thus, there was a good chance that most, if not all, of the individuals who came forward to testify that Lewy had committed perjury had been *encouraged* to do so. In the end, it was most unfortunate for Lewy that this dramatic development in the trial did not occur until close to the end, after all of the other witnesses had been called.

One has to question, moreover, the effectiveness of the defense attorneys' overall strategy in the trial. Appelbaum seems to have been more in touch with Konitz's social structure and town prejudices than his Berlin colleague, but he did not consistently pursue the trail of a campaign to recruit witnesses against Lewy. What he did do with consistency—in his closing, at least—was explicitly connect the prosecution of his client to the local construction of the killing of Ernst Winter as a Jewish ritual murder, the relentless newspaper campaign against the Lewy family, and the physical attacks by Konitz's Christian population on the Jewish community.[93] Ultimately, his strongest argument was to question the reliability of the witnesses who came forward to testify against Moritz Lewy on the grounds that they had been vulnerable to suggestion:

> Here in this hall, justice rules; but I ask: Does it also rule among the people? Did justice rule as the harassment against the accused was unleashed? Was not the entire population filled with hatred against the accused when one set out to find witnesses against the accused? And weren't the witnesses in fact influenced? . . . The witness testimony emerged from an agitated population, which found itself in deep turmoil. The population had taken up the

> notion that a religious community living in its midst indulges in criminal tendencies based on superstition. When one speaks about a single individual whose entire thinking is captured *a priori* by an idea, without being open to counter arguments, scientifically one is speaking about suggestion. . . . It is completely understandable, and also scientifically grounded, to speak about suggestion.[94]

In raising the image of individual and collective "suggestion," Appelbaum left himself open to a counterattack by any clever prosecutor who wished to avail himself or herself of the "I'm just a country lawyer" gambit: "I don't know anything about 'suggestion.'" And Schweigger was quick to take advantage of the opening.[95] More problematic, I think, was the extensive and highly technical legal argumentation put forward by Hugo Sonnenfeld in his own summation. Sonnenfeld went so far as to entertain the prosecution's own contention that Lewy committed perjury out of a fear that to tell the truth might have made him vulnerable to an even more serious criminal prosecution. Citing chapter and verse of the German criminal code, he led the jury through a scenario in which his client *might* have chosen to commit perjury out of a genuine fear that, to admit some kind of relationship with the victim, in the frenzied atmosphere in which Konitz was mired, would have dragged him and his family into an even more serious prosecution. Under such circumstances, Sonnenfeld reminded the jury, if his client were to be found guilty of perjury, he ought to receive a milder punishment.[96] Sonnenfeld's *plaidoyer* takes up forty-four pages of the printed trial transcript and reads very much like the lecture of the big-city lawyer that he was. His reading of the law may well have been correct. I cannot help but feeling, however, that what his intended audience heard was that Moritz Lewy may have had good reason to lie.

Finally, chief prosecutor Schweigger's conduct during the trial verged on the prejudicial. To the defense's argument that the whole atmosphere in the town had been poisoned by antisemitic agitation and harassment (*Hetze*)—referring mainly to the campaign against Jews waged by the *Staatsbürgerzeitung* and the *Konitzer Tageblatt*—Schweigger wished to point out that "the other side" was engaged in *Hetze* as well. He saw the case before him in terms of two mutually exclusive, antagonistic camps: Germans and Jews, each essentially at war with the other. More damning certainly was his leaping to correct a statement that had been made by the defense that the state admitted to having no proof of any participation by Moritz Lewy in the murder of Ernst Winter. "That is not what I said," he countered. "What I said was, for the moment I possess no evidence that would allow me to bring a charge against him. That is a giant difference."[97] In the end, Lewy was found guilty of perjury and sentenced to an unusually harsh term of four years. He was pardoned by the emperor some two years later, in October 1903. "Whatever his personal opinion of Jews," Helmut Smith writes, "he nevertheless understood that Lewy had been the victim of a community in the throes of anti-Semitic passion."[98]

Conclusion: A Debasement of the Coinage?

The police and prosecutors did not lack for other suspects and persons of interest in the Konitz affair. These included a local tailor, a cigar dealer, a teacher in the town's girls' school, and a prostitute and her jealous lover.[99] None of these leads proved successful, however, and some among the larger circle of investigators and prosecutors urged their colleagues in 1901 to turn their attention once more to the Christian butcher Gustav Hoffmann, a neighbor of the Lewy's, whose fifteen-year-old daughter Anna was known to have been courted by Ernst Winter. It seems that Hoffmann's alibi had developed an important hole—the block of time between 6 and 7 p.m.—and Lautz, the district attorney in Marienwerder, for one, theorized that Hoffmann had surprised his daughter and Winter *in flagrante delicto* in his shed by the lake. The daughter immediately fled, while the father, in a fit of rage, threw the young man to the ground where, in the heat of a struggle, he strangled or suffocated him.[100] The district attorney in Marienwerder was well aware that the popular mood in Konitz would not have greeted a renewed investigation of the highly regarded Hoffmann with equanimity, but he argued strongly for the need finally to solve the murder. Such was not to be the case, however. The newly appointed chief prosecutor—the same prosecutor Schweigger who presented the case against Moritz Lewy in February—turned down the request and closed the case against Hoffmann.[101]

Nor would this be the end of hot leads that went cold for one reason or another. Helmut Smith writes of a leaked report from 1904—most likely by the intrepid Berlin inspector Braun—suggesting that Bernhard Masloff was the actual murderer and that the crime had taken place in the small, two-bedroom apartment of his mother-in-law, Anna Ross, where he had caught Winter together with his wife. The time frame, the location of Ross's home, its access to the Mönchsee, and the fact that Masloff knew how to butcher sheep were all factors that appeared to support Braun's new theory. The Berlin police felt that now all of the pieces to the puzzle were falling into place and urged the district attorney in Konitz repeatedly to proceed against Masloff and his family. Again, chief prosecutor Schweigger declined to do so. Three years later, in 1907, Braun got word of an incident in Halberstadt (where Masloff and his family had since moved) in which a neighbor had overheard members of the family incriminating each other in the heat of an argument. Feeling that, finally, he had his "smoking gun," Braun appealed to the newly appointed district attorney in Halle to make an arrest. It turns out that the district attorney already knew something about the case from his previous position in West Prussia; Schweigger turned Braun down one last time.[102]

Watching the Konitz affair limp along to its unresolved conclusion, one wonders whether it is possible to call such an episode both ignominious and inconclusive. Konitz certainly shared some features with the temporally contiguous trials against Leopold Hilsner in Kutná Hora and Písek: a degraded political atmosphere, which actually rendered the chances for a not guilty verdict *more* difficult at the start of the new century than they had been in the 1880s and early 1890s; the apparent eagerness of townspeople to come forward with perjured, or imagined, eyewitness testimony; the ongoing and seemingly unresolved struggles between rival claimants to scientific expertise and between local practitioners and elite state institutions; and the poisoned, and now impossible, relations between Christians and Jews in what had been Jewish hometowns. And yet, one needs to be careful not to award historical contingency greater power than it deserves and not to underestimate the medium-term effects of the scientific assault on the blood libel. If Ernst Winter's scattered clothing had been discovered earlier, if the Danzig Medical Faculty's reexamination of the forensic evidence had been requested in January 1901, or if Schweigger had not replaced Settegast as chief prosecutor, Konitz might have been the story of justice somewhat delayed but ultimately rewarded. The Medical Faculty's intervention, together with that (again, ultimately) of Georg Puppe—even more so than the valiant efforts of Tomáš Masaryk and the Czech Medical Faculty in Prague in the Hilsner affair—did prove to be definitive, effectively ending any further pursuit of a Jewish perpetrator in Ernst Winter's murder. But this intervention came late. Moritz Lewy languished in prison. And Jewish life in Konitz had been rendered untenable.

Conclusion

New times bring new work, and that work, which understands what its time demands, is in the right place.

—Hans Gross, "Psychopatischer Aberglaube" (1902)

I aim to undermine the myth that what sets the modern world apart from the rest is that it has experienced disenchantment and a loss of myth. I am not claiming that industrialization never happened, nor am I denying that rationalization occurred in any cultural sphere; rather, I am interested in the process by which Christendom increasingly exchanged its claim to be the unique bearer of divine revelation for the assertion that it uniquely apprehended an unmediated cosmos and did so with the sparkling clarity of universal rationality.

—Jason Ā. Josephson-Storm, *The Myth of Disenchantment: Magic, Modernity, the Birth of the Human Sciences* (2017)

We come at last to the two major trials of the last decade of the 19th century. Finally, we find ourselves in the presence of proceedings that are more or less impartial—in any event, juridically legal—of precise and authentic documents, and of medical expertise that is serious and worthy of examination. Through these trials we can see what an important role forensic medical expertise was called upon to play in ritual murder affairs and what the principal questions were that one expected it to answer.

—Jules Marcus, *Étude Médico-Lêgale du Meurtre Rituel* (1900)

At noon on Sunday, 9 August 1903 (16 Av 5663 in the Jewish calendar), a few thousand people gathered in the courtyard outside the Old Synagogue of Kraków in Austrian Galicia, spilling out into the street beyond the walls of the courtyard and—if fortunate—occupying the seats of the synagogue itself, men on the ground floor and women in the balcony that stretched along the sides of the venerable sanctuary, there to witness a solemn ceremony.[1] Lit candles adorned the heavy candelabra; non-Jewish dignitaries mingled among the crowd; twenty-four police officers stood guard at the entrance to the synagogue. Dignitaries from the Kraków Jewish community gathered along the eastern wall of the sanctuary, while rabbis from communities across Europe and as far away as Egypt and Palestine stood, wrapped in prayer shawls (*talitot*), on the six steps that led to the ark. Among them was the chief rabbi (*Hakham Bashi*) of Alexandria, Eliyahu Hazan, decked out in his ceremonial garb—which included four decorations awarded by the Ottoman sultan—and Hayim Leibush Horowitz, chief rabbi of Kraków.[2]

Horowitz delivered the opening remarks, drawing attention to the feeling of crisis that seemed to envelop the Jewish world, particularly in Central and Eastern Europe. Toward the end of his talk, he urged his listeners to take advantage of this distinguished occasion "to demonstrate once and for all before the whole enlightened world our powerful and energetic rejection of this most despicable and false accusation, against this accusation that has caused much innocent blood from among us to spill. The terrible blood libel is so widespread, let us call upon the Lord, the God of Israel, as our witness that we are innocent of this awful crime. . . . Our purpose today is not for our benefit but for all of humanity. Not for us, but rather to cleanse all of humanity from the great sin of suspecting the pure."[3] The rabbi of Poltava, Eliyahu Akiva Rabinowitch, also rose to speak, and at the end of his remarks, printed sheets were distributed to all those assembled. Hayim Leibush Horowitz approached and opened the ark, removed a Torah scroll, turned to face the assembly, and, holding the Torah in his arms, read from the script that had been distributed.

> On Sunday, the 16th of Av, 5663, we, the rabbis who have gathered from many lands to the Old Synagogue here in Kraków, swear an oath of the Torah, with the knowledge of the Creator, blessed be He, and all of the inhabitants of the world, in the name of the God of Heaven and Earth who examines men's hearts and knows their thoughts, that the despicable libel which arouses disgust, the blood libel taught and dreamed up by treacherous evildoers, accusing the Jewish people for centuries that they use the blood of male and female Gentiles for a religious ritual, commandment or custom,

> or for any other purpose—this libel is an absolute falsehood. We have also never seen in any book from among the books of our holy Torah, either oral or written . . . and without exception, any law or custom or even the slightest hint regarding this heinous and despicable act. We, the rabbis, who have received from our fathers and grandfathers, the knowledge of Torah, commandments and customs in all their details, have never received or heard of any such despicable commandment or custom. We have also never heard that there are found among us any sect or private individuals who would, God forbid, perform this evil and disgusting thing. As we are making our oath in truth, in righteousness, and with a true heart, may God help us in all that we request, Amen. (A thunderous response breaks out from the congregation, "Amen.")[4]

This dramatic scene in the Old Synagogue of Kraków actually served as the opening ceremony of an international rabbinical conference—the brainchild of Aharon Mendel ben Natan Hakohen, rabbi of the Ashkenazi community of Cairo—which was called in order to address pressing concerns in the world of traditional Judaism, among them the lack of Jewish education for girls, mass immigration, growing religious indifference, and political radicalism.[5] But it was a recent bloody riot, the pogrom in the Bessarabian city of Kishinev, 6 to 7 April 1903, that formed the immediate backdrop to the ceremony. The riots were preceded by a series of antisemitic articles in the newspaper *Bessarabets* together with a groundswell of local rumors, which eventuated in an accusation of ritual murder—the purported victim being a Christian child from the nearby town on Dubossary. Preliminary investigations revealed that the child had not, in fact, been killed by Jews, but a violent mob attacked them, nevertheless. In the course of the rioting, forty-nine Jews were killed, possibly as many raped, and almost 600 were injured; 1,350 houses and 588 shops of Jews lay in ruins.[6]

This scripted, performative response to the ritual murder accusation—and to the violence that it could unleash—may have been unique in its evocation of a legal ceremony, a sacred oath, obliquely reminiscent of the *Kol Nidrei* liturgy of Yom Kippur. From this perspective, the Kraków ceremony might also be viewed as a traditional response, accessed through the literary and *halakhic* resources of rabbinic Judaism. At the same time, it can be said to have reprised the apologetic interventions of distinguished individuals from the Jewish historical past: Solomon ibn Verga in the early sixteenth century,

Menasseh ben Israel in the seventeenth century, Moses Mendelssohn toward the end of the eighteenth century, and Isaac Baer Levinsohn in the 1830s.[7] Solemn and, at the same time, seemingly unaware of the actual legal and rhetorical structures in which contemporary ritual murder investigations and trials were being carried out, the Kraków oath could evoke pathos and appear pathetic at the same time. By all accounts, it made no impression on the world outside the traditional Jewish street.

The Kraków declaration did frame itself, however, in terms of a certain kind of expertise—in this instance an exhaustive knowledge of traditional Jewish texts—and thereby touched upon one of the forms in which modern ritual murder trials were both articulated and contested: expert testimony. But here, too, the rabbis assembled in Kraków seemed not to know the implicit, typically unarticulated rules according to which expertise on Jewish practices, Jewish religious texts, or Jewish criminality could be presented. One key assumption was that the expert in question occupied a position of objectivity or, what one might call, critical neutrality. The expert, so it was claimed, had no personal stake in the outcome of his or her investigation. It was for this reason that Jewish communal leaders and newspaper editors, in an attempt to discredit the ritual murder accusation in the wake of the arrests of the Jews in Tiszaeszlár (and later), sought out and publicized the scholarly assessments of Christian—not Jewish—scholars of rabbinic texts; for this reason, that defense attorneys called Christian experts to the stand in Nyíregyháza and Xanten; and for this reason, of course, that Masaryk's relentless crusade against the Polná accusation was regarded as so valuable.[8] The opinions and interventions of non-Jewish criminologists, literary scholars, police investigators, forensic physicians, justices, and medical faculty carried weight. Those of a Talmudic scholar, for better or worse, did not.

The violence unleashed in Kishinev shocked public opinion in many parts of the world and had a convulsive effect on Jewish politics and culture. The nascent Zionist movement, in a crisis of confidence, momentarily turned its attention away from the long-term project of colonization in Palestine to consider a short-term asylum in East Africa for Jewish refugees. Hebrew poet Hayyim Nahman Bialik spent weeks in the city interviewing survivors of the pogrom, after which he produced the hugely influential poem "In the City of Killing" (*Be-ir ha-haregah*), characterized by Steven Zipperstein as "an unforgiving portrait of the weight of age-old persecution having recurred time and again, now in full view on Kishinev's streets and causing irreparable harm to the bodies and souls of contemporary Jews."[9] The psychological shock was undeniable but hardly final. The pace and scale of mob violence on Jewish communities in Russia would increase with each successive outbreak: 1905 to 1906 and during the civil war following the Bolshevik revolution, 1918 to 1921.

But Kishinev's murderous riot ought not to obscure the fact that no ritual murder trial took place in the wake of the boy Mikhail Rybachenko's death. Two autopsies were performed on the body, the first by a Jewish and the second by a Christian medical examiner. Both rejected theories of a ritual murder. Eventually, Mikhail's uncle, who stood to gain from an inheritance left by the boy's grandfather, was identified as the murderer. The work of the scientific experts in this case prevented any Jews from being arrested and brought to trial. But it was not, in the end, a strong enough counterweight to the relentless propaganda of newspapers such as *Bessarabets* and *Novoe vremia*—purportedly based on eyewitness accounts by residents of Dubossary—and could not prevent the outbreak of popular violence.[10] In many respects, the Bessarabian province of the Russian Empire was a world apart from the modernizing empires of Central Europe and does not offer an apt point of comparison. All the more striking, then, the relative speed with which the local authorities intervened in an attempt to suppress rumors of a Jewish ritual murder through the direct application of medical investigative techniques. Unlike Konitz, the state was not handicapped by competing judgments and an apparent loss of confidence. Unlike the Hilsner affair, forensic expertise did not butt heads with aggressive prosecutors, ambitious private attorneys, and a poisoned political atmosphere. Still, the outcome was horrific. Was the state's ability to discipline the ritual murder accusation failing?

Ten years after the Kishinev pogrom, on the eve of World War I, the last of Europe's formal trials against Jews on a charge of ritual murder—the infamous Beilis case—closed in Kiev, the capital of Russian Ukraine. The case, in which Mendel (Menachem) Beilis stood accused of the murder of thirteen-year-old Andrei Iushchinskii, gained immediate notoriety in Western Europe and North America, where it was widely regarded as emblematic of a corrupt and decaying tsarist system and engendered numerous editorial condemnations and public protests. Beilis, the thirty-nine-year-old, secular Jewish manager of a brick factory located in the vicinity of the cave where the boy's body was found, was not the first—and certainly not the most likely—suspect in the case, but he soon fell victim to a growing and increasingly voluble campaign to find and arrest "the Jew" who had perpetrated the murder as a ritual crime. The Justice Ministry and the Interior Ministry developed a keen interest in the investigation from the start—motivated in equal parts by a desire to maintain order in Kiev and other parts of the country, eagerness to both placate and tamp down radical right-wing groups such as the Black Hundreds, and, perhaps, the need to justify its restrictive Jewish policies to the world. Officials in St. Petersburg interfered in the local police investigation, ignoring the skepticism of grizzled detectives that the boy's murder had anything to do with ritual killing, juggling personnel when necessary, and closely reviewing strategy with the prosecutor's office in Kiev. The criminal investigation dragged on for two years, during which time Beilis languished in prison; it was botched at crucial junctures and laced with perjured testimony from numerous witnesses. The case was weak on its merits and appeared at several points to be heading for disaster. Finally, after nearly five weeks of trial proceedings, the jury of twelve men (half of whom came from the peasant estate) found Mendel Beilis *not guilty*—but with a twist.[11]

The Beilis affair laid bare the contradictions that inhered in Imperial Russia's efforts simultaneously to emulate Western and Central Europe's legal and scientific norms while sometimes demonstrating an almost paranoid antisemitism punctuated by a willingness to violate those very norms. The fact remains, however, that the various arms of the Russian government that were involved in the investigation of the murder and the prosecution of Beilis were often divided on the question of his guilt or innocence and unsure how to proceed. In the view of Robert Weinberg, Beilis's main problem may, in fact, have been that he fell victim to a police force and judiciary "intent on preserving law and order" at all cost, even if this meant bowing to the pressure of antisemites who were threatening physical violence against Jews.[12] Thus, while the historical record leaves no doubt that Beilis was framed and that prosecutors and investigators suborned perjury, it seems unlikely that the tsarist government conspired *in advance* to arrest and convict a Jew on the basis of the ritual murder accusation or that it did so in order to prop itself up against political and social pressures.

On 28 October 1913, the presiding judge in Kiev, Fyodor Boldyrev, instructed the jury to respond to two questions. The first was directed at the nature and physical features of the crime itself: that is to say, was the prosecution's characterization of the murder of Andrei Iushchinskii and the condition in which the boy's corpse was found *correct*? "Has it been proven," the court asked, that Andrei Iushchinskii

> was gagged and wounded by a pointed instrument in the parietal, occipital, and temporal lobes as well as on the neck with

> accompanying wounds to the cerebral vein, arteries of the left temple, and veins in the neck, resulting in abundant bleeding and then, after losing five glasses of blood, additional wounds were caused by the same implement to the torso, accompanied by wounds to the lungs liver, right kidney, and the heart, and that these wounds, which totaled forty-seven, caused Iushchinskii agonizing pain and led to the almost complete loss of blood and to his death?[13]

Note what the state was asking the jury to do in the first question: to confirm or reject the prosecution's forensic presentation. This was a highly unusual charge, a fact pointed out by the defense, which argued—unsuccessfully—that there was no basis in law for such a question. The wording of the question, moreover, while full of technical language and studious in its avoidance of the terms "ritual," "religion," "Jewish," and "Christian," was highly suggestive of a ritual crime. The court, then, was asking the jury to confirm—based solely on the forensic testimony given by expert witnesses for the prosecution, testimony that had taken up days in open court—that Andrei Iushchinskii had been the victim of a ritual murder. Members of the jury might well have asked themselves, who were they to contradict government experts? And, famously, most of the jury agreed with the prosecution that the manner in which the murder was carried out indicated a ritualistic crime. Most, but not all; remarkably, five of the twelve jurors voted *no.*[14]

It was the second question that addressed the guilt or innocence of the accused. Employing almost exactly the same language as the first, it added a preamble, which asked whether "Menachem-Mendel Tevye Beilis" was guilty of having colluded "with persons not yet discovered" to deprive Iushchinskii of his life "out of religious fanaticism." On this question, the jury returned a verdict of *not guilty.*[15] The split decision was widely understood at the time to be an endorsement of the accusation of Jewish ritual murder even if the culprit in this particular case did not happen to be Mendel Beilis. Upon hearing news of the verdict, Tsar Nicholas is said to have remarked, "It is certain that there was a ritual murder. But I am happy that Beilis was acquitted, for he is innocent."[16] The antisemitic newspaper the *Double-Headed Eagle* put it more succinctly, proclaiming boldly, "One Jew Is Acquitted, All Kikes Are Found Guilty."[17]

After Beilis, there would be no more state-sponsored trials against Jewish defendants in Europe on the charge of ritual murder. At the risk of stating the obvious, I want to be quick to add that the decline and ultimate demise of the modern ritual murder trial did not spell the end of popular violence against Jews; it did not prevent the rise of lethal, indeed genocidal, state-directed violence against this people; nor did states stop putting Jews *qua Jews* on trial, either collectively or individually. But this particular line of argument regarding Jewish criminality, this particular form of social and cultural knowledge, proved—after a span of some thirty years—to be spent, to have been incompatible with modern legal procedure, scientific method, and the self-consciousness of political and social elites. One might call this failure an epistemological collapse.

From the perspective of the main lines of argument in this study—the necessary coming together of discourses of modern rationality, scientific procedure, and Jewish ritual murder for the modern ritual murder trials to have worked in the first place—this collapse is paradoxical or at least surprising. Why a shelf life of only three decades? The answer to this question, I think, is that the discursive alliance that allowed for the trials to proceed was always inherently unstable and at risk of coming apart. Its reliance on forensic medicine and scientific language and procedures appeared to provide the ritual murder accusation with a "modern" scaffolding, but this same structural support would ultimately be its undoing. The very investigators, physicians, and scientists who seemed to be ready to bolster ritual murder prosecutions would inevitably turn against their supposed allies and subvert the methods and assumptions of the prosecutors. As I suggest, the coming together of scientific procedures, modern temperament, and investigations into Jews and ritual murder could only have been temporary and incomplete. In the Tiszaeszlár and Xanten cases, the state was actually divided against itself, and the accused were eventually acquitted. In the Polná and Konitz trials, one can see the discursive alliance beginning to tear apart at the seams—albeit with very different conclusions.

While I do not have a definitive answer as to why the trials begin in 1882 (or 1879) and end in 1913, I think it is instructive to consider the larger significance of the two "bookends" in the modern Jewish experience. The 1870s marked the completion of Jewish emancipation as a political process in Germany, Austria-Hungary, and Switzerland, to be followed shortly thereafter by the rise of political movements whose goal was to restrict the social effects of emancipation, if not to reverse the process. Accusations of Jewish ritual murder functioned in this context as a way of announcing the mortal danger posed by Jewish integration and legal equality. And they did so without relying necessarily on the new racial antisemitism that was also being disseminated around this time. In fact, one of the ingenious aspects of modern ritual murder discourse was that it could be expressed in part in the same idiom as political liberalism, that is to say, that Jewish *difference* from other Europeans was solely a function of culture and religion. Promoters of the fear of Jewish ritual murder pointed precisely to religion, religious texts, and religious fanaticism as the sources of a most dangerous expression of Jewish difference.

World War I stands at the end of the career of the modern ritual murder trial and, along with it, the collapse of the imperial states that had prosecuted these cases. The Habsburg, German, and Russian empires were replaced, in Central Europe, with postimperial "successor" states and, in Russia and parts of Eastern Europe, with the Soviet Union. Was it the new, national model of the successor states that proved to be the undoing of the ritual murder trial? The enormous violence of the war itself? The Soviet Union's prosecution of some of the major players in the Beilis affair? The relative indifference of National Socialist Germany toward the ritual murder accusation has always struck me as curious. While newspapers such as *Der Stürmer* devoted a couple of special issues to the trope of ritual murder in the 1930s, the Nazi state never took the trouble to mount any public trials against Jews on this charge. Perhaps, by then, it was all beside the point.

* * *

Max Weber is often credited with having provided the conceptual language to describe—and indeed to predict—the disciplining effects of modernity on traditional knowledge and belief. His famous Munich lectures of 1917 and 1919 explicitly applied the terms "rationality" (*Rationalität*) and "disenchantment" (*Entzauberung*) to historical processes that he had already identified in his pathbreaking studies of 1904 and 1905, *The Protestant Ethic* and *The Spirit of Capitalism*.[18] Working within a Weberian paradigm, one could argue that contemporary assumptions about—and commitments to—regularity, process, and predictability in law, in criminal investigation, and in forensic medicine produced a disciplining structure on ritual murder trials that, for a period of time, actually made the trials comprehensible and thus possible. But, as the decades wore on, the legal and scientific discourse of Jewish ritual murder became increasingly "illegible," even as anti-Jewish emotions appeared to be gaining in strength. As Paul Reitter and Chad Wellmon write in a recent new edition and translation of the lectures, "By refusing to accord explanatory power to ultimately unknowable forces, humanistic scholarship and the natural and physical sciences act as agents of disenchantment. Modern scholarship, whether philology or physics, strips the world of certain forms of magic and mysteries; it de- or un-magics, as the German term *Entzauberung* literally suggests."[19] Modern scientific language, assumptions, and procedures succeeded in *disenchanting*—in naturalizing, or "un-magicing," if you will—the ritual murder accusation for a certain period of time but, in the end, refused or failed to accord it explanatory power.

The literature on Weber's theory of modernity, indeed on the very categories of "rationality" and "disenchantment," is immense, and the model itself certainly has had its critics. I would imagine that it is more fashionable today in scholarly circles to deny rather than defend the notion of a single, historical process of modernization; to deny that the modern world *is* primarily rational in its assumptions, organization, or behavior; to emphasize, rather, the degree to which the world remains, in fact, *enchanted*.[20] This line of argument, it seems to me, would not have surprised Weber since his scholarly method was based on the need for abstraction in order to create pattern and general meaning out of the myriad of details left behind in the human record. It is not particularly difficult, after all, to uncover scores of examples to contradict one or more features of an ideal type. Moreover, the rapidly increasing specialization in the natural, human, and social sciences—an unavoidable if, perhaps, unfortunate fragmentation of knowledge—has rendered any quest for overarching certainty impossible. Weber expressed this tension in 1917 in the following way: "Increasing rationalization and intellectualization does *not*, in other words mean a greater general knowledge of the conditions we live under. Rather, it means something else: the knowledge, or belief, that we *could* find out if we *wanted* to; that in principle there are no mysterious incalculable forces intervening in our lives, but instead all things, in theory, can be *mastered* through *calculation*."[21] One could, then, in theory, calculate the entire distribution of individual human responses to a given situation. But that is not the same as an honest search for meaning.

It would be tempting to present the return of the ritual murder trial to the legal agenda of the modern European state as Exhibit A for the continued *enchantment* of modernity, the resistance or reassertion of *irrationality* in the face of rapid, disruptive, historical change. To be honest, this was my guiding assumption when I first began my own research into the modern ritual murder trial: how was it possible, I wanted to know, to promote irrationality and myth in the face of modern epistemology? I came to abandon this approach when it became clear to me that—with the exception of a few radical outliers—none of my actors, from defense attorneys to criminologists, police investigators to ministers of justice, expert witnesses to Jewish defense organizations, embodied this stance. To the contrary, for the vast majority, "modernity" very much existed and came with clear demands and expectations. These were people who were convinced that they occupied a radically different historical situation than that which had existed two or three centuries earlier, one in which not every belief could be made culturally legible, one that imposed implicit rules on procedure and even on expression.

It might also be possible, I suppose, to counter my claims concerning the discursive power of scientific methodology with the argument that at least some of the people involved in the prosecution of the modern ritual murder trial—expert witnesses, local medical examiners, and others—were simply engaging in bad science, or even "pseudoscience," rather than the real thing, mimicking scientific language and rhetoric while putting forward unsubstantiated claims based on faulty assumptions. An analogy that comes to mind would be that of so-called creation science and its Museum of Creation and Earth History, which opened in Petersburg, Kentucky, in 2007. The institution's public displays mimic those found in museums of natural history around the country, although its mission is to bolster an account of the origins of the universe and the diversity of species in the world in terms that are compatible with a fundamentalist understanding of the opening chapters of the Hebrew Bible.[22] As Michael Gordin persuasively argues, however, "pseudoscience" is a term "without real content," whose function is to police epistemological boundaries.

> On the imagined scale that has excellent science at one end and then slides through good science, mediocre science (the vast majority of what is done), poor science, to bad science on the other end, it is *not* the case that pseudoscience lies somewhere on this continuum. It is off the grid altogether. The process of demarcating science from non-science is a central and quite general aspect of all scientific activities, but pseudoscience attracts particular vehemence as compared to, say, non-science. . . . Pseudoscience is different. This is a combative notion deployed to categorize (and, its users hope, weaken or eliminate) doctrines that are non-science but pretend to be, aspire to be, or are simply mistaken for scientific. The effect of this demarcation . . . when it works, is to preserve the accepted boundaries of knowledge from intrusion.[23]

The arguments and controversies that swirled around the ritual murder trials of Europe's fin de siècle—and that were voiced in the practical work of the investigators, prosecutors, defense attorneys and appellants, experts, and justices—operated very much along Gordin's "imagined scale." They struggled over what was good science and what was bad, what was off the mark and needed improvement, what was inadequate and what was definitive. But there was little that was off the grid, little that offered an antiscientific or deliberately nonscientific set of arguments.

In the end, it was not only the investigations and trials of the turn of the century that operated within the era's rhetorical and institutional constraints; so, too, did the narrative accounts of ritual murder. During the high and late Middle Ages, narrative descriptions of Jewish murders of Christian children were certainly not devoid of blood and gore. Scenes of physical and psychological torture, piercings of the body with needles and knives, circumcisions, and exsanguination merged with symbolic reenactments of the crucifixion to produce narrative and visual representations of Jewish crime. But these representations were consistent with coherent theological understandings and expectations. Caroline Bynum reminds us that the theme of Christ's own exsanguination, the complete draining of blood from his body, was a salient element in late medieval piety.[24] And Ronnie Po-chia Hsia, whom we have encountered on more than one occasion, has stressed in his own writing how the sacrifice at the center of premodern ritual murder narratives was, in fact, a double sacrifice, in which the Jews, too, end up losing their lives; indeed, both sacrificial elements contain a message of redemption:

> By murdering the Christian family, Jews reenacted the Crucifixion, giving a historical event a salvific immediacy and power that the commemorative mass could not rival; by exposing the "crimes" of the Jews and avenging the "murders," sacrificing the evildoers to the offended deity, the townsfolk celebrated the triumph of Christianity and avenged and vindicated the historical Crucifixion of Jesus. A ritual murder discourse functioned as a form of *imitatio Christi*. Just as the Christian community dispensed justice, so, too, could pious Christians expect divine justice at the end of the world. . . . To German Christians of the late fifteenth century . . . the twin themes of murder-sacrifice and judgment must have represented the essence of the salvific message.[25]

The *naturalized* discourse of turn-of-the-century Jewish ritual murder, in contrast, contained no message of salvation. To borrow from Caroline Bynum's book title, the modern narratives retained all of the blood—and then some—but none of the wonder. Recall, if you will, the newspaper reportage from the Polná case, the imaginative re-creation of Anežka Hrůzová's last moments offered by the reporter from *Katolické listy*:

> When Anežka got to the top [of the hill], she began to walk slowly. The murderer grabbed her by the arm or by the throat, threw her down to the overgrowth, where a rope was tossed over her neck to prevent her from crying out. Her clothing was stripped down to her knickers, stockings, and shoes, and there in the thicket—six steps from the path—the act of cutting took place. The wound went from one ear to the other, straight and even, above the Adam's apple to the vertebrae: precisely the way in which cattle are (kosher-) slaughtered.[26]

This "disenchanted" narrative doubtless performed a variety of social, cultural, and political functions: it announced a renewed sense of "Jewish danger" to community, articulated a reasonably coherent argument against Jewish emancipation—one based *not* on fashionable racial theory but on the immutability of cultural difference—and the inevitably ensuing Jewish integration into different European societies, protested the weakening of small-town and village life in the face of increasing urbanization, and justified the very exclusion of Jews from their hometowns. It also sought to accommodate the disciplinary demands—the implicit rules—of the natural and social sciences. But as narrative, as a story that non-Jewish Europeans might tell themselves about how the world worked and what meanings they could derive from it, the naturalized discourse of ritual murder was a most impoverished vessel, containing little that was hopeful. It boiled down to butchers' cuts and blood, to someone else's religious fanaticism and depravity. It pointed to emptiness.

Notes

INTRODUCTION

1. For a synopsis of the ritual murder accusation since the Middle Ages, see Hillel J. Kieval, "The Blood Libel," in *Key Concepts in the Study of Antisemitism*, ed. Sol Goldberg, Scott Ury, and Kalman Weiser (London: Palgrave Macmillan, 2021), 53–64. For a recent, comprehensive study of the blood libel from the late Middle Ages through the eighteenth century, see Magda Teter, *Blood Libel: On the Trail of an Antisemitic Myth* (Cambridge, Mass.: Harvard University Press, 2020).

Other general studies of the ritual murder accusation include Daniil Khvol'son, *Die Blutanklage und sonstige mittelalterliche Beschuldigungen der Juden: Eine historische Untersuchung nach den Quellen* (Frankfurt: J. Kauffmann, 1901); Hermann L. Strack, *Das Blut im Glauben und Aberglauben der Menschheit mit besonderer Berücksichtigung der "Volksmedizin" und des "jüdischen Blutritus,"* 8th ed. (Munich: C. H. Beck, 1900) [translated as *The Jew and Human Sacrifice: Human Blood and Jewish Ritual. An Historical and Sociological Inquiry* (London: Cope and Fenwich, 1909)]; Alan Dundes, ed., *The Blood Libel Legend: A Casebook in Anti-Semitic Folklore* (Madison: University of Wisconsin Press, 1991); Rainer Erb, ed., *Die Legende vom Ritualmord: Zur Geschichte der Blutbeschuldigung gegen Juden* (Berlin: Metropol, 1993); and Susanna Buttaroni and Stanisław Musiał, eds., *Ritualmord: Legenden in der europäischen Geschichte* (Vienna: Böhlau Verlag, 2003). David Biale, *Blood and Belief: The Circulation of a Symbol Between Jews and Christians* (Berkeley: University of California Press, 2007), offers an interesting, comparative study of blood as symbol, practice, and provocation in Jewish and Christian (and Jewish-Christian) contexts.

2. On ritual murder trials in early modern Poland-Lithuania, see the discussion later in the Introduction and note 13 below.

3. Friedrich Frank, *Der Ritualmord vor den Gerichtshöfen der Wahrheit und der Gerechtigkeit* (Regensburg: G. J. Manz, 1901), 181–302. Frank's efforts to tabulate and describe ritual murder accusations against Jews, although serious, were somewhat arbitrary. For contemporary cases, he relied heavily on German and Austrian newspaper accounts. On occasion, he appears to have hewn closely to Leopold Auerbach, *Das Judenthum und seine Bekenner in Preußen und in den anderen deutschen Bundesstaaten* (Berlin: Sigmar Mehring, 1890). Frank seems not to have made use of Slavic sources and shows little awareness of the scores of accusations that transpired in Poland-Lithuania or the Russian Empire.

Frank's own position with regard to Jews was complicated. A conservative Catholic, he voiced his church's traditional theological teachings concerning the Jews—that they had been chosen by God to teach the belief in the one God and to give expression to the hope for a messianic redeemer but that they betrayed this mission, turning their backs on and, ultimately, crucifying the son of God. The metahistorical status of the Jews then switched from chosenness to abandonment and from blessing to curse. As late as 1892, Frank could write that Jews historically had committed crimes against their Christian neighbors but not, he argued, for religious purposes. (See Frank, *Die Kirche und die Juden: Eine Studie*, 2nd ed. [Regensburg: G. J. Manz, 1892].) It may well have been his own religious conservatism, his allegiance to official papal teaching, that caused Frank publicly to oppose the blood libel.

4. This assessment comes from Helmut Walser Smith, *The Butcher's Tale: Murder and Anti-Semitism in a German Town* (New York: W. W. Norton, 2002), 123, based on the bimonthly newsletter of the *Verein zur Abwehr des Antisemitismus*. Smith adds, "Of the seventy-nine accusations, fourteen escalated into some level of violence against Jews. In more than half the cases, specific charges were made against individual Jews, as opposed to the more general claim that 'the Jews did it.'"

5. On the connection between the mass-market press and accusations of Jewish criminality, see Daniel M. Vyleta, *Crime, Jews and News: Vienna 1895–1914* (New York: Berghahn Books, 2007).

6. John D. Klier, *Imperial Russia's Jewish Question, 1855–1881* (Cambridge: Cambridge University Press, 1995), 428. On the Kutaisi case, see *Mishpat Kutaisi: 100 shanim la-mishpat alilat ha-dam ha-rishon be-rusiyah, 1878–1978. Din ve-ḥeshbon stenografi*, ed. Gershon Megrelishvili (Tel Aviv: B'nai B'rith Trumpeldor, 1978), and Klier, *Imperial Russia's Jewish Question*, 428–33. On the judicial reform of 1864, see Benjamin Nathans, *Beyond the Pale: The Jewish Encounter with Late Imperial Russia* (Berkeley: University of California Press, 2002), 311–15.

7. On the Beilis affair, see, especially, Robert Weinberg, *Blood Libel in Late Imperial Russia: The Ritual Murder Trial of Mendel Beilis* (Bloomington: Indiana University Press, 2014), and Edmund Levin, *A Child of Christian Blood: Murder and Conspiracy in Tsarist Russia: The Beilis Blood Libel* (New York: Schocken Books, 2014). The brief quotes are taken from Levin, *A Child of Christian Blood*, 284. Other titles include Meir Kotik, *Mishpat Beilis: alilat dam ba-me'ah ha-esrim* (Tel Aviv: Melo, 1978); Mendel Beilis, *The Story of My Sufferings* (New York: Mendel Beilis Publishing Co., 1926); Ezekiel Leiken, *The Beilis Transcripts: The Anti-Semitic Trial That Shook the World* (Northvale, NJ: Jason Aronson, 1993), 217; Alexander B. Tager, *The Decay of Czarism: The Beilis Trial* (Philadelphia: Jewish Publication Society of America, 1935); and Maurice Samuel, *Blood Accusation: The Strange History of the Beiliss Case* (Philadelphia: Jewish Publication Society of America, 1966). For a more complete analysis of the trial, see the Conclusion.

8. There exists no single work on the ritual murder accusation in modern Europe. For Imperial Germany, see Johannes T. Groß, *Ritualmordbeschuldigungen gegen Juden im deutschen Kaiserreich (1871–1914)* (Berlin: Metropol, 2002). References for individual cases will be given in the chapters that follow.

9. On the medieval accusations concerning ritual crucifixion and ritual murder, see E. M. Rose, *The Murder of William of Norwich: The Origins of the Blood Libel in Medieval Europe* (Oxford: Oxford University Press, 2015); Mary D. Anderson, *A Saint at Stake: The Strange Death of William of Norwich, 1144* (London: Faber and Faber, 1964); Thomas of Monmouth, *The Life and Passion of William of Norwich*, trans. and ed. Miri Rubin (London: Penguin Books, 2014); Robert Chazan, "The Blois Incident of 1171," *Proceedings of the American Academy for Jewish Research* 36 (1968): 13–31; Hannah R. Johnson, *Blood Libel: The Ritual Murder Accusation at the Limit of Jewish History* (Ann Arbor: University of Michigan Press, 2012); Jeremy Cohen, *The Friars and the Jews: The Evolution of Medieval Anti-Judaism* (Ithaca, N.Y.: Cornell University Press, 1982), 42–44; idem, "The Jews as the Killers of Christ in the Latin Tradition, From Augustine to the Friars," *Traditio* 39 (1983): 1–27; Gavin Langmuir, "Thomas of

Monmouth: Detector of Ritual Murder," *Speculum* 59 (1984): 820–46 [reprinted in Langmuir, *Toward a Definition of Antisemitism* (Berkeley: University of California Press, 1990), 209–36]; idem, "The Knight's Tale of Young Hugh of Lincoln," *Speculum* 47 (1972): 459–82 [reprinted in Langmuir, *Toward a Definition of Antisemitism*, 237–62]; idem, "Ritual Cannibalism," in Langmuir, *Toward a Definition of Antisemitism*, 263–81; Robert C. Stacey, "From Ritual Crucifixion to Host Desecration: Jews and the Body of Christ," *Jewish History* 12 (1998): 11–28; Israel Jacob Yuval, *Two Nations in Your Womb: Perceptions of Jews and Christians in Late Antiquity and the Middle Ages* (Berkeley: University of California Press, 2006), 135–204; and Joshua Trachtenberg, *The Devil and the Jews: The Medieval Conception of the Jew and Its Relation to Modern Antisemitism* (New Haven, Conn.: Yale University Press, 1943, and later eds.).

On the host desecration charge, see, in addition to Stacey above, Miri Rubin, *Gentile Tales: The Narrative Assault on Late Medieval Jews* (New Haven, Conn.: Yale University Press, 1999), and Magda Teter, *Sinners on Trial: Jews and Sacrilege After the Reformation* (Cambridge, Mass.: Harvard University Press, 2011).

10. On the ritual murder accusation in pre-Reformation Germany (Holy Roman Empire), see R. Po-chia Hsia, *The Myth of Ritual Murder: Jews and Magic in Reformation Germany* (New Haven, Conn.: Yale University Press, 1988); idem, *Trent 1475: Stories of a Ritual Murder Trial* (New Haven, Conn.: Yale University Press, 1992); Teter, *Blood Libel*, 43–151; and Wolfgang Treue, *Der Trienter Judenprozeß: Voraussetzungen—Abläufe—Auswirkungen (1475–1588)* (Hannover: Hahnsche Buchhandlung, 1996). On the urban focus of early modern antisemitism, see, in addition to Hsia above, Hillel J. Kieval, "Antisemitism and the City: A Beginner's Guide," *Studies in Contemporary Jewry* 15 (1999): 3–18.

11. Hsia, *Myth of Ritual Murder*, 136.

12. Miri Rubin, *Gentile Tales*, 6.

13. The main sources for the history of the ritual murder accusation in Poland-Lithuania are Magda Teter, *Sinners on Trial*; idem, *Blood Libel*, 191–278; Daniel Tollet, *Accuser pour convertir: Du bon usage de l'accusation de crime rituel dans la Pologne catholique à l'époque moderne* (Paris: Presses Universitaires de France, 2000); Zenon Guldon and Jacek Wijaczka, "The Accusation of Ritual Murder in Poland, 1500–1800," *Polin* 10 (1997): 99–140; idem, *Procesy o mordy rytualne w Polsce w XVI–XVIII wieku* (Kielce: Wydawnictwo, 1995); Gershon David Hundert, *Jews in Poland-Lithuania in the Eighteenth Century* (Berkeley: University of California Press, 2004), 72–76; Mikhail Salman, "On the Question of the Origins and Frequency of Ritual Murder Trials in Poland," *Journal of the Academic Proceedings of Soviety Jewry* 1 (1986): 5–24; Hanna Węgrzynek, *"Czarna legenda" Żydów: Procesy o rzekome mordy rytualne w dawnej Polsce* (Warsaw: Wydawnictwo Bellonia; Wydawnictwo Fundacji Historia Pro Futurio, 1995); and Jacek Wijaczka, "Ritualmordbeschuldigungen und -prozesse in Polen-Lituaen vom 16. bis 18. Jahrhundert," in *Ritualmord: Legenden in der europäischen Geschichte*, 213–32.

14. For varying tabulations, see Tollet, *Accuser pour convertir*, 58, 227–46 (although the totals in the two places are slightly different); Guldon and Wijaczka, "The Accusation of Ritual Murder in Poland," 139; Węgrzynek, *Czarna legenda*, 161–76; and Hundert, *Jews in Poland-Lithuania*, 72, where he adds, "The actual number of victims may well have been higher."

15. On Sandomierz, see Teter, *Blood Libel*, 256–71, and Hundert, *Jews in Poland-Lithuania*, 73–75. For the ensuing Polish literature on Jewish ritual murder: Stefan Żuchowski, *Ogłos procesów kryminalnych na Żydach o różne ekscesy, także morderstwo dzieci* ([Sandomierz], 1700); idem, *Proces kryminalny o niewinie dziecię Jerzego Krasnowskiego. Już to trzecie roku 1710 dnia 18 sierpnia w Sendomirzu okrutnie od Żydow zamordowane* ([Sandomierz], 1713); Józef Załuski, *Morderstwa rytualne w Polsce do połowy XVIII wieku* (Warsaw, 1914).

16. Paweł Maciejko, *The Mixed Multitude: Jacob Frank and the Frankist Movement, 1755–1816* (Philadelphia: University of Pennsylvania Press, 2011).

17. Hundert, *Jews in Poland and Lithuania*, 77, n. 68. For an important, new analysis of the Ganganelli report, see Teter, *Blood Libel*, 323–44.

18. Guldon and Wijaczka, ""The Accusation of Ritual Murder in Poland," 140.

In the Russian Empire—following the partitions of Poland—significant reforms to the criminal code did not occur until the 1860s, and trials against Jews for ritual murder did take place from time to time. One notable example can be found in the Belarusian town of Velizh in 1823 to 1824. In a case that appeared to have been concluded at the local level within a year and a half, the surprising intervention of the Tsar Alexander I inaugurated a formal imperial investigation that stretched until 1835 before finally ending in the acquittal of all Jews accused. (See Eugene M. Avrutin, *The Velizh Affair: Blood Libel in a Russian Town* [New York: Oxford University Press, 2018].)

19. Pierre Birnbaum, *A Tale of Ritual Murder in the Age of Louis XIV: The Trial of Raphaël Lévy, 1669*, trans. Arthur Goldhammer (Stanford, Calif.: Stanford University Press, 2012).

20. On the Orkuta case, see Theodor Austerlitz, *Die letzte Folterprozedur in der öst.-ung. Monarchie: Der "Kodesch" von Orkuta* (Prešov: Jüdischer Museumverein, 1933); see also Edith Stern, "More on Ritual Murder Trials: The Ritual Murder Charge of Orkut, Greater Hungary, 1764," *Korot* 11 (1995): 132–35, although there are problems and inconsistencies in this article.

21. Austerlitz, *Die letzte Folterprozedur*, 29–40.

22. By far the best study of the Damascus Affair is Jonathan Frankel, *The Damascus Affair: "Ritual Murder," Politics, and the Jews in 1840* (Cambridge: Cambridge University Press, 1997).

23 *Der Blut-Prozeß von Tisza Eszlár in Ungarn. Vorgeschichte der Anklage und vollständiger Bericht über die Prozeß-Verhandlungen vor dem Gerichte in Nyíregyháza. Nach dem amtlichen, stenographischen Protocollen aus dem Ungarischen übertragen* (New York: Schnitzer Bros., 1883), i.

24. *Jewish Chronicle*, 26 January 1883, 11. Schiller-Szinessy also revealed that the original impulse to canvas the opinions of scholars in Hebrew and Rabbinics at the University of Cambridge came from the Budapest rabbinical board.

25. Letter of J. B. Dunelm, *Jewish Chronicle*, 26 January 1883.

26. Letter of J. J. Stewart Berowne, dean of Peterborough College, University of Cambridge, *Jewish Chronicle*, 2 February 1883.

27. Paul Nathan, *Xanten-Cleve: Betrachtungen zum Prozeß Buschhof. Separat-Abdruck aus der "Nation"* (Berlin: H. S. Hermann, 1892), 16.

28. I derive my use of the term "social knowledge" in part from the anthropologist Clifford Geertz, who writes that to engage in the sociology of knowledge is to regard "the community as the shop in which thoughts are constructed and deconstructed, history the terrain they seize and surrender" and, hence, to attend to such matters as "the representation of authority, the marking of boundaries, the rhetoric of persuasion, the expression of commitment, and the registering of dissent." (Clifford Geertz, "The Way We Think Now: Ethnography of Modern Thought," in Geertz, *Local Knowledge: Further Essays in Interpretive Anthropology* [New York: Basic Books, 1983], 153.)

On the social frameworks of knowledge and memory, see Maurice Halbwachs, *On Collective Memory*, ed., trans., and introd. Lewis A. Coser (Chicago: University of Chicago Press, 1992).

29. Peter Berger and Thomas Luckmann, *The Social Construction of Reality: A Treatise in the Sociology of Knowledge* (Garden City, NY: Doubleday, 1966), 21–22.

30. Ibid., 23.

31. Ibid., 30.

32. This process can also be viewed from the opposite direction (i.e., the production of knowledge as bound to social interaction). On this point, see Clifford Geertz: "The sociology of knowledge . . . is not a matter of matching varieties of consciousness to types of social organization and then running causal arrows from somewhere in the recesses of the second in the general direction of the first. . . . It is a matter of conceiving of cognition, emotion, motivation, perception, imagination, memory . . . whatever, as themselves, and directly, social affairs" (Geertz, "The Way We Think Now," 153).

CHAPTER 1

1. For a by now classic analysis of late medieval and early modern ritual murder trials in the Holy Roman Empire, see Hsia, *The Myth of Ritual Murder*. For the last of the medieval cases, see Hsia, *Trent 1475*; Teter, *Blood Libel*, 43–151; and Treue, *Der Trienter Judenprozeß*.

2. Adolf Buschhoff (1840–1912). On the Xanten ritual murder affair and the Kleve trial, see Chapter 3.

3. On the Tiszaeszlár case, see Chapter 2; the Polná case, Chapter 4; and the Konitz case, Chapter 5.

4. On the problem of applying general political and economic explanations to specific ritual murder accusations, see Hillel J. Kieval, "Middleman Minorities and Blood: Is There a Natural Economy of the Ritual Murder Accusation in Europe?" in *Essential Outsiders: Chinese and Jews in the Modern Transformation of Southeast Asia and Central Europe*, ed. Daniel Chirot and Anthony Reid (Seattle: University of Washington Press, 1997), 208–33.

5. György Enyedi, *Hungary: An Economic Geography* (Boulder, Colo.: Westview, 1976), passim; Tivadar Bernát, ed., *An Economic Geography of Hungary* (Budapest: Akadémiai Kiadó, 1989), 376–92.

6. C. A. Macartney, *Hungary* (London: Ernest Benn, 1934), 199.

7. Ibid., 199–200.

8. Robert E. Dickinson, *Germany: A General and Regional Geography* (New York: E. P. Dutton, 1953), 466.

9. Holger Schmenk, *Xanten im 19. Jahrhundert: Eine rheinische Stadt zwischen Tradition und Moderne* (Cologne: Bölau, 2008), 312; *Die Gemeinden mit 2000 und mehr Einwohnern im Deutschen Reich nach der Volkszählung vom 16. Juni 1925. Sonderhefte zu Wirtschaft und Statistik*, vol. 6 (Berlin Statistisches Reichsamt, 1926), 48–49. The latter publication compares data from the 1925 census to that of 1910.

10. Dickinson, *Germany*, 464–65.

11. Nathan, *Xanten-Cleve*, 1.

12. Zdeněk Jaroš, *Polná: kulturně historický* průvodce (Jihlava: Muzeum Vysočiny, 1989), 7–13.

13. Jaroš, *Polná*, 15; see also Břetislav Reyrich [Rérych], *Polná: Průvodce po městě a okolí* (Polná: Club Čs. Turistů, 1927), 6, and idem, "Židé a Polná," Typescript, n.d. (Muzeum Vysočina, pobočka Polná), 37.

14. Václav Kotyska, *Úplný místopisný slovník Království Českého* (Prague: Bursík & Kohout, 1895), 1044–45.

15. Bruno Schumacher, *Geschichte Ost- und Westpreußens*, 4th ed. (Würzburg: Holzner Verlag, 1959), 221, 281–82.

16. Karl Baedecker, *Deutschland in einem Bande: Handbuch für Reisende* (Leipzig: Baedecker, 1906), 60; referred to in Helmut Walser Smith, "Konitz, 1900: Ritual Murder and

Antisemitic Violence," in *Exclusionary Violence: Antisemitic Riots in Modern German History*, ed. Christhard Hoffmann, Werner Bergmann, and Helmut Walser Smith (Ann Arbor: University of Michigan Press, 2002), 95.

17. Schumacher, *Geschichte*, 286.

18. Max Aschkewitz, *Zur Geschichte der Juden in Westpreußen* (Marburg: Johann Gottfried Herder-Institut, 1967), 178; *Brockhaus' Konversationslexikon*, vol. 10 (Leipzig, 1908), 556 (cited in Hermann Greive, "Die gesellschaftliche Bedeutung der christlich-jüdischen Differenz: Zur Situation im deutschen Katholizismus," in *Juden im Wilhelminischen Deutschland 1890–1914*, ed. Werner E. Mosse [Tübingen: J. C. B. Mohr, 1976], 382); and Helmut Walser Smith, "Konitz, 1900," 95. Smith states that Poles made up less than 10 percent of the population of Konitz.

19. Jörg K. Hoensch, *A History of Modern Hungary, 1867–1986*, 2nd ed. (London: Longman, 1996), 10–16; on the Austrian-Hungarian Compromise: Hoensch, 16–19.

20. Tibor Frank, "Hungary and the Dual Monarchy, 1867–1890," in *A History of Hungary*, ed. Peter F. Sugar, Péter Hanák, and Tibor Frank (Bloomington: Indiana University Press, 1990), 259.

21. Ibid., 259–60.

22. Andrew C. Janos, *The Politics of Backwardness in Hungary, 1825–1945* (Princeton, N.J.: Princeton University Press, 1982), 127–28; Frank, "Hungary and the Dual Monarchy," 259.

23. Janos, *Politics of Backwardness*, 127–28, and Hoensch, *Modern Hungary*, 31, 36–43.

24. On the conquest of Ottoman Hungary, see Katalin Péter, "The Later Ottoman Period and Royal Hungary, 1606–1711," in *A History of Hungary*, 100–120; map, 139. On the Familiants laws, see Hillel J. Kieval, "Bohemia and Moravia," and Ivo Cerman, "Familiants Laws," both in *The YIVO Encyclopedia of Jews in Eastern Europe*, ed. Gershon D. Hundert, vol. 1 (New Haven, Conn.: Yale University Press, 2008), 205 and 493–94, respectively. The number of Jewish families that might legally reside was set (on the basis of a recent census) at 8,541 in Bohemia and at 5,106 in Moravia.

25. Victor Karády and István Kemény, "Les Juifs dans la structure des classes en Hongrie," *Actes de la Recherche en Sciences Sociales* 22 (June 1978): 28–29; Hoensch, *History of Modern Hungary*, 32. Jews from Bohemia and, especially, Moravia continued to migrate to Hungary through the first half of the nineteenth century, and it is not clear how much of the increase in immigration rates after 1780 was produced by Jews from Galicia. The Familiants Laws were not repealed until 1848.

26. Janos, *Politics of Backwardness*, 112–18; William O. McCagg, *Jewish Nobles and Geniuses in Modern Hungary* (Boulder, Colo.: East European Quarterly, 1972), 223. Similarly, in *A History of Habsburg Jews*, he describes the "alliance between the Magyar-speaking nobility and the reformer Jews" that was cemented in the 1860s (135).

27. There exist various descriptions of this process. See McCagg, *Habsburg Jews*, 123–139; idem, *Jewish Nobles and Geniuses*, 75–166; János Gyurgyák, *A zsidókérdés Magyarországon: Politikai eszmetörténet* (Budapest: Osiris Kiadó, 2001), 44–87, 263–82; and Tamás Ungvári, *The "Jewish Question" in Europe: The Case of Hungary* (Boulder, Colo.: Social Science Monographs/Atlantic Research and Publications, 2000), 61–90.

C. A. Macartney's summation of the noble-Jewish alliance in Hungary, while patronizing in tone, might still be apt: "The lordly Magyar warrior and the laborious and thrifty Hebrew complement one another's needs and proclivities in so providential a fashion that one is tempted to say, slightly paraphrasing Palacký, that if the Hungarian Jew had not existed it would have been necessary to invent him" (Macartney, *Hungary*, 208).

28. Hoensch, *History of Modern Hungary*, 37–38; McCagg, *Jewish Nobles and Geniuses*, 21–22 and passim.

29. András Gerő, *Modern Hungarian Society in the Making: The Unfinished Experience* (Budapest: Central European University Press, 1995), 182–84.

30. Ibid., 169–99.

31. Andrew Handler, *An Early Blueprint for Zionism: Győző Istóczy's Political Anti-Semitism* (Boulder, Colo.: East European Monographs, 1989), 33–36. Other works dealing with the early history of antisemitism in Hungary are Judit Kubinszky, *Politikai antiszemitizmus Magyarországon (1875–1890)* (Budapest: Kossuth Könyvkiadó, 1976); Nathaniel Katzburg, *Antishemiyut be-hungariyah 1867–1914* (Tel Aviv: Dvir, 1969), 53–105; Gyurgyák, *A zsidókérdés Magyarországon*, 314–39; and Friedrich Gottas, "Die antisemitische Bewegung in Ungarn im Zeitalter des Hochliberalismus," *Zeitgeschichte* 1 (1973–74): 105–19.

32. Handler, *An Early Blueprint*, 42–51. For the text of the speech, see Győző Istóczy, *Országgyülési beszédei, inditványai és törvényjavaslatai, 1872–1896* (Budapest: Buschmann, 1904), 42–63.

33. Istóczy, *Országgyülési beszédei*, 44; my translation is based on that of Handler (*An Early Blueprint*, 45) but with revisions, in part because his is somewhat abridged.

34. Ibid., 45–46.

35. On the *Kulturkampf* in Imperial Germany, see Helmut Walser Smith, *German Nationalism and Religious Conflict: Culture, Ideology, Politics, 1870–1914* (Princeton, N.J.: Princeton University Press, 1995); Michael B. Gross, *The War Against Catholicism: Liberalism and the Anti-Catholic Imagination in Nineteenth-Century Germany* (Ann Arbor: University of Michigan Press, 2004); and Ronald J. Ross, *The Failure of Bismarck's Kulturkampf: Catholicism and State Power in Imperial Germany, 1871–1887* (Washington, D.C.: Catholic University of America Press, 1998). On the entanglement of Jews in anti-Catholic polemics in Germany and France, see Ari Joskowicz, *The Modernity of Others: Jewish Anti-Catholicism in Germany and France* (Stanford, Calif.: Stanford University Press, 2014).

36. On the impact of the *Kulturkampf* on Catholic attitudes toward Jews, see Olaf Blaschke, *Katholizismus und Antisemitismus im Deutschen Kaiserreich* (Göttingen: Vandenhoeck & Ruprecht, 1997), 42–56, and Joskowicz, *The Modernity of Others*, 56–60.

37. Blaschke, *Katholizismus und Antisemitismus*, 30–41.

38. Barbara Suchy, "Antisemitismus in den Jahren vor dem Ersten Weltkrieg," in *Köln und das rheinische Judentum: Festschrift Germania Judaica 1959–1984*, ed. Jutta Bohnke-Kollwitz et al. (Cologne: J. P. Bachem, 1984), 266–67; see also Thomas Mergel, *Zwischen Klasse und Konfession: Katholische Bürgertum im Rheinland 1794–1914* (Göttingen: Vandenhoeck & Ruprecht, 1994), 258–59.

39. Ulrich Baumann, *Zerstörte Nachbarschaften: Christen und Juden in badischen Landgemeinden 1862–1940* (Hamburg: Dölling und Galitz, 2000), 138.

40. Suchy, "Antisemitismus," 266.

41. August Rohling, *Der Talmudjude: Zur Beherzigung für Juden und Christen aller Stände* (Münster: Adolph Russell, 1871). See also Hermann Greive, "Die gesellschaftliche Bedeutung der christlich-jüdischen Differenz: Zur Situation im deutschen Katholizismus," in *Juden im Wilhelminischen Deutschland 1890–1914*, ed. Werner E. Mosse (Tübingen: J. C. B. Mohr, 1976), 354–63. Greive argues that it was almost exclusively Catholic scholars and publicists who engaged in the public attack against the Talmud and rabbinic morality during the Second Empire and that the effects of this campaign lasted up to and through the Nazi period (355)

On Rohling's activity, see, in addition to Greive, I. A. Hellwing, *Der konfessionelle Antisemitismus im 19. Jahrhundert in Österreich* (Vienna: Herder, 1972), 71–183; Joseph S. Bloch, *My*

Reminiscences (Vienna: R. Löwit, 1922–23), 61–67; and Jacob Katz, *From Prejudice to Destruction: Anti-Semitism, 1700–1933* (Cambridge, Mass.: Harvard University Press, 1980), 219–20, 285–86. Publication and distribution figures are from Suchy, "Antisemitismus," 266, and *Acten und Gutachten in dem Prozesse Rohling contra Bloch*, vol. 1 (Vienna: M. Breitenstein, 1890), 3.

42. See, for example, the report in the *Jewish Chronicle*, 29 July 1892, 5–6.

43. Ibid. The *Chronicle* goes on to say: "It is further pointed out that as Jews are labouring under an everlasting curse, their hatred to Christians is equally everlasting, and the inference that the writer leaves his readers to draw is that the Ritual Murder is consequently a constant phenomenon in Jewish life. The discovery that this disgraceful work is now in circulation has produced considerable sensation in Germany, and Conservative organs like the *Kölnische Zeitung* join hands with Democratic newspapers like the *Frankfurter Presse* in severely condemning this literary outrage."

44. Ulrich Baumann, "The Development and Destruction of a Social Institution: How Jews, Catholics and Protestants Lived Together in Rural Baden, 1862–1940," in *Protestants, Catholics and Jews in Germany, 1800–1914*, ed. Helmut Walser Smith (Oxford: Berg, 2001), 297–315. See also Helmut Walser Smith, "The Learned and the Popular Discourse of Anti-Semitism in the Catholic Milieu of the Kaiserreich," *Central European History* 27 (1994): 315–28, particularly for his suggestions for distinguishing between Catholic and Protestant antisemitism in Imperial Germany.

Baumann notes that "occupational separation of professions along religious lines had little impact on neighborly helpfulness but played a large role in the way Christians perceived Jews. The professional and economic difference was less central to this perception than the difference between trade and farming, two areas that were also interconnected" (299). His research suggests that Christians and Jews maintained close and mutually supportive social ties into the first decades of the twentieth century but also that Christians verbalized certain moral judgments about the Jewish "attachment" to trade rather than to "work."

45. Ibid., 300. A Christian inhabitant from the predominantly Protestant town of Nonnenweier remembered seeing "Jewish men saying their early morning prayers at home and wearing straps around their arms." "The Jews," he observed, "were Christian" (300; based on Elfie Labsch-Benz, *Die jüdische Gemeinde Nonnenweier: Jüdisches Leben und Brauchtum in einer badischen Landgemeinde* [Freiburg: Mersch, 1981], 107).

46. Baumann, "Development and Destruction," 300. See also Baumann, *Zerstörte Nachbarschaften*.

47. Schumacher, *Geschichte Ost- und Westpreußens*, 284.

48. Ibid., 284–85.

49. Victor Karady, "Religious Divisions, Socio-Economic Stratification and the Modernization of Hungarian Jewry After Emancipation," in *Jews in the Hungarian Economy*, ed. Michael K. Silber (Jerusalem: Magnes Press, 1992), 170, 179. Karady points out that "Magyarization," as it was called, was virtually complete (over 90 percent) in the northern and eastern counties, including Szabolcs.

50. On the place of Jews in the Czech-German national conflict, see Hillel J. Kieval, *The Making of Czech Jewry: National Conflict and Jewish Society in Bohemia, 1870–1918* (New York: Oxford University Press, 1988); idem, *Languages of Community: The Jewish Experience in the Czech Lands* (Berkeley: University of California Press, 2000), 65–94, 114–58; Gary B. Cohen, *The Politics of Ethnic Survival: Germans in Prague, 1861–1914* (Princeton, N.J.: Princeton University Press, 1981), 76–85, 168–83, 217–73; and Michal Frankl, *"Emancipace od židů": Český antisemitismus na konci 19. století* (Prague: Paseka, 2007).

51. See Frankl, *"Emancipace od židů,"* 25–110; see also my discussion of the theme of "Death and the Nation" in *Languages of Community*, 181–97.

52. Reyrich, "Židé a Polná," 37. Such schools were referred to as *přelejvárny* (sing., *přelejvárna*), which, while difficult to translate precisely into English, might be rendered most closely as siphonings or decantings. See similar usages in *Radikální listy*, 26 June 1894, 6, and *Jizeran*, 27 May 1882, 3. My thanks to Michal Frankl for these references and linguistic suggestions.

In his published guide to the town, Reyrich noted with some bitterness that this two-grade German Jewish school had been better endowed in the 1870s than both of the five-grade Czech schools (Reyrich, *Polná: Průvodce po městě a okolí*, 48).

53. On the Protestant orientation in Czech nationalism, see Tomáš G. Masaryk, *The Meaning of Czech History*, ed., with an introduction, by René Wellek, trans. Peter Kussi (Chapel Hill: University of North Carolina Press, 1974); Milan Hauner, "The Meaning of Czech History: Masaryk versus Pekář," in *T. G. Masaryk (1850–1937). Vol. 3: Statesman and Cultural Force*, ed. Harry Hanak (Houndsmills: Macmillan, 1990), 24–42; and Karel Kučera, "Masaryk and Pekář: Their Conflict over the Meaning of Czech History and Its Metamorphoses," in *T. G. Masaryk (1850–1937). Vol. 1: Thinker and Politician*, ed. Stanley B. Winters (Houndsmills: Macmillan, 1990), 88–113.

54. On the origins of the German Jewish school system in Bohemia, see Kieval, *Languages of Community*, 37–64; Louise Hecht, "Die Prager deutsch-jüdische Schulanstalt 1782–1848," in *Jüdische Erziehung und aufklärerische Schulreform: Analysen zum späten 18. und frühen 19. Jahrhundert*, ed. Britta L. Behm, Uta Lormann, and Ingrid Lohmann (New York: Waxmann Münster, 2002), 213–52; and Michael K. Silber, "Josephian Reforms," in *The YIVO Encyclopedia of Jews in Eastern Europe*, ed. Gershon D. Hundert, vol. 1 (New Haven, Conn.: Yale University Press, 2008), 831–34. On Jewish acculturation in nineteenth-century Bohemia, see McCagg, *A History of Habsburg Jews*, 65–82; Kieval, *Languages of Community*, 65–94; and idem, "Bohemia and Moravia," 207–11.

55. These arguments are developed more fully in Kieval, *The Making of Czech Jewry*, 10–63.

56. On the legal and political underpinnings of Austrian nationality policy, see Gerald Stourzh, *Die Gleichberechtigung der Nationalitäten in der Verfassung und Verwaltung Österreichs, 1848–1918* (Vienna: Verlag der Österreichischen Akademie der Wissenschaften, 1985).

57. Bohumil Černý, *Justičný omyl: Hilsneriáda* (Prague: Magnet Press, 1990), 10. On the 1890 and 1900 censuses generally, see Kieval, *Making of Czech Jewry*, 60–63.

58. Károly Eötvös, *A nagy per*, vol. 2, 54–55, and Andrew Handler, *Blood Libel at Tiszaeszlar* (Boulder, Colo.: East European Monographs, 1980), 36, where he employs both terms in describing Jewish-Gentile relations.

Nathaniel Katzburg seems to combine Eötvös's and Handler's sentiments when he describes relations as "friendly, even if [they] contained a small measure of superiority" (Katzburg, *Antishemiyut be-Hungariya*, 107).

59. Paul Nathan, *Der Prozess von Tisza-Eszlár: Ein Antisemitisches Culturbild* (Berlin: F. Fontane, 1892), passim and 93–97.

60. Géza Ónody, *Tisza-Eszlár in der Vergangenheit und Gegenwart. Über die Juden im Allgemeinen. Jüdische Glaubensmysterien. Rituelle Mordthaten und Blutopfer. Der Tisza-Eszlárer Fall*, trans. Georg von Marcziányi (Budapest, 1883), 156.

According to Andrew Handler, Ónody had been forced to lease part of his estate (in fact, that part which lay outside of Tiszaeszlár) from its new, Jewish owners, Simon and György Pöhm. This humiliating situation turned into "a passionate, implacable hatred of Jews in general" (Handler, *Blood Libel*, 31).

61. Handler, *Blood Libel*, 36.

62. Ónody, *Tisza-Eszlár*, 156.

63. Ibid., 157.

64. *Der Blut-Prozeß von Tisza Eszlár in Ungarn*, 59.

65. Ibid., 110. At his trial, József Scharf identified Mrs. Bátori as the individual who worked as a "Sabbath Gentile" [Yiddish: *shabbesgoy*; Hebrew: *goy shel Shabbat*]. Ibid., 23.

66. Suchy, "Antisemitismus," 253, quoting from official police files. Suchy argues that one can conclude from the investigation reports that the murder had been sexual in character.

67. Schmenk, *Xanten*, 312; *Encyclopaedia Judaica*, vol. 16 (Jerusalem: Keter, 1972), 685–86.

Although always a small community, Xanten was sufficiently important to serve as the meeting place for the Jewish Diet of the Rhine beginning in 1690. In 1787, a special building (also containing a synagogue) was set aside for the assembly's meetings. After 1890, the Jewish population declined steadily: in 1916, it stood at thirty persons; by 1930, barely fourteen Jews remained (*Encyclopaedia Judaica*, vol. 16, 685–86).

68. *Der Xantener Knabenmord vor dem Schwurgericht zu Cleve, 4.–14. Juli 1892 Vollständiger stenographischer Bericht* (Berlin: Cronbach, 1893), 5–7. See the discussion of these points in Bernd Kölling, "Blutige Illusionen: Ritualmorddiskurse und Antisemitismus im niederrheinischen Xanten," in *Agrarische Verfassung und politische Struktur: Studien zur Gesellschaftsgeschichte Preußens 1700–1918*, ed. René Schiller (Berlin: Arno Spitz, 1998), 372.

69. Ibid., 3, 77.

70. *Der Fall Buschhoff: Aktenmäßige Darstellung des Xantener Knabenmord-Prozesses* (Frankfurt a.M.: C. Koenitz, 1892), 23, 35.

71. *Jewish Chronicle*, 22 July 1892, 9.

72. *Der Fall Buschhoff*, 23.

73. See Julius H. Schoeps, "Ritualmordbeschuldigung und Blutaberglaube: Die Affäre Buschhoff im niederrheinischen Xanten," in *Köln und das rheinische Judentum*, 287, 297–98 (where he quotes from the file of the district magistrate's office in Moers [Nordrhein-Westfällisches Hauptstaatsarchiv, Düsseldorf (HStAD), LA Moers, Nr. 547]).

74. Peter Letkemann, "Zur Geschichte der Juden in Konitz im 19. Jahrhundert," *Beiträge zur Geschichte Westpreußens* 9 (1985): 100–5.

75. Aschkewitz, *Westpreußen*, 23, 31–38, 177–79; *Brockhaus' Konversationslexikon*, vol. 10 (Leipzig, 1908), 556; Letkemann, "Juden in Konitz," 113.

76. On the riots in Pomerania and West Prussia, see Christhard Hoffmann, "Political Culture and Violence Against Minorities: The Antisemitic Riots in Pomerania and West Prussia," in *Exclusionary Violence*, 67–92; additional information in Stephen C. J. Nicholls, *The Burning of the Synagogue in Neustettin: Ideological Arson in the 1880s*, Research Paper No. 2 (Sussex: Centre for German-Jewish Studies, University of Sussex, 1999).

77. Nicholls, "Burning of the Synagogue," 1–2; Gerd Hoffmann, *Der Prozeß um den Brand der Synagoge in Neustettin: Antisemitismus in Deutschland ausgangs des 19. Jahrhunderts* (Schifferstadt: Gerd Hoffmann Verlag, 1998), 24–26.

78. Christhard Hoffmann, "Political Culture and Violence," 79–80; Nicholls, "Burning the Synagogue," 3.

79. Nicholls, "Burning of the Synagogue," 3–4; Gerd Hoffmann, *Der Prozeß um den Brand der Synagoge*, 50–197, for the trial proceedings.

80. Christhard Hoffmann, "Political Culture and Violence," 81–82.

81. Ibid., 82–84.

82. *Konitzer Tageblatt*, as reported in *Die Welt*, 18 May 1900, 8.

83. Max Aram, "Konitz," *Die Welt*, 21 September 1900, 1–2.

84. The collusion of the landed estate in Jewish efforts to circumvent the effects of Vienna's restrictive legislation has yet to be studied closely. For literature that does exist on the subject, see Josef Wertheimer, *Die Juden in Österreich*, vol. 1 (Leipzig, 1842), 187–94; Ludvík Singer, "Zur Geschichte der Toleranzpatente in den Sudetenländern," *Jahrbuch der Gesellschaft für Geschichte der Juden in der Cechoslovakischen Republik* 5 (1933): 236–37; Karel Adámek, *Slovo o židech* (Chrudim, 1899), 5–8; Adolf Stein, *Die Geschichte der Juden in Böhmen* (Brno, 1904), 86–90; and Kieval, "Bohemia and Moravia."

85. Reyrich, *Polná: Průvodce*, 34–36; Jaroš, *Polná*, 11.

86. Ibid., 56.

87. On Jewish population figures, see Jiří Fiedler, *Jewish Sights of Bohemia and Moravia* (Prague: Sefer, 1991), 139–40, and Ruth Kestenberg-Gladstein, "The Jews Between Czechs and Germans in the Historic Lands," in *The Jews of Czechoslovakia*, vol. 1 (Philadelphia: Jewish Publication Society of America, 1968), 29. On the Familiants Laws, see note 24 above.

88. Wolfgang Gasser, *Erlebte Revolution 1848/49: Das Wiener Tagebuch des jüdischen Journalisten Benjamin Kewall* (Vienna: Böhlau Verlag, 2010), 70–71. Benjamin Kewall (1806–1880), the author of this recently published diary—written originally in German in Hebrew script—was a native son of Polná who made his way to Vienna (possibly after rabbinical studies in Nikolsburg/Mikulov), where he worked at first as a tutor in a Jewish household and later as a journalist. He, too, was active in the Revolution of 1848 in that city.

89. On Jewish migration from the Czech countryside during the second half of the nineteenth century, see Kieval, *The Making of Czech Jewry*, 10–17; Kestenberg-Gladstein, "The Jews Between Czechs and Germans," 27–32 (with caution); Jan Heřman, "The Evolution of the Jewish Population in Bohemia and Moravia, 1754–1953," in *Papers in Jewish Demography, 1973*, ed. U. O. Schmelz, P. Glikson, and S. Della Pergola (Jerusalem: Institute of Contemporary Jewry, 1977), 191–206; and idem, "The Evolution of the Jewish Population in Prague, 1869–1939," in *Papers in Jewish Demography, 1977*, ed. U. O. Schmelz, P. Glikson, and S. Della Pergola (Jerusalem: Institute of Contemporary Jewry, 1980), 53–67.

For Polná's population figures, see J. Fiedler, *Jewish Sights*, 139–40.

90. The records of the Kutná Hora Regional Court (Krajský soud Kutná Hora) as well as of the Prague Criminal Court (Zemský soud trestní) are housed in the Státní oblastní archiv in Prague (SOA Praha). SOA Praha also maintains the records of the Hilsner murder investigations and trials—files generated by the Kutná Hora Prosecutor (SZ Kutná Hora), the Písek Prosecutor (SZ Písek), the Chief Prosecutor in Prague (VSZ Praha), and the Kutná Hora and Písek courts. I would estimate that the Kutná Hora and Prague courts together dealt with more than twenty criminal cases involving anti-Jewish agitation between 1883 and 1899.

91. The handwritten indictment and trial record are to be found in SOA Praha, KS Kutná Hora, C 1893/48.

92. Marc Raeff, *The Well-Ordered Police State: Social and Institutional Change Through Law in the Germanies and Russia, 1600–1800* (New Haven, Conn.: Yale University Press, 1983).

93. SOA Praha, KS Kutná Hora, C 1893/48.

94. Ibid.

95. Ibid.

96. Yuspah Shammash, *Minhagim de-kehilat kodesh Vermaisa*, ed. B. S. Bamberger, Eric Zimmer, and Y. M. Perles, vol. 2 (Jerusalem: Makhon Yerushalayim, 1988–1992), 86. Yuspah Shammash's discussion of the so-called first-born animal (*bekhor behemah*) appears in a section relating to the redemption of first-born male children. The father of a newborn male

child "redeemed" the child through a gift to *kohanim* (descendants of the priestly class) in the community. The *kohanim*, upon whom the formal responsibility for the maintenance of the "first-born animal" fell, were expected to make use of such gifts to pay the Gentile who tended the animal in the cemetery.

See the discussion of this source and of an engraving by the Christian artist Johannes Alexander Böner of the Jewish cemetery in Fürth in Richard I. Cohen, *Jewish Icons: Art and Society in Modern Europe* (Berkeley: University of California Press, 1998), 56–57.

97. Or, perhaps, *maykhl a bis / a bis maykhl* ("a little meal"). My thanks to Martin Jaffee for suggesting the first reading.

98. The fifth electoral curia included all males over the age of twenty-four. On the parliamentary elections of 1897, see Cohen, *Politics of Ethnic Survival*, 238, and Bruce M. Garver, *The Young Czech Party 1874–1901 and the Emergence of a Multi-Party System* (New Haven, Conn.: Yale University Press, 1970), 234–37.

99. SOA Praha, KS Kutná Hora C 1897/68. File contains the arrest record, dated 1 March 1897 (German); writ of indictment, dated 5 March 1897 (Czech); trial protocol, dated 15 March 1897 (Czech); verdict, same date (Czech); trial protocol in German; personal statement of the accused, signed with three crosses, dated 1 March 1897; written statements of two policemen; and personal statements of Marie Veselá and Anna Finková.

100. *Namlouvat si* can have the more formal meaning "to court" someone, but the colloquial expression *namlouvat si dívky* means to chase, or run after, girls; cf. Josef Fronek, *Česko-Anglický Slovník* (Prague: Státní Pedagogické Nakladatelství, 1993), 266.

101. SOA Praha, KS Kutná Hora C 1897/68; writ of indictment; trial protocol.

102. Ibid., statements of Marie Veselá and Anna Finková.

103. Ibid., statement of Jan Musil.

104. See Chapter 4.

CHAPTER 2

1. See the reliable narrative provided by Andrew Handler, based in large part on the memoirs of the lead defense attorney, Károly Eötvös, and the investigating magistrate, József Bary (Handler, *Blood Libel*, 40–46).

2. Handler, *Blood Libel*, 37–39.

3. See Scharf's trial testimony, day two: *Der Blut-Prozeß von Tisza Eszlár in Ungarn*, 22.

4. Handler's assertion that the meeting took place on the afternoon of April 2 (*Blood Libel*, 41) is contradicted by the trial testimony.

5. *Der Blut-Prozeß von Tisza Eszlár in Ungarn*, 24.

6. Testimony of Mrs. Gábor Solymosi, day four of trial proceedings: *Der Blut-Prozeß*, 73; also quoted in Paul Nathan, *Der Prozess von Tisza-Eszlár: Ein antisemitisches Culturbild* (Berlin: F. Fontane & Co., 1892), 100. In a Hungarian transcript, published serially in the Jewish newspaper *Egyenlőség*, Scharf's wife is referred to simply as "hat vékásné" (i.e., "Mrs. Six Bushels" or "the wife of Six Bushels") (*Egyenlőség*, 23 June 1883, 4). In the German transcript, the moniker "hat vékás" (for József Scharf) is left untranslated.

It seems that some of Tiszaeszlár's Jewish residents were given humorous (if somewhat derogatory) nicknames by their Christian neighbors. The journalist and novelist Kálmán Mikszáth, who covered the trial in Nyíregyháza, made note of this habit: "Jews also have their nicknames: old man Scharf has the name 'Six Bushels,' because he is a strong man, who once lifted up six bushels on Ónody's field; the nickname of the kosher butcher Schwarcz is 'chicken catcher,' while the blond Yid up yonder is 'dog whip'" (Kálmán Mikszáth, *Cikkek és karcolatok, XVI: 1883, ápr.–aug.* Vol. 66 of his *Collected Works* [Budapest: Akadémiai Kiadó, 1972], 221 [17 July]). My thanks to György Kövér, Michael Silber, and Lilla Vekerdy for helping me work my way through these colloquialisms and to György Kövér again for the Mikszáth reference.

7. *Der Blut-Prozeß*, 25; Nathan, *Der Prozess von Tisza-Eszlár* (in almost identical language), 101.

8. Handler, *Blood Libel*, 42–43; quotation is from 43.

9. *Der Blut-Prozeß*, iii.

10. Charles H. H. Wright, "The Jews and the Malicious Charge of Human Sacrifice," *Nineteenth Century* (November 1883): 757. Unaccountably, Wright insists that the fateful encounter between the Scharfs and the Solymosi sisters took place on 10 April.

11. Handler, *Blood Libel*, 42.

12. *Der Blut-Prozeß*, 24–25. Szeyffert's opening statement is recorded on 3–9; the reference to Tiszaszentimre is on 8. Szeyffert made it in the context of a highly critical overview of the recent surge in ritual murder accusations in Central Europe, including Hungary. Apparently, the Tiszaszentimre accusation had claimed that the victim was a Christian boy.

13. Ibid., 25.

14. Ibid.

15. Day nine of the trial proceedings; quoted in Nathan, *Der Prozess von Tisza-Eszlár*, 102.

16. Day fourteen of the trial proceedings; quoted in ibid., 103.

17. Nathan, *Der Prozess von Tisza-Eszlár*, 106–7.

18. As Hans-Joachim Neubauer writes, "The Christian child in the role of the crucified, the Jews as murderers of God: an implicit understanding by both common Christians and the elite which corresponds with this narrative pattern arises. People start saying what they have always known, indeed what everyone has always known. Often there is interplay and feedback between literary and oral descriptions and visual representation of similar events. . . . Foreknowledge and rumours symbolically co-ordinate an actual event and transfer it into another context" (Neubauer, *The Rumour: A Cultural History* [London: Free Association Books, 1999], 107–8).

19. Nathan articulates the first part of this analysis: "Both had grown up in the same intellectual atmosphere; both knew which prejudices, which superstitions, here and which there held sway" (Nathan, *Der Prozess von Tisza-Eszlár*, 107).

20. Jean-Noël Kapferer, *Rumors: Uses, Interpretations, and Images* (New Brunswick, N.J.: Transaction Publishers, 1990), 3.

21. Ibid., 4.

22. Ibid., 5.

23. Kapferer notes that when an investigation gets bogged down or a traumatic event goes unexplained, the affected community does not simply wait around for an official answer. Rather, "it seeks, through numerous discussions within the group, to forge its own answer or explanation. The latter is thus not the product of truth but rather of collective consensus" (Kapferer, *Rumors*, 172).

24. Handler, *Blood Libel*, 43–44.

25. Ibid., 44–45; József Bary, *A tiszaeszlári bűnper: Bary József vizsgálóbíró emlékiratai* (Budapest: Királyi Magyar Egyetemi Nyomda, 1933), 39–41. (The quote reported by Mrs. Pásztor is on 39.)

26. Handler, *Blood Libel*, 45–46; Nathan, *Der Prozess von Tisza-Eszlár*, 119–23. At the time of his appointment as investigating magistrate, Bary was still an assistant court clerk

(identified in several sources as a "vice notary"); he had not yet qualified as a judge. Nathan, for one, considered this appointment to have been a violation of Hungarian legal procedure.

27. Bary, *A tiszaeszlári bűnper*, 30. While Handler contends that Bary was "obsessed with the hatred of Jews" and that he was "particularly contemptuous of the Jews of Tiszaeszlár" (Handler, 47), Bary himself denied that the Tiszaeszlár prosecution involved the "blood libel" as conventionally understood, and he wished to distance himself from "true believers," such as Istóczy, Ónody, and Verhovay. It was not Jewry as a whole that stood accused at Nyíregyháza, he argued, but "a number of fanatical, cultureless, barbaric Jews of foreign practice and morality" who murdered Eszter Solymosi out of religious fanaticism (*A tiszaeszlári bűnper*, 30).

28. A number of elements in the boy's testimony seemed too improbable, even for those who were inclined to accept its overall veracity: he reportedly said that his father stuffed a white rag into Eszter's mouth, that a big Jewish man slashed her neck so that her head fell off, and that Samu's brother Móric then picked up the head and held it over a plate to collect the blood. Bary did take seriously, however, Samu's identification of one of the visiting candidates for the position of ritual slaughterer, Salamon Schwarcz, as the killer (Handler, *Blood Libel*, 207, n. 2; Bary, *A tiszaeszlári bűnper*, 72).

29. Károly Eötvös has described Recsky as someone who had the reputation for being able to extract confessions from even the most recalcitrant of suspects (*A nagy per*, 1:116).

30. Ibid., 1:105–7. See also Handler, *Blood Libel*, 53: "He was tired and frightened. Yet in a small room in Recsky's house, where the interrogation was resumed, he continued to insist on what he had already told them in Tiszaeszlár: he did not know Eszter Solymosi and the Jews did not kill her. Recsky, however, had not earned his reputation for being a scrupulous observer of the law. He suddenly struck Móric in the face with the handle of his whip and repeatedly knocked him to the floor. It was more than Móric could endure. When Recsky lifted up the limpid boy, he knew that the resistance of the stubborn Jewish boy had been broken. 'Did you know Eszter Solymosi?' 'Yes.' 'Did you speak with her on April 1?' 'Yes.' 'Is it true that the Jews killed her?' 'Yes.' 'Is it true that when Eszter walked past your window your father called her in and asked her to take some candles off the table because you Jews won't do things like that on Saturday?' 'Yes.'"

31. Handler, *Blood Libel*, 53–54. The text of Péczely's emergency telegram to Bary can be found in Nathan, *Der Prozess von Tisza-Eszlár*, 248–49.

32. For the second protocol, ibid., 252–55.

33. Handler, *Blood Libel*, 57; text of the letter in Iván Sándor, *A viszgálat iratai: Tudósítás a tiszaeszlári per körülményeiről* (Budapest: Kozmosz Könyvek, 1983), 103–5. See also the regular dispatches of its Budapest correspondent to the *Jewish Chronicle* of London beginning in June 1882.

A petition concerning the unlawful detention of Móric Scharf, which made its way to Prime Minister Kálmán Tisza in October 1882, explained that, after having spent three days at the house of the village head in Tiszaeszlár, Móric had been ordered taken to Nyíregyháza because the investigation was not yet complete. He was not being housed in the prison proper but in a room with prison guards (Magyar Nemzeti Levéltár, IM/K577—K5—1882–83, 197–203).

34. Primarily on the basis of Móric Scharf's testimony, four men were arrested on murder charges: Salomon Schwarcz, Ábrahám Buxbaum, Lipót Braun, and Hermann Vollner; six were charged with being accomplices to murder: József Scharf, Adolf Junger, Ábrahám Braun, Sámuel Lusztig, Lázár Weiszstein, and Emánuel Taub (Nathan, *Der Prozess*, 262–63). On Bary's frenetic activity following his arrival in the village, see Handler, *Blood Libel*, 48–49, 58–62.

35. In addition to Herskó, the other Jewish stewards were Jankel Smilovics, Amsel Vogel, and Nisen Mendelovics. Among the Gentile sailors and deck hands on board were György Csepkanics—who made the original discovery of the body—Ignác Matej, and György Drimus (Handler, *Blood Libel*, 78–79).

36. Edith Stern, *The Glorious Victory of Truth: The Tiszaeszlár Blood Libel Trial, 1882–3. A Historical-Legal-Medical Research* (Jerusalem: Rubin Mass, 1998), 14–15; Handler, *Blood Libel*, 69–70. A Reuter's telegram, dated Vienna, 19 June, was published four days later in the *Jewish Chronicle*. It read, "A dispatch from Pesth announces that the body of Esther Solymosi has been found in the River Theiss. The mysterious disappearance of this girl about a month ago from the village of Tisza Eszlar gave rise to a report that she had been murdered by Jewish butchers and formed the main pretext for the late anti-Semitic agitation in Hungary. The body has no external marks of violence" (*Jewish Chronicle*, 23 June 1882, 12).

37. This detail was potentially important, as Eszter Solymosi's employer had testified to investigators that she had sent the girl on an errand to buy paint and that she never returned. The blue paint did not receive mention in the official report of the first autopsy for reasons that are not clear (Stern, *Glorious Victory*, 15; Handler, *Blood Libel*, 69–70).

38. Handler, *Blood Libel*, 70–71; Stern, *Glorious Victory*, 15–16; and idem, "Gerichtsmedizinische Bezüge zu dem Ritualmordprozeß von Tiszaeszlar, Ungarn, 1882–83," *Monatsschrift für Kriminologie une Strafrechtsreform* 67 (1984): 42. A second viewing of the body for identification purposes was held the following day, 20 June, in Tiszaeszlár.

39. The three physicians were Soma Trajtler, Jenő Kiss (who had conducted the first examination in Tiszadada), and László Kéri Horváth. Géza Kéri Horváth was the assistant (Handler, *Blood Libel*, 73).

40. See the following section ("The Fury Before the Storm") for a more detailed discussion.

41. Handler, *Blood Libel*, 73–74.

42. Stern and Handler, op cit. Bary had posed eight questions to the medical commission, which it answered as follows:

1. The corpse ought to have been recognizable to those who had known her alive
2. Drowning could not have been the cause of death
3. Death could not have occurred earlier than ten days from the time of the postmortem exam
4. The corpse could not have been submerged in water longer than three to four days
5. Age of the corpse was estimated to be at least eighteen, but more likely twenty
6. The corpse was not only that of a non-virgin but of a woman who had engaged in sexual intercourse in an excessive manner
7. Probable cause of death was pneumonic anemia
8. Blood stains on the corpse could not have been the origin of the blood stains found on the clothes

(Handler, *Blood Libel*, 74).

43. Handler, *Blood Libel*, 75–77. Bary devotes a full 120 pages of *A tiszaeszlári bűnper* (158–276) to his reconstruction of the complicated "conspiracy" surrounding the so-called Csonkafüzes, or Tiszadada, corpse.

44. Handler, *Blood Libel*, 78–81. Vogel lodged a formal complaint to the Hungarian Ministry of Justice regarding the torture (Magyar Nemzeti Levéltár, Ministry of Justice, Elnöki iratok, 1882–1944: Tiszaeszlári vérvád, 1882–83 [IM/K577—K5—1882–83]).

45. As early as 20 May 1882, József Adamovics, a Catholic priest in Tiszaeszlár, wrote a story for the clerical newspaper *Magyar Állam* regarding "the mysterious disappearance of

a young girl." It was this story that formed the basis of Istóczy's interpellation of 24 May (Katzburg, *Antishemiyut be-hungariyah*, 112).

46. Handler, *Blood Libel*, 56–57; Judit Kubinszky, *Politikai antiszemitizmus*, 92; and Nathan, *Der Prozess von Tisza-Eszlár*, 7–8.

Ónody, himself, seems not to have taken part in the local elaboration of the case for "ritual murder" before sometime in May. Thereafter, his main role in this regard consisted of occasionally escorting the investigating team around the village and of selectively feeding reports of what were supposed to have been secret investigative proceedings of the Nyíregyháza court to *Függetlenség*.

47. See the *Jewish Chronicle*, 9 June 1882, 11 ("The 'Blood Accusation' in Hungary"). Bary's quick intervention following the discovery of the corpse on the Tisza River and his ordering of the arrest of the raftsmen had the effect of deflating any confidence that exculpatory evidence, in the form of Eszter's actual body, had now been found. See the Budapest correspondent's pessimistic lines written at the end of June 1882: "Whilst you were probably entertaining the belief that the body of Esther [*sic*] *Solymosy* had been found, we Jews in this city, and in Hungary generally, have been passing through a time of great anxiety and fear. Since Sunday, the 18th inst., that is to say, since the body of the pretended Esther was fished up in the Theiss, near Tisza-Dada, public opinion has undergone an unfavourable change, and instead of seeing the hope realized that the imprisoned Jews would be released from want of proof, we have had the daily misfortune to learn of fresh Jewish victims to the calumny" (*Jewish Chronicle*, 7 July 1882, 12).

48. Nathan, *Der Prozess von Tisza-Eszlár*, 45–50; Handler, *Blood Libel*, 63–65.

49. Handler, *Blood Libel*, 64–67; Eötvös, *A nagy per*, 2:88–90. The final defense team was headed by Eötvös and joined by four other attorneys: Ignác Heumann, Bernát Friedmann, Sándor Funták, and Miksa Székely. On the changing composition and characteristics of the defense team, see Nathan, *Der Prozess von Tisza-Eszlár*, 46–54.

50. See the discussion in Handler, *Blood Libel*, 224–25, based largely on Bary's memoirs. Bary appeared to have gained the upper hand initially, as the prime minister stepped in to orchestrate the removal of Egressy Nagy from his position as assistant prosecutor.

51. Handler, *Blood Libel*, 92, 225.

52. Eötvös published the petition, together with some related documents, in a German translation under the title *Sechs Aktenstücke zum Prozesse von Tisza-Eszlar* (Berlin: Leonh. Simion, 1882). See also Handler, *Blood Libel*, 92–103; Eötvös, *A nagy per*, 3: 1–88; and Edith Stern, *Glorious Victory of Truth*.

53. *Sechs Aktenstücke*, 3–97; this charge is found on 81.

54. Ibid., 86–87.

55. Ibid., 95–97.

56. For these definitions, I have relied on *Stedman's Medical Dictionary* (Philadelphia: Lippincott Williams & Wilkins, 2006). For a (not always satisfactory) discussion of their implications in this case, see Stern, "Gerichtsmedizinische Bezüge zu dem Ritualmordprozeß," 38–47, and idem, *Glorious Victory*, 17–18.

57. The court also arranged for numerous witnesses to the proceedings be present: Bary (as keeper of records); members of the medical team that had performed the first autopsy; Dr. András Józsa, chief medical officer of Szabolcs County; László Miklós, chief county clerk; Jenő Jármy, the *főszolgabíró* of Vencsellő; Ede Szeyffert, the deputy chief royal prosecutor; and Kálmán Lázár, assistant royal prosecutor. Members of the defense team were also invited to attend (Handler, *Blood Libel*, 94–95).

58. Handler, *Blood Libel*, 96.

59. Ibid., 96–97.

60. Ibid., 98.

61. See the discussion in Stern, *Glorious Victory*, 62–65, and Handler, *Blood Libel*, 99.

62. Stern, *Glorious Victory*, 66–67; Handler, *Blood Libel*, 100.

63. The estimation of age was made on the basis of a number of examinations: of hair, circumference and cavities of the skull, wisdom teeth, stage of development of the joints, and bone marrow.

64. Handler, *Blood Libel*, 100–1.

65. Letter of Ferenc Korniss to Minister of Justice Tivadar Pauler, 23 January 1883, cited in Stern, *Glorious Victory*, 68.

66. Handler, *Blood Libel*, 101–2.

67. Eduard Hofmann's extensive evaluation of by now numerous medical reports and rulings that had emerged from the case was published in a three-part series in the Vienna medical journal *Wiener medizinische Wochenschrift* (1883) and reissued as a single publication, *Gutachten über die am 18. Juni 1882 bei Tisza-Dada aus der Theisz gezogene, am 19. Juni gerichtlich obducirte und am 7. Dezember 1882 behufs neuerlicher Untersuchung exhumirte weibliche Leiche* (Budapest: Pester Buchdruckerei, 1883).

68. Handler, *Blood Libel*, 79–83; Bary, *A tiszaeszlári bűnper*, 158–276; Magyar Nemzeti Levéltár, Ministry of Justice, IM/K577—K5—1882–83.

69. Handler, *Blood Libel*, 106–7. Schwarcz, Buxbaum, and Braun were the three candidates for the vacant position of ritual slaughterer (*shoḥet*) who had been staying in Tiszaeszlár over the Sabbath of April 1, 1882. The job was awarded to Salamon Schwarcz. Hermann Vollner was a charity recipient from out of town (referred to in the legal proceedings and in journalistic accounts as a "beggar") who received hospitality that weekend in the home of József Scharf.

70. *Der Proceß von Tisza-Eszlar: Eine genaue Darstellung der Anklage, der Zeugenverhöre, der Vertheidigung und des Urtheils. Nach authentitischen Berichten bearbeitet* (Vienna: A. Hartleben's Verlag, 1883), 5–7. See also Eötvös, *A nagy per*, 3:176, who singles out Paul Nathan, correspondent for the Berlin paper *Die Nation*, for particular mention and praise.

71. Handler, *Blood Libel*, 117.

72. Eötvös, *A nagy per*, 3:162, 166; Handler, *Blood Libel*, 118.

73. Vogel, Smilovics, and Herskó had been among the raftsmen who discovered the body of a woman (presumably Eszter Solymosi) floating in the Tisza River in June 1882.

Andrew Handler consistently refers to thirteen defendants at Nyíregyháza, omitting—for reasons unknown—both Taub and Klein. All other sources, including *Magyar Zsidó Lexikon*, *Egyenlőség*, *Egyetértés*, Gyula Krúdy ("Tiszaeszlár, Fifty Years Later"), and Eötvös, *A nagy per*, name fifteen Jewish defendants.

74. One can find one version of the prosecutor's opening in *Der Blut-Prozeß*, 2–7; see also *Egyenlőség*, June 20, 1883, 3–4.

75. Handler, *Blood Libel*, 21.

76. Hungarian National Archives, Ministry of Justice, K577: Elnöki iratok; K5: Tiszaeszlári vérvád—1882–83, 132–45.

77. *Der Blut-Prozeß*, 3–4.

78. *Der Blut-Prozeß*, 7; see also the discussion in Nathan, *Der Prozess von Tisza-Eszlár*, 265–68.

79. *Der Blut-Prozeß*, 7; cf. *Der Proceß von Tisza-Eszlar*, 15.

80. Nathan, *Der Prozess von Tisza-Eszlár*, 268; *Der Blut-Prozeß*, 9.

81. Handler, *Blood Libel*, 146–51; Eötvös, *A nagy per*, 2:175–20.

82. Handler, *Blood Libel*, 149–50, 242–44.

83. *Der Blut-Prozeß*, 15. The topic was taken up again in somewhat greater detail on day two (*Der Blut-Prozeß*, 30–31). See also the detailed reporting and analysis of Móric's testimony in Paul Nathan, *Der Prozess von Tisza-Eszlár*, 262–79.

84. *Der Blut-Prozeß*, 16.

85. Ibid.

86. Ibid.

87. Ibid., 17.

88. Ibid., 18.

89. The defense attorney Friedmann interjected at this point that, if Móric could retell his story in German, he could thereby help to reassure the court that he had not in fact memorized a script. See Nathan, *Der Prozess von Tisza-Eszlár*, 276.

90. *Der Blut-Prozeß*, 18–19.

91. Ibid., 19 and 31 provide but two examples.

92. Ibid., 19–20. Braun and József Scharf were implying that Móric's use of the rather formal (and bureaucratic) "*jelen*" to indicate one's having been present at an event provided a further indication of his having been coached in a language that he did not fully command. More colloquially, one would have said something along the lines of "*ott volt*" or "*ott voltak*" (You were there!). *Jelen* means "present" in the sense of "present in the courtroom were . . ." or "in the present case" (*a jelen esetben*).

93. Ibid., 20–21. On the second day of testimony, Szeyffert questioned the father, József Scharf, on the same topic. Scharf indicated that Mrs. Bátori had been hired by the family to serve as what he called a "Saturday woman." When asked by Szeyffert whether there was a written contract, Scharf replied, "Not through a contract; rather, because it is forbidden to us Jews to milk the cow, or to carry the candlesticks back and forth—in other words, to work—she did this as a good neighbor" (*Der Blut-Prozeß*, 23).

On both the history and legal theory of the Sabbath Gentile, see Jacob Katz, *The "Shabbes Goy": A Study in Halakhic Flexibility* (Philadelphia: Jewish Publication Society of America, 1989).

94. *Der Blut-Prozeß*, 26.

95. Ibid., 26–27.

96. Ibid., 28.

97. Ibid.

98. Ibid., 28–29.

99. Ibid., 29. The command to honor one's father and mother is in fact the fifth commandment according to the traditional Jewish division of the biblical text, but it is the fourth commandment according to Catholic interpretation.

100. Ibid., 30.

101. Ibid.

102. Ibid., 31, 36–37.

103. Ibid., 37.

104. Ibid.

105. Ibid., 42; Eötvös, *A nagy per*, 3:106. In the published German transcript, the word for ritual fringes is rendered in Hungarian transliteration (*Cziczisz*) followed by the German *Schaufäden* in parentheses. None of this exchange is recorded in the weekly reporting of the Hungarian-language *Egyenlőség*.

106. *Der Blut-Prozeß*, 32–35.

107. Nathan, *Der Prozess von Tisza-Eszlár*, 280–88. For more on this line of questioning as it related to the Xanten and Polná cases, see Chapters 3 and 4.

108. *Der Blut-Prozeß*, 35.

109. See the coverage in *Egyenlőség*, 18 July 1883, 4–5 ("A helyszini szemle Tisza-Eszláron"); see also *Der Blut-Prozeß*, 175–77, and *Handler, Blood Libel*, 152–53.

110. *Egyenlőség*, 18 July 1883, 5.

111. On this point, see Handler, *Blood Libel*, 154, citing László Fayer, *A magyar bűnvádi eljárás mai érvényében* (Budapest: Franklin Társulat, 1887), 174.

112. *Der Blut-Prozeß*, 182–83.

113. Szeyffert's closing remarks are reproduced at length in *Der Blut-Prozeß*, 184–88, and more elliptically in *Egyenlőség*, 29 July 1883, 5–7. The prosecutor's closing is not included in the selections from the trial transcript published in the newspaper *Egyetértés* and reproduced in Judit Elek and Mihály Sükösd, eds., *Tutajosok: A tiszaeszlári per dokumentumai* (Budapest: Magvető Könyvkiadó, 1990).

114. *Der Blut-Prozeß*, 184.

115. Ibid., 184–85.

116. Ibid.

117. Ibid.

118. Ibid., 186.

119. Ibid.

120. Ibid., 187.

121. Ibid., 188.

122. Ibid.

123. Ibid.

124. Ibid. On Szalay's political affiliation, see Handler, *Blood Libel*, 159.

125. *Der Blut-Prozeß*, 188–89. Among the various claims made by Szalay in the course of his summation was the following: there is no pain, no torture in the world that could compel a person to confess to something that was "impossible." As to the "Swedish gulp" (*Schwedentrunk*) to which the raftsman Amsel Vogel was subjected, he declaimed, "drinking water is certainly not torture" (189).

126. Defense statements can be found in *Der Blut-Prozeß*, 189–201.

127. Ibid., 201. Eötvös's closing was published in a more complete version in Hungarian. See Judit Elek and Mihály Sükösd, *Tutajosok*, 219–51, taken from the daily reportage in *Egyetértés*. It is from this version (220) that "as a proposition" (*in thesi*) is taken.

128. *Der Blut-Prozeß*, 202.

129. Ibid., 203.

130. Ibid., 203–4.

131. Ibid., 204–5. For the complete Hungarian text of the verdict, see Eötvös, *A nagy per*, 3:223–50, and Elek and Sükösd, *Tutajosok*, 251–67.

132. *Der Blut-Prozeß*, 206.

CHAPTER 3

1. Handler, *Blood Libel*, 175–76. He draws largely on Kubinszky, *Politikai antiszemitizmus*, 105–6.

2. On the antisemitic violence of 1883, see especially Robert Nemes, "Hungary's Antisemitic Provinces: Violence and Ritual Murder in the 1880s," *Slavic Review* 66, no. 1 (Spring 2007): 20–44. The figure of thirty-two counties is found in Judit Kubinszky, "Adalékok az 1883.

évi antiszemitia zavargásokhoz," *Századok* 102 (1968): 176, but Nemes notes that the actual figure is probably higher, since many incidents may not have been reported to authorities (Nemes, "Hungary's Antisemitic Provinces," 22).

For an analysis of the antisemitic songs that accompanied the riots, see Daniel Véri, "Imagining Ritual Murder: Social Knowledge in the Making," in *Visual Antisemitism in Central Europe: Imagery of Hatred*, ed. Jakub Hauder and Eva Janáčová (Oldenbourg: De Gruyter, 2021), 37–60.

3. Nemes, "Hungary's Antisemitic Provinces," 34.

4. Ibid., 35.

5. Ibid., 35.

6. Ibid., 37.

7. Ibid., 24, 37–38.

8. There was an earlier, but isolated, journalistic report of the Tiszaeszlár "crime." József Adamovics, the Catholic priest of the village, published an article in the clerical paper *Magyar Állam* on 20 May under the headline "The Mysterious Disappearance of a Young Girl," in which he gave voice to Mária Solymosi's suspicions concerning the Jews and complained of the slow pace of the official investigation. But this single, barely read piece had minimal impact on the general, social knowledge of the event, which is more appropriately connected to the reportage in *Függetlenség* and the debates in the Hungarian Diet (see Katzburg, *Antishemiyut be-hungariyah*, 112).

9. On Ónody's purported expertise on Jewish matters, see Handler, *Blood Libel*, 31, 212–13, and Nathan, *Der Prozess von Tisza-Eszlár*, 26–27. Ónody's 1883 portrait of the Tiszaeszlár case (*Tißa-Eßlár in der Vergangenheit und Gegenwart*) bore the multilayered subtitle "Concerning the Jews in General. – Mysterious Beliefs of the Jews. – Acts of Ritual Murder and Blood Sacrifice. – The Tiszaeszlár Affair."

During the latter part of 1882, the Hungarian publicist Georg von Marcziányi, Ónody's principal German translator, issued a mass-circulation brochure on Tiszaeszlár based on Ónody's dispatches to *Függetlenség* (Marcziányi, *Esther Solymosi, oder Der jüdisch-rituelle Jungfrauenmord in Tißa-Eßlar.* Autorisierte deutsche Uebersetzung aus dem Ungarischen. Nebst einer Abbildung der Synagoge in T.-E. [Berlin: M. Schulze, n.d. (apparently summer or fall 1882)]).

10. Katz, *From Prejudice to Destruction*, 279–80; Katzburg, *Antishemiyut be-hungariya*, 207–9. See also the reports in the *Neue Freie Presse* (Vienna), 13 September 1882; *Abendblatt* (hereafter *AB*), 15 September 1882; and *Montagsblatt* (hereafter *MB*), 16 September 1882.

11. Iván Simonyi, *Der Antisemitismus und die Gesetze der menschlichen Gesellschaft* (Pressburg [Pozsony], 1884). Istóczy's pamphlet was published anonymously as *Manifest an die Regierungen und Völker der durch das Judenthum gefährdeten christlichen Staaten* (Chemnitz, 1882).

12. Presumably, Marcziányi's *Esther Solymosi, oder Der jüdisch-rituelle Jungfrauen-mord in Tißa-Eßlar.*

13. "Antisemiten-Congreß," *Neue Freie Presse*, *AB*, 13 September 1882.

14. "Antisemiten-Congreß." These narrative elements performed a crucial function for the anti-Jewish side of the debate on Tiszaeszlár. They accounted for the as-yet inconclusive nature of the criminal investigation, as well as for a central piece of evidence that appeared to contradict the charge of ritual murder, while preserving the overall coherence of its understanding of the events.

15. "Antisemiten-Congreß." Ónody's address to the Antisemitic Congress is reproduced, with elaborations, in his *Tisza-Eszlár in der Vergangenheit und Gegenwart* (Budapest, 1883), 156–80. (Paul Nathan indicates the date of publication as December 1882.) In this version, his depiction of the universality of the Tiszaeszlár crime is more vivid:

> This menacing danger flashes before us in its sinister magnitude from the point of the Tisza-Eszlar butcher's knife, [a knife] whose blade—in the moment that it was lowered horribly to cut through the neck of that innocent girl—struck simultaneously through the heart of humanity's spirit. Is it any wonder that the entire Christian world cries out in pain, clutches at its heart, and turns its uncertain sights to that modest Hungarian village, where the dark criminality of Rabbinism, paying homage to a wild, cannibalistic rite of antiquity, violently and ceremoniously opened the veins of its sacrificial victim—in the synagogue, a place for sacred worship—in order, wildly and out of a fanaticism born of Talmudic morality, to take the life of that poor, innocent Christian girl! Through this horrible and shameful human sacrifice, a bloody mark of humiliation has been imprinted for all time. (174)

16. "Antisemiten-Congreß"; Ónody, *Tiſsa-Eſslár in der Vergangenheit und Gegenwart*, 174.

17. *Tiſsa-Eſslár in der Vergangenheit und Gegenwart*, 174.

18. "Antisemiten-Congreß."

19. Ibid.; "Nachträge zum Antisemiten-Congresse," *Neue Freie Presse*, *MB*, 15 September 1882.

20. Nemes, "Hungary's Antisemitic Provinces," 32, 43, and passim. See also Hillel J. Kieval, "Antisémitisme ou Savoir Social? Sur la genèse du procès moderne pour meurtre rituel," *Annales: Histoire, Sciences Sociales* 49 (1994): 1091–105.

21. "Das 'Porträt' von Esther Solymossy," *Neue Freie Presse*, *MB*, 16 September 1882. For the complete story of the painting, see Daniel Véri, "The Tiszaeszlár Blood Libel: Image and Propaganda," in *Antisemitismus im 19. Jahrhundert aus internationaler Perspektive/Nineteenth Century Anti-Semitism in International Perspective*, ed. Mareike König and Oliver Schulz (Göttingen: Vandenhoeck & Ruprecht, 2019), 263–90.

22. Nathan, *Der Prozess von Tisza-Eszlár*, 39–40.

23. Ibid., 42. For a variation on the same theme, see 10:

> Everywhere one heard: Antisemitism is barbaric, and those who carry it out, the Russians, are barbarians. Perhaps one could reply in short: That may be, but the Jews are savages [*Karaïben*] and more bestial than the Russian barbarians. The daring attempt to divert attention from the fateful, Russian successes of antisemitism and to instill a little self-consciousness in the followers of the good cause through the idea that one was, in fact, fighting against cannibals was accomplished through the Tisza-Eszlár trial.

24. Ibid., 42–43.

25. A case in point: A few weeks after the close of the criminal trial, in August 1883, the Chomutov summer theater in Bohemia produced a five-act play about the affair, which caused great consternation in the governor's office. The play had been translated from Hungarian and was advertised in posters around the city as a "great sensation from the most recent past." The same advertisements referred to the Tiszaeszlár trial as "the most sensational event . . . which has captivated and claimed the attention of the entire world" (Národní Archiv, Prague [NA Praha], PM 1881–90, 8/1/9/1 [7194]).

26. On Rohling's role in the Talmud debate in Vienna, his self-promotion as an expert on Jewish behavior, and his desire to intervene in the Tiszaeszlár affair, see I. A. Hellwing, *Der konfessionelle Antisemitismus im 19. Jahrhundert in Österreich* (Vienna: Herder, 1972), 71–183;

Joseph S. Bloch, *Erinnerungen aus meinem Leben*, vol. 1 (Vienna: R. Löwit, 1922), 59–104; and *Acten und Gutachten in dem Prozesse Rohling contra Bloch* (Vienna: M. Breitenstein, 1890).

27. Rohling, *Meine Antworten an die Rabbiner, oder: Fünf Briefe über den Talmudismus und das Blut-Ritual der Juden* (Prague: Cyrillo-Method'schen Buchdruckerei [J. Zeman & Co.], 1883); idem, *Moje odpovědi rabínům aneb pět psaní o talmudu a židovské rituelní vraždě* (Prague: Cyrillo-Methodějské knihkupectví [G. Francl], 1883). There are slight but semantically significant differences in the German and Czech titles. The German edition uses the term "Talmudism," the Czech edition has "Talmud"; the German edition employs the phrase "blood ritual of the Jews," while the Czech edition uses "Jewish ritual murder."

28. The Presidium of the Bohemian Governor's Office had received numerous reports of the pamphlet's circulation together with worried predictions of popular violence, such as those that had already occurred in the Hungarian city of Pressburg/Pozsony. The Criminal Court in Prague ordered the work confiscated on 27 May 1883 (NA Praha, PM 1881–90, 8/1/9/1 [3169 and 4391]). See also *Acten und Gutachten*, 100–5.

29. Ibid., 103–4.

30. The text of the letter is reproduced in *Acten und Gutachten*, 105, and Hellwing, *Konfessionelle Antisemitismus*, 107–8.

31. *Acten und Gutachten*, 105, and Hellwing, *Konfessionelle Antisemitismus*, 107–8.

32. On the Rohling-Bloch controversy, see *Acten und Gutachten*; Bloch, *Erinnerungen aus meinem Leben*, vol. 1 (translated as *My Reminiscences* [Vienna: R. Löwit, 1923]); and Hellwing, *Konfessionelle Antisemitismus*, 160–83.

33. The declaration has been appended to the collection *Christliche Zeugnisse gegen die Blutbeschuldigung der Juden* (Berlin: Walther & Apolant, 1882), 55–58.

34. *Christliche Zeugnisse gegen die Blutbeschuldigung*.

35. On the intersection of Lagarde's scholarship and his politics, see, in particular, Fritz Stern, *The Politics of Cultural Despair: A Study in the Rise of Germanic Ideology* (Berkeley: University of California Press, 1961), 3–81. Information on the mutual polemic between Lagarde and the Jewish scholars can be found on 17.

36. *Christliche Zeugnisse*, 25.

37. "The Charge of Murder Against the Jews," *Times*, 24 January 1883, 10; reprinted in *Jewish Chronicle*, 26 January 1883, 11.

38. Ibid.

39. Ibid.

40. Letter of J. J. Stewart Berowne, *Jewish Chronicle*, 2 February 1883.

41. Quote is from the letter of C. Taylor to *Jewish Chronicle*, 2 February 1883.

42. *Jewish Chronicle*, 10 August 1883, 8.

43. Ibid.

44. Quoted in Hermann Hamburger, *Der Konitzer Mord: Ein Beitrag zur Klärung* (Breslau, 1900), 30.

45. "The anti-Semitic Press in Berlin, finding that all other weapons are unsuccessful, is trying to incite the German Christians against the Jews by a dose of "blood accusation." The *Kreuz-Zeitung* publishes a telegram from Constantinople reporting the murder at Mustapha Pacha of a girl eight years old by Jews and also of a Christian butcher who had discovered the first crime. The *Volk* improves on the method of its contemporary by reporting the perpetration of a murder by Jews for ritual purposes in Germany. The scene of the alleged tragedy is at Xanten, a town in Rhenish Prussia, and the victim is said to be a boy four [*sic*] years old" (*Jewish Chronicle*, 24 July 1891, 15).

46. *Jewish Chronicle*, 22 July 1892, 11.

47. Julius H. Schoeps, "Ritualmordbeschuldigung und Blutaberglaube: Die Affäre Buschhoff im niederrheinischen Xanten," in *Köln und das Rheinische Judentum: Festschrift Germania Judaica 1959–1984*, ed. Jutta Bohnke-Kollwitz et al. (Cologne: J. P. Bachem, 1984), 286–87.

48. *Der Xantener Knabenmord vor dem Schwurgericht zu Cleve, 4.–14. Juli 1892: Vollständiger stenographischer Bericht* (Berlin: Siegfried Cronbach, 1893), 21, and "Leichenschau-Protokoll," 457–58.

49. "Leichenschau-Protokoll," 457–58.

50. Kölling, "Blutige Illusionen," 360. The first quotation is taken from Schoeps, "Ritualmordbeschuldigung," 287; the second question paraphrases Dominick LaCapra, *Geschichte und Kritik* (Frankfurt a.M.: Fischer Verlag, 1987), 14.

51. Kölling, "Blutige Illusionen," 361.

52. *Berliner Tageblatt*, 15 July 1892, quoted in Kölling, "Blutige Illusionen," 361; *Jewish Chronicle*, 22 July 1892, 11. See also Hugo Friedländer, ed., *Der Knabenmord in Xanten vor dem Schwurgericht zu Cleve vom 4. bis 14. Juli 1892* (Kleve, 1892), 10–12.

53. *Der Xantener Knabenmord*, 22–23. See also Kölling, "Blutige Illusionen," 362.

54. "Obduktions-Protokoll," in *Der Xantener Knabenmord*, 461–66; quote is from 466.

55. Ibid., 466 (my emphasis).

56. "Gutachten des Kreisphysikus Dr. Bauer," in *Der Xantener Knabenmord*, 467.

57. Ibid., 467–68.

58. Ibid., 468.

59. Ibid., 469.

60. Ibid.

61. The most complete analysis of the Skurz case can be found in Johannes T. Groß, *Ritualmordbeschuldigungen gegen Juden im deutschen Kaiserreich (1871–1914)* (Berlin: Metropol, 2002), 33–50. Groß relies primarily on contemporary press reporting of the affair (from the *National-Zeitung*, the *Vossische Zeitung*, the *Berliner Tagblatt*, and the *Norddeutsche Allgemeine Zeitung*, primarily), including detailed reporting on the ensuing criminal trial.

Other printed sources include *Antisemitenspiegel: Die Antisemiten im Lichte des Christenthums, des Rechtes und der Wissenschaft*, 2nd ed. (Danzig: A. W. Kafemann, 1900), 445; Leopold Auerbach, *Das Judenthum und seine Bekenner in Preußen*, 58–64; and Friedrich Frank, *Der Ritualmord vor der Gerichtshöfen der Wahrheit*, 252–54.

62. Groß, *Ritualmordbeschuldigungen*, 33–34.

63. Ibid., 34; based on reporting in the *Norddeutsche Allgemeine Zeitung* of 23 April 1885, and Frank, *Der Ritualmord*, 253.

64. Groß, *Ritualmordbeschuldigungen*, 35.

65. Ibid.

66. Ibid., 35–36.

67. Ibid., 37.

68. Groß, *Ritualmordbeschuldigungen*, 38; Auerbach, *Das Judenthum und seine Bekenner*, 620.

69. Groß, *Ritualmordbeschuldigungen*, 38–39. In the eventual trial, a witness testified that Behrendt became unusually frightened and "completely pale" when someone told him that a new forensic method existed through which one could recover the face of a murderer from the pupils of the victim's eyes (Groß, 39, from trial coverage in the *Vossische Zeitung*, 23 April 1885).

70. Groß, *Ritualmordbeschuldigungen*, 39–40.

71. See, in this regard, the intriguing remarks of the German newspaper *Das Volk*, apparently explaining why the cut on Johann Hegmann did not appear really to be professional: "An

actual ritual cut was not necessary in order to accomplish the goal for which the Jews allegedly killed the boy Hegmann. This [ritual cut] is only made in order to allow the slaughtered cattle to bleed out as much as possible, so that its meat will be suitable, or fit, for eating. The Jews, however, did not want to eat the Christian lad" (*Das Volk*, 2 March 1892, in Kölling, "Blutige Illusionen," 367). The statement reveals the important symbolic linkage in the popular imagination between Jewish ritual slaughtering, the *Schächtschnitt*, and bleeding out of the slaughtered animal (or person). So, the cut did not have to be perfect, as the goal was not to eat the victim as meat. It only needed to be good enough to accomplish a successful bleeding.

72. See Robin Judd, *Contested Rituals: Circumcision, Kosher Butchering, and Jewish Political Life in Germany, 1843–1933* (Ithaca, N.Y.: Cornell University Press, 2007).

73. Judd, *Contested Rituals*, 89.

74. See the discussion in Judd, *Contested Rituals*, 64–67, 77, 95.

75. Ibid., 101–2.

76. Ibid., 113.

77. Kölling, "Blutige Illusionen," 355, based on reporting of the Kleve Prosecutor to the Prussian Minister of Justice, 19 December to 23 December 1892, in *Geheimes Staatsarchiv Prueßischer Kulturbesitz (GStAPK) Berlin*, Rep. 84a, Nr. 16763, 288–299, 370.

78. Kölling, "Blutige Illusionen," 357.

79. Ibid., 357–58; *Der Xantener Knabenmord*, 109. Numerous people in the town thought Wesendrup capable of murder, not least, apparently, because of the violence with which he had treated his deceased wife (Kölling, "Blutige Illusionen," 358, based on the report of the Kleve Prosecutor to the Prussian Minister of Justice, 4 May 1892 [GStAPK Berlin, Rep. 84a, Nr. 16763]).

80. Kölling, "Blutige Illusionen," 356.

81. Ibid., 358; Oberstaatsanwalt Köln to the Prussian Minister of Justice, 6 Oct 1893 (GStAPK Berlin, Rep. 84a, Nr. 16764, Bl. 42).

82. *Der Xantener Knabenmord*, 106; Hauptstaatsarchiv Düsseldorf, LA Moers, Nr. 547, cited in Schoeps, "Ritualmordbeschuldigung," 298. See the discussion in Groß, *Blutbeschuldigungen*, 56–57, and the dispatches of the Prosecutor Baumgard to the Prussian Minister of Justice in GStAPK, I. HA Rep. 84 a Justizministerium, Nr. 57 459.

83. Hauptstaatsarchiv Düsseldorf, LA Moers, Nr. 547; Groß, *Ritualmordbeschuldigungen*, 59.

84. Wolff's report was appended to *Der Xantener Knabenmord* as "Bericht des Kriminal-Komissars Wolff," 473–75. It is dated Xanten, 6 October 1891.

85. Wolff, "Bericht," 473.

86. Ibid., 474. The adult testimony was offered by a gardener, Hermann Mölders, six days after the murder. See Groß, *Ritualmordbeschuldigungen*, 54–55.

87. Wolff, "Bericht," 474.

88. Ibid., 475.

89. Ibid.

90. Groß, *Ritualmordbeschuldigungen*, 61. Wolff had urged Bushhoff's imprisonment, suggesting that he might seek to flee across the border to Belgium or Holland (Wolff, "Bericht," 473).

91. Groß, *Ritualmordbeschuldigungen*, 61–65; report of Attorney General Hamm to Minister of Justice Schelling, GStA PK, I. HA Rep. 84 a Justizministerium, Nr. 57 459, Bl. 46ff., 57 R (M); letter of Justice Minister Schelling to Attorney General Hamm, 31 December 1891, GStA PK, I. HA Rep. 84 a Justitzministerium, Nr. 57 459, Bl. 81 ff. (M). For the description of the accusations as "child's babble," see Nathan, *Xanten-Cleve*, 10, and Schoeps, "Ritualmord-beschuldigung," 287–88.

92. Groß, *Ritualmordbeschuldigungen*, 65–66.

93. Letter of Geheim Justitzrat Bietsch to Justice Minister Schelling, 18 January 1892, GStA PK, I. HA Rep. 84 a Justitzministerium, Nr. 57 459, Bl. 88ff (M). Brixius's letter to the State Prosecutor's Office and the official response have been reproduced in *Der Xantener Knabenmord*, 491–92.

On this episode, see also Nathan, *Xanten-Cleve*, 10, who writes, "[Brixius] saw things as they were, and his greatest crime was that he did not allow himself to be terrorized by antisemitic agitators. Such a judge had to be removed. Again, just as in Tiszaeszlár, they succeeded in Prussia in forcing this man from his position through agitation."

94. Groß, *Ritualmordbeschuldigungen*, 67–69.

95. I am referring here to the correspondence between the ministry and the prosecutor's office and the ministry and the court in Kleve, housed in the GStAPK, and to the discussion in Groß, *Ritualmordbeschuldigungen*, 51–88.

96. "Anklageschrift," in *Der Xantener Knabenmord*, 493.

97. Ibid., 501–2.

98. Ibid., 502.

99. Ibid., 503–4.

100. Ibid., 503. The official report of the Koblenz Medical faculty can be found in *Der Xantener Knabenmord*, 478–90.

101. "Anklageschrift," 502, 503. The court-appointed physicians (who had conducted the autopsy on Johann Hegmann) were of the opinion that the knife that was used "had to be particularly sharp and at least 20 cm long." All of the experts agreed that the knife that was used had a nicked, rounded edge, and a knife of this type had been found among Buschhoff's utensils. The court's doctors were of the opinion that the path of the cut revealed the sure handling of a butcher; the medical faculty disagreed (503).

102. Schmenk, *Xanten*, 347; Groß, *Ritualmordbeschuldigungen*, 76. The full transcript of the trial, including closing arguments and appendices, can be found in *Der Xantener Knabenmord vor dem Schwurgericht zu Cleve* (Berlin: Cronbach, 1893).

103. Groß, *Ritualmordbeschuldigungen*, 74; "Beschluß," of the Royal Criminal Court, dated May 28, 1892, in *Der Xantener Knabenmord*, 508.

104. Groß, *Ritualmordbeschuldigungen*, 74–75; concluding report of District Court Director Kluth to the President of the Superior Court in Cologne, 15 July 1892, GStAPK, I. HA Rep. 84 a Justitzministerium, Nr. 57 460, Bl. 166, 170R.

105. *Der Xantener Knabenmord*, 80.

106. Ibid., 382–83.

107. Ibid., 394.

108. Ibid., 386–96.

109. Ibid., 396–97.

110. Ibid., 399.

111. Ibid., 409.

112. Ibid., 407.

113. Groß, *Ritualmordbeschuldigungen*, 87.

114. Gavin Langmuir, *Toward a Definition of Antisemitism.*

115. Hsia, *The Myth of Ritual Murder.*

116. The early modern trials in Poland-Lithuania halted with the abolition of torture in judicial proceedings in 1776. See in particular Zenon Guldon and Jacek Wijaczka, "The Accusation of Ritual Muder in Poland," and idem, *Procesy o mordy rytualne w Polsce.*

CHAPTER 4

1. On the radicalization of Czech politics in the 1890s, see especially Michal Frankl, *"Emancipace od židů": Český antisemitismus na konci 19. století* (Prague: Paseka, 2007) and idem, "The Background of the Hilsner Case: Political Antisemitism and Allegations of Ritual Murder, 1896–1900," *Judaica Bohemiae* 36 (2000): 34–118. More generally, see Stanley B. Winters, "Kramář, Kaizl, and the Hegemony of the Young Czech Party, 1891–1901," in *The Czech Renascence of the Nineteenth Century*, ed. Peter Brock and H. Gordon Skilling (Toronto: University of Toronto Press, 1970), 282–314; Bruce M. Garver, *The Young Czech Party, 1874–1901, and the Emergence of a Multi-Party System* (New Haven, Conn.: Yale University Press, 1978); and Tomáš Vojtěch, *Mladočeši a boj o politickou moc v Čechách* (Prague: Academia, 1980).

2. The boycott movement in the Bohemian lands was known by the motto "Svůj k svému" (each to his own). In 1892, placards appeared in provincial cities and towns across central Bohemia on which the slogan "Nekupůjte od židů" (do not buy from Jews) was printed, perhaps marking the start of an economic boycott campaign directed at both Germans and Jews. This development prompted an investigation by the Kutná Hora regional court, which resulted in no criminal indictments (SOA Praha, KS Kutná Hora, B 1892/147).

3. A three-part series on "Svůj k svému" in the newspaper *Polaban* in 1893 attempted to make a coherent case for Czech economic nationalism and to rally popular support around the campaign. The Jews, *Polaban* emphasized, are not merely problematic; they are "our greatest enemy" (*největších našich odpurců*). So provocative, apparently, was its message that the paper's editor at the time, Josef Hejnic, was charged by the Kutná Hora criminal court with anti-Jewish agitation ("Svůj k svému," *Polaban*, 30 August 1893; for the criminal case, see SOA Praha, KS Kutná Hora, C 1893/518).

On the relationship between economic boycott and antisemitism, see Kieval, *The Making of Czech Jewry*, 64–83; Frankl, *"Emancipace od židů,"* 151–90; and idem, "The Background of the Hilsner Case," 92–95 and passim.

4. Kieval, *Languages of Community*, 181–97; Frankl, *Emancipace od židů*, 36–110, 191–99.

5. Cf. SOA Praha, KS Kutná Hora, C 1885/151, 190, 199, 201, 261, 272.

6. SOA Praha, KS Kutná Hora, C 1886/279. Appealing the court's verdict, Řezníček argued that his article had in no way advocated hatred against the Jews as a religious community but had merely offered statistical data on the Jews of the Czech lands according to the most recent Habsburg census. The court rejected his appeal, noting that the offending article contained not only statistical material but also the specific observation that the Jews "with very few exceptions stand among the ranks of our enemies, in fact, belong to the most fanatical of the enemies of our nation."

7. The records of the Zemský soud trestní (ZST) are housed in the Státní oblastní archiv (SOA) in Prague. To give just one example, when the Prague Criminal Court ordered the confiscation of the 15 June 1892 issue of *České zájmy*, it cited two inflammatory articles. In its *Miscellany* column, the paper had reported that "wherever Jews are in the majority"—such as in one small town in Bukovina—"they murder Slavic people without mercy." Another article judged to be deliberately provocative concerned "the usurer Popper." Pieces on such topics as "The Jews According to the Talmud," "On the Murder in Xanten," and "Jewish Impudence in the Czech Jerusalem—Rakovník," however, escaped specific censure (SOA Praha, ZST Praha, C 729/1892).

8. On the accusation in Corfu, see Hermann L. Strack, *The Jew and Human Sacrifice* (London: Cope and Fenwich, 1909), 213–15; Ludwig Corel, *Das Blutmärchen: Seine Entstehung*

und Folgen bis zu den jüngsten Vorgängen auf Korfu (Berlin: J. Gnadenfeld, 1891), 38–42; and Sakis Gekas, "The Port Jews of Corfu and the 'Blood Libel' of 1891: A Tale of Many Centuries and of One Event," *Jewish Culture and History* 7, nos. 1–2 (2004): 171–96.

9. SOA Praha, ZST Praha, C 613/1891. *Naše zájmy*, a monthly paper, carried the subtitle "Czech Political Journal" (*Český časopis politický*) followed by the slogans "Each to His Own!" (*Svojí k svému!*) and "Buy Only from Christians!" *České zájmy*, also published by Hušek, had the subtitle "Journal for National-Economic and Social Repair" (*Časopis pro opravy národohospodářské a společenské*). Both papers could be characterized as radical, state right (*státní právo*) nationalist, and populist. In addition to being pointedly antisemitic, Hušek's papers also voiced strongly Pan-Slavic sentiments. Each issue of *Naše Zájmy* carried two dates: the Julian and the Gregorian; both papers carried articles in Russian. Biographical information on Hušek can be found in Frankl, *"Emancipace od židů,"* 75–81.

10. Josef Deckert, *Ein Ritualmord. Aktenmäßig nachgewiesen* (Dresden: Gloß, 1893). Deckert remarks in his introduction, "Nonetheless, such blood crimes have been proven juridically and historically and cannot be denied by any historical researcher who loves the truth" (*Ein Ritualmord*, 3).

11. For more recent literature on the case of Simon of Trent, see Hsia, *Myth of Ritual Murder*, 42–65; idem, *Trent 1475*; Teter, *Blood Libel*, 43–151; and Wolfgang Treue, *Der Trienter Judenprozeß*.

12. The testimony in question came from a Jew named Engel:

> Asked how that is, he confessed that he heard that one proceeded in this manner in the murder of Christian children. He claimed further that the Jews allowed the blood of the Christian children to dry and used it in powdered from at the circumcision of their (male) children, sprinkling it over the circumcision wound. It served to close the wound and stop the bleeding. Rabbi Joseph de Riva, who had circumcised his children, possessed such Christian blood and used it for this purpose. (Deckert, *Ein Ritualmord*, 28).

13. Deckert, *Ein Ritualmord*, 35.

14. Ibid., 36–37.

15. The public prosecutor in fact ordered the booklet confiscated on March 23, 1893, on the usual grounds of incitement against a religious community. SOA Praha, ZST Praha, C 287/1893.

16. *Jewish Chronicle*, 1 July 1892.

17. Národní archiv, Praha, PM (1891–1900), 8/1/9/1 (3786).

18. Ibid. That *Polaban* was the source of the "news" that Havlínová had died, not by drowning but by a violent death, was confirmed by *Naše Zájmy*, the newspaper edited by Jaromír Hušek and sympathetic to *Polaban*.

19. Národní archiv, PM (1891–1900), 8/1/9/1 (3786).

20. Ibid. On the Kolín ritual murder accusation, see also Frankl, *"Emancipace od židů,"* 191–99.

21. Some evidence suggests that local wisdom in Kolín regarded the coroner's examination of Havlinová's corpse with skepticism and resisted the conclusion that the only violence she had suffered had been at her own hand. *Naše zájmy*, in an issue confiscated by the Prague Criminal Court, ridiculed the notion that the girl had simply "disappeared" or that she might have had reason to commit suicide. Alluding to the sexual connotations attached to suicide among young,

unmarried women, the paper countered that Havlinová had been "in all respects a happy and respectable girl." "And," the paper continued—in a revealing aside on the self-confirming role of collective memory in such episodes—"because the local population remembers other such mysterious cases, it considers this, too, to be a case of ritual murder" (*Naše zájmy*, 23 April 1893, 26; on the confiscation by the Prague Criminal Court, see ZST Praha, C 360/1893).

In Corfu (1891), some people responded to the fact that the victim of a violent death had herself been Jewish with a counternarrative suggesting that she had in fact been kidnapped from her Christian family of origin and subsequently been raised in a Jewish family in preparation for her eventual sacrifice (Corel, *Das Blutmärchen*, 39).

22. Georg Schroubek makes a similar claim in his essay "Der 'Ritualmord' von Polná": "There existed everywhere, in the city and the countryside, a high *expectation* for new 'ritual murder' cases—bound up with considerable 'knowledge' of their typical elements" (Georg R. Schroubek, "Der 'Ritualmord' von Polná: Traditioneller und moderner Wahnglaube," in *Antisemitismus und jüdische Geschichte: Studien zu Ehren von Herbert A. Strauss*, ed. Rainer Erb and Michael Schmidt [Berlin: Wissenschaftlicher Autorenverlag, 1987], 158).

23. Frankl, "Background of the Hilsner Case," 46–60.

24. Ibid., 52; Kieval, *Making of Czech Jewry*, 68.

25. Frankl, "Background of the Hilsner Case," 49–51.

26. Ibid., 52–53.

27. Kieval, *Making of Czech Jewry*, 68, quoted in Christoph Stölzl, *Kafkas böses Böhmen: Zur Sozialgeschichte eines Prager Juden* (Munich: Edition Text + Kritik, 1975), 61.

28. "Židé v národní naší společnosti," *Národní listy*, 12 March 1897, quoted in Frankl, "Background of the Hilsner Case," 55.

29. Good summaries of the controversies surrounding the Badeni language regulations can be found in Frankl, "Background of the Hilsner Case," 80, and Michael L. Miller, "Reluctant Kingmakers: Moravian Jewish Politics in Late Imperial Austria," in *Jewish Studies at the Central European University* 3 (2002–03), ed. András Kovács and Eszter Andor (Budapest: Jewish Studies Project, Central European University, 2004), 117–18. The most in-depth study of the language ordinances is Berthold Sutter, *Die Badenischen Sprachverordnungen von 1897: Ihre Genesis und ihre Auswirkungen vornehmlich auf die inneröstterreichischen Alpenländer*, 2 vols. (Graz: H. Böhlaus Nachf., 1960–65).

30. Frankl, "Background of the Hilsner Case," 80–81.

31. Ibid., 82–83; Helena Krejčová, "Pražský prosincový pogrom roku 1897," *Documenta Pragensia* 16 (1998): 73–78.

32. "Bouřlivý den v praze," *Národní listy*, 30 November 1897 and "Druhý den po německé provokáci," *Národní listy*, 1 December 1897.

33. For an elaboration of this argument, see Kieval, *Languages of Community*, 181–97.

34. The quotation is from Georg R. Schroubek, "Der 'Ritualmord' von Polná," 152. For literature on the Polná case, see Jiří Kovtun, *Tajuplná vražda: Případ Leopolda Hilsnera* (Prague: Sefer, 1994); Bohumil Černý, *Justičný omyl: Hilsneriáda* (Prague: Magnet, 1990); Arthur Nussbaum, *Der Polnaer Ritualmordprozess: Eine kriminalpsychologische Untersuchung auf aktenmässiger Grundlage* (Berlin: A. W. Hayn's Erben, 1906); idem, "The 'Ritual Murder' Trial of Polna," *Historia Judaica* 9 (1947): 57–74; Schroubek, "Der 'Ritualmord' von Polná," 149–71; and František Červinka, "The Hilsner Affair," *Leo Baeck Institute Yearbook* 13 (1968): 142–57, reprinted in Alan Dundes, ed., *The Blood Libel Legend: A Casebook in Anti-Semitic Folklore* (Madison: University of Wisconsin Press, 1991), 135–61.

35. Kovtun, *Tajuplná vražda*, 14–18.

36. Ibid., 29–32.

37. Nussbaum, *Der Polnaer Ritualmordprozess*, Appendix 1: "Tatbestandsaufnahme vom 1. April 1899," 211–13. See also the formal indictment against Leopold Hilsner (*Spis obžalovací*), in the printed trial transcript: *Přelíčení s Hilsnerem před porotou v Kutné Hoře pro vraždu v Polné. Doslovný otisk stenografických protokolů* (Prague: E. Beaufort, 1899), 6–48; German translation in Maximilian Paul-Schiff, *Der Prozess Hilsner: Aktenauszug* (Vienna, 1908), 11–27.

38. "Tatbestandsaufnahme vom 1. April 1899," 213.

39. Státní oblastní archiv [SOA] Třeboň (Vr 188/99/410), dated 7 August 1899, cited in Nussbaum, *Polnaer Ritualmordprozess*, 89, and in Kovtun, *Taluplná vražda*, 32.

40. *Katolické listy*, 11 April 1899, 5.

41. Ibid.

42. *Katolické listy*, 16 April 1899, 6. Similar terms of art were used on other occasions. On 16 May, the paper offered its readers "intimate details" about the family of "the unfortunate Anežka Hrůzová, murdered by means of kosher slaughtering (*košeráckým způsobem zavražděné*)" (*Katolické listy*, 16 May 1899, 4).

43. Kovtun, *Tajuplná vražda*, 43–44.

44. The text of the letter is reproduced in Nussbaum, *Polnaer Ritualmordprozess*, 8–9, and in Paul-Schiff, *Prozess Hilsner*, 2.

45. This trail of documents can be found in the State Regional Archive in Prague (Státní oblastní archiv [SOA] Praha), VSZ (Vrchní státní zastupitelství) III/c/8–9. It provides a fascinating account of bureaucratic ethos, politicization, and the legal and forensic framing of a sensational murder investigation.

46. On Baudyš and Schneider-Svoboda at this point in the investigation, see Kovtun, *Tajuplná vražda*, 72–91.

47. All three documents have been published in Nussbaum, *Polnaer Ritualmordprozess*, as *Anlage* I and III, 211–13, 215–20.

48. "Sektions-Protokoll vom 1. April 1899," in Nussbaum, *Polnaer Ritualmordprozess*, 215–19. For Nussbaum's analysis, see ibid., 68–90.

49. Ibid., 212.

50. Baudyš's request is reproduced in Paul-Schiff, *Der Prozess Hilsner*, 7–8. A handwritten copy can also be found in the Central Archives for the History of the Jewish People (CAHJP) in Jerusalem: A/W 333,7.

51. Nussbaum, *Polnaer Ritualmordprozess*, 219–20.

52. Ibid., 220.

53. One suspects that the reporter in question was Gustav Toužil, who had already made at least one trip to Polná and who would later publish a mass-circulation brochure on the case (see Kovtun, *Tajuplná vražda*, 105–6).

Records from the Kutná Hora Regional Court identify Toužil as the editor-in-chief of two local newspapers, *Volné Slovo* and *Věsna Kutnohorská*. He had appeared before the court on numerous occasions to answer charges relating to the contents of his papers; in 1895, for example, he was arraigned on separate occasions for having insulted a parliamentary deputy and for libeling the editor of the Czech national daily, *Národní listy*, Julius Grégr (SOA Praha. Katalog, KS Kutná Hora [1850–1897/98]).

54. See *Katolické listy* for 16, 19, 20, 21, 24, and 25 May 1899.

55. *Katolické listy*, 19 May 1899, 5.

56. The complete title was *Polná 29.3.1899: Popis vraždy Anežky Hrůzové a sensačního processu s Hilsnerem před porotou Kutnohorskou* [Polná, 29 March 1899: A Description of the

Murder of Anežka Hrůzová and of the Sensational Trial of Hilsner Before the Kutná Hora Jury] (Kutná Hora: Karel Šolc, n.d. [probably September 1899]). A version in German was published at the same time.

57. Toužil, *Polná 29.3.1899*, 19.

58. Ibid., 23–27.

59. Ibid., 25–27.

60. Ibid., 26–27.

61. Ibid., 78.

62. For depictions of Hilsner's background and early life, see Schroubek, "Der 'Ritualmord' von Polná," 152; Kovtun, *Tajuplná vražda*, 18–21; and Nussbaum, *Polnaer Ritualmordprozess*, 90–92.

63. Kovtun, *Tajuplná vražda*, 38–39.

64. SOA Praha, III/C/9/2.

65. Ibid.

66. See Jana Brabencová, "Zásluhy žen rychle stárnou: Anna Auředničková," in *Cesty k samostatnosti: Portréty žen v éře modernizace*, ed. Pavla Vošahlíková and Jiří Martínek (Prague: Historický ústav, 2010), 137–62, and Anna Auředničková, *Tři léta v Terezíně* (Prague: Hynek, 1945).

67. The typescript of a talk, "Před půl stoletím" ("A Half-Century Ago"), can be found in the Anna Auředníčková papers in the literary archive of the Památník národního písemnictví (PNP) in Prague. The somewhat more complete article version, "Kolem Hilsnerova procesu" ("Around the Hilsner Trial"), appeared in *Věstník židovské náboženské obce XI*, 15 (1949): 175–76, the typescript for which—together with a very close German version ("Noch immer Ahasver")—is also to be found in the Auředníčková papers at the PNP.

68. PNP, Auředníčková papers, with some variation among the three documents.

69. One of the first witnesses to come forward in the case was Johana Vomelová, the wife of the mayor of Malá Věžnice. She reported that, after spending part of the day in Polná on 29 March, she had been making her way back to the village from Polná along the path by the Březina woods when she was accosted by a young man, age twenty to thirty, dressed in an ash-gray suit and carrying a white stick, who muttered something about looking for a spruce tree before running off into the woods. The police set about looking for such a suit (eventually only the trousers) among Hilsner's possessions and those of his mother. In the meantime, when Hilsner was brought before Vomelová, she said she could *not* recognize him for sure as the man she saw. She stubbornly maintained this position throughout the trial. (Various sources: Kovtun, *Tajuplná vražda*, 37–43, 77–78; "Spis obžalovací" [Writ of Indictment], in *Přelíčení s Hilsnerem*, 33–36; trial testimony in ibid., 173–79).

70. Kovtun, *Tajuplná vražda*, 80–81; Nussbaum, *Polnaer Ritualmordprozess*, 94–95.

71. Nussbaum, *Polnaer Ritualmordprozess*, 98–99.

72. On Pešák's testimony, see Kovtun, *Tajuplná vražda*, 124–28, and Nussbaum, *Polnaer Ritualmordprozess*, 99–103.

73. The dueling expert testimonies are summarized in Nussbaum, *Polnaer Ritualmordprozess*, 101–2.

74. Kovtun, *Tajuplná vražda*, 127.

75. SOA Praha, VSZ Praha III/C/9/19. During the trial, Auředníček, Hilsner's defense attorney, would call this finding into question, stating to the court, "The judicial experts returned a positive opinion with regard to the stains [on the gray trousers] that, according to their composite elements, they come from human blood. But this conclusion is not clear, because experts have said to me regarding the question that the components may be those of

blood, but they cannot say whether or not they come from human blood. There is disagreement on this point." To this, Schneider-Svoboda replied, "The expert opinion is positive, clear, and certain. When the experts say that 'with the greatest probability' they [the stains] come from blood, they are able to say this because they could not get the last drop. Both experts have illustrious reputations" (*Přelíčení s Hilsnerem*, 264).

76. *Přelíčení*, 376–77.

77. Ibid., 380.

78. See, for example, ibid., 382, 384.

79. Ibid., 383. The reporter covering the trial for the Viennese Zionist weekly, *Die Welt*, appears to have reached a similar conclusion, writing in the week following the verdict, "The state's attorney made use of certain thoughtful turns of phrase, which were nothing other than unmistakable plays on 'ritual murder.'" "Der Mädchenmord in Polna," *Die Welt*, 22 September 1899, 8. Remarkably, the presiding judge repeated the words "according to her the Jew Hilsner persecuted (or, harassed) her and stared at her" in direct questioning of the accused (*Přelíčení*, 55).

80. On Karel Baxa (1863–1938), his early career, and his involvement in the Hilsner murder trials, see Frankl, "*Emancipace od židů*," 224, 240–42, 286–87, 299, and Kovtun, *Tajuplná vražda*, 51–52, 93–94, 112–21.

81. *Přelíčení*, 398.

82. Ibid., 399.

83. Ibid., 401.

84. Ibid., 302–3.

85. Ibid., 304–6.

86. T. G. Masaryk makes a similar point regarding the overall conduct of the trial in his 1900 publication *Die Bedeutung des Polnaer Verbrechens für den Ritualaberglauben*, recently reissued in Czech in T. G. Masaryk, *Hilsneriada: Texty z let 1898–1900*, vol. 2 (Prague: Ústav T. G. Masaryka, 219), 669–727.

Ostensibly, according to the public prosecutor, the motive behind the crime was beside the point. But antisemitic interests had ostentatiously pushed the question of motive to the foreground, so much so that the presumption of ritual murder had managed to shape the presentation of the facts of the case by the state and its experts. "In theory," Masaryk quipped, "we hear that motive was a side issue; in practice, it was the main issue" (Masaryk, *Die Bedeutung*, 50).

87. SOA, Praha, Sbírka Hilsner, KS Kutná Hora, Vr 188/99/457; *Přelíčení*, 374.

88. Ibid.

89. *Přelíčení*, 452–55.

90. "Vražda v Polné," *Českožidovské listy*, 15 September 1899, 3. The editors of *Českožidovské listy* claimed to have been able to find only two Czech-language newspapers in Bohemia that were openly skeptical of the charges.

91. Ignát Arnstein, "O našem stanovisku k sporu Dreyfusovu a Hilsnerovu," *Českožidovské listy*, 29 September 1899, 2.

92. Ibid. The Zionist newspaper, *Die Welt*, also reported on this meeting of the National Union of Czech Jews, although it was, in principle, closed. The paper's Prague correspondent heard the words of Arnstein rather differently, as calling only for the continued collaboration of Jews and Czech nationalists. Rather, it was the next speaker, Maxim Reiner, who expressed his complete disappointment at the "shameful behavior of the entire Czech nation" (N. P., "Prag," *Die Welt*, 6 October 1899, 8–9).

93. What had been a single institution, known as the Charles-Ferdinand University, in which lectures were given either in German or in Czech, was divided in 1882 into separate

German and Czech schools, although the name Charles-Ferdinand remained attached to each. The Czech institution was renamed Charles University in 1920.

94. "Münz, Sigmund," in *Jewish Encyclopedia* (http://www.jewishencyclopedia.com/articles/11227-munz-sigmund); "Münz, Sigmund (1859–1934), Schriftsteller und Journalist," in *Österreichisches Biographisches Lexikon und biographische Dokumentation* (http://www.biographien.ac.at/oebl/oebl_M/Muenz_Sigmund_1859_1934.xml).

95. Masaryk recounted the nature of the exchange with his former student numerous times over the course of his life, for example, in an interview with the *Jewish Chronicle* in 1901, in a speech to the Austrian Reichsrat in 1907, and in his later interviews with the Czech writer Karel Čapek—often with slight variations with each telling.

On Masaryk's involvement in the Hilsner case, see, especially, the recently published collection of sources: T. G. Masaryk, *Hilsneriada*; also Jan Herben, "T. G. Masaryk o židech a antisemitismu," in *Masaryk a židovství*, ed. Ernst Rychnovsky, with the collaboration of O. Donath and F. Thieberger (Prague: "Mars" Nakladatelství, 1931), 243–64; Ernst Rychnovsky, "Boj proti pověře o rituální vraždě," in *Masaryk a židovství*, 151–241; Kovtun, *Taluplná vražda*, 263–75; and Karel Čapek, *Talks with T. G. Masaryk*, trans. Dora Round, ed. Michael Henry Heim (North Haven, Conn.: Catbird Press, 1995), 167–68.

The *Masaryk a židovství* volume was issued at the same time in a German edition under the title *Masaryk und das Judentum* (Prague: Marsverlagsgesellschaft, 1931). An incomplete and somewhat less reliable English translation of the German (by Benjamin R. Epstein) appeared in 1945 as *Masaryk and the Jews* (New York: B. Pollak, 1945). Unless otherwise indicated, references are to the Czech edition.

96. *Neue Freie Presse*, 29 September 1899, 2, republished in Czech in T. G. Masaryk, *Hilsneriada*, vol. 1 (Prague: Ústav T. G. Masaryka, 2019), 392–93.

97. Quoted in Rychnovsky, "Boj proti pověře o rituální vraždě," 155, and, with some variations, in Kovtun, *Tajuplná vražda*, 268. Kovtun identifies Masaryk's interlocutor as Alois Zucker, a professor of law and former deputy in the Austrian Reichsrat from the Old Czech party. Zucker had served as the academic adviser to the Czech Jewish Student Association (Spolek českých akademiků-židů) when it was founded in 1876 (see Kieval, *Making of Czech Jewry*, 23).

98. T. G. Masaryk, *Nutnost revidovati proces polenský* (Prague: Čas, 1899; reissued in T. G. Masaryk, *Hilsneriada: Texty z let 1898–1900*, vol. 1 [Prague: Ústav T. G. Masaryka, 2019], 417–33). The German edition, *Die Notwendigkeit der Revision des Polnaer Processes*, was published as a supplement to the 11 November 1899 edition of the weekly *Die Zeit*.

99. T. G. Masaryk, *Die Bedeutung*, passim and "Foreword."

100. *Jewish Chronicle*, 3 May 1901, 13; already by this time, the *Jewish Chronicle* was referring to Masaryk as "the Czech Zola."

101. Čapek, *Talks with T. G. Masaryk*, 167–68.

Masaryk concluded this particular reminiscence with his own foray into a common anti-Jewish motif: "Yet during the war I came to realize how useful it had been. The world press is partly managed or financed by Jews; they knew me from the Hilsner case and repaid me by writing sympathetically about our cause—or fairly at least. That helped us a great deal politically" (168).

102. Bulova's report to the Prague police: SOA Praha, III/C/8/75. His main points later found their way to print in J[osef] A[dolf] Bulova, *Zum Polnaer Ritualmordprozess im Stadium vor dem zweiten Urteile: Ein Brief* (Berlin: G. E. Kitzler, 1900). A good summary of Bulova's background and intervention in the case can be found in Kovtun, *Tajuplná vražda*, 255–57, 366–70.

103. Baudyš to Vrchní Státní Zastuipitelství, Praha, 2 October 1899: SOA Praha, III/C/8/65. The letter is also quoted at length in Kovtun, *Tajuplná vražda*, 233–35.

104. Kovtun, *Tajuplná vražda*, 308–9. On the Ritter case, see Leopold Auerbach, *Das Judenthum und seine Bekenner in Preußen und in den anderen deutschen Bundesstaaten* (Berlin: Mehring, 1890), 64–69; J. Ch. Korn, *Der Talmud vor Gericht. Vorträge gehalten im Leseklub "Sciinta," zur Beantwortung der den Prozess Ritter betreffenden Fragen, insoweit der Talmud verantwortlich gemacht wurde* (Vienna: J. Ch. Korn, 1884); and Josef Rosenblatt, "Prozess Ritter," *Das Tribunal: Zeitschrift für praktische Strafrechtspflege* 1 (1885): 318–406, which includes official court documents.

105. Kovtun, *Tajuplná vražda*, 309.

106. SOA Praha, III/C/9/91. A manuscript copy in German can be found in the Jewish Museum of Prague, MS 10389. Printed texts of the report (*Gutachten der böhmischen medizinischen Facultät in der Strafsache Leopold Hilsner*) can be found in Nussbaum, *Der Polnaer Ritualmordprozess*, Appendix 4, 220–41, and Bulova, *Zum Polnaer Ritualmordprozess*, Appendices A and B, i–xxxv.

107. *Gutachten der böhmischen medizinischen Facultät*, passim. For a useful analysis, see Kovtun, *Tajuplná vražda*, 354–59.

108. A copy of the court's decision can be found in the Central Archives for the History of the Jewish People, Jerusalem: A/W 335,19. For a printed version, see Paul-Schiff, *Der Prozess Hilsner*, 46–48.

109. CAHJP A/W 335,19; Paul-Schiff, *Der Prozess Hilsner*, 47.

110. Kovtun, *Tajuplná vražda*, 359.

111. For an extensive analysis of the Písek trial, see Kovtun, *Tajuplná vražda*, 397–451; for the verdict itself, 449–51.

CHAPTER 5

1. On Khvol'son's career in general and his involvement in scholarship refuting the ritual murder accusation, see D. Chwolson, *Die Blutanklage und sonstige mitterlaterliche Beschuldigungen der Juden: Eine historische Untersuchung nach den Quellen* (Frankfurt: J.Kauffmann, 1901), ix–xv; Christoph Gassenschmidt, "Khvolson, Daniil Avraamovich," in *YIVO Encyclopedia of Jews in Eastern Europe*, http://www.yivoencyclopedia.org/article.aspx/Khvolson_Daniil_Avraamovich; and Andrew C. Reed, "For One's Brothers: Daniil Avraamovich Khvol'son and the 'Jewish Question' in Russia, 1819–1911," Ph.D. diss., Arizona State University, 2014.

2. D. Chwolson, *Die Blutanklage und sonstige mitterlaterliche Beschuldigungen der Juden*.

3. On Hans Gross's governmental and academic career, see *Hans Gross—Ein "Vater" der Kriminalwissenschaft: Zur 100. Wiederkehr seines Todestages*, ed. Christian Bachhiesl, Gernot Kocher, and Tohas Mühlbacher (Vienna: LIT Verlag, 2015); Roland Grassberger, "Pioneers in Criminology XIII—Hans Gross (1847–1915)," *Journal of Criminal Law, Criminology and Political Science* 47, no. 4 (Nov.–Dec. 1956): 397–405; and Daniel M. Vyleta, *Crime, Jews and News: Vienna 1895–1914* (New York: Berghahn Books, 2007), 203–9.

On the emergence of criminology as a social science during the last third of the nineteenth century, see Mary Gibson, *Born to Crime: Cesare Lombroso and the Origins of Biological Criminology* (Westport, Conn.: Praeger, 2002); Richard F. Wetzell, *Inventing the Criminal: A History of German Criminology, 1880–1945* (Chapel Hill: University of North Carolina Press, 2000); Peter Becker, *Verderbnis und Entartung: Eine Geschichte der Kriminologie des 19. Jahrhunderts als Diskurs und Praxis* (Göttingen: Vendenhoeck & Ruprecht, 2002); and Peter Becker and

Richard F. Wetzell, eds., *Criminals and Their Scientists: The History of Criminology in International Perspective* (Washington, D.C.: German Historical Institute and Cambridge University Press, 2006).

4. Lombroso, in addition to scattered references to Jews in his opus, *L'uomo delinquente* (*Criminal Man*; 1st ed., Milan, 1876; 5th ed., 1896), also published *L'antisemitismo e le scienze modern* (*Antisemitism and Modern Science*; Turin, 1894). Mary Gibson and Nicole Hahn Rafter, in their introduction to the English translation of *L'uomo delinquente* (*Criminal Man* [Durham, N.C.: Duke University Press, 2006]), write, "His own Jewish ancestry partially accounts for his refusal to characterize Jewish behavior in simple biological rather than more complex sociological terms. Aware of the frightening rise during the last decades of the nineteenth century of racial anti-Semitism in northern Europe, Lombroso argued that Jewish patterns of behavior derived from the historical legacy of persecution rather than from innate racial characteristics" (*Criminal Man*, 20).

5. Thus, for example, Hans Gross, "Buchbesprechung: Anonymous, *Der Konitzer Mord, Ein Beitrag zur Klärung* (Breslau, 1900)," *Archiv für Kriminal-Anthropologie und Kriminalistik* 4 (1900), 363–65; Gross, "Buchbesprechung: D. Chwolson, *Die Blutanklage und sonstige mittelalterliche Beschuldigungen der Juden. Eine historische Untersuchung nach den Quellen* (Frankfurt am Main, 1901 [1880])," *Archiv* 9 (1902), 240–41; Gross, "Buchbesprechung: Carl Mommert, *Menschenopfer bei den alten Hebräern* (Leipzig, 1905)," *Archiv* 24 (1906): 176; Gross, "Buchbesprechung: Maximilian Paul-Schiff, *Der Prozeß Hilsner. Aktenauszug* (Vienna, 1908)," *Archiv* 29 (1908): 314; Gross, "Buchbesprechung: Albert Hellwig, *Ritualmord und Aberglaube* (Minden: i.W. o.J.)," *Archiv* 59 (1914): 377.

6. "Buchbesprechung: *Die Blutanklage*," 241.

7. Ibid., 241.

8. Gross, "Buchbesprechung: *Der Konitzer Mord*," 363–65. The brochure was published anonymously, with a foreword by "H., M.D." The reference apparently is to Hermann Hamburger, a Breslau physician.

9. Gross, "Buchbesprechung: *Der Konitzer Mord*," 364.

10. Hans Gross, "Psychopathischer Aberglaube," *Archiv für Kriminal-Anthropologie und Kriminalistik* 9 (1902): 253–82, reprinted in Gross, *Gesammelte Kriminalistische Aufsätze*, vol. 2 (Leipzig: F. C. W. Vogel, 1908), 132–60, and Gross, "Zur Frage vom psychopathischen Aberglauben," *Archiv* 12 (1903): 334–40, reprinted in Gross, *Gesammelte Kriminalistische Aufsätze*, vol. 2, 161–67.

11. Gross, "Psychopathischer Aberglaube," 254–60; *Gesammelte Kriminalistische Aufsätze*, 133–38.

12. Quoted in Gross, "Psychopathischer Aberglaube," 260; *Gesammelte Kriminalistische Aufsätze*, 138.

13. Gross, "Psychopathischer Aberglaube," 260; *Gesammelte Kriminalistische Aufsätze*, 138.

14. Here I refer to the fifth edition: Hans Gross, *Handbuch für Untersuchungsrichter als System der Kriminalistik* (Munich: J. Schweitzer Verlag, 1908), 464–89. An English-language adaptation (not a faithful translation and without Gross's extensive reference notes) was published as *Criminal Investigation: A Practical Textbook for Magistrates, Police Officers and Lawyers*, adapted by John Adam and J. Collyer Adam (both public prosecutors in Madras, India), edited by Norman Kendal (London: Sweet & Maxwell, 1924). It continued to be reprinted into the 1960s.

15. Arthur Nussbaum, *Der Polnaer Ritualmordprozess: Eine kriminalpsychologische Untersuchung auf aktenmässiger Grundlage*, Mit einem Vorwort von Prof. Dr. Franz von Liszt (Berlin: A. W. Hayn's Erben, 1906). Nussbaum immigrated to New York in 1933 and eventually became

a professor of law at Columbia University. This book continues to be an important scholarly resource. See Elliott E. Cheatham et al., "Arthur Nussbaum: A Tribute," *Columbia Law Review* 57, no. 1 (1957): 1–7.

16. Arthur Nussbaum, "The 'Ritual Murder' Trial of Polna," *Historica Judaica* 9 (1947): 57–74; quote is from 65. His more extensive critique can be found in Arthur Nussbaum, "Der psychopatische Aberglaube," *Zeitschrift für die gesamte Strafrechtswissenschaft* 27 (1907): 350–75, and Nussbaum, "Über Morde aus Aberglauben," *Zeitschrift für die gesamte Strafrechtswissenschaft* 30 (1910): 813–52.

17. The *Obertertianeren* were students in the ninth, out of a total of thirteen, grades.

18. The two major monographic studies of the Konitz case are Christoph Nonn, *Eine Stadt sucht einen Mörder: Gerücht, Gewalt und Anstisemitismus im Kaiserreich* (Göttingen: Vandenhoeck & Ruprecht, 2002), and Helmut Walser Smith, *The Butcher's Tale: Murder and Anti-Semitism in a German Town* (New York: W. W. Norton, 2002). My narrative is also indebted to Johannes T. Groß, *Ritualmordbeschuldigungen gegen Juden im deutschen Kaiserreich (1871–1914)* (Berlin: Metropol, 2002), 89–145; Bernhard Vogt, "Die 'Atmosphäre eines Narrenhauses': Eine Ritualmordlegende um die Ermordung des Schülers Ernst Winter in Konitz," in *Zur Geshichte und Kulture der Juden in Ost- und Westpreußen*, ed. Michael Brocke, Margret Heitmann, and Harald Lordick (Hildesheim: Georg Olms Verlag, 2000), 545–77; Otto Steiner, *Ritualmord? Vier große Ritualmordprozesse* (Hamburg: Kriminalistik, 1955), 38–60; and Hugo Friedlaender, *Interessante Kriminal-Prozesse von Kulturhistorischer Bedeutung*, vol. 3 (Berlin: Hermann Barsdorf, 1911), 76–131.

19. Steiner, *Ritualmord?*, 38–40; "Motiviertes Gutachten vom 6. August 1900 von Dr. Mittenzweig und Dr. Störmer," in *Die Gutachten der Sachverständigen über den Konitzer Mord* (Berlin: Centralverein deutscher Staatsbürger jüdischen Glaubens, 1903), 31–32; "Gutachten des Königlichen Medizinal-Colllegiums der Provinz Westpreussen," in *Gutachten der Sachverständigen*, 44.

20. Steiner, *Ritualmord?*, 40; "Gutachten des Königlichen Medizinal-Colllegiums," 44.

21. "Gutachten des Königlichen Medizinal-Colllegiums," 54–55.

22. *Die Gutachten der Sachverständigen über den Konitzer Mord*, Nach den amtlichen Akten veröffentlicht vom Centralverein deutscher Staatsbürger jüdischen Glaubens (Berlin: Centralverein, 1903).

23. I have in mind here in particular the opinion offered by the forensic physician and *Privatdozent* at the University of Berlin, Dr. Puppe, and the report of the Royal Medical College at Danzig, which, when finally solicited in September 1901, provided a clear, critical, and reasoned analysis of all the medical examinations up to that time, arguing forcefully against any imputation of ritual murder to the events in Konitz.

24. Most of the archival holdings relating to Konitz are housed in the Geheimes Staatsarchiv Preußischer Kulturbesitz, Berlin-Dahlem (GStAPK); a significant file, found in the Brandenburgisches Landeshauptarchiv, Potsdam, was assembled by the criminal division of the Polizeipräsidium Berlin under the National Socialist government.

25. Gross, "Psychopathischer Aberglaube," 272; *Gesammelte Kriminalistische Aufsätze*, 150.

26. Gross, "Psychopathischer Aberglaube," 273; *Gesammelte Kriminalistische Aufsätze*, 150–51.

27. Gross, "Psychopathischer Aberglaube," 280; *Gesammelte Kriminalistische Aufsätze*, 158.

28. Gross, "Psychopathischer Aberglaube," 282; *Gesammelte Kriminalistische Aufsätze*, 160.

29. This view is also expressed by a number of other scholars writing after World War II, among them Otto Steiner, Christoph Nonn, Helmut Smith, and Bernhard Vogt (see note 18

above), but also as early as 1904 by Walter Zelle, a physician and freelance historian ([Walter] Zelle, *Wer hat Ernst Winter ermordet? Eine psychologische Studie* [Braunschweig: Richard Sattler, 1904]).

30. Nonn, *Eine Stadt*, 55.

31. Ibid., 55.

32. Ibid., 55.

33. The parts of Winter's body discovered in March and April 1900 (preserved first in ice and then in alcohol) underwent the typical sequence of preliminary examination followed by an official autopsy. A court-ordered follow-up autopsy (*Nachobduktion*) was performed by two court-appointed medical officers from Berlin (Drs. Mittenzweig and Störmer) on 16 and 17 May. In an effort to resolve discrepancies in expert testimony, especially regarding cause and time of death, Drs. Müller and Bleske were asked to provide a "directed" opinion (*motiviertes Gutachten*) the following month; more solicited opinions followed. Most of this material has been published in *Die Gutachten der Sachverständigen über den Konitzer Mord*, 5–78.

Most narratives of the Konitz case note that the very act of dismemberment suggested a ritual murder. I don't think this was necessarily the case or, at least, not without the accompanying verdicts of "expert hand" and exsanguination through a cut across the throat.

34. See, in particular, "Nachobduktion durch Dr. Mittenzweig and Dr. Störmer vom 16. Mai 1900" and "Motiviertes Gutachten vom 6. August 1900," in *Gutachten der Sachverständigen*, 15–21 and 31–38.

35. "Nachobduktion," 17.

36. Ibid., 19.

37. Ibid., 20.

38. "Motiviertes Gutachten," 31–38; quotation from 36.

39. "Zeugen- und sachverständigen- eidliche Aussage des Tierarztes Friedrich Wendt," in *Gutachten der Sachverständigen*, 42–43.

40. "Zeugen- und sachverständigen- eidliche Aussage," 43. Dr. Bleske did not claim to offer an expert opinion on this question. He only wished to observe that, with Winter, the pelvic area was separated from the chest, and the entrails were completely removed; they are still missing today (43).

41. Burkhard Madea, ed., *History of Forensic Medicine* (Berlin: Lehmanns Media, 2017), 137. In 1903, Puppe was appointed associate professor and director of the newly created Institute of Forensic Medicine at the University of Königsberg; he assumed the directorship of the Institute of Forensic Medicine in Breslau (today Wrocław) in 1921. In the field of forensic science, Puppe is credited with having created what became known as "Puppe's Rule," through which one could determine the sequence of injuries in skull fractures caused by repeated blows to the head. See Gunther Geserick, Klaus Krocker, and Ingo Wirth, "Puppe's Rule: A Literature Review," *Archiv für Kriminologie* 229 (2012): 34–43, and "Georg Puppe," *Wikipedia*, https://en.wikipedia.org/wiki/Georg_Puppe.

42. *Jewish Chronicle*, 14 September 1900, 9; Friedlaender, *Interessante Kriminal-Prozesse*, 82–85. See also Puppe's recollections, "Mündliches Gutachten des vereidigten Sachverständigen Gerichtsphysikus Dr. Puppe," in *Gutachten der Sachverständigen*, 81–87.

43. "Mündliches Gutachten des vereidigten Sachverständigen Gerichtsphysikus Dr. Puppe," 81–87; quotation is from 85.

44. Smith, *Butcher's Tale*, 188; "Gutachten des Königl. Medizinal-Collegiums der Provinz Westpreussen," in *Gutachten der Sachverständigen*, 65.

45. Ibid., 44–66.

46. Ibid., 59.

47. Ibid., 55–66.

48. Ibid., 64.

49. Ibid., 65.

50. Ibid., 65–66.

51. "The Konitz Murder: The 'Ritual Murder' Myth Officially Exploded," *Jewish Chronicle*, 18 October 1901 (but with the byline "Berlin, 15th September"), 12.

52. Helmut Smith makes a similar point when he writes regarding the amount of time the investigation was taking: "This opened a space for fears, for suspicions, for projections, even for settling scores. This was the space that antisemitism filled" (Smith, "Konitz, 1900," 93–122, here 117).

53. See Helmut Smith's excellent analyses of the Konitz riots in "Konitz, 1900" and *Butcher's Tale*, 33–53, as well as Christoph Nonn's, in *Eine Stadt sucht einen* Mörder, 31–54. Reports by the local police and public prosecutor can be found in GStAPK, Rep. 77 (Ministry of the Interior) and Rep. I/84a (Ministry of Justice). For the April 1900 riots, see Smith, "Konitz, 1900," 97–100, and Nonn, *Eine Stadt*, 31–36.

54. The regional president of the Marienwerder district of West Prussia reported that the event looked like a "stage play for the many thousands of onlookers" who had streamed into Konitz from nearby villages and towns (GStAPK, Rep. 77, Tit. 500, Bd. 1, bl. 251, Regierungspräsident Marienwerder, 31 May 1900, quoted in Smith, "Konitz, 1900," 100).

55. Smith, "Konitz, 1900," 100.

56. Smith, *Butcher's Tale*, 48. Hoffmann, it should be mentioned, used this occasion to publicize a full-fledged accusation against his neighbor, the Jewish butcher Adolf Lewy (see Nonn, *Eine Stadt*, 40–42).

57. On the trial of Bernhard Masloff and other members of his family, see Steiner, *Ritualmord?*, 38–60; Friedlaender, *Interessante Kriminal-Prozesse*, 87–115; and *Der Prozess gegen Masloff und Genossen (Konitz, 25. Okt.–10. Nov. 1900) nach stenographischer Aufnahme* (Berlin: H. G. Hermann, 1900).

58. Smith, "Konitz, 1900," 102.

59. Ibid., 102, quoting from GStAPK, Rep. 77, Tit. 500, no. 50, Bd. 1, bl. 222, LA Konitz, 4 June 1900.

60. Smith, *Butcher's Tale*, 49; GStAPK, Rep. I/84a (2.5.1), Nr. 16774, 134, Settegast, 10 June 1900.

61. Smith, *Butcher's Tale*, 49, and "Konitz, 1900," 102–3, quoting from GStAPK, Rep. 77, Tit. 500, no. 50, Bd. 2, 105, LA Konitz, 11 June 1900.

62. Smith, *Butcher's Tale*, 50, and "Konitz, 1900," 103–4.

63. Smith, *utcher's Tale*, 50–51, and "Konitz, 1900," 103–4.

64. Smith, "Konitz, 1900," 51–52, quoting here from GStAPK, Rep. 77, Tit. 500, no. 50, Bd. 2,2, report of LA Konitz, probably 10 June 1900.

65. Smith, *Butcher's Tale*, 52, and "Konitz, 1900," 104, quoting from GStAPK, Rep. 77, Tit. 500, no. 50, Bd. 2, 5, report LA Konitz, probably 10 June 1900.

66. Smith, *Butcher's Tale*, 2–53, and "Konitz, 1900," 105–6; Nonn, *Eine Stadt*, 48–49.

67. Nonn, *Eine Stadt*, 50.

68. Ibid., 42, 50; Torsten Lattki, *Benzion Kellermann: Prophetisches Judentum und Vernunftreligion* (Göttingen: Vandenhoeck & Ruprecht, 2016), 128.

69. Lattki, *Benzion Kellermann*, 114–17, 129–30; cf. Henry J. Kellermann, "From Imperial to National-Socialist Germany: Recollections of a German-Jewish Youth Leader," *Leo Beack Institute Yearbook* 39 (1994): 310.

70. Lattki, *Benzion Kellermann*, 131–32.

71. Nonn, *Eine Stadt*, 51; "Konitz," in *Encycopedia.com*, https://www.encyclopedia.com/religion/encyclopedias-almanacs-transcripts-and-maps/konitz.

72. Smith, "Konitz, 1900," 121.

73. On the testimonies offered by the Masloff family, see Steiner, *Ritualmord?*, 38–60; Friedlaender, *Interessante Kriminal-Prozesse*, 87–115; and Smith, *Butcher's Tale*, 68–75.

According to Friedlaender, Masloff was a gasfitter; Smith describes him as a bricklayer.

74. Steiner, *Ritualmord?*, 43; Friedlaender, *Interessante Kriminal-Prozesse*, 87.

75. Steiner, *Ritualmord?*, 43–44; Friedlaender, *Interessante Kriminal-Prozesse*, 87–88.

76. Steiner, *Ritualmord?*, 44–45; Friedlaender, *Interessante Kriminal-Prozesse*, 87–88.

77. Steiner, *Ritualmord?*, 45; Smith, "Konitz, 1900," 101.

78. Steiner, *Ritualmord?*, 45; Friedlaender, *Interessante Kriminal-Prozesse*, 87.

79. Steiner, *Ritualmord?*, 49.

80. *Der Prozess gegen Masloff und Genossen: (Konitz, 25. Oktober–10. November 1900) nach stenographischer Aufnahme* (Berlin: H. S. Hermann, 1900), quoted in Steiner, *Ritualmord?*, 49–50.

81. Friedlaender, *Interessante Kriminal-Prozesse*, 108–10.

82. Defense attorney Vogel in his closing argument: "Why has Moritz Lewy denied the relationship with Winter? This is suspicious" (Friedlaender, *Interessante Kriminal-Prozesse*, 111).

Steiner devotes quite a bit of space to teasing out the implications of this defense strategy (Steiner, *Interessante Kriminal-Prozesse*, 50–53); Smith, more briefly (Smith, *Butcher's Tale*, 75). Friedlaender offers a detailed summary of the accounts of the many witnesses, including Masloff himself, the forensic physicians, and townspeople (Friedlaender, *Interessante Kriminal-Prozesse*, 85–104).

83. Friedlaender, *Interessante Kriminal-Prozesse*, 111.

84. Ibid., 115.

85. Schwedowitz was accompanied on the bench by two associates. The prosecutor was first state's attorney Schweigger, who had taken over the position from Settegast, and the defense team comprised Hugo Sonnenfeld, from Berlin, and attorney Appelbaum, from Konitz. *Der Prozeß gegen Moritz Lewy (Konitz, 13.–16. Februar 1901) nach stenographischer Aufnahme* (Berlin: H. S. Hermann, 1901).

86. *Prozeß gegen Moritz Lewy*, days 1 through 3, 10–336.

87. Ibid., 4, 434.

88. Ibid., 358–60; cf. Friedlaender, *Interessante Kriminal-Prozesse*, 126; and Steiner, *Ritualmord?*, 59.

89. Steiner, *Ritualmord?*, 59–60.

90. *Prozeß gegen Moritz Lewy*, 289–307.

91. Friedlaender, *Interessante Kriminal-Prozesse*, 121.

92. *Prozeß gegen Moritz Lewy*, 316–18, on the request to have Zimmer removed from the courtroom, Appelbaum's information to the court, and the request to call Zimmer to the witness stand. The questioning and testimony are on 318–36.

93. Appelbaum's summation to the jury, *Prozeß gegen Moritz Lewy*, 361–76.

94. *Prozeß gegen Moritz Lewy*, 363, 367–68.

95. Ibid., 420–21.

96. Ibid., 377–420.

97. Schweiger gave his main summation to the jury on the morning of day four (*Prozeß gegen Moritz Lewy*, 344–60); his reply to the defense team's summations was given later that afternoon (*Prozeß gegen Moritz Lewy*, 421–34, here 421).

98. Smith, *Butcher's Tale*, 210.

99. See the survey of suspects in Smith, *Butcher's Tale*, 189–200.

100. Smith, *Butcher's Tale*, 202–5, based on GStAPK, Rep. 1/84a (2.5.1), Nr. 16777, 88–100, June and July 1901.

101. Smith, *Butcher's Tale*, 205.

102. Ibid., 210–14, based on GStAPK, Rep. I/84a, Nr. 16778, 39–49, Schweigger May 1904.

CONCLUSION

1. The Old Synagogue of Kraków, situated in the Kazimierz district of the city, dates from the fifteenth century. The description that follows is based principally on Aharon Mendel ben Natan Hakohen, *Sefer keneset ha-gedolah: maḥbarot agudat ha-rabanim*, 2 vols. (Alexandria: Hayim Mizrahi, 1901–1903), 2:25a–28a. Other sources include Shmuel Hakohen Shapira, *Asefat harabanim be-kraka* (Drohobycz: A. H. Żupnik, 1903); Menahem Mendel Hayim Landa, *Sefer mekits nirdamim* (Piotrkov: M. Tsederbaum, 1904); Jenő Horovicz, *Der Schwur des in Krakau am 9.–13. August 1903 abgehaltenen Rabbiner-Kongresses gegen die Blutbeschuldigung* (Vienna: J. Schlesinger, 1903), 13–18; and Gershon Bacon, "The Rabbinical Conference in Kraków and the Beginnings of Organized Orthodox Jewry," in *Let the Old Make Way for the New: Studies in the Social and Cultural History of Eastern European Jewry Presented to Immanuel Etkes*, ed. David Assaf and Ada Rapoport-Albert, vol. 2 (Jerusalem: Merkaz Zalman Shazar, 2009), 199*–225* [English section].

2. *Sefer keneset ha-gedolah*, 2, 25a.

3. Ibid., 2, 26b.

4. Ibid., 2, 27a. The translation, with the exception of a minor addition, is from Bacon, "Rabbinical Conference in Kraków," 214*. There is remarkable consistency in the various published versions of the 1903 oath, probably because the text had been distributed in advance. See also *Sefer mekits nirdamim*, 13, and, for a German version, *Der Schwur des in Krakau am 9.–13. August 1903 abgehaltenen Rabbiner-Kongresses*, 15–16.

I should point out that the idea of swearing a solemn oath to the falseness of the ritual murder accusation was a controversial one in Orthodox rabbinic circles because it crossed into the category of an oath given in vain (*shevu'at shav*). This was the view of the author of *Sefer mekits nirdamim*, who wrote, "It seems to us to be an oath given in vain, as when one makes an oath that a tree is a tree, or a stone is a stone" (11–12). These are statements of such obvious truth that they hardly require an oath, and to swear an oath on their reality would be to invoke God's name in vain. The same would hold for obvious falsehoods.

5. See the excellent discussion in Bacon, "Rabbinical Conference in Kraków."

6. On the Kishinev pogrom, see Edward H. Judge, *Easter in Kishinev: Anatomy of a Pogrom* (New York: NYU Press, 1992), and Wolf Moskovich, "Kishinev," in *YIVO Encyclopedia of Jews in Eastern Europe*, https://yivoencyclopedia.org/article.aspx/Kishinev. On Kishinev and its echoes in modern Jewish culture and memory, see Steven J. Zipperstein, *Pogrom: Kishinev and the Tilt of History* (New York: Liveright, 2018).

7. Menasseh ben Israel, *Vindiciae Judaeorum, or A Letter in Answer to Certain Questions Propounded by a Noble and Learned Gentleman, Touching the Reproaches Cast on the Nation of the Jewes* (London: R. D., 1656); Moses Mendelssohn, *Manasseh ben Israel Rettung der Juden (Aus dem Englischen übersetzt) nebst einer Vorrede Mendelssohns (1782)*, in Mendelssohn, *Gesammelte Schriften Jubiläumsausgabe*, vol. 8 (Stuttgart: Friedrich Frommann Verlag, 1983), xiii–xxiii, 1–71;

Isaac Baer Levinsohn, *Efes damim: Sefer hitnatslut neged alilat dam* (Warsaw: n.p., 1884 [Vilnius, 1837]); English translation: *Éfés Dammîm: A Series of Conversations Between a Patriarch of the Greek Church and a Chief Rabbi of the Jews Concerning the Malicious Charge Against the Jews of Using Christian Blood* (London: Longman, Brown, Green, and Longmans, 1841).

Solomon ibn Verga, while including seven separate vignettes of the ritual murder accusation in his historical opus, *Shevet Yehudah* (ca. 1520), never refers to any actual historical cases (not even the recent traumas of Trent [1475] or La Guardia [1490]), presenting instead fictional stories or folktales. See Jeremy Cohen, "The Blood Libel in Solomon ibn Verga's *Shevet Yehudah*," in *Jewish Blood: Reality and Metaphor in History, Religion, and Culture*, ed. Mitchell B. Hart (New York: Routledge, 2009), 116–35, and Cohen, *A Historian in Exile: Solomon ibn Verga, Shevet Yehudah, and the Jewish-Christian Encounter* (Philadelphia: University of Pennsylvania Press, 2017), 87–119.

8. It bears pointing out that Christian experts also came forward to condemn the ritual murder accusation of their own accord. Two individuals who stand out in this regard are the Berlin theologian Hermann Strack and the Russian orientalist Daniil Khvol'son (Daniel Chwolson). In contrast, August Rohling's intervention in the Tiszaeszlár case was undermined by his own obvious *parti pris*—as well as by his demonstrated ignorance of rabbinic texts.

9. Zipperstein, *Pogrom*, 107.

10. Judge, *Easter in Kishinev*, 30–48.

11. My narrative is indebted to two recently published books on the Beilis affair: Edmund Levin, *A Child of Christian Blood: Murder and Conspiracy in Tsarist Russia: The Beilis Blood Libel* (New York: Schocken, 2014), and Robert Weinberg, *Blood Libel in Late Imperial Russia: The Ritual Murder Trial of Mendel Beilis* (Bloomington: Indiana University Press, 2014). For reverberations of the Beilis affair in the Soviet Union, including Bolshevik retaliations against key players in the prosecution, see Elissa Bemporad, *Legacy of Blood: Jews, Pogroms, and Ritual Murder in the Lands of the Soviets* (New York: Oxford University Press, 2019), 35–56.

12. Weinberg, *Blood Libel*, 12–13.

13. Ibid., 161–62; Levin, *Child of Christian Blood*, 284. The translation is from Weinberg's version of the charge.

14. Levin, *Child of Christian Blood*, 284–85; Weinberg, *Blood Libel*, 63–67.

15. Levin, *Child of Christian Blood*, 284–85; Weinberg, *Blood Libel*, 65–67, text on 161–62.

16. Levin, *Child of Christian Blood*, 289.

17. Weinberg, *Blood Libel*, 67; text of editorial, 165.

18. *The Protestant Ethic and the Spirit of Capitalism* originally appeared as two separate essays in the *Archiv für Sozialwissenschaft und Sozialpolitik* in 1904 and 1905. A revised and expanded book edition appeared in 1920. For a recent English translation of the 1920 edition, see Max Weber, *The Protestant Ethic and the Spirit of Capitalism*, trans. and introduced by Stephen Kalberg (Oxford: Oxford University Press, 2011). The so-called Vocation lectures of 1917 and 1919 ("*Wissenschaft als Beruf*" and "*Politik als Beruf*") have typically been rendered in English as "Science as a Vocation" and "Politics as a Vocation." These lectures have recently been retranslated as "The Scholar's Work" and "The Politician's Work" in Max Weber, *Charisma and Disenchantment: The Vocation Lectures*, ed. and with an introduction by Paul Reitter and Chad Wellmon, trans. by Damion Searls (New York: New York Review of Books, 2020).

19. Reitter and Wellmon, "Introduction" to *Charisma and Disenchantment*, xiii.

20. To offer only a few examples, see Jason Ā. Josephson-Storm, *The Myth of Disenchantment: Magic, Modernity, and the Birth of the Human Sciences* (Chicago: University of Chicago Press, 2017); Richard Jenkins, "Disenchantment, Enchantment and Re-enchantment: Max

Weber at the Millennium," *Max Weber Studies* 1 (2000): 11–32; and Anthony J. Carroll, "Disenchantment, Rationality and the Modernity of Max Weber," *Forum Philosophicum* 16 (2011): 117–37. See also the helpful review essay by Michael Saler, "Modernity and Enchantment: A Historiographic Review," *American Historical Review* 111 (June 2006): 692–716.

21. Weber, "The Scholar's Work," 18.

22. See the discussions of creationism in Justin E. H. Smith, *Irrationality: A History of the Dark Side of Reason* (Princeton, N.J.: Princeton University Press, 2019), 138–58, and Michael D. Gordin, *The Pseudoscience Wars: Immanuel Velikovsky and the Birth of the Modern Fringe* (Chicago: University of Chicago Press, 2012), 135–62.

23. Gordin, *Pseudoscience Wars*, 1–2.

24. "Red and pulsating while poured out and left behind, blood could signal both Christ dying and Christ alive, both Christ present on earth (that is, shed—so to speak, *cruor*) and Christ gone to glory (that is, alive—so to speak, *sanguis*)." Caroline Walker Bynum, *Wonderful Blood: Theology and Practice in Late Medieval Northern Germany and Beyond* (Philadelphia: University of Pennsylvania Press, 2007), 165.

25. Hsia, *The Myth of Ritual Murder*, 41.

26. *Katolické listy*, 19 May 1899, 5.

Bibliography

ARCHIVAL COLLECTIONS

Alliance Israélite Universelle, Paris
  Correspondence with Dr. Josef Simon, Budapest
  Correspondence with the Israelitische Allianz, Vienna
Archiv Hlavního Města Prahy, Prague
  Jewish Religious Community—Antisemitism
  Prague newspaper collection
Archiv židovského Muzea v Praze, Prague
  Polná, Velké Mězíříčí, Kroměříž, Příbram, and Teplice collections
Bundesarchiv, Koblenz
  NL Harden (correspondence between Paul Nathan and Maximilian Harden)
Central Archives for the History of the Jewish People, Jerusalem (CAHJP)
  Archive of the Israelitische Kultusgemeinschaft (Jewish Religious Community) of Vienna (A/W): Hilsner investigation and trials
  Hungarian Collection: Antisemitic press (HU/45)
  Josef Samuel Bloch Archive (P 150)
  Newspaper clippings on the Xanten-Cleve trial (Inv/1066)
  H. Hildesheimer Collection on ritual slaughtering controversy (Inv/1417)
Central Zionist Archives, Jerusalem (CZA)
  Leo Motzkin Collection: Kiev Trial (A 126/38)
  Newspaper collection
Geheimes Staatsarchiv Preußischer Kulturbesitz, Berlin-Dahlem (GStAPK)
  HA Rep. 77 (Ministry of the Interior)
  HA Rep. 84a (Ministry of Justice)
Hauptstaatsarchiv Nordrhein-Westfallen, Düsseldorf
  Xanten trial
Leo Baeck Institute, New York
  Memoir Collection
  Gemeinde Konitz Collection
Literární archiv, Památník národního písemnictví, Prague
  Sbírka Anny Auředničkové
  Sbírka Emaneula Lešehrada
Magyar Nemzeti Levéltár (National Archives of Hungary), Budapest
  IM Igazságügyi Minisztérium—(Ministry of Justice K577: Elnöki iratok, 1882–1944; K.5: Tiszaeszlári vérvád, 1882–83)

Muzeum Vysočina, pobočka Polná
Břetislav Reyrich, "Židé a Polná," Typescript, n.d.
Postcard collection (Hilsner Affair)
Národní archiv, Prague (NA Praha)
Confidential Proceedings of the Presidium of the Bohemian Governor's Office: PMT 1881–1910
Archive of the Presidium of the Bohemian Governor's Office: PM 1881–1910
Országos Széchényi Könyvtár (National Séchényi Library), Budapest
Manuscript Division—Fol. Hung. 1384 (Eötvös Károly: *A Nagy Per*)
Fol. Hung. 1847: 1882–83, Bary József nagyváradi Kir. törvenyszéki elnöknek a tiszaeszlári perre vonatkozó iratai (Documents of József Bary pertaining to the Tiszaeszlár trial deposited with the Praesidium of the Nagyvárad Royal Court)
Österreichisches Staatsarchiv. Allgemeines Verwaltungsarchiv, Vienna
K. k. Justitzministerium Sig. VI, H 4652: Hilsner case
Parlamentsarchiv, Vienna
Interpellations concerning the Hilsner case
Státní oblastní archiv v Praze (SOA Praha)
Hilsner Collection:
Státní zastupitelství Kutná Hora; Krajský Soud Kutná Hora; Státní zastupitelství Písek; Krajský Soud Písek; Vrchní státní zastupitelství Praha (Records of the Kutna Hora and Prague criminal courts)
Szabolcs-Szatmár-Bereg Megyei Levéltár (Szabolcs-Szatmár County Archives), Nyíregyháza
Collection: IV. B.: Szabolcs vármegye alispánjának iratai, 1872–1944 (Documents of the Szabolcs County Sheriff, 1872–1944)

NEWSPAPERS

Allgemeine Zeitung des Judenthums
Čas
České zájmy
Českožidovské listy
Die Welt
Dr. Bloch's Oesterreichische Wochenschrift
Egyenlőség
Függetlenség
Humoristické listy
Jewish Chronicle
Katolické listy
Národní listy
Naše doba
Naše zájmy
Neue Freie Presse
Ostdeutsche Tageszeitung. Konitzer Anzeiger.
Polaban
Radikální listy

The Times
Wiener medizinische Wochenschrift

PRINTED PRIMARY SOURCES

Adámek, Karel. *Slovo o židech* Chrudim: A. Eckert, 1899.

Adler, Bruno. *Kampf um Polna: Ein Tatsachenroman.* Prague: Kacha Verlag, 1934.

Antisemitenspiegel: Die Antisemiten im Lichte des Christenthums, des Rechtes und der Wissenschaft. 2nd ed. Danzig: A. W. Kafemann, 1900.

Antisemitenspiegel: Die Antisemiten im Lichte des Christenthums, des Rechtes und der Wissenschaft, edited by Curt Bürger. Berlin: Verein zur Abwehr des Antisemitismus, 1911.

Aram, Max. "Konitz," *Die Welt,* 21 September 1900, 1–2.

Arnstein, Ignát. "O našem stanovisku k sporu Dreyfusovu a Hilsnerovu," *Českožidovské listy,* 29 September 1899, 2. [As offprint: Prague: Národní jednota českožidovská, 1899.]

Auerbach, Leopold. *Das Judenthum und seine Bekenner in Preußen und in den anderen deutschen Bundesstaaten.* Berlin: Sigmar Mehring, 1890.

Auředničková, Anna. *Tři léta v Terezíně.* Prague: Hynek, 1945.

Baedecker, Karl. *Deutschland in einem Bande: Handbuch für Reisende.* Leipzig: Baedecker, 1906.

Bary, József. *A tiszaeszlári bűnper: Bary József vizsgálóbíró emlékiratai.* Budapest: Királyi Magyar Egyetemi Nyomda, 1933.

Beilis, Mendel. *The Story of My Sufferings.* New York: Mendel Beilis Publishing Co., 1926.

Bloch, Joseph S. *Acten und Gutachten in dem Prozesse Rohling contra Bloch.* Vienna: M. Breitenstein, 1890.

———. *Erinnerungen aus meinem Leben.* 2 vols. Vienna: R. Löwit, 1922.

———. *My Reminiscences.* Vienna: R. Löwit, 1922–23.

Borowka, Bruno. *Aus Sage und Geschichte von Konitz: Ein Heimatbuch.* Konitz: Schmolke, 1919.

Brockhaus' Konversationslexikon. Vol. 10. Leipzig: Brockhaus, 1908.

Bulova, Josef Adolf. *Zum Polnaer Ritualmordprozess im Stadium vor dem zweiten Urteile: Ein Brief.* Berlin: G. E. Kitzler, 1900.

Čapek, Karel. *Talks with T. G. Masaryk,* translated by Dora Round and edited by Michael Henry Heim. North Haven, Conn.: Catbird Press, 1995.

Christliche Zeugnisse gegen die Blutbeschuldigung der Juden. Berlin: Walther & Apolant, 1882.

Chwolson, Daniel [Daniil Khvol'son]. *Die Blutanklage und sonstige mittelalterliche Beschuldigungen der Juden: Eine historische Untersuchung nach den Quellen.* Frankfurt: J. Kauffmann, 1901.

Code pénal hongrois des crimes et des délits (28 Mai 1878) et Code pénal hongrois des contraventions (14 Juin 1879). Paris: Imprimerie Nationale, 1885.

Corel, Ludwig. *Das Blutmärchen: Seine Entstehung und Folgen bis zu den jüngsten Vorgängen auf Korfu.* Berlin: J. Gnadenfeld, 1891.

Deckert, Josef. *Ein Ritualmord. Aktenmäßig nachgewiesen.* Dresden: Gloß, 1893.

Der Blutmord in Konitz, mit Streiflichtern auf die staatsrechtliche Stellung der Juden im Deutschen Reiche. Berlin: Deutschnationale Buchhandlung und Verlags-Anstalt, [1901].

Der Blut-Prozeß von Tisza Eszlár in Ungarn. Vorgeschichte der Anklage und vollständiger Bericht über die Prozeß-Verhandlungen vor dem Gerichte in Nyíregyháza. Nach dem amtlichen, stenographischen Protocollen aus dem Ungarischen übertragen. New York: Schnitzer Bros., 1883.

Der Fall Buschhoff: Aktenmäßige Darstellung des Xantener Knabenmord-Prozesses. Frankfurt a.M.: C. Koenitz, 1892.

Der Fall Buschhoff: Die Untersuchung über den Xantener Knabenmord. Von einem Eingeweihten. Berlin: Vaterländische Verlags-Anstalt, 1892.

Der Knabenmord in Xanten vor dem Schwurgericht zu Cleve vom 4. bis 14. Juli 1892, edited by Hugo Friedländer. Kleve: L. A. Knipping, 1892.

"Der konitzer Mord: Kriminalstudie von Kühleborn," *Antisemitisches Jahrbuch für 1901.* Berlin: W. Giese, 1901, 162–98.

Der Meineidsprozess in Konitz: Eine kritische Untersuchung. Berlin: Hermann Walther, 1901.

Der Mord in Konitz am 11. März 1900. Die öffentlichen Gerichtsverhandlungen in der konitzer Mordaffaire u.s.w., edited by Georg Zimmer. Chemnitz: E. A. Hager; Konitz: Georg Zimmer, [1900].

Der Prozess gegen Masloff und Genossen (Konitz, 25. Okt.–10. Nov. 1900) nach stenographischer Aufnahme. Berlin: H. S. Hermann, 1900.

Der Prozeß gegen Moritz Lewy (Konitz, 13.–16. Februar 1901) nach stenographischer Aufnahme. Berlin: H. S. Hermann, 1901.

Der Xantener Knabenmord vor dem Schwurgericht zu Cleve, 4.–14. Juli 1892 Vollständiger stenographischer Bericht. Berlin: Cronbach, 1893.

Desportes, Henri. *Le mystère du sang chez les juifs de tous les temps.*Préface d'*Édouard Drumont.* Paris: Albert Savine, 1889.

Die Gemeinden mit 2000 und mehr Einwohnern im Deutschen Reich nach der Volkszählung vom 16. Juni 1925. Sonderhefte zu Wirtschaft und Statistik. Vol. 6. Berlin: Statistisches Reichsamt, 1926.

Die Gutachten der Sachverständigen über den Konitzer Mord. Nach den amtlichen Akten veröffentlicht vom Centralverein deutscher Staatsbürger jüdischen Glaubens. Berlin: Centralverein, 1903.

Elek, Judit, and Mihály Sükösd, eds. *Tutajosok: A tiszaeszlári per dokumentumai.* Budapest: Magvető Könyvkiadó, 1990.

Eötvös, Károly. *A nagy pér, mely ezer éve folyik s még sincs vége.* Budapest: Révai Testvérek, 1935.

———. *Sechs Aktenstücke zum Prozesse von Tisza-Eszlar.* Berlin: L. Simion, 1882.

Fayer, László. *A Magyar bűnvádi eljárás mai érvényében.* Budapest: Franklin Társulat, 1887.

Frank, Friedrich. *Der Ritualmord vor den Gerichtshöfen der Wahrheit und der Gerechtigkeit.* Regensburg: G. J. Manz, 1901.

———. *Die Kirche und die Juden: Eine Studie.* 2nd ed. Regensburg: G. J. Manz, 1892.

Friedländer, Hugo. *Interessante Kriminal-Prozesse von Kulturhistorischer Bedeutung.* Vol. 3. Berlin: Hermann Barsdorf, 1911.

Gasser, Wolfgang. *Erlebte Revolution 1848/49: Das Wiener Tagebuch des jüdischen Journalisten Benjamin Kewall.* Vienna: Böhlau Verlag, 2010.

George, Gustav. *Enthüllungen zur Konitzer Mordaffair auf Grund eignener Ermittlungen und Beobachtungen.* Berlin: Georg Koenig, [1902].

Gibt es einen jüdischen Ritualmord? Verhandlungen über die Judenfrage im Hause der österreichischen Abgeordneten am 10. und 16. November 1899. Lorch-Württemberg: Karl-Rohm-Verlag, [1899].

Gross, Hans. "Buchbesprechung: Albert Hellwig, *Ritualmord und Aberglaube* (Minden: i.W. o.J.)," *Archiv für Kriminal-Anthropologie und Kriminalistik* 59 (1914): 377.

———. "Buchbesprechung: Anonymous, *Der Konitzer Mord, Ein Beitrag zur Klärung* (Breslau, 1900)," *Archiv für Kriminal-Anthropologie und Kriminalistik* 4 (1900): 363–65.

———. "Buchbesprechung: Carl Mommert, *Menschenopfer bei den alten Hebräern* (Leipzig, 1905)," *Archiv für Kriminal-Anthropologie und Kriminalistik* 24 (1906): 176.

———. "Buchbesprechung: D. Chwolson, *Die Blutanklage und sonstige mittelalterliche Beschuldigungen der Juden. Eine historische Untersuchung nach den Quellen.* (Frankfurt am Main, 1901 [1880])," *Archiv für Kriminal-Anthropologie und Kriminalistik* 9 (1902): 240–41.

———. "Buchbesprechung: Maximilian Paul-Schiff, *Der Prozeß Hilsner. Aktenauszug* (Vienna, 1908)," *Archiv für Kriminal-Anthropologie und Kriminalistik* 29 (1908): 314.

———. *Handbuch für Untersuchungsrichter als System der Kriminalistik.* Munich: J. Schweitzer Verlag, 1908.

———. "Psychopathischer Aberglaube," *Archiv für Kriminal-Anthropologie und Kriminalistik* 9 (1902): 253–82.

———. "Zur Frage vom psychopathischen Aberglauben," *Archiv für Kriminal-Anthropologie und Kriminalistik* 12 (1903): 334–40.

Hakohen, Aharon Mendel ben Natan. *Sefer keneset ha-gedolah: maḥbarot agudat ha-rabanim.* 2 vols. Alexandria: Hayim Mizrahi, 1901–1903.

Hamburger, Hermann. *Der Konitzer Mord: Ein Beitrag zur Klärung.* Breslau, 1900.

Hellwig, Albert. *Ritualmord und Blutaberglaube.* Minden: J. C. C. Bruns, 1914.

Herben, Jan. "T. G. Masaryk o židech a antisemitismu," in *Masaryk a židovství*, edited by Ernst Rychnovsky, with the collaboration of O. Donath and F. Thieberger, 243–64. Prague: "Mars" Nakladatelství, 1931.

Hofmann, Eduard. *Gutachten über die am 18. Juni 1882 bei Tisza-Dada aus der Theisz gezogene, am 19. Juni gerichtlich obducirte und am 7. Dezember 1882 behulfs neuerlicher Untersuchung exhumirte weibliche Leiche.* Budapest: Pester Buchdruckerei, 1883.

Horovicz, Jenő. *Der Schwur des in Krakau am 9.–13. August 1903 abgehaltenen Rabbiner-Kongresses gegen die Blutbeschuldigung.* Vienna: J. Schlesinger, 1903.

Istóczy, Győző. *Manifest an die Regierungen und Völker der durch das Judenthum gefährdeten christlichen Staaten.* Chemnitz: Schmeitzner, 1882.

Korn, J. Ch. *Der Talmud vor Gericht. Vorträge gehalten im Leseklub "Sciinta," zur Beantwortung der den Prozess Ritter betreffenden Fragen, insoweit der Talmud verantwortlich gemacht wurde.* Vienna: J. Ch. Korn, 1884.

Kotyska, Václav. Úplný místopisný slovník Království Českého. Prague: Bursík & Kohout, 1895.

Krúdy, Gyula. "Tiszaeszlár, Fifty Years Later," in *Krúdy's Chronicles: Turn-of-the-Century Hungary in Gyula Krúdy's Journalism*, selected, edited, and translated by John Bátki, with an introductory essay by John Lukacs, 1–12. Budapest: Central European University Press, 2000.

Landa, Menahem Mendel Hayim. *Sefer mekits nirdamim.* Piotrkov: M. Tsederbaum, 1904.

Levinsohn, Isaac Baer. *Efes damim: Sefer hitnatslut neged alilat dam.* Warsaw: 1884 (Vilnius, 1837). [English translation: *Éfés Dammîm: A Series of Conversations Between a Patriarch of the Greek Church and a Chief Rabbi of the Jews Concerning the Malicious Charge Against the Jews of Using Christian Blood.* London: Longman, Brown, Green, and Longmans, 1841.]

Lieberman, Natan. *Megilat Eslar.* Munkács: P. Blayer, 1883.

Lombroso, Cesare. *Criminal Man*, translated by Mary Gibson and Nicole Hahn Rafter. Durham, N.C.: Duke University Press, 2006.

Marcziányi, Georg von. *Esther Solymosi, oder Der jüdisch-rituelle Jungfrauen-mord in Tißa-Eßlar.* Autorisierte deutsche Uebersetzung aus dem Ungarischen. Nebst einer Abbildung der Synagoge in T.-E. Berlin: M. Schulze, n.d. [apparently summer or fall 1882].

Marcus, Jules. *Étude Médico-Lêgale du Meurtre Rituel.* Paris : L. Boyer, 1900.

Masaryk a židovství, edited by Ernst Rychnovsky, in collaboration with O. Donath and F. Thieberger.Prague: Marsverlagsgesellschaft, 1931. [German ed.: *Masaryk und das Judentum*. Prague: Marsverlagsgesellschaft, 1931; English ed.: *Masaryk and the Jews*. New York: B. Pollak, 1945.]

Masaryk, Tomáš G. *Die Bedeutung des Polnaer Verbrechens für den Ritualaberglauben*. Berlin: H. S. Hermann, 1900. [Czech ed.: *Význam procesu polenského pro pověru rituální*. Prague: J. Heben, 1900. Confiscated.]

———. *Dvě povídky*. Prague: Milena Herbenová, 1930.

———. *Hilsneriada: Texty z let 1898–1900*, edited by Luboš Merhaut. 2 vols. Prague: Ústav T. G. Masaryka, 2019.

———. *The Meaning of Czech History*, edited and with an introduction by René Wellek. Translated by Peter Kussi. Chapel Hill: University of North Carolina Press, 1974.

———. *Nutnost revidovati proces polenský*. Prague: Čas, 1899.

Menasheh ben Israel. *Vindiciae Judaeorum, or A Letter in Answer to Certain Questions Propounded by a Noble and Learned Gentleman, Touching the Reproaches Cast on the Nation of the Jewes*. London: R. D., 1656.

Mendelssohn, Moses. *Manasseh ben Israel Rettung der Juden (Aus dem Englischen übersetzt) nebst einer Vorrede Mendelssohns* (1782), in Mendelssohn, *Gesammelte Schriften Jubiläumsausgabe*. Vol. 8. Stuttgart: Friedrich Frommann Verlag, 1983, xiii–xxiii, 1–71.

Mikszáth, Kálmán. *Cikkek és karcolatok, XVI: 1883, ápr.–aug*. Budapest: Akadémiai Kiado, 1972.

Mishpat Kutaisi: 100 shanim la-mishpat alilat ha-dam ha-rishon be-rusiyah, 1878–1978. Din ve-ḥeshbon stenografi, edited by Gershon Megrelishvili. Tel Aviv: B'nai B'rith Trumpeldor, 1978.

Monmouth, Thomas of. *The Life and Passion of William of Norwich*, translated and edited by Miri Rubin. London: Penguin Books, 2014.

Nathan, Paul. *Der Prozess von Tisza-Eszlár: Ein Antisemitisches Culturbild*. Berlin: F. Fontane, 1892.

———. *Xanten-Cleve: Betrachtungen zum Prozeß Buschhof. Separat-Abdruck aus der "Nation."* Berlin: H. S. Hermann, 1892.

Nussbaum, Arthur. *Der Polnaer Ritualmordprozess: Eine kriminalpsychologische Untersuchung auf aktenmässiger Grundlage*. Mit einem Vorwort von Prof. Dr. Franz von Liszt. Berlin: A. W. Hayn's Erben, 1906.

———. "Der psychopatische Aberglaube," *Zeitschrift für die gesamte Strafrechtswissenschaft* 27 (1907): 350–75.

———. "The 'Ritual Murder' Trial of Polna," *Historica Judaica* 9 (1947): 57–74.

———. "Über Morde aus Aberglauben," *Zeitschrift für die gesamte Strafrechtswissenschaft* 30 (1910): 813–52.

Ónody, Géza. *Tisza-Eszlár in der Vergangenheit und Gegenwart. Über die Juden im Allgemeinen. Jüdische Glaubensmysterien. Rituelle Mordthaten und Blutopfer. Der Tisza-Eszlárer Fall*. Translated into German by Georg von Marcziányi. Budapest, 1883.

Paul-Schiff, Maximilian. *Der Prozess Hilsner: Aktenauszug*. Vienna: L. Rosner, 1908.

Polná 29.3.1899: Popis vraždy Anežky Hrůzové a sensačního processu s Hilsnerem před porotou Kutnohorskou. Kutná Hora: Karel Šolc, n.d. (probably September 1899).

Přelíčení s Hilsnerem před porotou v Kutné Hoře pro vraždu v Polné. Doslovný otisk stenografických protokolů. Prague: E. Beaufort, 1899.

Prozeß Buschhof. Der Xantener Knabenmord vor dem Schwurgericht zu Cleve vom 4. bis 14. Juli 1892. Hagen i. W.: Wrietzner, 1892.

Rohling, August. *Der Talmudjude: Zur Beherzigung für Juden und Christen aller Stände.* Münster: Adolph Russell, 1871.

———. *Meine Antworten an die Rabbiner, oder: Fünf Briefe über den Talmudismus und das Blut-Ritual der Juden.* Prague: Cyrillo-Method'schen Buchdruckerei (J. Zeman & Co.), 1883. [Czech ed.: *Moje odpovědi rabínům aneb pět psaní o talmudu a židovské rituelní vraždě.* Prague: Cyrillo-Methodějské knihkupectví (G. Francl), 1883.]

Reyrich [Rérych], Břetislav. *Polná: Průvodce po městě a okolí.* Polná: Club Čs. Turistů, 1927.

Rychnovsky, Ernst. "Boj proti pověře o rituální vraždě," in *Masaryk a židovství*, edited by Ernst Rychnovsky, with the collaboration of O. Donath and F. Thieberger, 151-241. Prague: "Mars" Nakladatelství, 1931.

Rys, Jan. *Hilserniáda a TGM: Ke čtyřicátému výročí* vražd polenských. Prague: Alois Wiesner, 1939.

Sello, Dr. "Der Neustettiner Synagogenbrand," *Das Tribunal: Zeitschrift für praktische Strafrechtspflege* 1 (1885): 5–59.

Shammash, Yuspah. *Minhagim de-kehilat kodesh Vermaisa*, edited by B. S. Bamberger, Eric Zimmer, and Y. M. Perles. Jerusalem: Makhon Yerushalayim, 1988–92.

Shapira, Shmuel Hakohen. *Asefat harabanim be-kraka.* Drohobycz: A. H. Żupnik, 1903.

Simonyi, Iván. *Der Antisemitismus und die Gesetze der menschlichen Gesellschaft: Rede, gesprochen am 1. Antisemiten-Kongresse zu Dresden am 10. Sept. 1882.* Pressburg, 1884.

Spät, Franz. *Die Gutachten der Sachverständigen über den Konitzer Mord.* Offprint from: *Münchener Medizinische Wochenschrift*, no. 51 (1903).

Strack, Hermann L. *Das Blut im Glauben und Aberglauben der Menschheit mit besonderer Berücksichtigung der "Volksmedizin" und des "jüdischen Blutritus."* 8th ed. Munich: Beck, 1900. [Translated as *The Jew and Human Sacrifice: Human Blood and Jewish Ritual. An Historical and Sociological Inquiry.* London: Cope and Fenwich, 1909.]

Sutor, Gustav. *Der Konitzer Mord und seine Folgen: Ein Mahnruf zur Vernunft.* Berlin: Hugo Schildberger, 1900.

———. *Die konitzer Prozesse: Ein weiteres Wort zur Aufklärung.* Konitz: Ostdeutsche Tageszeitung, 1900–1901.

Tager, Alexander B. *The Decay of Czarism: The Beilis Trial.* Philadelphia: Jewish Publication Society of America, 1935.

Wright, Charles H. H. "The Jews and the Malicious Charge of Human Sacrifice," *Nineteenth Century* (November 1883): 753–78.

Załuski, Józef. *Morderstwa rytualne w Polsce do połowy XVIII wieku.* Warsaw: Ksieg. Kroniki Rodzinnej, 1914.

Zelle, Walter. *Wer hat Ernst Winter ermordet? Eine psychologische Studie.* Braunschweig: Richard Sattler, 1904.

Żuchowski, Stefan. *Ogłos procesów kryminalnych na Żydach o rózne ekscesy, także morderstwo dzieci.* [Sandomierz], 1700.

———. *Proces kryminalny o niewinie dziecię Jerzego Krasnowskiego. Już to trzecie roku 1710 dnia 18 sierpnia w Sendomirzu okrutnie od Żydow zamordowane.* [Sandomierz], 1713.

Zum Meineids-Prozeß gegen Moritz Lewy in Konitz Westpr. Verteidigungsrede des Rechtsanwalts Hugo Sonnenfeld in Berlin, mit einem Vorwort des Justizrats Dr. Erich Sello in Berlin. Berlin: H. S. Hermann, 1901.

SECONDARY SOURCES

Anderson, Mary D. *A Saint at Stake: The Strange Death of William of Norwich, 1144.* London: Faber and Faber, 1964.

Aschkewitz, Max. *Zur Geschichte der Juden in Westpreußen.* Marburg: Johann Gottfried Herder-Institut, 1967.

Austerlitz, Theodor. *Die letzte Folterprozedur in der öst.-ung. Monarchie: Der "Kodesch" von Orkuta.* Prešov: Jüdischer Museumverein, 1933.

Avrutin, Eugene M. *The Velizh Affair: Blood Libel in a Russian Town.* New York: Oxford University Press, 2018.

Bachhiesl, Christian, G. Kocher, and T. Mühlbacher, eds. *Hans Gross—Ein "Vater" der Kriminalwissenschaft: Zur 100. Wiederkehr seines Todestages.* Vienna: LIT Verlag, 2015.

Bacon, Gershon. "The Rabbinical Conference in Kraków and the Beginnings of Organized Orthodox Jewry," in *Let the Old Make Way for the New: Studies in the Social and Cultural History of Eastern European Jewry Presented to Immanuel Etkes,* Vol. 2, edited by David Assaf and Ada Rapoport-Albert, 199*–225* [English lang. section]. Jerusalem: Merkaz Zalman Shazar, 2009.

Baumann, Ulrich. "The Development and Destruction of a Social Institution: How Jews, Catholics and Protestants Lived Together in Rural Baden, 1862–1940," in *Protestants, Catholics and Jews in Germany, 1800–1914,* edited by Helmut Walser Smith, 297–315. Oxford: Berg, 2001.

———. *Zerstörte Nachbarschaften: Christen und Juden in badischen Landgemeinden 1862–1940.* Hamburg: Dölling und Galitz, 2000.

Becker, Peter. *Verderbnis und Entartung: Eine Geschichte der Kriminologie des 19. Jahrhunderts als Diskurs und Praxis.* Göttingen: Vendenhoeck & Ruprecht, 2002.

Becker, Peter, and Richard F. Wetzell, eds. *Criminals and Their Scientists: The History of Criminology in International Perspective.* Washington, D.C.: German Historical Institute and Cambridge University Press, 2006.

Bemporad, Elissa. *Legacy of Blood: Jews, Pogroms, and Ritual Murder in the Lands of the Soviets.* New York: Oxford University Press, 2019.

Berger, Peter, and Thomas Luckmann. *The Social Construction of Reality: A Treatise in the Sociology of Knowledge.* Garden City, N.Y.: Doubleday, 1966.

Bernát, Tivadar, ed. *An Economic Geography of Hungary.* Budapest: Akadémiai Kiadó, 1989.

Biale, David. *Blood and Belief: The Circulation of a Symbol Between Jews and Christians.* Berkeley: University of California Press, 2007.

Birnbaum, Pierre. *A Tale of Ritual Murder in the Age of Louis XIV: The Trial of Raphaël Lévy, 1669.* Translated by Arthur Goldhammer. Stanford, Calif.: Stanford University Press, 2012.

Blaschke, Olaf. *Katholizismus und Antisemitismus im Deutschen Kaiserreich.* Göttingen: Vandenhoeck & Ruprecht, 1997.

———. *Offenders or Victims? German Jews and the Causes of Modern Catholic Antisemitism.* Lincoln: University of Nebraska Press and the Vidal Sassoon International Center for the Study of Antisemitism, 2009.

Brabencová, Jana. "Zásluhy žen rychle stárnou: Anna Auředničková," in *Cesty k samostatnosti: Portréty žen v éře modernizace,* edited by Pavla Vošahlíková and Jiří Martínek, 137–62. Prague: Historický ústav, 2010.

Buttaroni, Susanna, and Stanislaw Musial, eds. *Ritualmord: Legenden in der europäischen Geschichte.* Vienna: Böhlau Verlag, 2003.

Bynum, Caroline Walker. *Wonderful Blood: Theology and Practice in Late Medieval Northern Germany and Beyond*. Philadelphia: University of Pennsylvania Press, 2007.

Carroll, Anthony J. "Disenchantment, Rationality and the Modernity of Max Weber," *Forum Philosophicum* 16 (2011): 117–37.

Cerman, Ivo. "Familiants Laws," in *The YIVO Encyclopedia of Jews in Eastern Europe*, Vol. 1, edited by Gershon D. Hundert, 493–94. New Haven, Conn.: Yale University Press, 2008.

Černý, Bohumil. *Justičný omyl: Hilsneriáda*. Prague: Magnet Press, 1990.

Černý, Bohumil, et al. *Hilsneriáda (k 100. výročí 1899–1999)*. Polná: Linda–Jan Prchal, 1999.

Červinka, František. "The Hilsner Affair," *Leo Baeck Institute Yearbook* 13 (1968): 142–57.

Chazan, Robert. "The Blois Incident of 1171," *Proceedings of the American Academy for Jewish Research* 36 (1968): 13–31.

Cheatham, Elliott E., et al. "Arthur Nussbaum: A Tribute," *Columbia Law Review* 57, no. 1 (1957): 1–7.

Cohen, Amnon. "Ritual Murder Accusations Against the Jews During the Days of Suleiman the Magnificent," *Journal of Turkish Studies* 10 (1986): 73–78.

Cohen, Gary B. *The Politics of Ethnic Survival: Germans in Prague, 1861–1914*. Princeton, N.J.: Princeton University Press, 1981.

Cohen, Jeremy. "The Blood Libel in Solomon ibn Verga's *Shevet Yehudah*." In *Jewish Blood: Reality and Metaphor in History, Religion, and Culture*, edited by Mitchell B. Hart, 116–35. New York: Routledge, 2009.

———. *The Friars and the Jews: The Evolution of Medieval Anti-Judaism*. Ithaca, N.Y.: Cornell University Press, 1982, 42–44.

———. *A Historian in Exile: Solomon ibn Verga, "Shevet Yehudah," and the Jewish-Christian Encounter*. Philadelphia: University of Pennsylvania Press, 2017.

———. "The Jews as the Killers of Christ in the Latin Tradition, from Augustine to the Friars," *Traditio* 39 (1983): 1–27.

Cohen, Richard I. *Jewish Icons: Art and Society in Modern Europe*. Berkeley: University of California Press, 1998.

Dickinson, Robert E. *Germany: A General and Regional Geography*. New York: E. P. Dutton, 1953.

Dundes, Alan, ed. *The Blood Libel Legend: A Casebook in Anti-Semitic Folklore*. Madison: University of Wisconsin Press, 1991.

Enyedi, György. *Hungary: An Economic Geography*. Boulder, Colo.: Westview, 1976.

Erb, Rainer, ed. *Die Legende vom Ritualmord: Zur Geschichte der Blutbeschuldigung gegen Juden*. Berlin: Metropol, 1993.

Feder, Ernst. *Paul Nathan: Ein Lebensbild*. Berlin: Deutsche Verlagsgesellschaft für Politik und Geschichte, 1929.

———. "Paul Nathan, the Man and his Work," *Leo Baeck Institute Yearbook* 3 (1958): 60–80.

Fiedler, Jiří. *Jewish Sights of Bohemia and Moravia*. Prague: Sefer, 1991.

Flusser, David. "'Alilat ha-dam neged ha-yehudim le'or ha-hashkafot shel ha-tekufah ha-helenistit," in *Yehudim ve-yahadut be-einei ha-olam ha-helenisti*, edited by Menahem Stern, 187–207. Jerusalem: Merkaz Zalman Shazar, 1974.

Frank, Tibor. "Hungary and the Dual Monarchy, 1867–1890," in *A History of Hungary*, edited by Peter F. Sugar, Péter Hanák, and Tibor Frank, 252-66. Bloomington: Indiana University Press, 1990.

Frankel, Jonathan. *The Damascus Affair: "Ritual Murder," Politics, and the Jews in 1840*. Cambridge: Cambridge University Press, 1997.

Frankl, Michal. "The Background of the Hilsner Case: Political Antisemitism and Allegations of Ritual Murder, 1896–1900," *Judaica Bohemiae* 36 (2000): 34–118.

———. *"Emancipace od židů:" Český antisemitismus na konci 19. Století*. Prague: Paseka, 2007.

Garver, Bruce M. *The Young Czech Party 1874–1901 and the Emergence of a Multi-Party System*. New Haven, Conn.: Yale University Press, 1970.

Gassenschmidt, Christoph. "Khvolson, Daniil Avraamovich," in *The YIVO Encyclopedia of Jews in Eastern Europe*, Vol. 1, edited by Gershon D. Hundert, 890–91. New Haven, Conn.: Yale University Press, 2008.

Geertz, Clifford. "The Way We Think Now: Ethnography of Modern Thought," in Geertz, *Local Knowledge: Further Essays in Interpretive Anthropology*, 147–63. New York: Basic Books, 1983.

Gekas, Sakis. "The Port Jews of Corfu and the 'Blood Libel' of 1891: A Tale of Many Centuries and of One Event," *Jewish Culture and History* 7, nos. 1–2 (2004): 171–96.

"Georg Puppe," *Wikipedia*, June 23, 2020. https://en.wikipedia.org/wiki/Georg_Puppe (accessed January 3, 2021).

Gerő, András. *Modern Hungarian Society in the Making: The Unfinished Experience*. Budapest: Central European University Press, 1995.

Geserick, Gunther, K. Krocker, and I. Wirth. "Puppe's Rule: A Literature Review," *Archiv für Kriminologie* 229 (2012): 34–43.

Gibson, Mary. *Born to Crime: Cesare Lombroso and the Origins of Biological Criminology*. Westport, Conn.: Praeger, 2002.

Gibson, Mary, and Nicole Hahn Rafter. *Criminal Man*. Durham, N.C.: Duke University Press, 2006.

Gordin, Michael D. *The Pseudoscience Wars: Immanuel Velikovsky and the Birth of the Modern Fringe*. Chicago: University of Chicago Press, 2012.

Gottas, Friedrich. "Die antisemitische Bewegung in Ungarn im Zeitalter des Hochliberalismus," *Zeitgeschichte* 1 (1973–74): 105–19.

Grassberger, Roland. "Pioneers in Criminology XIII—Hans Gross (1847–1915)," *Journal of Criminal Law, Criminology and Political Science* 47, no. 4 (1956): 397–405.

Greive, Hermann. "Die gesellschaftliche Bedeutung der christlich-jüdischen Differenz: Zur Situation im deutschen Katholizismus," in *Juden im Wilhelminischen Deutschland 1890–1914*, edited by Werner E. Mosse, 349–88. Tübingen: J. C. B. Mohr, 1976.

Groß, Johannes T. *Ritualmordbeschuldigungen gegen Juden im deutschen Kaiserreich (1871–1914)*. Berlin: Metropol, 2002.

Gross, Michael B. *The War Against Catholicism: Liberalism and the Anti-Catholic Imagination in Nineteenth-Century Germany*. Ann Arbor: University of Michigan Press, 2004.

Guldon, Zenon, and Jacek Wijaczka. "The Accusation of Ritual Murder in Poland, 1500–1800," *Polin* 10 (1997): 99–140.

———. *Procesy o mordy rytualne w Polsce w XVI–XVIII wieku*. Kielce: Wydawnictwo, 1995.

Gyurgyák, János. *A zsidókérdés Magyarországon: Politikai eszmetörténet*. Budapest: Osiris Kiadó, 2001.

Ha-Kohen, Menaḥem. *Mishpatim ve-alilot dam: mishpetei ra'avah ve-alilot dam neged yehudim*. [Tel Aviv]: Misrad Habitaḥon, 1967.

Halbwachs, Maurice. *On Collective Memory*, edited, translated, and with an introduction by Lewis A. Coser. Chicago: University of Chicago Press, 1992.

Handler, Andrew. *Blood Libel at Tiszaeszlar*. Boulder, Colo.: East European Monographs, 1980.

———. *An Early Blueprint for Zionism: Győző Istóczy's Political Anti-Semitism*. Boulder, Colo.: East European Monographs, 1989.

Harris, Ruth. *Murders and Madness: Medicine, Law, and Society in the Fin de Siècle*. New York: Oxford University Press, 1989.

Hauner, Milan. "The Meaning of Czech History: Masaryk versus Pekář," in *T. G. Masaryk (1850–1937). Vol. 3: Statesman and Cultural Force*, edited by Harry Hanak, 24–42. Houndsmills: Macmillan, 1990.

Hellwing, Isak Arie. *Der konfessionelle Antisemitismus im 19. Jahrhundert in Österreich*. Vienna: Herder, 1972.

Heřman, Jan. "The Evolution of the Jewish Population in Bohemia and Moravia, 1754–1953," in *Papers in Jewish Demography 1973*, edited by U. O. Schmelz, P. Glikson, and S. Della Pergola, 191–206. Jerusalem: Institute of Contemporary Jewry, 1977.

———. "The Evolution of the Jewish Population in Prague, 1869–1939," in *Papers in Jewish Demography 1977*, edited by U. O. Schmelz, P. Glikson, and S. Della Pergola, 53–67. Jerusalem: Institute of Contemporary Jewry, 1980.

Hilsnerova Aféra a česká společnost 1899–1999, edited by Miloš Pojar. Prague: Židovskê Museum v Praze, 1999.

Hoensch, Jörg K. *A History of Modern Hungary, 1867–1986*. 2nd ed. London: Longman, 1996.

Hoffmann, Christhard. "Political Culture and Violence Against Minorities: The Antisemitic Riots in Pomerania and West Prussia," in *Exclusionary Violence: Antisemitic Riots in Modern German History*, edited by Christhard Hoffmann, Werner Bergmann, and Helmut Walser Smith, 67–92. Ann Arbor: University of Michigan Press, 2002.

Hoffmann, Gerd. *Der Prozeß um den Brand der Synagoge in Neustettin: Antisemitismus in Deutschland ausgangs des 19. Jahrhunderts*. Schifferstadt: Gerd Hoffmann Verlag, 1998.

Hrabal, Bohumil. *Dancing Lessons for the Advanced in Age*. Translated by Michael Henry Heim. New York: Harcourt Brace & Co., 1995.

———. *Murder Ballads and Other Legends*. Translated by Timothy West. Bloomington, Ind.: Slavica, 2018.

Hsia, R. Po-chia. *The Myth of Ritual Murder: Jews and Magic in Reformation Germany*. New Haven, Conn.: Yale University Press, 1988.

———. *Trent 1475: Stories of a Ritual Murder Trial*. New Haven, Conn.: Yale University Press, 1992.

Hundert, Gershon. *Jews in Poland-Lithuania in the Eighteenth Century*. Berkeley: University of California Press, 2004.

Janos, Andrew C. *The Politics of Backwardness in Hungary, 1825–1945*. Princeton, N.J.: Princeton University Press, 1982.

Jaroš, Zdeněk. *Polná: kulturně historický průvodce*. Jihlava: Muzeum Vysočiny, 1989.

Jenkins, Richard. "Disenchantment, Enchantment and Re-Enchantment: Max Weber at the Millennium," *Max Weber Studies* 1 (2000): 11–32.

Jersch-Wenzel, Stefi. "Zur Geschichte der jüdischen Bevölkerung in der Provinz Posen im 19. Jahrhundert," in *Juden in Ostmitteleuropa von der Emanzipation bis zum ersten Weltkrieg*, edited by Gotthold Rhode, 73–84. Marburg/Lahn: J. G. Herder-Institut, 1989.

Johnson, Eric A. *Urbanization and Crime: Germany 1871–1914*. Cambridge: Cambridge University Press, 1995.

Johnson, Hannah R. *Blood Libel: The Ritual Murder Accusation at the Limit of Jewish History*. Ann Arbor: University of Michigan Press, 2012.

Josephson-Storm, Jason Ā. *The Myth of Disenchantment: Magic, Modernity, and the Birth of the Human Sciences.* Chicago: University of Chicago Press, 2017.

Joskowicz, Ari. *The Modernity of Others: Jewish Anti-Catholicism in Germany and France.* Stanford, Calif.: Stanford University Press, 2014.

Judd, Robin. *Contested Rituals: Circumcision, Kosher Butchering, and Jewish Political Life in Germany, 1843–1933.* Ithaca, N.Y.: Cornell University Press, 2007.

Judge, Edward H. *Easter in Kishinev: Anatomy of a Pogrom.* New York: NYU Press, 1992.

Kapferer, Jean-Noël. *Rumors: Uses, Interpretations, and Images.* New Brunswick, N.J.: Transaction Publishers, 1990.

Karády, Victor. "Religious Divisions, Socio-Economic Stratification and the Modernization of Hungarian Jewry after Emancipation," in *Jews in the Hungarian Economy 1760-1945*, edited by Michael K. Silber, 161-84. Jerusalem: Magnes Press, 1992.

Karády, Victor, and István Kemény. "Les Juifs dans la structure des classes en Hongrie," *Actes de la Recherche en Sciences Sociales* 22 (June 1978): 25–59.

Katz, Jacob. *From Prejudice to Destruction: Anti-Semitism, 1700–1933.* Cambridge, Mass.: Harvard University Press, 1980.

———. *The "Shabbes Goy": A Study in Halakhic Flexibility.* Philadelphia: Jewish Publication Society of America, 1989.

Katzburg, Nathaniel. *Antishemiyut be-hungariyah 1867–1914.* Tel Aviv: Dvir, 1969.

Kellerman, Henry J. "From Imperial to National-Socialist Germany: Recollections of a German-Jewish Youth Leader," *LBIYB* 39 (1994): 305–30.

Kestenberg-Gladstein, Ruth. "The Jews Between Czechs and Germans in the Historic Lands," in *The Jews of Czechoslovakia*, Vol. 1, 21–71. Philadelphia: Jewish Publication Society of America, 1968.

Kieval, Hillel J. "Antisemitism and the City: A Beginner's Guide," *Studies in Contemporary Jewry* 15 (1999): 3–18.

———. "Antisémitisme ou Savoir Social? Sur la genèse du procès moderne pour meurtre rituel," *Annales: Histoire, Sciences Sociales* 49 (1994): 1091–105.

———. "The Blood Libel," in *Key Concepts in the Study of Antisemitism*, edited by Sol Goldberg, Scott Ury, and Kalman Weiser, 53–64. London: Palgrave Macmillan, 2020.

———. "Bohemia and Moravia," in *The YIVO Encyclopedia of Jews in Eastern Europe*, edited by Gershon D. Hundert, 202–11. New Haven, Conn.: Yale University Press, 2008.

———. *Languages of Community: The Jewish Experience in the Czech Lands.* Berkeley: University of California Press, 2000.

———. *The Making of Czech Jewry: National Conflict and Jewish Society in Bohemia, 1870–1918.* New York: Oxford University Press, 1988.

———. "Middleman Minorities and Blood: Is there a Natural Economy of the Ritual Murder Accusation in Europe?" in *Essential Outsiders: Chinese and Jews in the Modern Transformation of Southeast Asia and Central Europe*, edited by Daniel Chirot and Anthony Reid, 208–234. Seattle: University of Washington Press, 1997.

———. "The Rules of the Game: Forensic Medicine and the Language of Science in the Structuring of Modern Ritual Murder Trials," *Jewish History* 26 (2012): 287–307.

———. "Yahrzeits, Condolences, and Other Close Encounters: Neighborly Relations and Ritual Murder Trials in Germany and Austria-Hungary," in *Ritual Murder in Russia, Eastern Europe, and Beyond: New Histories of an Old Accusation*, edited by Eugene M. Avrutin, Jonathan Dekel-Chen, and Robert Weinberg, 110–29. Bloomington: Indiana University Press, 2017.

Klenovský, Jaroslav. *Židovské město v Polné*. Polná: Linda–Jan Prchal, 2000.

Klier, John D. *Imperial Russia's Jewish Question, 1855–1881*. Cambridge: Cambridge University Press, 1995.

Kölling, Bernd. "Blutige Illusionen: Ritualmorddiskurse und Antisemitismus im niederrheinischen Xanten," in *Agrarische Verfassung und politische Struktur: Studien zur Gesellschaftsgeschichte Preußens 1700–1918*, edited by René Schiller, 349–82. Berlin: Arno Spitz, 1998.

Kotik, Meir. *Mishpat Beilis: alilat dam ba-me'ah ha-esrim*. Tel Aviv: Melo, 1978.

Kovtun, Jiří. *Tajuplná vražda: Případ Leopolda Hilsnera*. Prague: Sefer, 1994.

Kövér, György. "Performációk I. 'Zsidó társadalom' Tiszaeszláron a nagy per előestéjen," *Korall: Társadalomtörténeti folyóirat* 17 (September 2004): 5–42.

———. *A tiszaeszlári dráma: Társadalomtörténeti látószögek*. Budapest: Osiris, 2011.

Krejčová, Helena. "Pražský prosincový pogrom roku 1897," *Documenta Pragensia* 16 (1998): 73–78.

Kubinszky, Judit. *Politikai antiszemitizmus Magyarországon (1875–1890)*. Budapest: Kossuth Kőnyvkiadó, 1976.

Kučera, Karel. "Masaryk and Pekář: Their Conflict over the Meaning of Czech History and Its Metamorphoses," in *T. G. Masaryk (1850–1937). Vol. 1: Thinker and Politician*, edited by Stanley B. Winters, 88–113. Houndsmills: Macmillan, 1990.

Labsch-Benz, Elfie. *Die jüdische Gemeinde Nonnenweier: Jüdisches Leben und Brauchtum in einer badischen Landgemeinde*. Freiburg: Mersch, 1981.

LaCapra, Dominick. *Geschichte und Kritik*. Frankfurt a.M.: Fischer Verlag, 1987.

Langmuir, Gavin. "The Knight's Tale of Young Hugh of Lincoln," *Speculum* 47 (1972): 459–82. [Reprinted in Langmuir, *Toward a Definition of Antisemitism*, 237-62. Berkeley: University of California Press, 1990.]

———. "Ritual Cannibalism," in Gavin Langmuir, *Toward a Definition of Antisemitism*, 263–81. Berkeley: University of California Press, 1990.

———. "Thomas of Monmouth: Detector of Ritual Murder," *Speculum* 59 (1984): 820–46. [Reprinted in Gavin Langmuir, *Toward a Definition of Antisemitism*, 263-81. Berkeley: University of California Press, 1990.]

Lattki, Torsten. *Benzion Kellermann: Prophetisches Judentum und Vernunftreligion*. Göttingen: Vandenhoeck & Ruprecht, 2016.

Leiken, Ezekiel. *The Beilis Transcripts: The Anti-Semitic Trial That Shook the World*. Northvale, N.J.: Jason Aronson, 1993.

Letkemann, Peter. "Zur Geschichte der Juden in Konitz im 19. Jahrhundert," *Beiträge zur Geschichte Westpreußens* 9 (1985): 99–116.

Levin, Edmund. *A Child of Christian Blood: Murder and Conspiracy in Tsarist Russia: The Beilis Blood Libel*. New York: Schocken Books, 2014.

Macartney, C. A. *Hungary*. London: Ernest Benn, 1934.

Maciejko, Paweł. *The Mixed Multitude: Jacob Frank and the Frankist Movement, 1755–1816*. Philadelphia: University of Pennsylvania Press, 2011.

Madea, Burkhard, ed. *History of Forensic Medicine*. Berlin: Lehmanns Media, 2017.

McCagg, William O. *A History of Habsburg Jews, 1670–1918*. Bloomington: Indiana University Press: 1994.

———. *Jewish Nobles and Geniuses in Modern Hungary*. Boulder, Colo.: East European Quarterly, 1972.

Mergel, Thomas. *Zwischen Klasse und Konfession: Katholische Bürgertum im Rheinland 1794–1914*. Göttingen: Vandenhoeck & Ruprecht, 1994.

Miller, Michael L. "Reluctant Kingmakers: Moravian Jewish Politics in Late Imperial Austria," in *Jewish Studies at the Central European University* 3 (2002–2003), edited by András Kovács and Eszter Andor, 111-23. Budapest: Jewish Studies Project, Central European University, 2004.

Moskovich, Wolf. "Kishinev," in *The YIVO Encyclopedia of Jews in Eastern Europe*. https://yivoencyclopedia.org/article.aspx/Kishinev (accessed January 3, 2021).

Nathans, Benjamin. *Beyond the Pale: The Jewish Encounter with Late Imperial Russia*. Berkeley: University of California Press, 2002.

Nemes, Robert. "Hungary's Antisemitic Provinces: Violence and Ritual Murder in the 1880s," *Slavic Review* 66, no. 1 (Spring 2007): 20–44.

Neubauer, Hans Joachim. *The Rumour: A Cultural History*. London: Free Association Books, 1999.

Nicholls, Stephen C. J. *The Burning of the Synagogue in Neustettin: Ideological Arson in the 1880s*. Research Paper No. 2. Sussex: Centre for German-Jewish Studies, University of Sussex, 1999.

Nonn, Christoph. *Eine Stadt sucht einen Mörder: Gerücht, Gewalt und Anstisemitismus im Kaiserreich*. Göttingen: Vandenhoeck & Ruprecht, 2002.

———. "Zwischenfall in Konitz: Antisemitismus und Nationalismus im preußischen Osten um 1900," *Historische Zeitschrift* 266 (1998): 387–418.

Péter, Katalin. "The Later Ottoman Period and Royal Hungary, 1606–1711," in *A History of Hungary*, edited by Peter F. Sugar, Tibor Frank, and Peter Hanák, 100–120, map 139. Bloomington: Indiana University Press, 1994.

Peukert, Will-Erich. "Ritualmord," in *Handwörterbuch des deutschen Aberglaubens*, Vol. 7, edited by Hanns Baechtold-Staeubli and E. Hoffmann, 727–39. Berlin: W. de Gruyter & Co, 1927.

Raeff, Marc. *The Well-Ordered Police State: Social and Institutional Change Through Law in the Germanies and Russia, 1600–1800*. New Haven, Conn.: Yale University Press, 1983.

Reed, Andrew C. "For One's Brothers: Daniil Avraamovich Khvol'son and the 'Jewish Question' in Russia, 1819–1911." Ph.D. diss., Arizona State University, 2014.

Reich, Emil. "The Magyar County: A Study in the Comparative History of Municipal Institutions," *Transactions of the Royal Historical Society* 7 (1893): 37–53.

Ritual Murder in Russia, Eastern Europe, and Beyond: New Histories of an Old Accusation, edited by Eugene M. Avrutin, Jonathan Dekel-Chen, and Robert Weinberg. Bloomington: Indiana University Press, 2017.

Rohrbacher, Stefan. "Die 'Hep-Hep Krawalle' und der 'Ritualmord' des Jahres 1819 zu Dormagen," in *Antisemitismus und jüdische Geschichte*, edited by Rainer Erb and Michael Schmidt, 135–47. Berlin: Wissenschaftlicher Autorenverlag, 1987.

———. "Volksfrömmigkeit und Judenfeindschaft: Zur Vorgeschichte des politischen Antisemitismus im katholischen Rheinland," *Annalen des Historischen Vereins für den Niederrhein* 192/193 (1990): 125–44.

Rohrbacher, Stefan, and Michael Schmidt. *Judenbilder: Kulturgeschichte antijüdischer Mythen und antisemitischer Vorurteile*. Reinbeck: Rowohlt Verlag, 1991.

Rose, E. M. *The Murder of William of Norwich: The Origins of the Blood Libel in Medieval Europe*. Oxford: Oxford University Press, 2015.

Ross, Ronald J. *The Failure of Bismarck's Kulturkampf: Catholicism and State Power in Imperial Germany, 1871–1887*. Washington, D.C.: Catholic University of America Press, 1998.

Rubin, Miri. *Gentile Tales: The Narrative Assault on Late Medieval Jews*. New Haven, Conn.: Yale University Press, 1999.

Saler, Michael. "Modernity and Enchantment: A Historiographic Review," *American Historical Review* 111 (June 2006): 692–716.

Salman, Mikhail. "On the Question of the Origins and Frequency of Ritual Murder Trials in Poland," *Journal of the Academic Proceedings of Soviet Jewry* 1 (1986): 5–24.

Samuel, Maurice. *Blood Accusation: The Strange History of the Beiliss Case.* Philadelphia: Jewish Publication Society of America, 1966.

Sándor, Iván. *A viszgálat iratai: Tudósítás a tiszaeszlári per körülményeiről.* Budapest: Kozmosz Könyvek, 1983.

Schmenk, Holger. *Xanten im 19. Jahrhundert: Eine rheinische Stadt zwischen Tradition und Moderne.* Cologne: Bölau, 2008.

Schmidt, Michael. "Ritualmordbeschuldigungen und exemplarisches Wissen," in *Stereotypvorstellungen im Alltagsleben: Beiträge zum Themenkreis Fremdbilder—Selbstbilder—Identität,* edited by Helge Gerndt, 44–56. Munich: Münchner Vereinigung für Volkskunde, 1988.

Schoeps, Julius H. "Ritualmordbeschuldigung und Blutaberglaube: Die Affäre Buschhoff im niederrheinischen Xanten," in *Köln und das rheinische Judentum: Festschrift Germania Judaica 1959–1984,* edited by Jutta Bohnke-Kollwitz et al., 286–99. Cologne: J. P. Bachem, 1984.

Schroubek, Georg R. "Der 'Ritualmord' von Polná: Traditioneller und moderner Wahnglaube," in *Antisemitismus und jüdische Geschichte: Studien zu Ehren von Herbert A. Strauss,* edited by Rainer Erb and Michael Schmidt, 149–71. Berlin: Wissenschaftlicher Autorenverlag, 1987.

Schumacher, Bruno. *Geschichte Ost- und Westpreußens.* 4th ed. Würzburg: Holzner Verlag, 1959.

Silber, Michael K. "Josephian Reforms," in *The YIVO Encyclopedia of Jews in Eastern Europe,* Vol. 1, edited by Gershon D. Hundert, 831–34. New Haven, Conn.: Yale University Press, 2008.

Singer, Ludvík. "Zur Geschichte der Toleranzpatente in den Sudetenländern," *Jahrbuch der Gesellschaft für Geschichte der Juden in der* Čechoslovakischen *Republik* 5 (1933): 231–311.

Smith, Helmut Walser. *The Butcher's Tale: Murder and Anti-Semitism in a German Town.* New York: W. W. Norton, 2002.

———. *German Nationalism and Religious Conflict: Culture, Ideology, Politics, 1870–1914.* Princeton, N.J.: Princeton University Press, 1995.

———. "Konitz, 1900: Ritual Murder and Antisemitic Violence," in *Exclusionary Violence: Antisemitic Riots in Modern German History,* edited by Christhard Hoffmann, Werner Bergmann, and Helmut Walser Smith, 93–122. Ann Arbor: University of Michigan Press, 2002.

———. "The Learned and the Popular Discourse of Anti-Semitism in the Catholic Milieu of the Kaiserreich," *Central European History* 27 (1994): 315–28.

Smith, Justin E. H. *Irrationality: A History of the Dark Side of Reason.* Princeton, N.J.: Princeton University Press, 2019.

Soukupová, Blanka. "Národněpolitické protižidovské stereotypy v české společnosti na konci 19. století," in *Protižidovské stereotypy a křesťanská společnost na přelomu 19. a 20. století,* edited by Zbyněk Vydra, 13–49. Pardubice: Univerzita Pardubice, 2007.

Spector, Scott. *Violent Sensations: Sex, Crime, and Utopia in Vienna and Berlin, 1860-1914.* Chicago: University of Chicago Press, 2016.

Stacey, Robert C. "From Ritual Crucifixion to Host Desecration: Jews and the Body of Christ," *Jewish History* 12 (1998): 11–28.

Stedman's Medical Dictionary. Philadelphia: Lippincott Williams & Wilkins, 2006.

Stein, Adolf. *Die Geschichte der Juden in Böhmen.* Brünn: Jüdischer Buch- und Kunstverlag, 1904.

Steiner, Otto. *Ritualmord? Vier große Ritualmordprozesse.* Hamburg: Kriminalistik, 1955.

Stern, Edith. "Gerichtsmedizinische Bezüge zu dem Ritualmordprozeß von Tiszaeszlar, Ungarn, 1882–83," *Monatsschrift für Kriminologie und Strafrechtsreform* 67 (1984): 38–47.

———. *The Glorious Victory of Truth: The Tiszaeszlar Blood Libel Trial, 1882–3: A Historical-Legal-Medical Research.* Jerusalem: Rubin Mass, 1998.

———. "Legal-Medical References to the Blood Libel (Ritual Murder) Trial in Tiszaeszlar, Hungary 1882–83," *Korot* 10 (1993–94): 102–11.

———. "More on Ritual Murder Trials: The Ritual Murder Charge of Orkut, Greater Hungary, 1764," *Korot* 11 (1995): 132–35.

Stern, Fritz. *The Politics of Cultural Despair: A Study in the Rise of Germanic Ideology.* Berkeley: University of California Press, 1961.

Stölzl, Christoph. *Kafkas böses Böhmen: Zur Sozialgeschichte eines Prager Juden.* Munich: Edition Text + Kritik, 1975.

Stourzh, Gerald. *Die Gleichberechtigung der Nationalitäten in der Verfassung und Verwaltung Österreichs, 1848–1918.* Vienna: Verlag der Österreichischen Akademie der Wissenschaften, 1985.

Suchy, Barbara. "Antisemitismus in den Jahren vor dem Ersten Weltkrieg," in *Köln und das rheinische Judentum: Festschrift Germania Judaica 1959–1984*, edited by Jutta Bohnke-Kollwitz et al., 252–85. Cologne: J. P. Bachem, 1984.

———. "The Verein zur Abwehr des Antisemitismus (I): From Its Beginnings to the First World War," *Leo Baeck Institute Yearbook* 28 (1983): 205–39.

Sutter, Berthold. *Die Badenischen Sprachverordnungen von 1897: Ihre Genesis und ihre Auswirkungen vornehmlich auf die innerösterreichischen Alpenländer.* 2 vols. Graz: H. Böhlaus Nachf., 1960–1965.

Tatar, Maria. *Lustmord: Sexual Murder in Weimar Germany.* Princeton, N.J.: Princeton University Press, 1995.

Teter, Magda. *Blood Libel: On the Trail of an Antisemitic Myth.* Cambridge, Mass.: Harvard University Press, 2020.

———. *Sinners on Trial: Jews and Sacrilege after the Reformation.* Cambridge, Mass.: Harvard University Press, 2011.

Timmermans, Stefan. *Postmortem: How Medical Examiners Explain Suspicious Deaths.* Chicago: University of Chicago Press, 2006.

Tollet, Daniel. *Accuser pour convertir: Du bon usage de l'accusation de crime rituel dans la Pologne catholique à l'*époque moderne. Paris: Presses Universitaires de France, 2000.

Toury, Jacob. "Defense Activities of the Österreichisch-Israelitische Union Before 1914," in *Living with Antisemitism: Modern Jewish Responses*, edited by Jehuda Reinharz, 167–92. Hanover: University Press of New England, 1987.

Trachtenberg, Joshua. *The Devil and the Jews: The Medieval Conception of the Jew and Its Relation to Modern Antisemitism.* New Haven, Conn.: Yale University Press, 1943.

Treue, Wolfgang. *Der Trienter Judenprozeß: Voraussetzungen—Abläufe—Auswirkungen (1475–1588).* Hannover: Hahnsche Buchhandlung, 1996.

Trost, Ralph. *Eine gänzlich zerstörte Stadt: Nationalsozialismus, Krieg und Kriegsende in Xanten.* New York: Wazmann, 2004.

Ungvári, Tamás. *The "Jewish Question" in Europe: The Case of Hungary.* Boulder, Colo.: Social Science Monographs/Atlantic Research and Publications, 2000.

Véri, Daniel. "Imagining Ritual Murder: Social Knowledge in the Making," in *Visual Antisemitism in Central Europe: Imagery of Hatred*, edited by Jakub Hauder and Eva Janáčová, 37–60. Oldenbourg: De Gruyter, 2021.

———. "The Tiszaeszlár Blood Libel: Image and Propaganda," in *Antisemitismus im 19. Jahrhundert aus internationale Perspektive/Nineteenth Century Anti-Semitism in International Perspective*, edited by Mareike König and Oliver Schulz, 263–90. Göttingen: Vandenhoeck & Ruprecht Unipress, 2019.

Vogt, Bernhard. "Die 'Atmosphäre eines Narrenhauses': Eine Ritualmordlegende um die Ermordung des Schülers Ernst Winter in Konitz," in *Zur Geshichte und Kultur der Juden in Ost- und Westpreußen*, edited by Michael Brocke, Margret Heitmann, and Harald Lordick, 545–77. Hildesheim: Georg Olms Verlag, 2000.

Volkov, Shulamit. "Antisemitism as a Cultural Code: Reflections on the History and Historiography of Antisemitism in Imperial Germany," *Leo Beack Institute Yearbook* 23 (1978): 25–46.

Vojtěch, Tomáš. *Mladočeši a boj o politickou moc v* Čechách. Prague: Academia, 1980.

Vydra, Zbyněk. "Krvavé obvinění a moderní společnost: Tradiční protižidovský stereotyp na konci 19. století," in *Protižidovské sterotypy a křest'anská společnost na přelomu 19. a 20. století*, edited by Zbyněk Vydra, 51–72. Pardubice: Univerzita Pardubice, 2007.

Vyleta, Daniel M. *Crime, Jews and News: Vienna 1895–1914*. New York: Berghahn Books, 2007.

Wagner, Benno. "Kafkas Polná: Schreiben jenseits der Nation," in *Juden zwischen Deutschen und Tschechen: Sprachliche und Kulturelle Identitäten in Böhmen 1800–1945*, edited by Marek Nekula and Walter Koschmal, 152–72. Munich: R. Oldenbourg, 2006.

Weber, Max. *Charisma and Disenchantment: The Vocation Lectures*, edited and with an introduction by Paul Reitter and Chad Wellmon, translated by Damion Searls. New York: New York Review of Books, 2020.

———. *The Protestant Ethic and the Spirit of Capitalism*, translated and introduced by Stephen Kalberg. Oxford: Oxford University Press, 2011.

Węgrzynek, Hanna. *"Czarna legenda" Żydów: Procesy o rzekome mordy rytualne w dawnej Polsce*. Warsaw: Wydawnictwo Bellonia; Wydawnictwo Fundacji Historia Pro Futurio, 1995.

Weinberg, Robert. *Blood Libel in Late Imperial Russia: The Ritual Murder Trial of Mendel Beilis*. Bloomington: Indiana University Press, 2014.

Wertheimer, Josef. *Die Juden in* Österreich. Leipzig, 1842.

Wetzell, Richard F. *Inventing the Criminal: A History of German Criminology, 1880–1945*. Chapel Hill: University of North Carolina Press, 2000.

Wijaczka, Jacek. "Ritualmordbeschuldigungen und -prozesse in Polen-Litauen vom 16. bis 18. Jahrhundert," in *Ritualmord: Legenden in der europäischen Geschichte*, edited by Susanna Buttaroni and Stanisław Musiał, 131–172. Vienna: Böhlau Verlag, 2003.

Winters, Stanley B. "Kramář, Kaizl, and the Hegemony of the Young Czech Party, 1891–1901," in *The Czech Renascence of the Nineteenth Century*, edited by Peter Brock and H. Gordon Skilling, 282–314. Toronto: University of Toronto Press, 1970.

Wodziński, Marcin. "Blood and the Hasidim: On the History of Ritual Murder Accusations in Nineteenth-Century Poland," *Polin: Studies in Polish Jewry* 22 (2010): 273–90.

Yuval, Israel Jacob. *Two Nations in Your Womb: Perceptions of Jews and Christians in Late Antiquity and the Middle Ages*. Berkeley: University of California Press, 2006.

Zipperstein, Steven J. *Pogrom: Kishinev and the Tilt of History*. New York: Liveright, 2018.

Index

Page numbers in italics indicate figures or tables.

Acknowledgments

This project, the culmination of more than two decades of research and writing, has incurred many debts—scholarly, intellectual, fiscal, and emotional—all of which I gratefully acknowledge. My hope is that, in so doing, I have not failed to mention any individual or institution.

Let me begin by thanking the following sources of institutional funding: ACLS/SSRC Joint Committee on Eastern Europe; IREX (International Research and Exchanges Board); the Herbert D. Katz Center for Advanced Judaic Studies, University of Pennsylvania; The Hebrew University of Jerusalem, Faculty of the Humanities (Lady Davis Visiting Professorship); my home institution, Washington University in St. Louis; and my former home, the University of Washington, Seattle.

The following archives were gracious enough to open their collections to me, either in person or online: in Berlin, the Geheimes Staatsarchiv Preußischer Kulturbesitz; in Budapest, the National Archives of Hungary (Magyar Nemzeti Levéltár); in Düsseldorf, the Hauptsaatsarchiv Nordrhein-Westfallen; in Jerusalem, the Central Archives for the History of the Jewish People and the Central Zionist Archives; in Koblenz, the Bundesarchiv; in New York, the archives of the Leo Baeck Institute; in Nyíregyháza, the Szabolcs-Szatmár-Bereg Megyei Levéltár; in Paris, the archives of the Alliance Israélite Universelle; in Polná, the Muzeum Vysočina, pobočka Polná; in Prague, Archiv Hlavního Města Prahy, Archiv Židovského muzea v Praze, Literární archiv of the Památník národního písemnictví, Národní archiv, and Státní oblastní archiv v Praze; and in Vienna, the Österreicisches Staatsarchiv and the Parlamentsarchiv. I also spent many hours working in various libraries, among which are the National Széchényi Library in Budapest, the library of the Jewish Museum in Prague, the Herbert D. Katz Center for Advanced Judaic Studies in Philadelphia, the Van Leer Jerusalem Institute, and the National Library of Israel, which has been a home away from home for me for many years and to which I owe enormous thanks.

Numerous colleagues and friends at home and abroad have engaged with this work in one form or another, offering comments, advice, emotional support, and criticisms. My thanks go to Eugene Avrutin, Israel Bartal, Pamela Barmash, John Bátki, Elissa Bemporad, Richard Borbás (for research assistance), Petr Brod, Kateřina Čapková, Flora Cassen, Jeremy Cohen, Richie Cohen, Jonathan Dekel-Chen, David Feldman, John Findlay, Jonathan Frankel (z"l), Michal Frankl, Hayim Goldgraber, Zeev Gries, György Haraszti, Martin Jacobs, Marty Jaffee, Adam Kepecs, John Klier (z"l), András Kovács, György Kövér, Joe Loewenstein, Ezra Mendelsohn (z"l), Joel Migdal, Steve Miles, Michael Miller, Sowandé Mustakeem, Arno Pařík, Tim Parsons, Attila Pók, Alexandr Putík, David Rechter, Emily Rose, Moshe Rosman, Miri Rubin, David Ruderman, Dmitry Shumsky, Michael Silber, Helmut Walser Smith, Robert Stacey, Lynne Tatlock, Magda Teter, Daniel Unowsky, Scott Ury, Petr Vašíček, Daniel Véri, Lilla Vekerdy (with additional gratitude for being my first Hungarian teacher), and Robert Weinberg.

I wish also to recognize the students and former students of mine—many of whom by now are colleagues at other institutions—who read, discussed, and offered their own original insights into versions of the book's chapters, its sources, and historical questions. Thanks, then, to Mary Andino, Amber Aragon, Anruo Bao, Mark Beirn, Lorraine Berry, Kate Brown, Matthew Brown, Tomasz Cebrat, Ashley Walters Cohen, Sara Jay, Cree Johannsen, Jacob Labendz, Jen Mabray, Mary Neuberger, Keith Pickus, Jill Storm, Beverly Tsacoyianis, and Janek Wasserman. Special thanks to Jen Mabray for her professional assistance with maps, photos, and the cover.

Jerry Singerman, Senior Humanities Editor at the University of Pennsylvania Press, deserves special thanks for his long-term and unflinching interest and support. I truly appreciate the faith that he has had in this project.

Happily, my own family has managed to grow and thrive since the earliest stages of research and writing. I am grateful at this point in my life to be able to thank Michael and Carla, Shira and Dan, Isabelle, Leslie, and Kiran for their love, encouragement, gentle teasing, and critical eye. Love and deep thanks, finally, to my wife Debbie, to whom this book is dedicated. You never did ask when it would be finished. You just knew.

CPSIA information can be obtained
at www.ICGtesting.com
Printed in the USA
JSHW050809261221
21519JS00001B/1